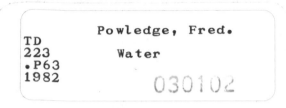

WATER

Water

The Nature, Uses,
and Future of Our
Most Precious
and Abused
Resource

Fred Powledge

Farrar Straus Giroux

NEW YORK

For Clara Powledge Worsley

Copyright © 1982 by Fred Powledge
All rights reserved
Printed in the United States of America
Published simultaneously in Canada by
McGraw-Hill Ryerson Ltd., Toronto
Designed by Constance Fogler
Second Printing, 1983

Library of Congress Cataloging in Publication Data
Powledge, Fred.   Water: the nature, uses, and future
of our most precious and abused resource.
1. Water-supply—United States.   2. Water—
Pollution—United States.   I. Title.
TD223.P63   1982   333.91'0973   82-7471   AACR2

A section of this book was first published,
in slightly different form, in *The Nation*

Acknowledgments

A great many people were very helpful to me as I undertook this project, and I am deeply grateful to them all for their interest, encouragement, patience, and generosity. Many of them knew, even as they were helping me, that we had sharply differing notions of what constituted the proper stewardship of Earth's water, but they were generous anyway, and for that I am particularly appreciative.

The following people deserve special thanks:

David F. Abelson, Bruce Adams, Terry Agriss, Susanna Ashton, Robert Atchison, Peter Barrett, Dick Beamish, John Bennett, Dan R. Bishop, Brent Blackwelder, Peter Bloch, Essie Borden, Stewart H. Brehm, Howard Brown, Mitch Burak, Peter Carlson, Gino Carlucci, Wally Chadow, William Chandler, Joseph Codispoti, Jeffrey P. Cohn, Ed Cross, William Cummings, Abel Davis, Alfred Davis, Sue Davis, John DeGrove, James Dragna, Mark Dubois, William Du Bois, Lyn Edwards, Mike Edwards, Mohammed El-Ashry, Rae Ely, Ed Essertier, Enzo Fano, Efrain Fernandez, Karl Fleming, Joanne Foster, Stewart Freeman, John Galloway, Francisco Garcia, Claude M. Gehman, Michael Gilberti, Kiki Goodwin, Samuel McC. Goodwin, Brian Gorman, Diane Graves, Michael Greenberg, Ed Greene, Harvey Wm. Greisman, Jack Gualco, Louis Gwin, David Hall, Ellen Stern Harris, Robert H. Harris, Deirdre Hazelrigg, Susan Herman, Gladwyn Hill, Kathy Hinds, Chuck Hoffman, Oscar Holt, Jan Horvath, Gardner Hunt, George Ihrig, Caroline Isber, Tom Johnson, T. Richard Johnson, Irwin Kantrowitz, Steven Kasower, Don Kelly, Barry Kohler, Ebba Kraar, Donald Krumm, C. Laurence Linser, Ross Lockridge,

John McAllister, Francis X. McArdle, Joynes McFarlan, James W. MacFarland, Carol McKeown, Gene McNeill, John Marlin, Donald Maughan, Jill Maunder, Pat Messigian, Donald Middleton, Lawrence G. Moncher, Derek Morgan, Naomi Morrison, Annie Murray, Francis Murray, Bronius Nemickas, Larry O'Neill, Charles Osolin, Donald Owen, Mary Painter, Andy Paszlor, George W. Pendygraft, P. K. Pettus, Wolfgang Pindur, Zyg Plater, Charles Pou, Pauline Powledge, Mike Principe, George Pring, Robert Quayle, Joan Raines, Stephen Reynolds, David Rich, Ronald Robie, Paul B. Rohne, Jr., Paul Sarkisian, William Shawn, Herb Shuman, Larry Silverman, Kerala Snyder, Richard Snyder, Peter Steen, Wesley Steiner, Brad Swanson, Shirley Taylor, Dean Thompson, Mindy Trossman, Pat Tyson, Frank Velkas, Jacqueline M. Warren, Cheryl Washburn, Kit Weigel, Judith Weigell, Katie Weimer, Frank Welsh, William H. Westray, Eva White, Bob Williams, and Robert Witzeman.

For three great friends, the encouragement and generosity stretched through the entire project, from beginning to end and beyond, and for them I have gratitude of a special degree. They are Pat Strachan, my editor; Claire Cooper, my wonderful friend and commiserater; and Tabitha Powledge, my wife.

Contents

I

The Substance and the Crisis

1

The United States has entered a period of grave emergency in its supply of water. The crisis is not confined to this nation or even, as one might expect, to the highly industrialized regions. Rather, the problem is one of global magnitude, one that helps to demonstrate the fact, which we often overlook, that the world's tenants are very dependent upon one another, whether they be rich or poor, developed or developing. The entire world has a water crisis.

In the United States, however, the emerging dilemma is likely to be felt with particular intensity. Americans, to a degree inconceivable to many of the world's other inhabitants, are accustomed to having unlimited supplies of inexpensive, clean water at their immediate disposal. It is almost always there whenever we turn on a tap, whether we want it for drinking, bathing, irrigating our farmland or our backyards or our windowsill herb gardens, for running our factories or washing our cars, or even just for looking at, in public fountains. We can, and often do, allow a gallon or so of pure drinking water to run down the drain while we brush our teeth, and we think nothing of it.

We have acted as if water were like air—free, so omnipresent as to exist beyond our conscious thought; so unquestionably necessary to life on this planet that it would be foolish to spend any time or energy thinking about it. And yet water is one of the most intimate substances in our lives. Setting aside the fact that it is necessary for life (as if it were possible to set aside such an important matter), water remains an extremely pleasurable, gratifying substance. When we are thirsty—*really* thirsty, that is—it is not a soft drink that we want, or a glass of iced tea with lots of ice, or a beer, but cold, clear "tasteless" water, and as we drink it down we remind ourselves that there's nothing like it, nothing quite so good. As humans, we are rather fragile when it comes to temperature ranges; we often use water (in radiators, or perhaps as a source of electrical energy) to warm ourselves in winter and (in big air conditioners and swimming pools) to cool ourselves in summer. And it is water, rather than some other substance, which we have chosen to give ourselves one of our most sensuous pleasures—the ritual, which we repeat with great frequency, of removing our clothes and stepping naked, in specially set-off, private areas of our homes, into gleaming reservoirs of clear water, or perhaps standing beneath stinging sprays of the stuff. And yet it is the ritual that we think of at such moments, not the water that makes the ritual possible. In bathing as in our other uses of water, it is easy to forget the actual substance, for there is so very much of it.

Water *is* abundant. No one knows with any certainty how much there is in, on, and above the planet during the various phases of the hydrologic cycle, but the estimates all agree that the amount is so huge as almost to defy our thinking about it. One of them, the result of a calculation made for a 1977 United Nations water conference, is that Earth contains 1.4×10^9 cubic kilometers of water, in all its forms. That figure, which is expressed in scientific notation to keep the numbers more manageable, means 1.4 multiplied by 10 multiplied by itself nine times, or 1,400,000,000 cubic kilometers of water. The superscript (in this case, ^{9}) indicates the number of spaces which the decimal should be moved to the right. (A kilometer is a little more than six-tenths of a statute mile in length. To visualize a cubic kilometer, the time-honored device of football fields may be used: Each of the six square sides of a cubic kilometer would occupy about the same space as the playing surface of eleven football fields laid end to end in one direction and twenty and one-half fields laid side by side in the other.)

The estimated 1.4×10^9 cubic kilometers is the equivalent of 335,860,000 cubic miles—or, to put it in a way that is even closer to home, about 369,820,250,000,000,000,000 gallons of water. That is 369 quintillion 820 quadrillion 250 trillion gallons. It would be enough to fill Lake Superior, the largest of the Great Lakes, about 115,814 times, or to fill Lake Erie, the smallest, a little under 3 million times. It would provide each resident of Earth with something like 85,586,728,000 gallons of water, which is not too far from a trillion gallons per capita and which is surely a plentitude.

With such an abundance of water around, it may be difficult to understand how a crisis can be developing. But one is, and it threatens to alter our styles of living just as much as, and quite possibly more than, the crisis in energy which we entered a few years ago and which seems destined to affect our lives profoundly from now until as long as our world shall exist. Because of what's happening to water now, and even more because of the ways we have treated water in the past, the nation finds itself in a position in which it never again can take water for granted.

Just as we woke one morning a few years ago to the realization that fuel for our cars, factories, and homes was no longer cheap, and never again would be, that we would never again be able to conduct our lives oblivious to thoughts of *energy* (the awakening was almost a literal one; the transition occurred that quickly), now we are about to awake to the understanding that water, in the forms we require and of the quality and quantities we desire, is no longer, and almost certainly never again will be, a free good, to be taken and used with hardly a second thought. We are going to have to start paying for the water we use, both in terms of actual cash outlays that bear a more realistic relationship to the real cost of water and in terms of having to go to some trouble to get it when we want it. (Those with enough money, of course, will always be able to hire someone else to go to their trouble for them.) Some of us, perhaps many of us, are going to become sick and die because of problems with the substance that we always considered not only a free good but a *pure* free good. Some of what we have come to count among our basic liberties —the farmer's right to cultivate what he wants, with the technical and financial assistance of government; the politician's right to produce income for his supporters, and thus to extract loyalty from them, by bringing home expensive public-works water projects of arguable value; the individual's right to set up housekeeping anyplace in the nation that strikes his or her fancy, even in the floodplain of a river, and to expect bountiful, inexpensive supplies of potable water, even if the house is built on the desert—a number of these seemingly self-evident truths are going to come under attack, and they are going to have to be altered or abandoned, in coming years. And in some cases and in some places, the changes have already started.

We are, in sum, about to suffer a bit with respect to water. We are, to use a slightly tattered term from a recent era, soon to have our consciousnesses raised about the substance. It's about time. We have abused Earth's enormous, but finite, supply of water for a very long time now. While there may be 369,820,250,000,000,000,000 gallons of it on the planet with us, we have been poisoning and damaging the usable supply at a rate that has been increasing with shameful speed.

The crisis has many components. This should not be surprising, since water has so much to do with all life on Earth. What *may* be surprising, however, is the speed with which the multitude of water problems has been thrust on the planet and particularly on the United States.

The most dramatic of the current and recent troubles with the quality of water have been the ones involving toxic wastes —and of those, the most dramatic has been the case of Love Canal, in which housing and a school were built near a former toxic chemical dump. It was just the sort of thing, some might think, that could be expected to happen at Niagara Falls, New York, in a region that is the home of some of the heavier and more pollution-prone industrial processes, including many that involve dangerous chemicals and compounds. Less dramatic than the events at Love Canal, but perhaps equally scary in the long run, have been the discoveries of problems with toxic chemicals at scores of other places in the nation, including some regions far removed from industrial blight. Often the first people to detect the presence of such chemicals beneath the earth are the owners of nearby homes who, after noticing that their well water "tastes funny," have it tested and learn that it is too dangerous to drink or even to wash clothes with. The chemicals have percolated down through the soil into the aquifers. These underground reservoirs of water are not the "vast underground lakes" of popular literature, but rather cells of rock or sand that are porous (and thus collect and hold water) below the earth's surface and above a layer of non-porous rock. Whether the material of the aquifer is beach sand deposited thousands of years ago, or sandstone (sand that's cemented together), or gravel, shattered rock, or limestone, it is saturated with water. Because the material beneath it is non-porous, the water in the aquifer is supported from below, just as water in a lake on the earth's surface is held up by its relatively impermeable bottom. The aquifer is recharged by rainwater that leaches, or percolates, down through the soil from above, and it moves downhill, obeying the laws of gravity, at what is usually an extremely slow rate, appearing on the surface again in the form of springs, or pouring into lakes and streams, or in some cases thrusting out under the ocean floor, where it eventually mixes with seawater. When wells are sunk, it is these cells of groundwater from which they draw. No one really knows how fast water moves through the aquifers, but it is generally accepted that anything that is done to an aquifer —such as contaminating it—will take a very long time to undo. It has been estimated that the horizontal movement of groundwater on New York's Long Island, when the place was in its natural state, ranged from a few feet to a few hundred feet each year, and that water now being extracted from the aquifers (the source of all fresh water on the island) may have been moving through the system for hundreds or thousands of years.

Other problems with the quality of the water have manifested themselves in recent years in what seem to be almost geometrically increasing numbers. Herbicides and pesticides have turned up in public drinking water supplies. Whole towns and sections of big cities have had their systems shut down for a few days, and their residents have been advised to drink bottled water, while harmful chemicals or organisms of undetermined origin are flushed out of the pipes. Americans, like everyone else, have been using rivers as sewers for centuries, but until very recently two other sources of water—groundwater from aquifers and precipitation from the sky—have generally been considered to be about as close to purity as humans are likely to find. Now it is not unusual for rain to fall that is as acid as vinegar (it carries sulfuric acid picked up, many scientists believe, from coal-burning industries, particularly the power-producing plants in the center of the nation). Nor is it any longer surprising when an announcement is made that an aquifer has become, or is in serious danger of becoming, polluted and that no one has the slightest idea what caused the condition or whether anything can be done about it. For decades the residents of Long Island have been pouring their human, agricultural, and industrial wastes into an aquifer that underlies their homes, farms, schoolhouses, and businesses, and then taking their drinking water from the same source. Realizing what they were doing, they have now started trying to get their water from an even deeper aquifer, which also is becoming tainted with the wastes of a highly developed civilization that has not yet learned that there is really no such thing as "out of sight, out of mind."

Many of the present-day problems with water—and ones that lately have been quite apparent to residents of the New York metropolitan area—have to do with its quantity: often it is a case of too much or too little; of floods or of drought. Rarely is it found in the exact quantities that its human users would prefer. Traditionally, quantity problems have occurred in America's West, where the rainfall is generally a small percentage of that in the East. In 1977, a two-year drought in California, the most severe in the state's history, was broken by rains that caused flooding and mudslides and millions of dollars' worth of damage. Farmers between Phoenix and Tucson, Arizona, have been withdrawing water from aquifers —to use in irrigating crops they are growing on the desert—at such a rate that the surface of the earth is cracking and falling several feet a year. Pumping out more groundwater than normally would trickle down from the surface and recharge the aquifers naturally is referred to as "mining water," and the farmers in Arizona (and other places) mine it just as surely and deliberately as the state's copper miners remove ore from the ground. In downtown Phoenix, meantime, a normally dry riverbed which cuts through the city has gotten into the habit of flooding with great violence in the late winter, despite the fact that a series of dams has been constructed upstream.

The notion that water *quality* problems belong to the developed, densely populated Eastern United States and that *quantity* problems are peculiar to the West is being challenged by recent developments. Synthetic organic chemicals, of the sort that have been turning up in toxic waste dumps and tests of contaminated wells in the East, have been found in public wells serving thousands of people in California's San Gabriel Valley. The pesticide dibromopropane, or DBCP, has been discovered in groundwater supplies in two dozen California counties, most of them in the San Joaquin Valley. DBCP is believed to cause sterility and cancer. Long Island is "mining water" in much the same way that the Arizona farmers are, and water planners in much of Florida, from Tampa Bay to the Keys, are deeply embroiled in water quantity issues and controversies. In the older cities of the Northeast, including New York, the condition of the underground infrastructure by which clean water is delivered and waste water taken away— the pipes that serve as the cities' circulatory system—has deteriorated greatly because of the aging process, because of the weight of traffic passing overhead, and because of neglect on the part of politicians.

Agriculture, for all its symbolic and actual connections with people's well-being, is under attack as never before for what some perceive as its widespread waste and abuse of water through irrigation, applications of herbicides and pesticides, and contamination from the fecal matter of livestock. Another constituent of human life, the production of energy to run our cars, furnaces, stoves, and television sets, is part of the water crisis as well. As the nation attempted to decrease its reliance on oil imported from the Persian Gulf, there was increased interest in energy that can be produced at home—from coal, hydroelectric power, and nuclear fission, among others. Each of these processes has profound effects on both the quality and the quantity of water. And when efforts are made, as some have been in recent years, to turn government policy toward the vigorous pursuit of what is called "energy independence," the danger increases that the sizable body of environmental-protection law, regulation, and custom that has been built up over the past decade or so will be sacrificed.

The danger, and all the others that go into the burgeoning crisis in water, would not be so severe if it were not for another problem that runs straight through every issue of quantity and quality. It is the fact that government, so far, has been an abject failure at recognizing the water crisis, planning for it, protecting its citizens against it, informing them of it, or figuring out what to do about it. Government in the United States has stood by, almost inert, as caches of poisons have been discovered beneath the ground and atop drinking water supplies; as rain has turned to acid as powerful as lemonade; as greed has mined water from the ground to the degree that the earth has collapsed above it; as the networks of pipes that carry water to city dwellers have cracked and disintegrated; as highly productive farmland has been confiscated and flooded, its graves robbed, and its owners forced to flee, so that dams can be built which will not control floods, not produce very much electricity, and not do much of anything else except enrich some land speculators and perpetuate a vast government bureaucracy which feels it must destroy nature in order to survive.

This failure of government is at the bottom of the crisis in water, but it cannot continue in its careless, irresponsible role much longer, for the simple reason that we can't play many games with water much longer. Real estate, people, and even supplies of fuel can be manipulated by bureaucrats and cartels a great deal, and life goes on. But drinking water is different. If we don't have it for a day, we start feeling very uncomfortable. If we don't have it for a few days, we die.

2

Water is the most commonly found and easily recognized substance on earth. Everybody knows it by sight and taste and feel, and it is likely that more people can quote its scientific name, H_2O, than that of any other substance, even though many of them may not know what H_2O represents—a molecule made up of two atoms of hydrogen and one of oxygen.

Water is the only substance on earth that can, and does, exist in all three physical states—liquid, gas, and solid—under normal conditions of climate. That water is abundant is quite clear, but what makes it so *important* is its unique set of physical properties. Because of the manner in which two hydrogen atoms fix themselves to an oxygen atom, the resulting molecule of water has its electrical charges arranged in a way that gives it a great deal of what scientists call chemical bonding strength. Because of this bonding, water does many things that other substances don't do. As its temperature is lowered toward 4° Celsius (a little more than 39° Fahrenheit), for example, water contracts, as do most other substances. But if its temperature is lowered even more toward its freezing point of 0° Celsius, its hydrogen atoms push the molecules apart and the water expands, becoming less dense. (Other substances become heavier as they pass from the liquid to the solid state.) This attribute of water is a beneficial one, since it means that ice is lighter than liquid water. If the opposite were true, lakes would freeze from the bottom up, rather than from the top down, and fish would not be able to survive the cold winter.

Water's bonding strength—the tendency for its molecules to hold on to each other—also gives it great surface tension, a sort of stickiness that allows it to defy gravity through capillary action and that causes it to cling to particles of soil, thus making possible the growing of crops. The fact that the water molecule possesses uneven electrical charges gives it the power to break through other substances by more or less forcing its way into them. Thus water has become nature's greatest solvent. Another of water's characteristics, and one that is not widely appreciated, is its capacity for absorbing great quantities of heat without becoming extremely hot iself.

H. Baldwin and L. B. Marman, Jr., writing in a pamphlet on water that is published by the United States Geological Survey, the federal agency with the most abiding interest in water as it exists in its natural states, offer as an illustration of this last property the example of a pan resting on the burner of a stove. If it is empty and the heat is switched on beneath it, the metal pan will quickly heat up—will turn red and eventually will burn up. "But put water in the pan and the water will absorb heat from it," write Baldwin and Marman. "The pan will become hot, but not as hot as before, and the temperature of the water, even if it boils, will rise only a small amount compared to the temperature of the pan." It is this capacity for holding heat that makes the world's oceans so important in controlling climate. Huge bodies of water absorb heat when it is present, during the day and during summertime, and release it at night or during the winter. If it were not for the moderating influence of water in this way, Earth would be subject to painful extremes of heat and cold, and we who live on it might start feeling like that pan that sat atop the hot stove.

Water has been around since the beginning of the world, or at least the beginning of the world as we know it. One theory is that when the earth began cooling down from a molten state 4,000,000,000 or so years ago, it had an atmosphere made up of many gases. Some of them would have been quite poisonous to life, but others included the constituents of water. As the cooling process continued, a new atmosphere developed, and water vapor was formed. Eventually the oceans were born, and in them, it is widely believed, were spawned the ancestors of all the creatures on earth.

Humans made their way out of the watery environment and started breathing air many eons ago, but the intensity of our dependence on water is second only to our need for that air. The adult human's body is around 65 per cent water (babies are wetter than grownups). Our blood is about 83 per cent water, and the liquid makes up close to three-quarters of our brains. Water in our bodies does most of the things that it does for our societies—it lubricates, cools, carries nutrients around from one place to another, and, just like far too many of our rivers and streams, carries off our wastes. It is impossible to say how much water a human must have each day in order to go on living, because too many variables come into play—the person's size and weight and metabolism, the ambient temperature, the individual's rate of exercise, and other factors that influence the degree with which he or she loses water and, thereby, needs it replaced. Under normal conditions, the average human needs between two and three quarts of water each twenty-four hours. But that statistic, like a surprising number of others associated with water in all its complex manifestations, is wrong about as much of the time as it is right. A walker carrying a thirty-five-pound backpack, traversing mile after mile of hilly terrain in a western desert where there is intense heat and bright sunlight and little or no shade, may not feel comfortable unless he or she has consumed more than a gallon and a half a day. People have been known to drink so much water that they have died—the condition is called psychogenic polydipsia, or compulsive water drinking—and some of its victims, who have suffered convulsions and coma, have said that they were trying to cleanse themselves of sin. While it might be difficult to document the often-quoted admonition that one can drown in a teacup, the point is well made that it is not hard for water to overcome and damage the body it normally keeps alive. Its superior ability to act as a solvent makes water one of the best agents of hygiene and medicine, but the same characteristic means that water is an excellent vehicle for the transmission of disease.

We take a lot of water into our bodies simply by eating food. The U.S. Department of Agriculture has calculated the water content for hundreds of foods, including apples, which are about 85 per cent water; choice beef chuck, 61 per cent; beer, 92 per cent; cola-type soft drinks, 90 per cent; diet cola-type soft drinks, 100 per cent; herring (Atlantic), 69 per cent, and herring (Pacific), 79 per cent; potatoes, 80 per cent; hot dogs, 56 per cent; lean reindeer, 73 per cent; spinach, 91 per cent; boysenberries, 90 per cent. Peanut butter contains very little water—less than 2 per cent, according to the Agriculture Department—which helps explain why a sandwich made of it goes so well with a glass of milk (87 per cent for whole, 91 per cent for skim).

Considering how valuable it is, relatively little is actually said about water in normal, daily conversation unless it is in very short supply or unless it suddenly becomes overabundant. Still, humans have managed, by their actions, to hint at the respect that they have for the substance. American Indians, whose lives have always been closer to nature than other Americans', have treated rivers with the greatest awe. Some tribes believed that fast-flowing springs were sacred and that the bubbles that issued from them were caused by the breathing of spirits. Water is important, too, in the organized religions of the white man. In one of them, it is even called "holy water." In some parts of the United States the seriousness with which a churchgoer takes his religion is felt by some to be correlated directly with the amount of water used in the baptismal ritual. The Koran states, simply and truthfully: "By water everything lives." And today, Americans spend upward of four dollars a gallon on bottles of water imported from other nations, which they drink and discuss with almost religious fervor at cocktail parties.

Water *does* exert an almost holy influence on our emotions and actions, whether we admit it or not. It is difficult to hike through the western slopes of the Great Smoky Mountains in western North Carolina, a place where vast amounts of rain fall, without feeling emotional about the effects of all that water on the environment. The treeless rounded tops of some of the mountains, called "balds" locally, are vibrant green from grasses and heathery vegetation. In the hollows the growth is jungle-like, and along the sides of the mountains the traveler is likely to be quite moved by the trickles, springs, and outpourings he encounters. The mountain seems to be weeping, there is so much water inside it. The rock seems to be made of water. And the water that pours forth all goes downhill, pulled by gravity, to sustain the planet's life.

At the base of El Morro National Monument, in west-central New Mexico, is a sight that must have been an emotional one for thirsty travelers: a small pool of water, perhaps 200,000 gallons of it, blooming in the hot, dry, high plains. The pool rests at the foot of a tall, tan mesa, and since it is the only reliable body of water for miles around, it has attracted pilgrims since prehistoric times. Because it is on the rock's north side, the pool is protected from much of the sun's evaporative powers. Its major, and almost only, source of recharge is the rain that falls in July, August, and September, along with some snow in winter. For hundreds of years trails have carried travelers by the mesa, and many of them have carved their name into the soft sandstone alongside the refreshing green water. Don Juan de Oñate, the first governor of New Mexico, passed by in 1605. General Don Diego de Vargas added his name, as did dozens of emigrants to California in the 1850s. What made the rock worth stopping at, of course, was the almost miraculous supply of the life-sustaining substance at its base.

Unfortunately, water also has inspired those who view it not as a precious substance, worthy of feelings approaching devotion, but rather as something to be *dealt with*; something to *overcome*. These people, most of whom seem to be employed by, or to serve as consultants to, government agencies, always speak of "managing" water. (They are the ones who also speak of "managing" wildlife, wetlands, and alligator populations, by which they generally mean "exploiting" them.) Thanks to them, "managing" and "management" have become the two most overworked terms in Washington—and, simultaneously, the least meaningful. Water can no more be "managed" than can alligators or rainfall, despite the fact that the bureaucrats keep trying to convince each other that it can. A recent report to the Secretary of Commerce from his "Weather Modification Advisory Board" (titled, of course, "The Management of Weather Resources") advises of the need for "an extraordinary—if relatively modest—national commitment to an effort to improve our ability to manage one small but important aspect of the human environment—our weather resources." And a commissioner of the Bureau of Reclamation clearly demonstrated his feelings for nature as well as the language when he advised Congress that "A major research thrust in atmospheric water resources management has yielded promising information which could be used to overcome the relative inefficiency of nature in producing precipitation at the times and places where it can be better utilized for man's benefit." Luckily for nature, bureaucrats and weather modification advisory boards evaporate relatively quickly, while the weeping mountains and desert oases stay around a bit longer.

We have conducted trials with water, allowing a river or a boiling vat to serve as a suspected witch's judge and jury, and often as the executioner as well. We have made our favorite mythological figures rise out of, and live in, water. We have hurled human sacrifices into water. The Greeks used to put coins into the mouths of the dead so that they might pay their ferryboat fare across the Styx. Our early explorers tasted and reported on the water before they checked into anything else, and even today it is evidence of water, in the form of ice crystals, that excites us most when our spacecraft send back information on our fellow planets. When the premier cities of the world were constructed, almost all of them were built beside bodies of water; in Paris, it was a series of village wells that provided the magnet. When the promoters of San Antonio, Texas, which is not premier, wanted to make their city less secondary, they naturally lit on water as the logical way to increase municipal self-esteem and visitors' attention. They picked a neglected stream—it was more like a sewer—that ran through the center of town. Now the river and accompanying walkway are the focal point for the city, with a properly classy name (Paseo del Rio) and with smart shops and eating places along its banks and barges that may be chartered for weddings and parties.

All around the nation, and particularly along the East Coast, towns and cities that once relied on water for their trade, their intellectual stimulation, and quite often for their very existence, but that had lost touch with their watery beginnings, recently have rebuilt waterfronts, installed parks and marinas and promenades, and in general have reaffirmed their dependence on water. New York City could hardly be oriented more toward water, situated as it is at the confluence of one major and several lesser rivers and an ocean. But through the years the city has lost most of its connection with the liquid that is all around it, to the point where a citizen has a difficult time getting close to the stuff. Only now is New York showing interest in trying to rescue its badly decayed waterfront. The city's exact course of action has not yet been set (any deliberations concerning the control of real estate are bound to drag on for years in New York), but the preliminary indications are that much of the "rediscovery" will accrue to the benefit of private speculators and builders, and that when they finish "saving" the waterfront the ordinary citizen will be the last in line to be allowed to see and use it.

Water, in the form of rivers and the larger lakes, serves frequently as a boundary between states and nations that is handy and easily recognizable (although streams do tend to wander as time goes by, and the nationality of at least one community along the Rio Grande, where it serves as the border between the United States and Mexico, is in dispute). Every once in a while, water seems to bring out some of the less desirable characteristics of humans. Clean drinking water at easily affordable prices is not always easy to find in parts of southernmost Texas, and until very recently poor Americans of Mexican ancestry, who lived in rural communities known as *colonias*, were condemned to get their water from shallow, salty wells of questionable purity, or from irrigation ditches where it could be polluted with pesticides, or to haul it from the homes of friends and relatives in the towns. The attitude of those who run things in south Texas, who are almost all Anglos, is generally that there is not only no such thing as a free lunch, but not even a free glass of water. When the city of McAllen ran a fresh-water line out to an industrial complex it was building a few years ago, the line passed beneath Colonia Balboa, a Mexican-American settlement that was contiguous to, and in every way except ethnicity a part of, the city itself; yet McAllen refused at first to allow Balboa's residents to tap into the line. Later a compromise was effected, but meanness remains a way of life in water issues in much of the Southwestern part of the nation.

Water, more than any other substance, clearly has dictated where we may grow our food, build our homes, live, and, in some cases, die. And yet, most of the time we hardly think about water, either in our personal lives or in the most far-reaching plans and proclamations of our governments. Water seems to be almost *too* abundant, *too* cheap, too easily taken for granted. Although there are moments, some of them painfully long ones, during which water becomes scarce, we tend—especially we in the United States—to treat such periods as aberrations, as departures from a norm in which water is precisely as plentiful as we want it to be. A recently completed government study, which sought to examine the probable changes in the world's population, its natural resources, and its environment through the end of the twentieth century, and which was titled *The Global 2000 Report to the President*, examined this aspect of water and noted, with the usual flourishes about "management":

"While the identification of water as an important natural resource seems beyond argument, water has not always been viewed as a resource in the same sense as coal, petroleum, mineral ores, timber, and crops. In fact, the management and utilization of water has followed patterns distinctly different from those of other economic resources. The differences may stem from the relative abundance of water in many parts of the world, or from ambiguity concerning the resource nature of water."

A resource, said the authors of the study (who included experts from agencies as diverse as the Council on Environmental Quality, Department of State, Environmental Protection Agency, National Science Foundation, and National Oceanic and Atmospheric Administration), is usually thought of as "something that can be used for supply or support." Most elements of the physical environment would come under that definition. "Resources that attract the attention of analysts and policymakers, however," continued the report, "are those that display an additional characteristic—scarcity. If all resources were available in unlimited quantity wherever and whenever desired, resource planning and resource management would not be required. Most resources are scarce in some sense, and these scarce (or economic) resources are the legitimate object of national and global concern. . . .

"The concept of water as an economic resource, subject to scarcity and dependent upon rational management, is not universally shared. Water has often been ignored in resource planning efforts or has been presumed to obey economic laws different from those that apply to other resources. The planning and construction of water supply works, the allocation of water among users, the pricing of water—these and other activities have been frequently influenced by the notion that water is virtually 'free goods,' which should be provided as cheaply as possible in any quantity desired."

The study then went on to list six general properties of water as a resource: Water, it said, is ubiquitous on the earth; its existence "is a fundamental assumption." With its different forms and characteristics, it is perhaps the least homogeneous of all the natural resources. It is renewable. Unlike mineral resources, it may be common property. It is used in vast quantities. And it is very inexpensive. All these qualities, said the government report, make it difficult to deal with water resources as one would deal with, say, coal or petroleum. In listing those properties, the study seemed to be seeking some sort of a *political* definition of water, rather than the more frequently encountered scientific-physical one. The very fact that government thinkers, charged with peering into the future, were attempting to probe such relatively uncharted territory seemed to underscore the fact that our perceptions of water are changing; that the time has come when we must begin thinking differently about the substance.

3

One of the reasons we have thought so little about water until now is the fact that there is so much of the liquid—so much that it is beyond our ability to measure it. The United Nations estimate of the total world volume of water in all forms, 1.4×10^9 cubic kilometers, is based on figures from A. Baumgartner and E. Reichel in their 1975 publication in Munich of *The World Water Balance*. Other estimates would seem to be fairly close; the U.S. Geological Survey uses 326,000,000 cubic miles, which translates into about 1.36×10^9 cubic kilometers. A 1967 estimate by C. A. Doxiadis, the Greek big thinker, is also about 1.36×10^9. The difference between 1.36×10^9 and 1.4×10^9 cubic kilometers may seem trifling, but actually it works out to about 10.5 quintillion gallons of water, or approximately enough to make the Mississippi River flow at its normal volume for almost 70,000 years.

The suspected quantities of water as it exists in its various forms are equally staggering. Baumgartner and Reichel estimate that, of the 1.4×10^9 cubic kilometers on the planet, 97.3 per cent, or 1.36×10^9 cubic kilometers, is in the oceans at any given moment. The remainder, which constitutes roughly the world's fresh-water supply, is 3.78×10^7 cubic kilometers of water, or 9,068,220 cubic miles, or almost 10 quintillion gallons. Of that remainder, an estimated 77.2 per cent, or 2.92×10^7 cubic kilometers, is stored in polar ice caps and glaciers. The largest body of frozen water, the Antarctic ice cap, is about 6,000,000 square miles in area and between 6,000,000 and 7,000,000 cubic miles in volume. The Geological Survey has calculated that if the Antarctic cap were melted at a uniform rate it could fill either the Mississippi River for more than 50,000 years, all U.S. rivers for about 17,000 years, the Amazon River for about 5,000 years, or all the rivers of the world for about 750 years.

About 22.4 per cent of the fresh water is in groundwater and soil moisture. About two-thirds of the groundwater is believed to lie deeper than 750 meters, or 2,461 feet, beneath the surface of the earth, and thus is very hard to get at. (In fact, hydrologists generally calculate that only about 1 per cent of the global supply of water is readily available for human use.) An estimated 0.35 per cent of the fresh water is found in lakes and swamps. The atmosphere accounts for relatively little of the world's water at any given moment—0.04 per cent of the non-ocean supply. The Geological Survey has calculated that if all the water in the atmosphere were to fall at once as rain, the earth would be submerged to a depth of only one inch.

(There is a certain fascination to be had in dealing with statistics concerning water—one brought on, no doubt, by the sheer enormousness of the substance in question. The USGS has also figured that if all the water in the world were poured on the fifty states—not just all that in the atmosphere, but also all that in the oceans, rivers, and aquifers—the nation would find itself beneath 90 miles of water. The agency does not explain whether British Columbia, which stands between the lower forty-eight and Alaska, would be similarly sodden.

(Inasmuch as football fields are so useful in demonstrating the relative sizes of large objects, it seems reasonable that quantities of water might be reckoned in terms of bathtubs. There is no truly standard-sized bathtub, but the Kohler Corporation, which makes a lot of the devices, says that most people seem to buy models that are 5 feet long and either 14 or 16 inches deep and hold 35 and 42 gallons of liquid, respectively. The suspected total world supply of water, then, would fill 10 quintillion, 566 quadrillion, 293 trillion bathtubs of the 35-gallon variety, provided they were loaded to the overflow vent. The amount of water that would slop down the drain if people got into all those tubs at the same moment is too awesome to consider.)

Only 0.01 per cent of the water that is not in the oceans at any given moment is believed to be in streams and rivers. Compared to the other forms and receptacles in which water may be found, the quantity in streams seems relatively tiny. But it isn't. The figures for streamflow, like statistics for everything else watery, are enormous: New York's Hudson River discharges 9,000,000 gallons each minute as it flows past Manhattan (up north at Glens Falls, much closer to its source at Lake Tear of the Clouds in the Adirondack Mountains, the Hudson runs at 2,000,000 gallons a minute). The Ohio River, whose drainage area includes parts of Ohio, Indiana, Kentucky, West Virginia, Pennsylvania, Illinois, Tennessee, New York, Maryland, and North Carolina, produces 125,000,000,000 gallons a day. The Mississippi River, into which the Ohio feeds, is the United States' largest, carrying about 40 per cent of all the nation's rainfall to the sea. The river collects the drainage from 1,232,000 square miles, (or about 40 per cent) of the land area of the lower forty-eight states. It discharges 133 cubic miles of water a year into the Gulf of Mexico. That works out to 620,000 cubic feet per second.

And the Mississippi is almost a sluggish brook compared with the Amazon, which runs 2,348 miles through Brazil. The Amazon discharges more than 11 times the volume of the Mississippi, or 1,664,191,100,000,000 gallons a year.

Water in all of its forms—in the rivers, in the atmosphere, and even in the glaciers—is constantly moving through a process called the hydrologic cycle, which is one of the less complicated natural processes on the planet. Water that is on the earth's surface—in lakes, rivers, and reservoirs, but particularly in the oceans—evaporates because of the sun's heat. It floats into the air as vapor; when the vapor cools, it condenses and returns to earth as precipitation. After falling as rain, snow, sleet, or hail, the water again collects in large bodies, where the cycle continues. Although the cycle sounds devilishly simple, humankind manages to do a great deal with the water during the time it is on Earth's surface. We pounce upon it as soon as it falls and capture and impound it, drink it, put it on our crops, run it through our air conditioners and over our bodies, employ it to carry off our wastes, sail our boats in it, boil our eggs and potatoes in it, wash our cars and our dogs in it, make electricity with it, barge coal and refrigerators on it, ski on it, cool nuclear reactors with it, swim in it, search for trout and catfish in it, and, finally, we swear at it when it comes down too quickly or not often enough. We treat water even worse than dirt.

Because of the things we do to water as it goes through the cycle, and because of the other substances with which water comes in contact, the thing that we call "water" can hardly ever be a pure combination of two atoms of hydrogen and one of oxygen. James Wilson, in a booklet titled *The Inorganic Constituents of Natural Water*, published by the Academy of Natural Sciences of Philadelphia, explains that H_2O picks up numerous other chemicals in its time in, on, and over Earth, including bicarbonate and carbonate, calcium, silica, sulfate, chloride, sodium, magnesium, manganese, potassium, phosphate, nitrate, and iron. Wilson further declares: "Pure water—that is, water consisting only of water molecules—*does not* and *cannot* exist in nature. Nature simply will not allow it to exist. At the very second it is formed, a drop of liquid water is in immediate contact with the gases in the atmosphere; the very second it touches . . . earth, the properties which make it a 'universal' solvent cause it to acquire 'impurities' from virtually every natural feature with which it comes in contact, from dust to tree leaves to minerals from rock formations thousands of feet below the earth's surface."

Evaporation is not the only method by which water gets into the atmosphere. A great deal is released from the surface of the earth by the process known as transpiration, in which moisture moves up plants' roots, through their trunks or stems, and out through tiny holes on the undersides of their leaves.

Luna B. Leopold and Walter B. Langbein, in a Geological Survey publication called *A Primer on Water*, note that transpiration is one of the more important sources of water vapor. An acre of corn, they say, releases 3,000 to 4,000 gallons of water each day, and a large oak tree can produce about 40,000 gallons a year. Scientists sometimes combine transpiration and evaporation into a single word, evapotranspiration, to account for all the Earth-based sources of water vapor.

The hydrologic cycle has a certain uncomplicated purity, functioning as it does with the assistance of such basic working components as solar energy and gravity. A Geological Survey pamphlet on the cycle calls it "a natural machine, a constantly running distillation and pumping system. The Sun supplies heat energy, and this together with the force of gravity keeps the water moving; from the Earth to the atmosphere as evaporation and transpiration, from the atmosphere to the Earth as condensation and precipitation, and between points on the Earth as streamflow and groundwater movement. As a cycle, this water system has neither beginning nor end, but from man's point of view, the oceans are the major source, the atmosphere is the deliverer, and the land is the user." The cycle also helps explain two points about water that are often overlooked: The first is that water is not used up, nor is it created. The same water is around now that was around a hundred, a thousand, or a billion years ago. (As some researchers are wont to say, the water with which Christ was baptized, and which Cleopatra used to float her barge, is still here.) We can boil a kettle of water until the liquid disappears, but it will be back someday. We recycle water whether we want to or not. Our continuing use and reuse of water are, of course, greatly influenced by our efforts, or lack of them, to keep the substance clean.

The second point about water, having considered its volume, that is obvious but not often thought about is that, strictly speaking, there is little difference between salt water and fresh water. Humans, most animals, many other creatures of the earth, and many plants cannot tolerate water in which very much salt is dissolved. The rule of thumb about salinity seems to be that a concentration of 500 milligrams per liter of dissolved solids in water is acceptable. A milligram, which is a measure of weight, is one-thousandth of a gram. A gram is less than four-hundredths of an avoirdupois ounce. (Expressions of milligrams per liter, or mg/l, are roughly comparable to parts per million.) Hydrologists tend to refer to all the solids that are dissolved in water—which can include such substances as calcium, magnesium, sulfate, and others as well as chloride —as "salts." The 500 mg/l concentration is considered "recommended" by the U.S. Public Health Service and the "highest desirable level" by the World Health Organization. But it is possible for humans to consume considerably higher concentrations and survive, or even thrive. The World Health Organization sets 1,500 mg/l as its "maximum permissible level," and the Public Health Service has stated that quite a few public water supplies in the nation provide water with concentrations greater than 2,000 mg/l. "Newcomers and casual visitors would certainly find these waters almost intolerable," said the agency, but "many are able to tolerate if not to enjoy these highly mineralized waters." Only a relatively few fish have evolved systems that allow them to thrive in waters that are alternately fresh or as salty as seawater. But in the larger sense, the water that is salty today may be fresh tomorrow, and the fresh water that we drink today may be part of the ocean tomorrow—a literal fact if we live in New York City, San Francisco, or any other coastal community.

Prodigious quantities of water are involved in the hydrologic cycle. Each year, according to calculations by Swedish experts Malin Falkenmark and Gunnar Lindh, the sun causes 453,000 cubic kilometers of water to rise from the seas and 73,000 cubic kilometers to evaporate from the land. Most of the evaporated seawater, 412,000 cubic kilometers of it, returns to the sea as rain—a fact that is not surprising, since oceans cover seven-tenths of the earth's surface. The remaining 114,000 cubic kilometers of evaporated moisture from the sea and the land fall as precipitation over land. Of that quantity, 73,000 cubic kilometers return to the atmosphere as evaporation or transpiration. The remaining 41,000 cubic kilometers run down the rivers and seep through the underground aquifers to the sea, completing the cycle.

Falkenmark and Lindh calculate that, on the inhabited continents, there are about 38,000 cubic kilometers of water available in the form of river runoff. This is a very large amount of water—10,037,978,000,000,000 gallons, more or less—but, as the authors point out in their book *Water for a Starving World*, not all of it is considered usable by humans. Because some of it is passed down to the seas in the form of floodwater, only around 35 per cent of the runoff may be thought of as "stable." The authors figure the world's stable supply of runoff, then, at about 14,000 cubic kilometers each year. The figure is not really as small as it sounds, inasmuch as water flowing down a river is almost always used and reused several times, by the populations of several communities or even nations, on its way to the sea. Also, floodwater can be and is captured in reservoirs and stored for use in dry periods. With all those conditions in mind, and assuming the most efficient utilization of water as it moves through the cycle (Israel currently holds the world's record in this category), Falkenmark and Lindh figure that a maximum of 70 per cent of the total runoff might conceivably be extracted and used by humans. This leaves us (literally, if the calculations are correct) with about 27,000 cubic kilometers of usable water, or about 7 quadrillion gallons per year.

Numerous methods have evolved for measuring such large quantities of water (hardly anyone goes around talking about quadrillions of gallons). The United Nations, which has shown interest in global water supplies for many years, tends to count in terms of cubic kilometers and other forms of metric measurement. One cubic kilometer is equal in volume to 0.2399 cubic mile, and in one cubic mile of water there are 1.1011143×10^{12} gallons.

The flow of rivers is frequently measured and expressed in terms of the number of cubic feet of water that pass a certain point in one second. One cubic foot per second, which would appear to be just a trickle in a stream, translates into about 449 gallons per minute, or 646,315 gallons per day. During the Western gold-mining era, a unit of measurement called the "miner's inch" was popular, but it also was very confusing, inasmuch as the Western states couldn't seem to agree on what a miner's inch *was*. It was defined as the amount of water that would flow through a one-inch-square hole while under a certain pressure. It was the certain pressure that varied among the states, so that one cubic foot per second equaled 50 miner's inches in Idaho, Utah, northern California, and some other places; or it equaled 40 miner's inches in Arizona, Oregon, Montana, and *southern* California; or it equaled 38.4 miner's inches in Colorado. The system was obviously insane, and it has given way in the West to the widespread use of acre feet as a measure of large amounts of water, particularly irrigation water. An acre foot of water is the amount needed to cover one acre, which is 43,560 square feet, to a depth of one foot—or 43,560 cubic feet. One cubic foot of water contains 7.480519 gallons, so an acre foot contains a bit more than 325,851 gallons. In the West this amount is generally thought of as representing the personal water needs of a family of five for one year.

The arithmetic seems fairly neat, even when it's being converted back and forth among metric measure, U.S. customary units, and acre feet. So it should not be surprising that government is hard at work unsimplifying it all. The State of California lately has begun quoting water volume in "cubic dekametres," which are not too far from acre feet, but which nobody else ever heard of. "Cubic dekametres" do not appear in standard conversion tables issued by the Geological Survey or the U.S. Bureau of Standards, and the Institute of Electrical and Electronics Engineers, Inc., in its widely used handbook of metric standards, suggests that the "deka" prefix should be "avoided where practical." The term does, however, have the attractive quality of requiring more bureaucratic time and paper in order to translate.

Publications on water routinely round off measurements. (An acre foot, says an otherwise handy little water-volume slide rule produced by the Metropolitan Water District of Southern California, is 325,900 gallons. That is actually 49 gallons too much. It may seem like a small error, unless one is talking, as the Metropolitan Water District frequently is, in terms of a million acre feet, in which case the error is 49,000,000 gallons.) One consequence of the difference in numbers is that calculations are rarely precise. This is just as well, because water experts admit, when asked, that theirs is a very imprecise science. "We have no idea whatsoever how much water there is in the ground, in the air, or in the streams," said one of them, a Westerner who works for the U.S. Geological Survey, not long ago. "It's amazing, considering how much we rely on the stuff, but it's real hard to measure. Most of the time nobody's very interested in coming up with an exact figure. It's only when it gets scarce that people start talking about gallons and cubic feet instead of acre feet and cubic miles."

Another way to measure water, and one that is familiar to anyone who listens to weather reports following a rainfall, is in inches. An inch of rain is the amount that it takes to cover one acre to a depth of one inch. It equals 27,143 gallons and weighs a little more than 100 metric tons.

The Geological Survey, which always seems to be trying to make water and its characteristics more understandable, has set forth a "water budget" for the nation that expresses in inches some of the same hydrological principles that others have applied, in cubic kilometers, to the global water supply. The Survey estimates that about 30 inches of rain, or about 1,430 cubic miles of water, falls on the United States each year. Since one inch of rainfall falling on the entire country would cover the nation to a depth of one inch, 30 inches, if it all happened at the same time, would leave the United States under two and one-half feet of water.

Of the 30 inches that fall annually onto the nation, according to the Geological Survey's calculations, rivers carry about 9 inches back to the seas (about 3.5 inches are carried by the Mississippi River alone). The amount of precipitation that seeps back to the seas through groundwater is unknown, but it is believed to amount to less than 0.1 inch out of the 30. Evapotranspiration accounts for 21 inches. The water that is available for Americans' use—the water in stream runoff and in the ground, where it may be obtained by pumping, amounts to an average of 1.3×10^{12} gallons of water per day, or more than 6,000 gallons a day for each resident of the country.

4

Globally, the supply of fresh water has been estimated at about ten times the demand, a calculation that would seem to reinforce the notion that there is so much water around that we hardly need to think about it. Another projection, made in the mid-1970s, was that there were about 10,000 cubic meters, or 2,642,000 gallons, of water available per year for each person in the world. Those numbers have little real meaning because of the seasonal nature of water and because it frequently isn't where the people are who need it. Many citizens of the world have very little water available to them and many others have far more than they could ever use. A United Nations expert on water supplies, Enzo Fano, wrote in the mid-1970s that "almost 80 per cent of the population of the developing countries lack adequate water supply and this tragic situation has shown very little improvement during the last decade."

The great majority of the water, perhaps 80 per cent of it, that is used globally is used in agriculture. Beyond that, information on world water quantity and quality is hard to find and, when it does turn up, it illustrates the uncertainties associated with the art and science of studying water. The amount of water believed to be stored in the ground to a depth of 4,000 meters (one way of categorizing the groundwater that is relatively easily obtained) has been estimated both at 8.1×10^6 and at 10.5×10^6 cubic kilometers—a difference of almost 634,000,000,000,000,000 (634 quadrillion) gallons. Products of erosion carried annually by world streams have been calculated at between 12,000,000,000 and 51,000,000,000 metric tons, another rather large spread.

In March, 1977, a United Nations Water Conference was held at Mar del Plata, Argentina, and it attracted representatives from 116 nations. The meeting was one of a series of UN-sponsored "megaconferences" on issues of world concern (others have been held on the topics of human environment, population, food, human settlements, desertification, science and technology for development, and new and renewable sources of energy). The very first recommendation printed in the conference report referred to the worldwide scarcity of reliable information on water. It said: "In most countries there are serious inadequacies in the availability of data on water resources, particularly in relation to ground water and water quality. Hitherto, relatively little importance has been attached to its systematic measurement. The processing and compilation of data have also been seriously neglected." The conference participants recommended that nations take several steps to improve their collection of water information.

There is no shortage of data on how water is used in the United States. Very often the information is conflicting and confusing, but it is certainly abundant. Every five years, the U.S. Geological Survey calculates the ways in which the nation's water supply is used. The most recent compilation of these statistics, for the year 1975, was published in 1977 by hydrologists C. Richard Murray and E. Bodette Reeves. In it, the authors asserted that the nation's water use had grown to about 420,000,000,000 gallons a day, or about 1,900 gallons per person per day. (There is some of the usual statistical confusion over the number of total gallons withdrawn. Elsewhere in their report, the hydrologists use 416,000,000,000 gallons, and if their statistics for the various categories of use are added up, the result is yet another figure.)

The amount used, wrote Murray and Reeves, represents the water that is withdrawn from surface and ground supplies for public purposes (including domestic, commercial, and industrial applications), for rural domestic and livestock use, for irrigation, and for self-supplied industrial use in the United

States, Puerto Rico, and the U.S. Virgin Islands. The 1,900 gallons-per-person-per-day represents the per capita disposition of all the water that's withdrawn in the nation. (The amount of water that is used strictly in people's homes, for drinking, cooking, tooth brushing, and the like, is, of course, much lower. One study places the range at 10 to 80 gallons per person per day.) If only fresh-water supplies are counted (many industrial processes use saline water), the national per capita average falls to 1,600 gallons per day. The per capita total (including saline water) for 1975 was 100 gallons per day more than the average for 1970, and it was approximately double the usage of twenty years before. But it represented the smallest percentage of increase since the USGS started conducting its five-year assessments in 1950.

Hydrologists sometimes refer to the *consumption* of water; by that they mean the water that is made unavailable for further use after its withdrawal because of evaporation (as in storage ponds), transpiration (as through the leaves of agricultural crops), ingestion by humans or animals, or incorporation into foods or products. In the 1975 assessment, the hydrologists determined that 95,000,000,000 gallons (or 96,000,000,000, according to another part of their report) of the total 420,000,000,000 withdrawn each day in the United States were consumed. That represented a 10 per cent increase over the 1970 figure.

The calculations on withdrawal did not include another 3,300,000,000,000 gallons a day that are drawn from surface supplies to create hydroelectric power. Such supplies are considered "in-channel" uses, since they put the withdrawn water immediately back into the stream. (There is some consumption, however, due to evaporation. A 1962 USGS hydrological paper estimated that principal reservoirs and regulated lakes in the seventeen western states gave up 11,000,000,000 gallons a day, or more than 4,000,000,000,000 gallons a year, in evaporation.) Withdrawals for hydropower in 1975 constituted a 20 per cent increase over the 1970 figures.

Of the water that was withdrawn in the United States, wrote Murray and Reeves, almost two-thirds of it came from fresh surface waters (such as lakes and rivers) and 20 per cent from fresh groundwater. Seventeen per cent came from saline surface waters, and very small portions came from saline groundwater and reclaimed sewage. ("Saline" water, in this case, is defined as water containing more than 1,000 milligrams of dissolved solids per liter of solution, regardless of the sort of minerals that produce the solids.) The nation continued a trend, in the meantime, of obtaining more and more water from below-the-ground supplies. Between 1950 and 1975, according to the report, the nation's population rose from 150,700,000 to 217,500,000, a 44 per cent increase; during the same time, withdrawals from groundwater went from 34,000,000,000 to 82,000,000,000 gallons a day, a 141 per cent increase, while withdrawals from surface water went from 160,000,000,000 to 260,000,000,000 gallons a day, a 63 per cent rise.

The total withdrawals equaled more than one-third of the nation's average streamflow, which hydrologists consider a rough measure of the total amount of water that is available to humans. That ratio may seem to provide a comfortable margin, but reality, in this case as in most others, is much less neat than statistics. Some portions of the nation which have large streamflow and modest demands use very little water available to them. Others, including sections of the middle Atlantic, Missouri Basin, Texas and Gulf, Rio Grande, lower Colorado, and California regions, withdrew more water than what the Geological Survey likes to call the "locally dependable supply."

Twenty-nine billion gallons a day of the water withdrawn in the nation in 1975, according to the hydrologists, went into public supplies. This includes water for drinking, bathing, cooling, firefighting, street cleaning, municipal swimming pools, and the like. About one-third of the public supply is sold to commercial and industrial users. A shockingly large portion of the total disappears from the system through dripping faucets, leaking water mains and hydrants, and errors in measurement: a Geological Survey publication in 1960 placed the figure for waste from public systems at 20 per cent of the total use, although estimates made by the water utilities generally run to about half that.

The 29,000,000,000 gallons estimated for public use represent about 7 per cent of the nation's total water withdrawals, and that works out to 168 gallons per day per user. Twenty-three per cent of the public supplies withdrawn was consumed.

Rural uses accounted for 2,800,000,000 gallons a day for domestic purposes, of which half was consumed, and 2,100,000,000 gallons a day for livestock, 95 per cent of which was consumed. In all, rural uses added up to a little more than 1 per cent of all national withdrawals. The per capita rate at which rural people use their domestic water was much lower than the public water supply—only 66 gallons per day.

Farm irrigation is a big user of water; for 1975 the usage was 140,000,000,000 gallons a day, or 34 per cent of the national total, applied to 54,000,000 acres of farmland. About 56 per cent of the irrigation water withdrawn was consumed, and 16 per cent of it was lost in conveyance. The U.S. Water Resources Council, a federal body made up of several cabinet heads that is charged by a 1965 law with keeping track of the nation's water assets, has used existing drainage basins to establish twenty-one water regions for the nation, eighteen of them in the coterminous states. The 1975 statistics showed that the nine Western regions used 93 per cent of the nation's irrigation water.

The great bulk of all the water used by industry, something like 94 per cent of it, does not come from public systems but rather is obtained by the industry itself. Hydrologists call this "self-supplied" water. In 1975, according to Murray and Reeves, such water accounted for 240,000,000,000 gallons, or 58 per cent, of the nation's daily withdrawals. Of that amount, 78,000,000,000 gallons a day were from saline sources. In contrast to the heavy withdrawal of water for irrigation purposes in the West, some 85 per cent of the self-supplied industrial water in the nation was obtained in the Eastern United States. Eighty-one per cent of it, or close to 200,000,000,000 gallons a day, was used in thermoelectric power plants, and virtually all of *that* was used for condensing spent generator steam. Wrote Murray and Reeves: "Not only does the power industry withdraw the largest quantity of water for off-channel use, but the rate of increase in usage by thermoelectric power plants makes self-supplied industrial use the fastest growing of the major withdrawal uses." Relatively little of the water used in thermoelectric plants is consumed—the USGS report is confusing on the subject, but seems to be saying 1 or 1.5 per cent—while 11 per cent of the self-supplied water used by other industries is consumed. One reason for this difference is that power plants, for reasons of economy and because of environmental regulations, tend to cool the water they use in ponds or towers, so that it may be reused.

Of the 96,000,000,000 or so gallons a day that were consumed, according to the 1975 survey, 84 per cent was spent in the seventeen Western states, largely because of irrigated agriculture. California alone accounts for the consumption of 23,000,000,000 gallons a day, the most of any of the states. Per capita domestic use from public supplies was greater, too, in the drier West, by 27 per cent. Even when commercial and industrial uses were figured in, the West used 19 per cent more. For all withdrawal except hydropower, Western Americans used two times as much water as Easterners, and when hydropower was included they used three times as much.

Alaska was the state with the highest per capita rate of withdrawal from public supplies, with 442 gallons per day. Utah was second with 331 and Nevada used 321 per capita, while Kentucky used 101, New Hampshire, 115, and Virginia, 119. The national average from public supplies was 168 gallons per day. New York State's rate was close to this, at 154 gallons, while Connecticut used 134 and New Jersey, 145.

Western states came in with very large per capita figures

when the water withdrawals, excluding hydropower, came from all sources, not just public supplies. In this case, the national average was about 1,600 gallons per capita per day; it was greatly exceeded by Idaho, with 21,000 gallons, and Wyoming and Montana, with 17,000 gallons each. Rhode Island had the lowest withdrawal rate, 160 gallons per capita per day. "High per capita values," wrote Murray and Reeves, "are characteristic of thinly populated states having large acreages of irrigated land."

These are enormous quantities of water, by any standard of measurement. Calculations involving the amount of water in the ground, or in the seas, or coming down a river, have been, up until recently, fun for operators of slide rules and pocket calculators. They produced such large numbers that they seemed to really not have much meaning; it was like looking at a clear summer night's sky and announcing that there are "billions" of stars out there. When the numbers that reflected estimated usage were projected against the total quantities of water that hydrologists believe exist on the planet, it quickly became evident that the world, and America, were in little danger of running out of water.

That is still the case. The supplies of water on Earth are quite adequate to support life, as well as all conceivable sorts of human endeavor, far into the predictable future. But that no longer is the point. The point of the crisis in which we now are beginning to find ourselves is that no longer will we be able to take water for granted, either in terms of its quality or in terms of its quantity. As a 1976 document for the UN Water Conference put it, from now on "water may be present in the wrong place, it may be available at the wrong time, and it may not be of the right quality (i.e., it may be polluted)."

Even though the supply of water is vast, we are finding that we are tapping, and using, and wasting, the easily obtained portion of it. We have been skimming the cream for a very long time. Water that is cheap and easily obtained is getting scarce. From now on, we are going to be paying increasingly more for our water and going to more trouble to get it. This will have the effect of reducing the quantity of cheap water. At the same time, we are polluting vast portions of our available supply of water (and, in some cases, such as those involving the deep aquifers, the water that is not easily available to us and that might be essential to future generations) with organic and inorganic wastes, some of which are deadly poisons. This, too, has the effect of decreasing the quantity of our water, for water that is poisoned surely must be subtracted from our calculations. We are, in effect, creating our own drought.

All this is happening at a time, furthermore, when competition for usable water seems to be increasing, both nationally and globally. The world rate of population growth is believed to be slowing somewhat, but there are so many people now on the planet that even a slowed rate will result in just a few years in vastly increased demands for food, and therefore for water. Most of the population growth that is expected in the near future will occur in the less developed countries, where adequate food even now is something of a luxury. Coupled with this is the continuing decline in worldwide cropland, a product of increased human development (and need for land on which to put the houses for all those people) and erosion of the soil. One UN document asserts that one-third of the world's arable land will disappear in the next twenty years. Another survey says that continuing deterioration in the land and water environments that produce the things we want and need, together with population growth, has resulted already in a decline in the per capita production of resources such as cattle, grain, fish, and wood.

One way of putting all this is in a phrase used by some experts: We are approaching the world's "carrying capacity," its manageable limits. If this is so, then one sign of the approach might be an increase in unexpected calamities involving water. For much of the world, almost invariably the poorer part, such calamities have been happening for so long that they have almost become the norm. But such thinking is new to the United States. Here, it is an *assumption* that when we turn the faucet on water will come out of it, and it is another assumption that the water that comes out will be of the highest quality.

Those assumptions no longer have unquestioned validity. Calamities are starting to happen with increasing frequency in the United States. Sometimes nothing comes out of the faucet, and—even worse—we are just beginning to learn now that what does come out may be harmful. Those distressing situations, and the overall, nationwide emergency that water supply and quality is turning into, have caught not only the public unawares, but also the engineers, the professionals, the scientists, and, most of all, the people who run the government and who are supposed to protect the health and welfare of the population. Although the crisis is well upon us, we have not yet learned to treat water with the respect that it deserves, or with the awe that it deserves, either. Water, the substance that we have taken for granted for so long, turns out to have, until now at least, very few defenders.

5

Unfortunately, there have been several recent and dramatic illustrations of the degree to which we are approaching our "carrying capacity" for water. One of the most dramatic occurred in New Jersey in the summer and fall of 1980.

New Jersey is the most densely industrialized state in the nation, and much of that industry is closely related to chemicals —the petroleum products and by-products, the solvents and degreasers and processing fluids that are in such great demand by the nation and, in particular, by the New York metropolitan region, of which New Jersey is a distinct and major part. Only Texas, with its enormous petroleum industry, is more involved with chemicals than New Jersey. In addition, many of New Jersey's 7,836 square miles are devoted to suburbia—to providing living space for people who work in New York City or Philadelphia. Suburbia here, as elsewhere, grew rapidly after World War II, and the developers, speculators, and politicians who encouraged it to grow did so with what seems now, with hindsight, to have been minimal attention to what that growth was doing to the environment. They filled in the marshes; they built tract housing within the floodplain, which is the geographical zone which might be expected to be inundated during normal seasonal floods; they spent little time trying to figure out where the sewage and other waste from the new populations would go. Nor did they devote much thought to ensuring safe, centrally operated water supplies for the new people; many residents obtained their water, as do millions of suburban and rural residents around the world, from backyard wells. Some communities—towns or townships or cities—

invested in public-supply wells to serve larger numbers of people, and some of them built reservoirs in the Ramapo Mountains in northwestern New Jersey.

That part of New Jersey that lies alongside New York City —along the Upper New York Bay and the industry-tortured Arthur Kill (*kill*, from the Dutch, means channel or creek), which forms the political boundary between New Jersey and Staten Island—that part of the state had long attracted the sort of industry that seriously threatens the environment with its discharges into the air, the soil, and the water. And the older cities of the northeastern border had similarly insulted the environment by flushing their sewage and other wastes into bodies of water that once had supported great varieties of life. The state takes sewage sludge, 1,700,000 tons of it a year, and much of it from the urban strip along the northeast, and dumps it a dozen miles out into the Atlantic Ocean, at costs to the environment that are only beginning to be calculated.

It has been easy—almost fashionable—to consider northeastern New Jersey a lost cause, an environmental disaster that was too far gone to be repaired; or possibly one that we'd get around to dealing with some day in the distant future. Perhaps the best way to handle the problem, some might conclude, would be to knock everything down and start over from scratch.

The more newly grown New Jersey, the New Jersey of the suburban towns and private wells and commuters, did not start out with the same sort of pestilential industry that has ruined much of the northeast. But it developed industry nevertheless. The costs of maintaining suburbia, with its police departments, firemen, schools, and highway repair crews, are high, and the people who govern those places are forever talking about "broadening the tax base." That means bringing in industry.

Suburbia did not want the same sort of heavy, smelly industry that dominated the northeastern border, but it did welcome smaller, seemingly cleaner manufacturers and processors who had decent payrolls and paid their local taxes on time—the firms whose names smacked of "technology," and which used processes the layman never heard of, and which occupied low, modern buildings that blended in with the landscape and had no ugly smokestacks. If the work these outfits did involved getting rid of large quantities of waste water that was laced with compounds that had strange-sounding names, nobody seemed to worry too much. The state of New Jersey was eager to attract new industry so that the tax base might be broadened, and environmental laws had never been held in terribly high esteem in the state, and so it was not unusual that some of the firms piped their waste materials directly into waterways or into the ground, and that nobody penalized them for it.

The state has long been a leading observer of two other time-honored traditions that go hand in hand—corruption in politics and efforts by practitioners of organized crime to insinuate themselves into, and to dominate, seemingly legitimate businesses—and this added to the state's arsenal of what is fashionably being called "environmental time bombs."

The time bombs have been exploding for several years now. Since the middle 1970s there have been frequent discoveries of chemicals and compounds in New Jersey drinking water, from both private wells and public supplies, which have forced residents—or those residents who could afford it—to shift to some other source of drinking water. In late 1978 suspected carcinogenic substances were found in water from wells serving the public in Mahwah. Not long afterward came the news that the state, in a study of groundwater (about half of the drinking water for New Jersey's 7,400,000 residents comes from wells), had found at least traces of hazardous substances in every well tested, and that it decided to condemn hundreds of wells.

One of the most hazardous metals in general use today is mercury. It developed that for thirty-six years, according to state officials, a processing plant had been dumping mercury into the soil and water of the Hackensack Meadowlands, within a mile of the Giants football stadium and the Meadowlands

Racetrack. According to one estimate, 300 tons of the poisonous metal were believed to be in the ground and in Berry's Creek, which runs through the area. The substance was found as far as six feet down in the soil. A consulting firm (which discovered the poisons while surveying the area for the proposed sports complex) reported in 1976 that "The available data indicate that the streams and wetlands of the Hackensack Meadowlands district are more severely contaminated with mercury than any other area known in the world."

Chloroform, which has been called a carcinogen, was discovered in early 1979 in four of the sixteen wells that provide Fair Lawn, a northern New Jersey suburb-and-industry town, with its drinking water. Chlordane, a pesticide that was banned years ago because it is believed to cause cancer, was discovered in fish in Camden County, and the county health officer said that someone who ate those fish, caught in an area between the New Jersey Turnpike and the Delaware River, might get sick. In early 1980, three firms that specialized in disposing of industrial waste were accused by a grand jury of disposing of them through a seventy-five-foot-long underground pipe that fed into the Arthur Kill. The indictment said that the wastes, 40,000,000 gallons a day of them, came from fifty industrial firms in New Jersey, New York, Pennsylvania, Delaware, and Connecticut.

More than 50,000 customers of a water company in West Orange were told to boil all their drinking water in August, 1980, after a break in a main. Not far away, in West Caldwell, Jersey City, Hoboken, and Lyndhurst, 300,000 residents were left without a supply of clean water after engineers discovered that diesel oil had seeped into an aqueduct near a water treatment plant and reservoir. Newark Bay was fouled with raw sewage. About 150 persons, most of them children, came down with intestinal problems after swimming in a lake in Ringwood State Park in the summer of 1980. A health official said the culprit was probably fecal contamination from a storm-drainage pipe that emptied into the lake.

As the horror stories mounted, and as more and more

residents of New Jersey found themselves forced to purchase their drinking water at grocery stores for a day, a week, or two weeks because of some mysterious, unexpected, and not very well defined "problem with the water," the official reports started coming out. In 1977, Rocco D. Ricci, then the state's environmental commissioner, announced that New Jersey had 12,000 industries that dumped toxic wastes into the water and sewer systems and that some of the wastes were turning up in people's drinking water. Two years later a governor's commission on hazardous waste, headed by Ricci (now departed from the state job and heading a regional sewerage commission), said there was an "imminent threat" to the state's welfare from the improper handling of 4,000,000 to 5,000,000 tons of such waste per year. The number of businesses producing toxic waste was now placed at 10,000, and the commission said it believed 60 per cent of the product was dumped in the Atlantic and that much of the remainder was disposed of illegally. By 1980, another state official was saying that New Jersey had 15,000 companies that produced 1,200,000,000 gallons of liquid chemical wastes per year, along with 350,000 tons of chemical sludges. Ninety per cent of that is disposed of properly, said the official, Edwin H. Stier, who was the director of the state's Toxic Waste Investigation-Prosecution Unit. If the figures were correct, that would mean that 120,000,000 gallons of liquid and 35,000 tons of chemical sludges were *not* disposed of properly each year.

Chemical waste in New Jersey, said Diane Graves, who chaired the state chapter of the Sierra Club, in the summer of 1979, "is a gigantic and hideous problem." And, as it has turned out, it is a problem that can and does strike anywhere. When improper disposal of toxic wastes first came dramatically to the attention of the general public in 1977 and 1978, with the revelation of the Love Canal tragedy, it seemed possible to explain part of the problem away by noting that, after all, Love Canal was up there by Buffalo, New York, in an area that was notorious for its abuse of the environment. *Of course* there were "problems" at Love Canal. It was possible to be similarly unsurprised when toxic chemicals and heavy metals started turning up in the soil and water of northeastern New Jersey. After all, that's what that part of the state is all about.

But what about Rio Grande, New Jersey? And what about Jackson Township? Rio Grande is a tiny town on the southernmost tip of New Jersey, less than eight miles from Cape May Point. The terrain around Rio Grande is one of seashore and marshland, not the heaviest of industries. But homeowners who drew their drinking water from wells found a few years ago that there was as much as five inches of refined oil floating on top of the water table. Oil penetrated the walls and floors of their houses, and fumes from the waterborne substance caused them headaches. Near their homes are two huge oil tanks with a total capacity of 700,000 gallons.

Jackson Township is in the Jersey Pine Barrens, which is a jewel of a natural area, nearly 1,000,000 acres in size, that is situated near the center of the state. The Barrens, which are anything but barren, are covered with forests of pine and oak and filled with blueberries and cranberries, both of which are harvested as commercial crops. This environmental wonder has been under steady, unrelenting attack over the years by politicians and developers who would turn it into, among other things, industrial wasteland, retirement homes, and an airport for Philadelphia. But somehow the Barrens have endured. An immense rural area so close to the New York and Philadelphia metropolitan areas is an oddity itself, but the Pine Barrens offer even more: Much of the plant life there is representative of southern species at their northernmost point in America, and of northern species at their most southern point. And there is the water. Beneath the Pine Barrens there is a relatively shallow aquifer, the Cohansey, that contains, by one estimate, 17,700,000,000,000 gallons of water. The water in the Cohansey has been described by a federal agency as comparable in its quality to uncontaminated rain or melted glacier ice. The Cohansey collects its precious burden with relative ease; rainfall works its way quickly through the sandy, spongy soils of the Pine Barrens. Of course, anything else of a soluble nature that is placed on top of the soil will work its way quickly down to the aquifer as well.

Starting in 1972, according to the state's Department of Environmental Protection in a civil lawsuit it brought against Jackson Township and several individuals, the township had operated a landfill; as a condition of obtaining state registration for the dump, the operators were prohibited from accepting or disposing of "liquid or solid industrial materials," such as chemical wastes. The landfill was not insulated from the underlying aquifer or from nearby surface waters. But since 1975, said the suit, "Jackson Township has known, or should have known, that dangerous chemicals were leaching from the landfill into the groundwater," with the result that there has been a "discharge into the Cohansey aquifer of carcinogenic, toxic, or otherwise poisonous chemicals which contaminate the groundwaters, and which also pose immediate and potential risks of serious illness, cancer, deformity, and even death to persons exposed to such pollution." Furthermore, said the state, the township "continues to fail to operate the landfill in a manner to prevent such pollution."

Since November, 1978, neighbors of the landfill have been advised not to drink their well water. Some of the residents have sued the township as well. The cases are pending.

The plight of a relative handful of families in Jackson Township has been easy for the public to ignore. The families live in an isolated part of the world, even if it is smack in the middle of the East Coast megalopolis, and it is not difficult for the rest of the world to overlook the fact that the residents had to get their drinking water from a cruising tank truck, or that the township that operated the dump offered them the use of showers in a schoolhouse five miles away between the hours of 6 and 8 p.m. on Tuesdays and Thursdays. Those who suffer from water problems, like the water itself, are also the victims of the "out of sight, out of mind" syndrome.

That situation changed a bit in the spring of 1980 when a toxic chemicals storage dump burned and exploded at Elizabeth, New Jersey. Elizabeth, unlike Jackson Township, is close to New York City. The fire, which burned out of control for about half a day, made good television footage; clouds of smoke seemed headed, for a while, toward New York. And there was the fact that the 2.2-acre site was filled with thousands of drums of explosives and toxic wastes, many of them illegally stored. The fire, at a dump that had been operated by the Chemical Control Corporation, was not strictly a *water* problem, although it took place beside the Elizabeth River. (After the fire, officials said they found concentrations of up to 2,000 parts per billion of thirteen chemicals in the river water, but the state health department seemed not alarmed, noting that the river had been polluted all along anyway.) But the fire, which commanded considerable press attention, did demonstrate conclusively, to people in the New York metropolitan area at least, that toxic chemicals were all around them, that little was being done to protect them against the poisons, and that the storage and presumed disposal of such chemicals are fraught with illegalities as well as incompetence—that, in short, Love Canal was not the isolated, upstate incident that many hoped it would turn out to be.

The State of New Jersey had known about problems at the Chemical Control site for at least three years, according to Joseph F. Sullivan in *The New York Times*. Sullivan also wrote that, after an investigation in which the state alleged that the firm had illegally dumped wastes (which other firms were paying it to dispose of legally) in streams, streets, vacant lots, and in sewers in and around northern New Jersey, the president of the company was convicted of creating and maintaining a public nuisance and sentenced to three years in prison. The company pleaded guilty to operating without a permit and was fined the shockingly small sum of $75,000. In 1977 Chemical Control's new president promised to clean the place up. A year and a half later the state checked the site again, found that the cleanup was not progressing, and started doing the job itself. The removal of the drums was under way (many of them were being sent, in one of the many ironies that seem to inflict themselves on the whole toxic waste situation, to another processing plant, said to be a "secure" one, at Niagara Falls, two miles from Love Canal) when the April, 1980, fire broke out. The federal Environmental Protection Agency had planned earlier in the week, according to the press, to use the Elizabeth site as a backdrop for a press conference at which its chief executive, Douglas Costle, was to announce the agency's new regulations to control hazardous wastes. The corroded steel drums of mysterious, dangerous chemicals, reasoned those who were staging the announcement, would look good behind the administrator. But after the fire and explosions, the plan was dropped for safety reasons. At that point, EPA was two years behind its congressionally mandated schedule for issuing the regulations, and it could be argued that if the agency had acted more quickly, then other situations like the Chemical Control fire—situations that are sure to develop, as more and more "toxic time bombs" explode—might be averted.

The Chemical Control fire, along with dozens of other incidents in which aquifers have been tainted, pipelines shut down, and poisonous substances found in the water that people depend on for life, have served to inform New Jerseyites and others in the metropolitan area, if they needed any informing, that they had a serious problem of water quality—perhaps, because of the region's heavy dependence on the manufacture and use of chemicals, the most serious such quality problem in the nation. By the middle of the summer of 1980, the severity of that threat to water quality should have been apparent to anyone. And that was about the time New Jersey started noticing that it had a problem with water *quantity* as well.

The summer was a very dry one for much of the Northeast. There were many days in which rain threatened; the skies became heavy with moisture, but the rain did not fall. Slowly but surely, the reservoirs that held the water for millions of northern New Jersey residents became drier. Other parts of the metropolitan area experienced the drought, too—New York City's situation worsened as winter approached—but its effects on them were not so severe because their reservoirs were situated farther away, where rain did fall, or they were larger, or they existed as part of systems, with built-in interconnections, so that water could be shifted from one storage point to another. This was not the situation in northern New Jersey, where a plethora of private, municipal, and state water systems attempted to serve millions of homes and businesses, with little provision for interconnection.

By mid-September, 1980, the state was urging residents in 114 northern towns to conserve water, and by the end of the month Governor Brendan Byrne had imposed mandatory rationing that was designed to cut water usage by 25 per cent. Households were told they could use no more than 50 gallons per day, and commercial and industrial firms were ordered to cut their use by one-quarter. Penalties for violating the rationing order included jail, fines, surcharges on water bills, and the threat that authorities might install a flow restrictor on a miscreant's water line. The state offered tips on ways to conserve water, tips that had been used before in places like California where droughts were not unusual: Take showers instead of tub baths; catch the shower runoff in a bucket and use it for watering plants; don't let the water run while shaving or brushing teeth; eat off paper plates every once in a while in order to save dishwashing water.

The drought seemed to catch many New Jerseyites by surprise, even though there had been a similar period of dryness (one that affected much of the rest of the metropolitan area) as recently as the mid-1960s. It caught the state government by surprise, too; Trenton obviously had done even less planning for a drought than it had done for the possibility that industrial poisons would contaminate people's drinking water supplies. Following the previous drought, the state had built a reservoir, Round Valley, with a 55,000,000,000-gallon capacity, but had not had the foresight to install pipes to carry its water away to the users. That was but one of the ironies of New Jersey's water supply as the new decade got under way. Another was that some of the same communities whose water supplies only lately had been shut down for reasons of quality, while poisons and chemicals were purged from them, now were having problems with quantity. They were being told that there wasn't enough water to go around. Water was becoming, for them, truly valuable.

6

Nineteen-eighty was the year that much of the nation learned what New Jersey had just found out: that toxic wastes were a problem, that the problem was enormous, and that government at all levels was hopelessly confused over how to solve that problem, if indeed it could be solved. Not only had the same sort of technology that had put us on the moon and given us shiny plastics and powerful glues and efficient spot removers ended up pouring millions of gallons of poisons into the streams and into the earth above our drinking water; it and the technocrats who had promoted it now were unable to tell us how to undo the damage.

Almost overnight, those citizens who kept themselves reasonably well informed realized that deadly chemicals could be anywhere in the environment and, most insidiously, that they could be in the groundwater supplies. The realization came relatively quickly, in the closing moments of the seventies and the beginnings of the eighties, as horror story after horror story unfolded in newspapers and the evening broadcast news. Love Canal was the most outrageous example, of course—a community built by a pit full of industrial poisons, a community that was ignored, lied to, and mistreated—despised, really—by governments at all levels. But it is a community that has persisted, despite the miscarriages and kidney disorders, and that serves as a living reminder of just what we have gotten ourselves into—or, perhaps, as the tip of an iceberg that we are starting only now to probe.

Idaho's Teton Dam, which was built by the U.S. Bureau of Reclamation on porous rock in an earthquake zone, burst in the spring of 1976 and flooded 300 square miles downstream. Chemicals, including DDT and PCB (polychlorinated biphenyl, which was widely used in electrical insulators; it is a poison whose chemical structure is similar to that of the pesticide DDT), had been stored close to the Snake River, and when the dam broke they were washed downstream. Researchers found high levels of the chemicals in fish and wildlife below the dam. Residents of North Miami Beach, Florida, were told for two days in 1977 to avoid drinking water from their home faucets after pesticides showed up in the municipal water supply. In 1974, Robert H. Harris of the Environmental Defense Fund reported that he had discovered a strong statistical connection between the toxic substances found in drinking water drawn from the Mississippi around New Orleans and increased rates of cancer.

For the seventeen years ending in 1970, according to a document prepared for the Senate, a battery manufacturer in Cold Spring, New York, discharged cadmium and nickel into Foundry Cove, on the Hudson River across from West Point. High levels of the heavy metals have been found in mammals, fish, birds, and vegetation there. Sometime in the mid-thirties someone buried, at Perham, Minnesota, a quantity of a substance used for killing grasshoppers. It contained arsenic. In 1972, a contractor dug a well twenty feet from the site, and homeowners started drinking the water. After several of them became ill, the water was tested and it was found to contain as much as 21,000 parts per billion of arsenic (50 parts per billion is considered a safe level). A new, public well was drilled and the poisoned one sealed, reported a government document, but the original contaminant has not been removed because of the costs involved.

A pharmaceutical and chemical firm manufactured hexachlorophene, which was used as a skin cleaner, near Aurora, Missouri, from 1969 until 1972, according to the government. Dioxin, a deadly poison, is a by-product of the manufacturing process. In the spring of 1980 residents of the town were told by government officials that dozens of drums of dioxin had been found stored on a nearby farm in a dump that the firm had used for its wastes, that the drums were leaking, and that the poison might find its way into the town's drinking water. By that time, as is so often the case in toxic waste matters, the firm that produced the poison was out of business, and officials said they weren't sure who would pay for a cleanup or even how a cleanup should be undertaken.

There was so much liquid hazardous waste at the dump at Bumpass Cove, Tennessee, said the government report, that workmen used some of it to wet down the dust on the entrance road. When heavy rains came to the area, barrels of the chemical and other industrial waste were swept down the Nolichucky River, poisoning drinking water supplies downstream.

In Renfrow, Oklahoma, Eva and Lloyd White got about 2,000 gallons of high-octane gasoline from their drinking water well. Their automobile engine had a chronic ping when run on regular gasoline, said Mrs. White in a recent interview, but the irksome noise disappeared when they used the product of the wells. "The wells are probably ruined for years," said Mrs. White. "It's a shame, because we had a good well." A lot of people joked at the time, the winter of 1978, about the free gasoline, but, Mrs. White said later, "gasoline didn't cost but 50 cents a gallon then and we had to go to a lot of trouble to get water, in the blizzards and everything. It cost us more than five hundred dollars to hook up to the regular water supply. I told people we'd be willing to *pay* for our gasoline—we don't drive very much anyway—and I'd rather have the well. The state water resources board held some hearings on it, after a lot of investigations and spending jillions of dollars and man-hours, and they said it came from a storage tank in a gas station about two or three blocks away." There was no talk of restitution, she said. "Nothing was done, but we met a lot of nice people, mostly reporters."

The state of California in 1979 accused the Aerojet General

Corporation and a subsidiary, Cordova Chemical Company, of discharging toxic wastes into the groundwater of Sacramento County since 1963. Throughout Montgomery County, Pennsylvania, and neighboring Bucks County, wells were closed after quantities of trichloroethylene and perchloroethylene were found in the water. Trichloroethylene is a chemical that cuts grease exceptionally well. It is used widely in industry and has been readily available to the public for use in cleaning septic tanks. It causes cancer in animals, and it is assumed to be carcinogenic to humans. Perchloroethylene is a similar chemical. Trichloroethylene has shown up in drinking water supplies all over the country, and it may be the most widespread poison in the current water crisis.

Woburn, Massachusetts, may turn out to be more seriously afflicted by toxic wastes than Love Canal. According to an article by Michael Knight in *The New York Times*, the small city just north of Boston has discovered, starting in 1979, "almost every known major form of hazardous waste pollution," including illegal dumping, wells contaminated with solvents, industrial lagoons containing heavy metals, chloroform in the municipal drinking water supply, radioactive wastes in the town dump, and two firms that recycle drums that contain hazardous waste—one of them by washing the drums and letting the rinse water soak into the ground. Woburn's residents have an abnormally high rate of cancer, and the indications are that drinking water is the source.

When the Ohio River flooded in December, 1978, people noticed a large number of bad-smelling fifty-five-gallon drums bobbing in Stump Gap Creek, about twenty miles southwest of Louisville. It developed that the drums had floated downstream from a farm where about 20,000 other drums full of chemicals were stored. The seven-acre site had been owned by a waste hauler who "trucked the drums to the location, emptied them, and then stored or resold the containers," according to a report by the Library of Congress's Congressional Research Service. The site became known as the Valley of the Drums.

Initial testing of the contents, said the report, revealed that there were 197 organic chemicals and 28 metals, most of them at low concentrations. Twenty-one of them were suspected carcinogens; or mutagens, which cause mutations or heritable changes in the genetic material of cells; or teratogens, which means monster-producing and which causes defects in embyros while they are developing in pregnancy.

At Austin, Texas, said the same report, paper bags containing powdered pesticides, including DDT, had been dumped into a landfill over a period of time. As often happens, the landfill area later was used for another purpose; in this case bulldozers came along in 1979 and scraped the land for a baseball field. The chemicals were unearthed, and rainfall washed them into a nearby pond, killing the fish there. The contaminated soil had to be removed, at considerable expense, before construction could proceed on the baseball field.

A major component of the toxic waste problem concerns the dumping of such poisons into municipal waste systems—either into sewage systems, which were not built to handle synthetic chemicals, or into city storm sewers, which often are just convenient conduits into the nearest river. When someone, whose identity was unknown to the authorities, poured an estimated 2,500 gallons of a cyanide solution into a storm drain in Illinois, the toxic mixture went into a stream which is the public water supply for the town of Newton, sixty miles downstream. Forty thousand fish died in the first thirty miles, said one account, along with five cattle.

In 1978 a man pleaded guilty to dumping more than 730,000 gallons of chemical wastes into a Philadelphia storm sewer. The chemicals then went into the Delaware River near the intake for a water treatment plant that provides about half of Philadelphia's drinking water. The chemicals (which contained traces of eight substances that are believed to cause cancer) entered the river at a waste treatment plant, according to a study by the Environmental Protection Agency. Then they moved seven miles upstream into the intake pipe of the water treatment plant. A congressional report on the incident explained how the poisons defied the nominal flow of the river: "This occurred because Philadelphia is located at the mouth of the Delaware River, which is subject to tidal changes from the Chesapeake Bay. As the tide rises, it sweeps the chemical wastes upstream to the intake pipes for the city's . . . drinking water plant, in what some local officials were described as calling 'a chemical engineering nightmare.'"

New York City, whose residents through the years have not been reluctant to look with disdain, and sometimes fear, on the environmental degradations of their neighbors in New Jersey, has had its share of problems with toxic and hazardous substances, and on several occasions has been revealed as a nest fouler of some note. At about the time of the Chemical Control fire in Elizabeth, New Jersey, a lagoon full of chemical wastes (including the very toxic PCB) on city-owned land in Queens burst repeatedly into flames. A spokesman for the city's Department of Environmental Protection said the wastes had been dumped there two years previously and that the city had been looking for a proper way to dispose of them. Not long before, it had been revealed that the city had about 100 drums of pesticides, insecticides, suspected carcinogens, oils, and unknown other chemicals stored not far away from the lagoon, in the leftover New York State Pavilion from the 1964–65 World's Fair. One overriding theme of that exposition was mankind's proud entry into the future on the wings of technology—the same sort of technology that produced all those chemicals that the city said it was now trying to dispose of.

The twisted, poison-filled drums in the Chemical Control fire were still hot when New York City announced plans to clean up a four-acre site on Staten Island that contained solvents and other chemical wastes that, the city said, had been dumped there illegally. Texaco, the oil and chemical conglomerate, owned the property, but had leased it to another outfit and had denied having any responsibility for the chemicals. But now, with the environmental tragedy in Elizabeth making front-page news, Texaco agreed to pay for an inventory and cleanup of the site, at costs that were estimated at from $200,000 to $2,000,000. "We feel we do have a civic duty," a Texaco vice-president was quoted as saying.

A report by the New York State Health Department quotes another state agency, the Department of Environmental Conservation, as reckoning that, in 1978, 2,032,697 gallons of gasoline had been reported spilled in 255 separate events throughout the state. Of the total, said the state, 50,400 gallons were recovered and recycled. According to the report, 21 of the incidents occurred in New York City, with spills totaling 1,067,146 gallons, or about 53 per cent of the state total, of which none was recovered. The agency said another 190,108 gallons of hazardous wastes or toxic substances were known to have been spilled in the state in 1978, of which 24,091 gallons were spilled in New York City.

The city has been identified as a serious polluter, and would be one even if it were possible to overlook the 105,000,000,000 or so gallons of raw sewage it pipes each year into the Hudson and East Rivers. In the spring of 1980 the United States Supreme Court rejected an argument by the city that it was not subject to the federal law against discharging oil into navigable waterways. The Coast Guard had fined the city $1,200 for dumping oil into the water on five occasions. In 1981 the city fought in federal court for the continued right to dump 260 tons of sewage sludge each day into a nearby section of the Atlantic Ocean that already is horribly polluted.

Not all of the problems of toxic and hazardous wastes are related to clandestine dumping or bureaucratic responsibility-ducking. Some are the unforeseen by-products of programs and processes that most people would consider beneficial to society. In much of that part of the nation that is subjected to freezing wintertime temperatures, for example, municipalities, counties, and state highway departments use chlorides, or unrefined salts, to melt ice on roadways. Often the salt is stored in large piles until it is used. In numerous cases the salt has leached into the groundwater supply, contaminating it. A University of Massachusetts study of two adjacent communities in the Boston metropolitan area, one with a high level of salt in its water supply, the other with a low level, turned up increased rates of blood pressure in residents who drank the more saline water. The elevated rates were found even in high school students.

A landfill in Washington County, Pennsylvania, accepted, from a company that made air pollution devices, sludges containing the dangerous heavy metals lead, cobalt, and chromium. A congressional committee determined that leachate from the landfill had descended into the groundwater and had contaminated a farm well and a nearby spring. In February of 1980, the federal Environmental Protection Agency recommended "immediate caution but not alarm" in removing from the marketplace components of water-softening machines that, they said, might contain radioactive material. And a bizarre example of our inability to keep pace with our technological "advances" occurred in New England in early 1980. Acidic, or "soft," water supplies in many New England communities tend to corrode iron and lead pipes, and so several years ago pipes made of a mixture of concrete and asbestos were introduced into the region. Then researchers learned more about the carcinogenic qualities of asbestos in its airborne state, and vinyl liners were fitted into the pipes in order to protect the public from any possible asbestos contamination. Now it seems that a solvent used in installing the liner, tetrachloroethylene, which is a toxic chemical, has been found in water systems in various parts of New England.

7

Accompanying the horror stories, the lists of toxic "incidents," and the confusing sets of initials, the PCBs and TCEs and PBBs that now have become part of our lives, has been the realization of a few unfortunate facts. One of them is that the toxic waste problem, and our initial efforts at understanding what it might do (or might already have done) to our supply of usable water, came upon us relatively recently and suddenly —we were unprepared for it.

Another is that we are practically overwhelmed by the sheer *statistics* of the problem—the volume of poison that is out there on our planet, the numbers of dump sites, the immense sums of money involved in assessing the damage, much less cleaning it up.

A third major factor is that the revelations have been accompanied by a shocking lack of leadership from elected and appointed officials and by equally shocking efforts by elements of industry—the inventors, producers, promoters, and conveyors of these toxic wastes—to avoid responsibility for what they have done.

And, largely because of the lack of proper leadership and the failure of industry, we are faced with great uncertainties over what to do next. We had, as 1982 began, little reason to be confident that the poisonous chemicals that would be manufactured in the future would be handled properly, even in the light of our recent but certain knowledge that the issue was of transcendent importance. And we had absolutely no reason to suspect that the poisons of the past would or ever could be removed from our drinking water or intercepted before they penetrated the precious aquifers—that they all would be discovered and neutralized, their victims properly compensated for their suffering (and perhaps for the suffering yet to come of their unborn children), their perpetrators punished.

And, worst of all, we knew, or should have known, that the poisoning of our drinking water was not just an isolated calamity, like a shipwreck or a volcano's eruption, and that it was not even a *set* of isolated incidents. We had learned that it was something that could and might happen anywhere, and not just along the stinking industrial gutters of upstate New York's Niagara Frontier or the environmental disaster that is New Jersey's northeastern border (both of them places that produce the goods and services that society enjoys and demands and has come to depend on). There is no escaping America's water crisis now, anywhere in America.

There were quite a few clues—industry certainly was aware of what it was doing, and those state agencies charged with the responsibility for issuing licenses and permits surely knew what was happening—but we managed to ignore the hazardous waste problem as long as possible. An official atlas of Long Island's water resources was published in 1968 by the New York State Water Resources Commission, which described itself as "the central policy-making body for water in New York State." But the atlas had little to say about the poisons that since have been found to afflict much of Long Island's water supply. Its authors were far more concerned with the traditional issues: the island (which gets practically every drop of its fresh water from aquifers) was pumping water out of wells at a high rate ("mining" it), and there were dangers of increased salt-water intrusion into the fresh-water supplies. In 1976 the U.S. Geological Survey issued a report on groundwater in California. Little was known about industrial water pollution, said the Survey, "for the subject has received little attention from industry and is of apparently little interest to the general public." (It was about then that our great era of innocence was ending; heavy rains were causing dozens of industrial chemicals, eleven of them believed to be agents of cancer, to begin to bubble out of the ground at Love Canal.)

One reason for the recent and sudden nature of our discoveries was that hazardous and toxic chemicals hadn't been around all that long. The "toxic time bombs" that have exploded recently are, apparently, the first of the batch. Much of what society used, until about the end of World War II, in industry, government, and homes, had been made out of "natural" ingredients. The advertising business in recent years has perverted the meaning of "natural" until its use has come almost to serve as a tip-off that a product is artificial, but what is meant in this case is chemicals, compounds, and substances that existed in nature. After the war there was a dramatic increase in synthetic materials, many of which do not break down readily under normal conditions and quite a few of which are dangerous to human life. A May, 1981, report to the President by the Toxic Substances Strategy Committee, made up of representatives of every federal agency with an interest in the subject, noted that the nation's production of synthetic organic chemicals was less than 1,000,000,000 pounds in 1941, but that by 1978, "production of the top 50 organic chemicals alone had risen to 172,000,000,000 pounds." The report continued:

"Synthetic organic chemicals, virtually unknown before World War II, have come to serve many essential and beneficial functions in modern society, from weed killers to pacemakers to rubber tires to synthetic fabrics. Modern society has come to depend upon chemicals for health and safety, scientific and technological achievement, environmental quality, recreation, and other benefits. Most chemicals, chemical mixtures, and chemical products are not known to cause harm under safe and normal conditions of use and exposure. Yet many have had unforeseen or harmful effects on humans and the environment. Some require extreme caution in use, or they may be too dangerous to use at all. Cleaning compounds, paint removers, and insecticides are examples of potentially toxic chemicals in common use; these and many other common chemicals may have harmful effects if used improperly or under the wrong circumstances."

Even though not much has been *done* about poisonous substances that affect our water, government has been at work for several years defining them. "Hazardous waste," according to the federal Resource Conservation and Recovery Act of 1976, is "a solid waste, or combination of solid wastes, which because of its quantity, concentration, or physical, chemical, or infectious characteristics may (A) cause, or significantly contribute to, an increase in mortality or an increase in serious irreversible, or incapacitating reversible, illness; or (B) pose a substantial present or potential hazard to human health or the environment when improperly treated, stored, transported, or disposed of, or otherwise managed." (Although the act refers to such wastes as solids, the definition is generally understood to include liquids as well.) Already the euphemizers are at work in these matters, and in several places, including New Jersey and Tennessee, "toxic" or "hazardous" wastes are now officially known as "special wastes."

"We're just now coming out of the dark ages," said Gardner S. Hunt not long ago as he stood beside a hazardous waste site in Gray, Maine, where unwanted oils and other chemicals had been "processed." Hunt was the director of part of the State of Maine's effort to keep its water clean—specifically, he headed the Division of Laboratory and Field Services of the Bureau of Water Quality Control, which is part of the state's Department of Environmental Protection. The site where he stood was surrounded by a chain link fence that was not very tall and not very sturdy-looking and that had a few strands of barbed wire at the top and an inexpensive-looking lock on its gate. Inside the fence was a shallow-looking lagoon full of a liquid which obviously was not water. There were iridescent swirls in the emerald-green liquid, and it almost looked pretty. There were two tall tanks that looked like farm silos; two short tanks with capacities of about 25,000 gallons each; six long, horizontal tanks which would hold about 20,000 gallons each; an odd-looking machine that, Hunt explained, was an incinerator; and large numbers of the containers that have come to symbolize the toxic waste scandal, rusting fifty-five-gallon metal drums. It was a colorless, wet day in the fall of 1979 after the leaves had turned and had started to fall. The small site itself, except for the lagoon, was colorless and ugly, and a passerby would have felt the ugliness even if he had not known what the barrels contained. The place was known as the McKin site, after the industrial waste disposal company that had operated there.

Visible, through the trees that bordered the McKin site on three sides, were a number of one-story houses set on lots of one or one and a half acres. The houses were not expensive-looking but they were well kept. In almost every yard there was evidence—a tricycle, a set of swings, a bright plastic toy that had been left outside—of the youth of the families that lived in them.

The neighborhood was known as East Gray, but it was really just a small addition to Gray, itself a small town north of Portland, almost directly on the Maine Turnpike. Gray was incorporated in 1778, according to a sign at its border, and although it is situated precisely in what should be suburbia, it is, more than that, a nice-looking, old town. It is one of those New England towns that cause a visitor to remark that they must be populated with hard-working people (as opposed to those towns that one sometimes encounters that obviously, from the looks of the architecture and the quantities of fresh white paint, obviously serve as the homes of hard-working, *well-to-do* people).

It was in 1973, according to local people who have compiled a history of the East Gray situation, that a resident of one of the houses beyond the trees noticed that her laundry was discolored and that the drinking water (which came from a modern, enclosed backyard well) had a bad odor. The problems persisted, and in the following year the resident sent a water sample to a testing laboratory. The lab reported finding two "unidentified insoluble volatiles." Other homeowners complained, too, and by 1977, according to the residents' history, more detailed tests were showing that their well water contained trichloroethylene, trichloroethane, dimethyl sulfide, acetone, and alcohol. The McKin site was inferred as the cause of the contamination. (A report by the federal Council on Environmental Quality said that trichloroethane "was found in the groundwater aquifer under the East Gray section of the town, apparently due to storage and operations by an oil tank cleaning firm, the McKin Company.")

As Gardner Hunt reconstructed it, businesses felt a need from time to time to have their storage tanks—the tanks that held the oils and chemicals and other substances on which much of modern society thinks it must depend—cleaned, and it was the job of McKin's operator, Richard Dingwell, to clean them. The operator's "disposal technique," said the state official, "was to put the chemicals on the ground and burn them, and that that didn't burn up just sort of disappeared." Exactly how all this worked has become the subject of several lawsuits, whose outcomes have not yet been reached. Although one of the horrors of the current toxic waste crisis is that we have little information on where or how chemicals were disposed of, it is likely that the techniques employed at McKin were fairly standard. There was, until recently, little government interest in, and particularly no regulation of, the disposal of such waste.

The chemicals disappeared, according to a lawsuit some of the residents later brought against Dingwell and McKin, into "the groundwater table and thereafter spread in all directions within the water table to the properties of the Plaintiffs, resulting in the contamination of water" in the plaintiffs' wells and in a wider area. This happened, said the suit, because of "negligence" on the part of Dingwell or his employees, and it happened with "malicious and intentional disregard of the laws of the State of Maine and the health of the Plaintiffs" and others.

After the defendants made their discoveries and peppered officials with complaints, the state closed and fenced off the site, and the residents of East Gray had to drink water brought to them by tank trucks until a pipe could be laid from Gray.

Then, in January of 1978, traces of some of the chemicals were found in the water supply for Gray itself. For about a week, the entire town experienced what the residents of East Gray had gone through—taking their showers in the high school and getting their drinking water from a tank truck—and then tests showed that the chemicals had disappeared. It still is not known what happened, or precisely where the chemicals came from.

In the case of East Gray, though, said Gardner Hunt, most people assumed a connection between the McKin site and the contaminated wells. During much of the time the site was operating, he said, the state had no licensing procedure for such an operation. The activities engaged in by the processor at East Gray, said the state official, "are probably very little different from others in the waste oil business." The differences, he said, were that the McKin site was discovered, that it was situated over very porous ground, and that there were drinking water wells nearby. Another factor was that the discovery in East Gray took place at a time when tests were being perfected that could isolate traces of chemicals in water that had neither been isolated nor even looked for a few years before. The tests, utilizing very sophisticated and expensive machines such as the mass spectrometer, which can identify substances by their molecular weight, are capable now of detecting concentrations of chemicals as weak as one part per billion. It is likely, then, that as the tests become more sophisticated, and as the machinery becomes more widely available, more chemicals will be found in more water supplies. Richard Woodhull, a water expert with the Connecticut Health Department, was quoted in January, 1979, as saying, "With more testing going on, I suspect more will be found in the water." Already his suspicion has been verified in dozens of places across the country. Several years ago, for example, many detergents were reformulated because they had ingredients that did not biodegrade, or break down readily, once they entered the environment as part of society's treated effluent. Now, with newer tests that are capable of more finely probing the products, scientists are discovering that the replacement ingredients themselves are not as biodegradable as had originally been thought.

Douglas M. Costle, the administrator of the Environmental Protection Agency in the Carter administration, discussed the matter of testing technology when he appeared before the House Appropriations Committee in February, 1979, to argue EPA's budget requests. "This last year," said Costle, "we took our first crack at developing standards for the presence of organic chemicals in drinking water. In the last ten years, our instrumentation for detecting and measuring toxic chemicals in very small amounts has become almost embarrassingly good. Our knowledge of what to do about it has progressed less rapidly. The fact of the matter is, we took a look at the drinking water supplies in over eighty cities and found an alarming number of man-made chemicals, albeit in small quantities, appearing in finished drinking water—that is, after it has been treated for delivery to the taps. In Cincinnati alone, for example, we found 700 synthetic organic chemicals—man-made chemicals. Cincinnati draws much of its drinking water out of the Ohio River."

Congressman Edward P. Boland of Massachusetts interjected: "I would expect to see that in Cincinnati." Costle noted that the presence of chemicals in water was a relatively new phenomenon, and continued:

"As you move from Cincinnati to rural New Jersey or rural Kansas . . . agricultural chemicals and pesticides in the shallow aquifers show up in drinking water. We find that, as a result of underground injection of waste in[to] the shallow aquifers of the Miami area, there is increasing presence of organic chemicals in drinking water there, as well as severely contaminated wells in New Jersey. The latency period for cancer can be as much as forty years. We know very little about carcinogenistic reaction between chemicals. We can, for example, take a chemical that is a known carcinogen—and I might add that several of those organic chemicals in the Cincinnati system are known carcinogens—and a chemical that is not a carcinogen and put them together and one acts as a promoter of the other."

Congressman Boland asked if the incidence of chemicals in Cincinnati's water had been the highest of all of the eighty cities.

"If I remember correctly," replied Costle, "New Orleans was a little bit worse, but Cincinnati was pretty high."

A year later, Costle seemed less cocky about the "embarrassingly good" results of his testing. "We are not even sure if, not to mention how, chemical contaminants can be removed," he told *Time* magazine. "It takes sophisticated testing just to determine if there are chemicals present at all."

One of the several controversies in progress at present in the world of technocracy has to do with just such advanced testing techniques and machinery. If a substance is believed to cause cancer or some other disease in humans (that is, if it *does* cause cancer in animals in controlled laboratory experiments), and if that substance is found to exist in the human environment—in, say, hot dogs or hair dryers or drinking water—then, most technocrats agree, it should be regulated or eliminated, if possible, from the human environment, or at the least, people should be warned about it. But then the road comes to a fork. Some technocrats believe that there should be a limit of zero on such substances—that none of it should be allowed, on the grounds that even a tiny amount of something harmful is harmful. Others feel just as strongly that there is a threshold of harmfulness, a level beyond which the substance should not be allowed to grow, and that there should be a declaration that science has found that more than a certain amount of this harmful substance presents a health risk to humans. There are multitudinous problems with both arguments, one of the chief ones being that it is easy for a lay person to become enraged at the technocrats on both sides for what might be perceived as their fiddling while Rome burns (or while people die of cancer).

The invention of machinery that can detect one part of a harmful chemical in a billion parts of drinking water doesn't help resolve the confusion over whether there should be a threshold for such chemicals and, if so, what it should be. "Being a chemist, and having a little bit of knowledge about chemical things," said Gardner Hunt that afternoon in Maine, "I know that any chemical, even if it's the most terrible chemical in the world, if you take a small enough quantity of it, it won't hurt you. It's the long-term, cumulative thing that counts." Of course, he agreed, there's that devilish question of how small a "small enough" quantity should be. And the other question, one that seems to be becoming more and more important as we increase our knowledge of what harms us and what doesn't: the matter of the synergistic effect of various elements in our environment and our daily lives. A worker who handles asbestos on the job, for example, is considered to be more susceptible to the known harmful effects of the mineral, one of which is lung cancer, than the general public. If the worker handles asbestos and is a cigarette smoker, the susceptibility is believed to be greatly increased.

"Two years ago, before Gray," said Gardner Hunt, "our department didn't have the instrumentation to examine for the materials that we're doing here. Nowhere in the state did we have that capability. We do have it now, and we're enlarging our concerns and our monitoring and our sites to other areas of the state."

Gray, Maine, is also an example of the second in our list of unfortunate facts. It is a statistic, one of a growing list of numbers of toxic waste sites—and of victims—that have been surfacing over the last few years; of towns and communities whose drinking water wells may no longer be trusted, whose citizens have been told by their elected and appointed officials (in some cases the same ones who earlier had said not to worry) to stop drinking the water for a while, to buy their water in expensive one-gallon lots at the supermarket, and to take their showers in the high school gym or at the National Guard armory.

We live in a time of big numbers. A generation or so ago, a million of something was a shocking amount; today, petty criminals rip off a million dollars and judges hardly stir. Still, the statistics associated with toxic wastes, and with the toxic pollution of our water supplies, are shocking. They are also largely guesswork, since no government agency has done a proper job of keeping track of them.

The number of chemicals in and around the environment is phenomenal. In late 1977, said a report by the nation's Council on Environmental Quality, "the registry of chemicals maintained by the American Chemical Society listed 4,039,907 distinct chemical compounds—and the registry includes only chemicals reported in the literature since 1965. The list has been growing at a rate of 6,000 per week. . . . The number of chemicals currently in commercial production in the United States may be as high as 70,000; fifty are produced in quantities greater than 1,300,000,000 pounds per year. One hundred and fifteen thousand establishments are involved in the production and distribution of chemicals . . . and the business is worth $113,000,000,000 per year, about 7 per cent of the nation's Gross National Product."

That report was dated December, 1978. Since that time the list of compounds has continued to grow—to 5,566,102 by the end of 1981. The American Chemical Society estimates that an additional 2,000,000 substances, which are not on the list, were around before the registry was started but have not been mentioned in the literature since then.

The Council on Environmental Quality, an executive branch agency whose job it was to "formulate and recommend national policies to promote the improvement of the quality of the environment" (and which has been practically dismantled by the Reagan administration), went on to note that the statistics associated with chemical production suggest two things: "One is the astonishing dependence of modern life on chemicals that are synthesized or isolated from natural products. A second is the staggering task that faces industry and government in regulating the production and distribution of so many different entities. Many, indeed probably the majority, of the tens of thousands of chemicals in commerce are innocuous, and their benefits are great. Yet our ignorance about them is also great. The continuing discovery of previously unsuspected hazards from one chemical or another underscores the point."

The Environmental Protection Agency, the federal agency which has the most responsibility for identifying, keeping tabs on, and regulating the disposal of toxic and hazardous matter (and another one whose energies and mission have been seriously altered by Reagan), has estimated that 35,000,000 metric tons, or a little more than 77,000,000,000 pounds, of hazardous waste are generated each year in the United States, of which only 10 per cent, or almost 8,000,000,000 pounds, are disposed of in environmentally safe ways. That estimate, if correct, would mean that some 31,500,000 metric tons of waste were *not* disposed of properly each year. Carrying EPA's estimate further (and assuming, again, that the federal agency's figures are correct, which is an assumption that not everyone shares), that would translate into about 19,192 pounds of improperly disposed of hazardous waste each year on every square mile of the land and water surface of the United States, including Alaska and Hawaii.

As might be expected, the chemical industry has statistics that are at variance with EPA's. In an August, 1980, speech, Irving S. Shapiro, then the chairman of E. I. du Pont de Nemours & Company, a major manufacturer and user of chemicals, said that 4,000,000,000 tons of solid wastes were disposed of in the United States each year, of which "more than 2,500,000,000 tons are animal and agricultural wastes, another 1,000,000,000 tons are from mining or mineral extraction, and about one-third billion are from municipal and commercial sources. Only about one-eighth billion ton is from all manufacturing industry, including the chemical industry. Only about one-tenth of total chemical industry waste is hazardous. Among the large chemical companies, an estimated 94 per cent of process wastes are disposed of within the plant site that produced it. And among the fifty-three major chemical companies, 99.4 per cent of all hazardous and non-hazardous wastes generated over the past thirty years can be traced to known disposal sites either on or off plant."

EPA, in an inventory of toxic substances that are produced "commercially in significant amounts," came up with a list of more than 43,000 items, and those did not include chemical mixtures, foods, drugs, cosmetics, pesticides, and chemicals that are otherwise regulated. Only a relative handful of those chemicals have been tested for carcinogenicity. In another survey, EPA is reported to have found 181,000 man-made lagoons containing liquid wastes at industrial and municipal sites. Studies of 8,200 of them revealed that close to three-quarters were not lined, and that 700 of the unlined ones were within one mile of wells. Lagoons that are not lined—asphalt or plastic or semi-impervious clays are often used in lining— are likely to leach their contents into the soil and, thus, into whatever groundwater lies beneath them.

In New York State, as at the federal level, information on toxic materials and where they are stored is profoundly disturbing. As early as 1978, the state said it knew of 20 toxic waste dumps that it considered to be of major concern. Half of the sites were in Niagara County, which is where Love Canal is. A year later the state released a survey showing that industries produced 1,200,000 tons of hazardous waste each year, almost half of it in Erie and Niagara Counties, and that about 30 per cent of the waste was not being disposed of properly. (If the amount and percentages were correct, that would mean that 16,000 pounds of hazardous waste were produced annually for every square mile in New York State.) And in 1980 the state's Department of Environmental Conservation released an inventory of 680 known and suspected chemical dump sites. Of the total number of sites, 157 were said to "raise public health or environmental concern." As is usual in these cases, there was no explanation for the large difference in the reports' statistics.

The number of toxic waste sites should provide some clue to the dangers being faced by our groundwater supplies. Unfortunately, no one seems to have the slightest idea how many sites there are or where they are situated. A survey by EPA that was released in 1980 by the House Committee on Government Operations reported that the agency had found 2,100 sites that contained "at least one unlined impoundment located above a usable groundwater source with no barrier reported between the wastes and the ground water." Two hundred and fifty of the sites were said to contain "potentially hazardous contaminants" and were said to be situated within a mile of a "potential water supply well." In yet another EPA report, this one quoted by a federal task force on toxic wastes, the agency said there might be between 32,000 and 50,000 dump sites across the country that contained hazardous wastes, of which 500 to 800 might be abandoned.

Such large spreads, from 32,000 to 50,000 and from 500 to 800, might raise some questions about the quality of EPA's research. Unfortunately, such questions appear to be routine in matters involving toxic wastes and the water supply. An example of the quality of the data which is being ordered, assembled, and paid for by federal agencies, and which finds its way into other documents and serves as the basis for decisions affecting public policy, may be seen in a forty-seven-page report produced by EPA in 1979 titled "Preliminary Assessment of Cleanup Costs for National Hazardous Waste Problems." It is in that paper that the estimate of 32,000 to 50,000 sites appears.

The contractor who did the report for EPA's Office of Solid

Waste came up with its estimated number of dump sites by collecting replies from each of EPA's regional offices to a letter from headquarters requesting "a rough estimate" of the number of sites that "*may* contain hazardous wastes in any quantity which now or potentially could cause adverse impact on public health or the environment." The letter asked for another "rough estimate" of the number of sites that "*may* contain *significant* quantities of hazardous wastes which could cause *significant* imminent hazard to public health." (The emphasis was in the EPA memo.) The contractor took the replies, added them to other data (which it referred to as "hazardous waste problem prevalence data"), and came up with the estimate. Where information was lacking, the contractor made estimates.

The total number of supposed sites reported by the EPA regional offices was 32,254. The contractor, using something it called an "alternative prevalence methodology" that was not fully explained in the report, came up with another figure: 50,644. Thus the purported range of sites—32,000 to 50,000—was established.

A glance at the data supplied by the EPA offices shows that the government's participation in the whole project was a farce. The ten regional offices differed greatly in their definitions of a hazardous waste site. One office proceeded under the assumption that all landfills might contain hazardous waste, while another concluded that all *municipal* landfills did. One failed to include pits, ponds, and lagoons, while another didn't include places where pesticides were disposed of. The numbers of "sites" sent in by the regional offices ranged from 14,000, for the office serving the Southwest, to 25, for the office covering the mountain states. The report said that "most of the Regions stated that they could not provide verifiable, quantitative estimates for any of these sites, due to a lack of information on the nature, location, and condition of sites and the frequent problems of what wastes in various quantities constitute a health hazard."

The report was apparently sufficiently embarrassing to

prompt its author to insert a warning: "All available data were evaluated to the extent possible within the short time frame of this contract, but, because of such constraints, the accuracy of the data base cannot be vouchsafed." And EPA added its own disclaimer on the front page of the report: "This report describes work performed for the Office of Solid Waste under contract no. 68–01–5063 and is reproduced as received from the contractor. The findings should be attributed to the contractor and not to the Office of Solid Waste." Someone who might want to follow EPA's admonition, however, would find that the report does not bear the name of the contractor.

Despite alibis and disclaimers, the highly arguable numbers in the report have seeped into the literature of toxic waste, just as poisons dumped upon the ground leach into the water supply, and they are being quoted as quasi facts—even by those who issue the disclaimers. "EPA recently estimated" the number of dump sites at between 32,000 and 50,000, said a report to the President by the Toxic Substances Strategy Committee in May, 1980. The Environmental Protection Agency, which stuck the disclaimer on the data, is itself a member of the strategy committee. More recently the figures were quoted in a General Accounting Office report on toxic wastes. The pseudo-statistics have popped up on several other occasions as well, and they are almost always treated as if they were facts rather than highly unscientific estimates. Indeed, the more they are unquestioningly quoted, by presumably well-intentioned and reputable agencies and individuals who are believed to be responsible and objective sources of information, the more fact-like they become. And they are hardly more "facts" than would be a handful of digits drawn from a table of random numbers.

As the statistics, or estimates, or guesses, come out, so do the official exclamations of horror over what is happening, and might happen in the future, to our water supplies. Several agencies of the government, particularly congressional committees, conducted investigations into the situation as the decade began, and their conclusions were uniformly laced with dire predictions. Most of them acknowledged the direct connection between toxic substances and water, as in this 1979 report of the oversight and investigations subcommittee of the House Committee on Interstate and Foreign Commerce: "The volume and toxicity of the materials dumped at these sites and the inadequate disposal methods used have resulted in significant environmental damage already and pose additional threats for the future. The most pervasive damage done to the environment at these sites has been the contamination of ground water."

Eckardt C. Beck, then the EPA assistant administrator for water and waste management, told a congressional subcommittee in midsummer, 1980, that harmful substances were threatening much of the nation's drinking water supply: "I come before you today with the distressing news that one of this nation's most vast and vital natural resources is in serious jeopardy. Our groundwaters, long considered virtually pollution-free, are threatened by ruinous contamination. The problem is national, for the potential sources and routes of contamination may be found wherever people live and work. The problem is serious, for the intruding contaminants are often highly toxic, sometimes cancer-causing. More than 100,000,000 of our citizens depend in whole or in part on underground sources of drinking water. Each day more than 10,000,000,000 gallons of groundwater are withdrawn for use in American homes. Another 70,000,000,000 gallons are drawn for agricultural purposes. The prospect that that water may contain high concentrations of toxic chemical compounds compels our immediate attention and action. The story of hazardous wastes and vulnerable groundwaters is just beginning to be written, but the opening chapter is enough to predict that this will become the environmental horror story of the eighties— with aftereffects reaching into the next millennium."

Not long before Beck delivered that chilling warning, the Committee on Environment and Public Works of the Senate issued a thick catalogue of environmental horrors and noted, in summary, that "damage to natural resources in the United States by toxic chemicals is substantial and enduring. Historic and invaluable waterways . . . are injured. The Great Lakes are contaminated by a variety of toxic and hazardous substances which have dealt a severe blow to the commercial and sport fishing industries there. Groundwaters on which millions depend for drinking water are contaminated."

The House Committee on Government Operations, in the introduction to its report on the 2,100 presumed toxic waste sites, observed that "Groundwater is one of America's most valuable and plentiful natural resources. This water, which lies unseen beneath the earth's surface, is used every day by over 100,000,000 Americans. We drink, bathe in, grow and cook our food with this liquid. It is absolutely essential to life and our agricultural and economic sustenance." The committee said that the nation is using more and more groundwater for various purposes, especially irrigation, and added: ". . . just at the time our reliance on groundwater resources for pure drinking water and other vital economic activities is increasing, so is its contamination—and at a distressing rate. Clean groundwater—still bountiful in many areas—is seriously threatened by overuse, indiscriminate dumping of hazardous wastes, improper disposal in unlined pits, ponds, and lagoons, and the use of toxic degreasing agents in septic tanks."

Time magazine made toxic substances the subject of its major story in September, 1980, with a gruesome drawing on the cover. The magazine quoted Dr. Irving Selikoff, the director of the Environmental Sciences Laboratory in New York City's Mount Sinai Medical School, as saying, in agreement with Eckardt Beck, that "Toxic waste will be the major environmental and public health problem facing the U.S. in the eighties." Dr. Julius Richmond, the Surgeon General, in a statement to Congress that same month, said, "We believe that toxic chemicals are adding to the disease burden of the United States in a significant, although as yet not precisely defined, way. We believe that the magnitude of the public health risk associated with toxic chemicals currently is increasing and will continue to do so until we are successful in identifying chemicals which are highly toxic and controlling the introduction of these chemicals into our environment." And Representative Albert Gore, Jr., of Tennessee, one of the more articulate residents of Capitol Hill, has commented on what he calls a national "blind spot"—"an almost total ignorance of the real and potential consequences for land pollution. Until very recently," said Gore, "land was perceived to be an awesome sponge, a resilient reservoir which would readily absorb any chemical concoction that man could brew."

8

"Blind spot" is the term that Albert Gore used, but other observers of the situation, including some of his colleagues in Congress, would employ much harsher language to describe the conspicuous lack of national leadership in the crisis that has been brought on by toxic chemicals. One manifestation of that void, and one that might come as a surprise to the ordinary citizen, is the poor quality of the information that government and its contractors and subcontractors generate about the issue. EPA's disclaimed report on the number of toxic waste sites is, unfortunately, not just an isolated example of such sloppiness.

When the House Committee on Government Operations released, in September of 1980, the report on groundwater contamination that identified 2,100 waste sites, of which 250 were said to pose serious threats to drinking water, Representative Toby Moffett, the Connecticut Democrat who runs the committee's environment, energy, and natural resources subcommittee, was quoted as saying groundwater contamination "will become the most volatile domestic issue of the 1980s. It touches virtually every state. Nothing comes close to rivaling the issue of contaminated water." All that was quite likely true, but the report which Representative Moffett's own subcommittee compiled did little to add to a rational understanding or discussion of the problem, and in fact detracted from such a discussion, inasmuch as it was based on sketchy, quite unreliable data. The information was provided to the subcommittee by the Environmental Protection Agency, and EPA, in another of what seemed to be its series of efforts to sidestep responsibility for the information it produced, advised Representative

Moffett of certain "limitations": The material, wrote EPA
Administrator Costle, "was intended to provide a *first-round
approximation* [the emphasis is his] of the magnitude of the
potential groundwater problems associated with surface impoundments. ["Surface impoundment" is an EPA and industry
euphemism for a form of waste dump.] It was never intended
to provide information specific enough to lead to conclusions
relative to specific sites and their practices." Much of the data,
wrote Costle, was secondhand, having been gleaned from
"permit files, responses to questionnaires, trade associations,
industrial directories, and other similar sources." The "few
attempts that have been made to verify the data," wrote the
administrator, have demonstrated that the inventory and assessment are not sufficiently precise to yield reliable data on a site-
by-site basis." In other words, a cynic might conclude, the
information is virtually worthless—except as ammunition for
those who feel the toxic dumps problem has been exaggerated
and who can cite EPA's and Congress's work as an example of
shoddy and biased research.

Some elements of the chemical manufacturing industry
wasted no time doing just that. The waste-site report was
released as Congress debated the merits of legislation designed
to apportion the cost of cleaning up toxic waste dumps (and,
therefore, to some extent the blame for creating them)—the
issue known as the "Superfund" controversy—and the chemical
industry was quite sensitive to the criticism. One official of a
chemical manufacturers' lobbying association said at the time:
"If industry—not just the chemical industry, but any part of industry that's been involved in all this hazardous waste issue—
if industry used the sort of bad and misleading data that EPA
has used in the Superfund controversy, we'd be thrown in jail."
And less than a week after Representative Moffett released his
report, the senior vice-president for environmental policy for
the Monsanto Company, Monte C. Throdahl, issued a statement condemning the EPA-congressional effort as "confusing,
misleading, and substantially inaccurate." He called it a docu-

ment that "pursued short-term political gain at the cost of increased public misunderstanding of hazardous waste problems." Throdahl continued: "It is a sad but increasingly typical example of how hastily collected, quick-and-dirty data can distort facts and exaggerate hazards. It may get a few votes come election time, but the price in terms of escalating public fears and confusion will be awesome. This kind of 'sky-is-falling' scare tactic serves only to distract the many dedicated government and industry scientists who are trying to work together on solutions to the real problems involved with waste disposal."

In that case, the reputation of an industry, and of its environmental stewardship, was involved. In another, the Love Canal chromosome study, much more was at stake—not only the physical health but also the psychological well-being of a group of residents who had been given the runaround for years by government at every level. Also involved were the efforts by the federal government to make a solid case against the Hooker Chemical Corporation, which put most of the toxic chemicals into the canal.

EPA had done a crude, heartless job of "research" in 1979, when it put out a report saying that someone living over the edge of the filled-in dump had as much as a one-in-ten chance of getting cancer from airborne chemicals. A few days later EPA called the report a "draft" and said the original calculations had been "too high by a factor of ten."

But EPA's darkest hour thus far occurred in the spring of 1980, when it hurriedly released a report, done by a Houston consulting firm called Bionetics, claiming that 11 of 36 Love Canal residents had "very rare chromosomal aberrations" of a sort that are "frequently linked to cancer." The report put Love Canal back on the front pages, and within a few days President Carter declared a state of emergency at Love Canal so that 710 families could receive government aid in finding temporary housing outside the contaminated area.

There was widespread controversy over the methodology

used in the Bionetics research—among other things, there were no control groups used, the selection of subjects did not follow normal scientific procedures, and the usual devices to prevent researcher bias were not employed—and in October of 1980 a panel of respected scientists who had been asked by Governor Hugh Carey to look into the matter reported back that, after reviewing the EPA and other documents, they believed "chronic effects of hazardous wastes exposure at Love Canal have neither been established nor ruled out as yet, in a scientifically rigorous manner," and that "The studies conducted in the past two years have been inconclusive in demonstrating long-term health effects due to hazardous wastes exposure." Of EPA's handling of the chromosome report and of the report itself, they said that "this study represents a paradigm of administrative ineptitude . . ." "[S]uch a poorly designed investigation as this one should not have been launched in the first place," wrote the physicians. "With so much at stake for the residents involved, to have set up experiments that lead to public conclusions of such magnitude, without prior review of the protocol by qualified uninvolved peer scientists, and without any after-the-fact, independent review by competent scientists before release of the results, was a disservice to the citizens most intimately concerned and, as well, to the public at large. The damage done by this EPA effort is perhaps beyond mending; many of the Love Canal residents have by now become so distrustful of governmental agencies and their scientific reliability that they are unwilling to believe anything except the worst of news about themselves."

The panel dismissed another report by professionals, commissioned by the Love Canal residents themselves, as "literally impossible to interpret." Two agencies, one federal and one state, should continue the research at Love Canal, said the investigators, but the federal government should not be represented by EPA, which had "not demonstrated the capacity to design and implement health effects studies in a scientifically rigorous manner." The physicians who reported to the governor had impressive credentials; they included the chancellor of Memorial Sloan-Kettering Cancer Center, the dean of the New York University Medical Center and the chairman of the center's department of environmental medicine, and the physician-in-chief of Rockefeller University Hospital.

By the time the chromosome study episode had lost most of its news appeal, it had become quite apparent that many of the professionals and technocrats involved were largely interested in covering their own hides, polishing their hindsight lenses, allocating the blame to others, and furthering their own political and philosophical positions, and that the innocent victims of the Love Canal tragedy were once again the big losers. Almost lost in the shuffle was a later statement by another respected expert on genetics that, whatever its limitations in methodology, Bionetics' interpretation of the original chromosome data was a reasonable one.

Many reports and studies on the toxic substances issue, including some of those that are critical of some of the others, are poorly put together, employing a writing style that appears to be a slurry of technical jargon and bureaucratic nonsense words, along with a plethora of inadequately explained charts, tables, and diagrams that often are lifted from other, equally unintelligible, reports. The growth of photocopying and offset printing, which has encouraged anyone with a pair of scissors and a pot of rubber cement to become a compositor, apparently has had a lot to do with this.

Often the numbers in such reports don't add up properly, footnotes and citations are incorrect, the sources of data are missing, and the methodology is unexplained, leading a reader to wonder if it existed at all—and these faults may be found in high-priced documents produced by and for scientists and government officials who make public policy on very serious matters, such as the quality of drinking water and the causes of cancer.

One things that is clear about these documents (indeed, it may be the only thing that is clear about them) is that they never went through the editing process; no one ever asked the authors if they really meant to say what they appear to be saying and if there were perhaps a better way to say it. One by-product of this is writing that sometimes is ridiculous; a two-volume, hardbound study of water on Long Island that cost $5,200,000 contains, along with much information that is useful and enlightening, the revelation that "Ducks have an aquatic orientation." A publication by the American Chemical Society on chemicals and the environment, discussing a research technique that measures lethal doses, notes that while such a method provides "a useful measure of toxicity, death is a crude, uninformative, and often inappropriate indicator of organic damage." Another by-product is unbelievability. Much of the data that is presented on toxic waste dumps and the like comes from the chemical industry itself. Even that portion of the information that is in government's own hands is spread quite thin; there are about two dozen federal statutes covering chemicals and the environment, and they are supposed to be administered by six federal agencies. One government study of the situation argued that "The soundness and efficiency of the federal effort to control toxic substances could be vastly enhanced by coordinated data systems to provide all agencies ready access to information on chemicals." Such a network, said the study, "does not yet exist. Rather, over the years the many agencies involved in chemical research and regulation have independently developed more than 220 separate systems, each serving different needs and organized in a different way. Some are sophisticated computer systems; others are simply manual files."

The shoddiness and inadequacy of some research threaten to erode even further what some observers see as a growing disenchantment by the public with those who do the research. The hucksters of science and technology have never exactly *denied* that the universe would be a dramatically better place if the public placed more faith and taxpayers' money in them and their ways of thinking—ways that include systems analysis, use of cost-benefit and risk-benefit analysis, and computer "models" of problems that need solving. Unfortunately, however, technology and science keep failing us, possibly because common sense is so rarely included in their analyses. They tell us that saccharine gives us cancer, and then they change their minds. Then they do the same thing with the additives in our bacon. With great regularity, science produces substances that it widely promotes as the solutions to some of our most serious problems—the Pill virtually eliminates unwanted pregnancies, Valium enables us to handle depression, atomic energy reduces our dependence on "foreign oil"—and it is only later that we discover, as we always do, that there is no such thing as a free lunch: That the Pill increases the chance of stroke, that Valium has become the most overprescribed drug in the world, that we have no notion of how to protect ourselves against nuclear energy's leftovers or its accidents. And science and technocracy produce with the same abandon "statistics" and "studies" and "reports" that bear the imprimatur of what high-schoolers are taught is the "scientific method" but that really amount to little more than guesswork and in some cases are high-paid quackery. The statistics that are more widely quoted than any others in the entire nation—the Environmental Protection Agency's estimates of gasoline mileage for new automobiles—are about as far from actuality as could be imagined. Everybody seems to know they are fabrications; EPA acknowledges that the averages bear little relationship to actual driving conditions and attaches one of its by now routine disclaimers to them; and yet no one seems able to *do* anything about these pseudo-scientific numbers. Nor does anyone seem able to do anything about numerous other fiascos brought about by the use of meaningless data, sloppy research, and inadequate methodology.

One inevitable result of all this is a growing cynicism about science and technology on the part of the public. This may well be a healthy development, for science and technology have never been nearly as pure as their practitioners wanted the public to believe they are, but it also means that research that *is* worthy may have a harder time getting financed and its conclusions believed. The panel of scientists who examined and dismissed the EPA's chromosome study in the Love Canal disaster concluded, among other things, that "The design, implementation and release of the EPA chromosome study has not only damaged the credibility of science but exacerbated any future attempts to determine whether and to what degree the health of the Love Canal area residents has been affected."

The entire Love Canal problem, wrote the governor's panel, was a "paradigmatic example of government decision-making at the outer bound of scientific knowledge. With a literally exponential growth in information and awareness concerning environmental contaminants and human health has also come a greater appreciation of the limitations of what we can know with certainty. Dialogues of hazardous wastes, air pollution, water quality, nuclear wastes, and other environmental problems now center on such imponderable and ambiguous subjects as risk assessment, acceptable levels of voluntary and involuntary risk, and benefit/cost analysis. While the Panel believes it is important to improve public awareness of the current limitations of science with respect to environmental hazards, the critical failure in the past two years has been the inconclusiveness of studies carried out to date. Where improvements in public and decision-maker understanding might have been achieved, only further questions and debates on scientific credibility have been the result."

Many reputable scientists are concerned about such issues, and about the bad name that is being given the scientific method, but they seem currently to be outnumbered (or outshouted) by technocrats who control the financing and direction of research and by those among their own colleagues who seem to be trying to *use* the scientific method to make public-policy points or to please the technocrats.

The lack of national leadership manifests itself in quite a few other ways, most of which point to a shocking failure on the part of government in general to face up to the problems of groundwater contamination. A grand jury in Rockland County, New York—the sort of investigative body that might be expected to explore problems of school lunch programs or conditions in the local jail—spent eight months in 1979 looking into toxic wastes and concluded that "The evidence indicates the response of federal, state, and local governments to the problems posed by hazardous waste has been characterized by ignorance, neglect, laxity, and fractionalization of responsibility." Former EPA Assistant Administrator Beck, speaking not long ago about groundwater problems, identified the federal government as the perpetrator of "the most grievous errors in judgment we as a nation have ever made." Others have narrowed the blame down to EPA itself.

The Environmental Protection Agency's failure is widespread and enduring, and it seemed, as toxic waste was revealed as a growing problem, that the White House was of little mind to encourage the agency to improve itself. And this was the situation even before the Carter administration was replaced by another which has practically performed a lobotomy on the agency. Early in 1980, EPA began to look very much as if it had become one of those government bodies that were not on the consumer's side and not on industry's side, but rather on their own side—bureaucratic entities dedicated mainly to preserving themselves. For decades citizens have tolerated such instincts, and even developed a sense of humor about them, when they occurred in the government offices that regulate tractor-trailer loads, tobacco allotments, and bank robbery, but it was unusual to see the same crassness in the agency that is supposed to keep our drinking water from killing us. We seem to be left, as the anxieties grow over the chemical poisoning of our groundwater, with the conclusion that government is simply not competent to handle a problem of this nature. But with water, as with perhaps no other component of our lives, there is no other way to do it—no other organization with the finances and authority to do the job, no other body in which we might place—must place—such an enormous amount of our trust.

Mostly because of the thunderous lack of leadership, we are faced with our fourth big unfortunate realization: that there is great uncertainty about what to do next. The public has recently been exposed on almost a daily basis to ample evidence that its water is endangered, but there is little indication that anybody knows what to do about it. While EPA stumbles along in its congressionally mandated assignment to keep strict tabs on the toxic substances that are manufactured in the future, Congress has debated what to do about the chemicals that are already in and on the ground, in or headed inexorably toward the pure waters that lie in the priceless aquifers.

Estimates of what it could cost to clean up present toxic dumps seemed, by the winter of 1980–81, to be about as well grounded as estimates of the number of sites that need cleaning up, which is to say in the neighborhood of uneducated guesswork. Barbara Blum, EPA's deputy administrator at the time, told a congressional committee in March, 1979, that costs could go as high as $50,000,000,000. One thing that *was* certain was that the costs would rise the longer the nation put off doing something about the problem. EPA administrator Costle was quoted by *Time* in 1980 as saying that in 1975, when the poison Kepone was discovered in Virginia's James River, it could have been cleaned up for $250,000, but that because of delays the polluter had paid out $13,000,000 in damage claims. Now the estimates were that it would cost $2,000,000,000 to clean up the river, if indeed it can be cleaned up at all.

Other estimates are similarly astronomical. The Agriculture Department has estimated that if it had the power to force a cleanup of PCBs in old equipment in meat-, poultry-, and egg-processing plants, the price tag for the industry would be between $20,000,000 and $40,000,000. And another estimate, made in 1979, was scarier but also possibly closer to the mark: Jack Bails, the chief of the enforcement division of Michigan's

Department of Natural Resources, was quoted as saying, "Chemical contamination may be so widespread and pervasive that we can't afford to clean it up."

Although the government had ample authority to use the courts to force polluters to clean up their messes, relatively little was accomplished. Between 1972 and 1980, when much of the lasting damage was being done to the environment, the federal government filed only thirty toxic waste suits, and they were aimed at the operators of the dumps themselves. It was not until mid-1980 that the government brought legal action against the manufacturers of the chemicals. In that action, eleven corporations, with big names such as U.S. Steel, Dow, Shell, Exxon, and Allied Chemical, were sued for allegedly contributing their chemicals to two Louisiana dumps that EPA said were dangerous to human health. The suits asked for a halt to the dumping operation, a cleanup, and fines—$10,000 each—which the companies could easily pay out of petty cash.

A year and a half later, with an administration in place that was firmly pro-big business and very anti-regulation, little had been done on the Louisiana suits. An EPA lawyer handling the case said "some" of the defendants (he could not remember the exact number) had agreed, after negotiations, to put up a total of $218,000 so that stopgap measures could be taken to keep the mess from being made worse by floods, hurricanes, or other natural events. That work, said an EPA spokesperson in January, 1982, was "starting now." Still somewhere in the future were negotiations on actually cleaning up the site. It seemed clear that the EPA of Ronald Reagan was not much interested in pursuing the matter aggressively, and that a settlement in the matter, if it ever comes, will probably not put much of a strain on the polluters

Congress, in 1980, was debating legislation that would finance the cleanup of the toxic waste sites that probably pose the greatest threat to groundwater supplies—the inactive or abandoned sites that exist around the nation in unknown number. The legislation would create the "Superfund," to which both government and the chemical and oil industries would contribute and which would be used for cleaning up what the technocrats call "orphaned" sites. President Carter proposed such a fund (totaling $1,400,000,000, with industry contributing 80 per cent and provisions for emergency government response to crises and for compensation for victims) in the summer of 1979, but little happened until the Elizabeth, New Jersey, Chemical Control fire in the spring of 1980. A House bill that soon emerged would have created a $1,200,000,000 fund, with industry paying 80 per cent and no compensation for victims. A Senate version called for $4,200,-000,000 over six years, with compensation. Congress adjourned for the fall, 1980, election break without taking final action, and when it returned it passed a law that represented a compromise.

The chemical industry's reaction to the proposed legislation was a muted one, possibly because its leaders realized that the public mood was not exactly one of benevolence toward people and corporations that were responsible for pouring cancer-causing materials into the drinking water supply. Some of those leaders did, however, try to argue the somewhat strange point that the general public enjoyed the fruits of those toxic substances (that is, we degreased things, cleaned out septic tanks, drank decaffeinated coffee, killed pests, and brushed teeth with them) and, therefore, the general public should pay the bill for cleaning up. "If this is a matter of public concern," said Robert A. Roland, the president of the Chemical Manufacturer's Association, "we ought to use the public money to solve the problem."

Dr. Louis Fernandez, another spokesman for the chemical association and vice-chairman of the Monsanto Company, told Congress that he detected a thread that weaved its way through the proposed Senate legislation, a false assumption "that the chemical industry is evil, that it needs to be punished for the sins of the past, that it does not care about its workers or the citizens of this country, and that it has enormous 'profits' which can be tapped indefinitely to solve societal ills." As for those who dumped their chemical wastes illegally (a large percentage of all dumpers, according to many reports), Fernandez fell back on the rather weak explanation that "There will always be some bad apples in the barrel."

Irving S. Shapiro, the Du Pont chairman, advocated the granting of what might sound to some like a blanket pardon for any of those bad apples of the past. In an interview with *Time*, he said: "Let's start with today, not worry about who did what in the past. Government and industry should work together, rather than get emotional. We've got to work together rather than get emotional. We've got to get going rather than sitting around trying to figure out who's wearing the black hat and who's wearing the white hat."

Representative Albert Gore, Jr., replied to some of the industry arguments with the comment that the chieftains of the chemical business often made handsome profits off the "petrochemical revolution," that they knew something of the effects of their discoveries on the environment, that they chose to use "the cheapest disposal practices available, with little apparent consideration of the environmental effects of their actions," and that it now is "cynical, absurd, and offensive to propose that the chemical companies should bear less responsibility for the consequences of that recklessness than a consumer who simply bought the household cleaners the companies produced."

Not only does nobody want to pay for the cleanup; nobody, not even an environmentalist, wants a hazardous dump site, even a legal one, next door. In 1975, EPA gave the Minnesota Pollution Control Agency $3,700,000 to build and operate a chemical landfill in an environmentally safe manner. But no community would allow the plant to be built, and the demonstration project was scuttled. The solution, for many states and communities, seems to lie in shipping their own toxic problems somewhere else, which is a masterful application of "out of sight, out of mind" thinking. A comprehensive study of water on Long Island, where copious amounts of toxic wastes are produced, states rather stuffily: "Public health and environmental considerations suggest that Long Island disposal of hazardous wastes is the least acceptable of several alternatives. The need to protect the deep flow aquifers, in order to maintain a potable water supply, and the shallow flow system, to prevent degradation of productive marine waters, provides a strong argument for out-of-area disposal."

Where, then, should it be dumped? What constitutes the magical "out-of-area disposal"? Who'll volunteer to inform the out-of-area recipients of the delicacies that are headed their way? One of industry's bright ideas (and one that was worrying the State Department in the late seventies) was that such wastes be shipped to, and stored in, developing countries of Africa and Latin America. Another solution, far less legal but widely used, is to dump it on Pennsylvania, and particularly in Pennsylvania's abandoned coal mines and quarries. From there the poisons leach into streams and aquifers that serve as community and individual water supplies. Pennsylvania has long been an environmental disaster, a state always inclined to look the other way rather than enforce an environmental law, but the situation has gotten even worse in recent years. Congressman Marc L. Marks, who represents a district in the northeastern section of Pennsylvania, complained in 1979 that 65 to 70 per cent of the hazardous waste from New Jersey was being dumped in his state. "The reason for this is simple," he said. "New Jersey has enacted strict laws regulating the disposal of hazardous wastes. Pennsylvania has not. Therefore, to avoid the expense and effort of complying with New Jersey's laws, hazardous waste generators in that state simply send their hazardous wastes to Pennsylvania. Undoubtedly, other states are following the same pattern."

And, finally in our list of discouraging realizations, there is the fact that there is no easy escape from the plague of toxic chemicals. They are all around us, and the only way we can avoid them is to change our attitudes about them.

The groundwater aquifers, which once we held in awe as the practically eternal custodians of water in its most pristine condition, water cleansed and made almost magically pure through the centuries as it moved through the filter of the earth's own crust, popping to the surface from time to time in springs (*springs:* Their name has an almost unworldly sense to it)—these aquifers are turning out to be contaminated, tainted by chemicals that science and technology have heaped on us in such vast, unregulated profusion, and that we have accepted so willingly, convinced that they would simplify our existence —would improve, as the saying goes, our "quality of life." Now we are finding them in our drinking water and we know, despite all the conflicting claims and testimony and "scientific" reports and hasty "studies," that they could not possibly be anything but bad for us.

We are learning that there is no escaping the poisons that are in the aquifers, at least with our current technology. Eckardt Beck of EPA told Congress not long ago that "treating contaminated groundwater is not a viable option for most systems. . . . The hard economic realities would lead to the . . . conclusion: Shut down the water wells."

But we are also learning that there is no escaping the aquifers that are poisoned; that no longer may we think of poisoned water as a problem of just New Jersey, or just Pennsylvania. The chemicals are showing up practically everywhere tests have been made.

Gardner Hunt, the water official for the state of Maine, unfolded a wrinkled topographical map on that fall day in 1979 and spread it on the trunk of his venerable car. "Where we are, at the McKin site, is right here," he said, pointing to a spot not far from the center of the town of Gray. The map was of a scale that showed the subtle elevations of the area, and the roads and even individual houses. "We've found a spring on the west bank of the Royal River, a mile or so to the east, that has the chemicals in it that we have here." Nearby was a drum that was typical of those stored at the site. Its label said that it contained fifty-four gallons of "Tri-Ethane (inhibited) 1,1,1-Trichloroethane," and that it was made by PPG Industries, Inc., Pittsburgh. The label also said: "Caution! Vapor May Be Harmful. Technical Grade." Tricholoroethane, which the National Cancer Institute has classified as a carcinogen, is sometimes used as a degreaser.

Hunt pointed to another place on the map, to the north and west of Gray. "We've found them in the groundwater here, too," he said. The contour lines of the map, which traced elevations in ten-foot increments like a section of a cutaway onion, showed that the place was uphill from the McKin site. Chemicals that leached into the ground at Gray could easily move, by gravity, down to the Royal River. But no such explanation was possible to the northwest. Hunt's visitor asked if any industries were situated there.

"Nope," he said. "What we're finding is that these degreasers are ubiquitous in our society. One gallon of something that causes trouble at one part per billion can screw up a lot of water." He said he had no idea where the chemicals had come from, only that they seemed to be virtually everywhere.

In that case, his visitor asked, wasn't he pessimistic about the future of water?

"We live in an industrial society," said Hunt, "and we accept certain risks for the benefits that we derive from it. What we want, though, is to know what the odds are. What we need to know is what the risks are, what the relative costs are if we do or if we don't, and then let us make our choices. . . . As I said earlier, I think we're really coming out of the dark ages and into the dawn of enlightenment."

So, said the visitor, Hunt was actually rather optimistic?

"Gotta be," he said as he stood there beside the chemical dump. "You gotta be, otherwise you're just going to go stick your head in the sand and somebody's going to come kick you in the behind. No man is an island unto himself. There's just no way you can do it. There isn't any escape. If you want to try to solve some of the world's problems, which are your own problems, too, you've got to get in there and pitch. If I were a bachelor I guess that'd be one thing. But I've got two kids. That's got to make you look a little differently at things. Because it's not only for me; I could end my life today and be rid of all these hard problems, but I can't do that because my life is my kids', not mine."

II

The Exploiters

9

The horrible prospect of toxic chemicals oozing from their rusting fifty-five-gallon containers into the aquifers and streams that form our drinking water supplies is one that is very real and very great, and it is made all the more horrifying by the facts that in most cases we cannot see or taste or feel the poisons; that we have only begun to learn how to design tests to determine whether they are present and in what concentrations, not to mention the effects of those concentrations on human life; that only now, years after industry and government started dumping the poisons into the ground, are we seeking out, digging up, and taking inventories of the sites. We know that no one, in government or out, seems to have the slightest idea of what to do even after the sites are uncovered, and we know, too, that public disclosure and outrage over the illegal dumping have not stopped the dumpers from pouring more of the poisons, millions of gallons of it a day, into the earth and the streams. And we know—this is perhaps the scariest realization of all—that we have no idea of when we will start paying the physical and emotional prices for the damage that has been done. Poisonous chemicals move through the aquifers with the same deliberate slowness as the purest of water, at speeds and in ways which we have never been able, for all our storied command of technology, to figure out. And human exposure to cancer-causing substances, as we have learned from studies of asbestos in industry, sometimes does not manifest itself in observable symptoms for decades. The ticking of the toxic "time bombs" may go on, then, in our reservoirs and wells and inside our bodies, long after we have discovered them and dug them out of the ground. The horror that started with the revelations about Love Canal is certain to profoundly affect our lives, and the water we drink, for a long, long time.

But there is more to the current water situation, and to our water crisis, than toxic chemicals dumped upon the earth by irresponsible industry, arrogant government, and outlaw contractors. Our most precious substance is threatened, in quantity and in quality, in a number of other ways, each of them of enormous importance and complexity, each tied in intimately with our national goals and with the quality of American life. As with the Love Canals, our comprehension of these threats has come to us only relatively recently, although the makings of the problems have been clearly visible for a very long time to anyone who really wanted to see them. Hardly any aspect of our life has escaped being part of the crisis. Involved are the food we eat, the work we do, the sort of government we have, and the places in which we choose to live.

There are relatively safe, inexpensive substitutes for many of the toxic substances that currently are plaguing us. The work of chemical degreasers used to be done, and still could be done, for instance, with what used to be called elbow grease. But there are no easy substitutes for food. Agriculture accounts for about 80 per cent of the water the world uses, and for almost 90 per cent of that withdrawn in some of the Western United States, and so the potential for *misuse* is high, as is agriculture's susceptibility to criticism. In fact, there has developed in the United States in recent years, and particularly in the West, an *opposition* to agriculture and to its technology, its practices, and its practitioners. That opposition might be shocking in its intensity when it is encountered by someone who was raised with the notion that farms, farmers, and farming—concepts that could best be summed up in the phrase "family farm"—are in the same general category with motherhood and apple pie. Much, perhaps most, of the criticism is phrased in terms of attacks on large-scale agriculture, which often is called "agribusiness" and frequently is referred to as "corporate agriculture." The assumption behind the opposition is that farms run by corporations are less moral, decent, and caring than those run by families, and that in the process of becoming, foremost, a businessman (or, more likely, an employee of a businessman), the American farmer has somehow forfeited his traditional claim to being a good steward of the land. The land belongs to the corporation now—to the oil companies and railroads and to their stockholders, who never see it and certainly never work it—rather than to the farmer's children and their children after that. And so, in the eyes of those who are critical about agribusiness and corporate farming, the American farmer is fast forgetting the old rule about putting more back into the soil than he takes out of it.

Unfortunately, that criticism appears to have a substantial basis in fact; in the case of water, the farmer in several parts of the nation is literally taking more from the soil than nature returns to it—"mining" or overdrafting the groundwater aquifer. Such mining has been practiced routinely but almost exclusively in the drier portions of the Western United States for years, but now it is becoming a national problem. It is a simple, exploitative practice; a U.S. Geological Survey paper on groundwater supplies in California, published in 1976, put it this way: "All water discharged from a well must be balanced by a loss of water somewhere, and this loss is always to some extent, and may be largely, from storage in the aquifer. . . . Thus some depletion of ground water storage is an inevitable result of exploitation." The authors of the professional paper, H. E. Thomas and D. A. Phoenix, further noted that "For more than half a century the California region has led all others in North America in pumping of ground water as well as in the area, variety, yield, and export of crops irrigated by water from wells. It has led in the development and use of deep-well turbine pumps for large yield and in the drilling of water wells to great depths." At the same time, wrote the hydrologists, California was also the leader in producing the harmful side effects of groundwater mining.

An example of those side effects, and of the sort of groundwater exploitation that California introduced to the rest of the Western states, may be found in the fertile San Joaquin Valley, the wide, long flatland that stretches from below San Francisco to above Los Angeles and from the Sierra Nevada to the Coast Ranges. A state publication asserts that about 2,000,000 acre feet of ground water, or about 651,702,000,000 gallons, is pumped out of the earth of the valley each year, while only 500,000 acre feet is recharged, or finds its way back into the aquifers from the surface, either from rainfall or from streams passing through. As when an overdraft occurs in one's bank account, the consequences here can be unhappy ones. "Because of overdraft," said the publication, "groundwater levels are dropping, causing an increase in energy use and higher pumping costs. In coastal areas, salt-water intrusion is threatening the quality of some aquifers." The study by the federal hydrologists referred, in addition, to another problem caused by water mining: subsidence of the land over aquifers that have been pumped out and that, therefore, no longer hold the surface of the earth up.

The references to energy cost and salt-water intrusion are heard frequently in discussions of groundwater mining. As water tables decline due to increased pumping from the surface, the pumps must reach deeper to get adequate quantities of water. The deeper they go, the harder the pumps must work to bring the water to the surface. And the harder the pumps work, the more energy they must use, and so more fuel must be burned. Salt-water intrusion is a problem that is often found in connection with groundwater overdraft, and not just along the seashore. Both in coastal areas and inland, fresh-water aquifers serve as buffers against cells of saline water. Inland, the cells are simply aquifers themselves, but made salty by dissolved minerals, while along the coasts they are layers of the more familiar sea-type water that are fed by the oceans. If pressure in the neighboring fresh-water aquifers is reduced (as it is by ovedrafting), the salty water enters ("intrudes," in the language of self-centered man) to fill the partial vacuum. In the process, the remaining fresh water in the aquifer can become more saline, often to the point where it is no longer potable—until it is made undrinkable by humans and useless for agriculture.

The ruination of farmland by salinization, waterlogging, erosion, and other forms of poor stewardship, along with the growth of housing developments, highways, and shopping centers, have been cited as components in what some analysts see as a dangerous reduction in the amount of arable land available for world food production. Iowa cropland, for instance, loses 200,000,000 tons of soil per year from erosion, according to an Iowa State University study quoted by Lester R. Brown, the president of the Worldwatch Institute in Washington, in a pamphlet, *The Worldwide Loss of Cropland.* One of Brown's conclusions is that "Agricultural land can no longer be treated as a reservoir, an inexhaustible source of land for industry, urbanization, and the energy sector. Cropland is becoming scarce. In a world of continuously growing demand for food, it must be viewed as an irreplaceable resource, one that is paved over or otherwise taken out of production only under the most pressing circumstances and as a result of conscious public policy."

The water that runs beneath or alongside farmland is also tainted by various agricultural chemicals, including pesticides and herbicides, which leach through the soil into the aquifers and surface waters. Some are not man-made chemicals: Animal wastes, concentrated in quantity on crowded feedlots, threaten nearby water supplies. Nitrates, from nitrogen fertilizer and from animal wastes, also enter the water. Although nitrogen is an essential nutrient, both infants and cattle who drink water contaminated with it may become ill and die; in both cases their stomachs convert the nitrate to nitrite, which alters the blood hemoglobin in such a way that it cannot properly carry oxygen from the lungs to the tissues. A result, in humans, is "blue-baby disease."

Pesticides are a major problem. One estimate, made by an association of professional chemists, is that more than 1,600,000,000 pounds of pesticides are produced in the United States each year and that such a vast quantity of poison poses serious problems in terms of accidents, possible by-products, and what to do with "empty" containers. "The 116,000,000 pounds of pesticides used in California alone in 1971," said the report, ". . . were accompanied by more than 17,000,000 containers—from paper bags to 55-gallon steel drums" (including about 10,000,000 that entered the home as containers of household products), and "if each 'empty' container were to retain only 1 per cent of its original contents, California, for example, would be dealing with more than 1,000,000 pounds of 'waste' pesticides annually from this source alone."

Some problems with pesticides have been much more direct in their threats to the environment. There are numerous examples of groundwater contamination caused by pesticides; in one of them, the pesticide dibromochloropropane, or DBCP, was found in heavy concentrations in half the irrigation and drinking water wells tested in the San Joaquin Valley in 1979. Two years before, the Environmental Protection Agency had banned the use of DBCP on nineteen fruit and vegetable crops when tests showed it caused sterility in some of the workers who manufactured it, as well as cancer in laboratory animals. EPA's concern was tempered, however; a federal document reported that the agency "has allowed continued use of an estimated 10,000,000 pounds of DBCP annually in the U.S. on crops such as soybeans, citrus fruits, grapes and nuts."

For about six years, farmers in Long Island's $30,000,000 potato industry spread quantities of the pesticide aldicarb on their fields in an effort to wipe out the golden nematode, which attacks potatoes. Aldicarb, manufactured by Union Carbide under the trade name Temik, attacks people as well as parasites; in humans, the compound inhibits an enzyme that transmits data from muscles to nerves, and can cause weakness, sweating, nausea, and slurred speech. By March of 1980, the poison had been found in one-fourth of the samples of well water tested in Suffolk County, and the state health department recommended that residents near potato fields buy their water in bottles from the grocery store. Union Carbide asked the Environmental Protection Agency to withdraw its certification of Temik from the Suffolk County market, and the corporation offered to pay for filtration of some home water supplies.

The potato farmers were quoted as complaining about not being able to use the poison anymore. EPA reported that the farmers had been coating the earth, and therefore the groundwater, with twice as much of the poison per acre as did farmers elsewhere in the nation. Temik remains in use, as a matter of fact, in potato and other farming in other parts of the United States, said a Union Carbide official in 1982. Among the reasons it caused such a problem on Long Island, he said, were the vulnerability of the aquifer, the fact that the Suffolk farmers doused the ground with so much of it, and the fact that they planted almost continuous crops of potatoes, each of which required—in their estimation—more poison.

For all the trouble they cause, pesticides may turn out eventually to be of limited value at doing what they are supposed to do. *The Global 2000 Report* on projected world conditions noted that some estimates of world food supplies assume that a 100 per cent increase in food production by 2000 will be accompanied by a doubling in the rate of pesticide application generally, and, in the less developed countries, a quadrupling. Massive increases, warned the report, would "definitely increase" the chances that pests would strengthen their resistance to pesticides, "as has happened already in cotton." On California farms, said the report, seventeen out of the twenty-five "major agricultural pests are now resistant to one or more types of pesticides, and the populations of pest predators have been severely retarded."

Of course, not everyone takes such a dim view of pesticides. The Committee on Environmental Improvement of the American Chemical Society, which is a non-profit association of professional chemists and chemical engineers, has published a book titled *Cleaning Our Environment: A Chemical Perspective*, which deals in a straightforward manner with many of the issues of the environment and chemicals. A section on pesticides, however, seems out of place in its defense of the poisons. "Pesticides by design are biologically active and may be hazardous if misused," says the book. "Nevertheless, the number of illnesses and deaths known to have been caused by accidental or deliberate misuse of the materials is far outweighed by the benefits these chemicals have brought in controlling disease-bearing pests and in increasing food and fiber production. In addition, there is no evidence to date that long-term, low-level exposure to pesticides in the concentrations found in our diet or in the environment in the U.S. has had a harmful effect on people, although extensive research is continuing." A skeptic might wonder if membership on the author committee by representatives of Dow Chemical may have contributed to the book's lack of anxiety over the pesticide issue. Dow, a Michigan-based firm, is the world's seventh-largest chemical company and the second-largest in the United States. Its more than $9,000,000,000 in net sales in 1979 included sales of some $471,000,000 worth of agricultural chemicals, among them insecticides and herbicides.

Another problem that until now, like the mining of groundwater, has been peculiar to the Western United States is the matter of determining how the region's supplies of ground and surface water shall be divided up. For residents of much of the Eastern part of the country, it may be difficult to understand why dividing it up is necessary at all. But the Western states receive quantities of rainfall that are meager in comparison with the East's. The Environmental Data Service of the U.S. Department of Commerce published, in 1968, a handsome oversized book called *Climatic Atlas of the United States*. In it, page after page of maps show precipitation, sunshine, dew points, degree days, relative humidity, sky cover, prevailing wind, lake evaporation, and the other components of climate in a nation that is rich in geographical diversity. There are many distinctions between the East and the West, but none is sharper than that shown on the maps depicting normal annual precipitation across the country. Rainfall and snowfall averages for the period 1931–60 are measured in inches, with areas of identical annual precipitation connected by lines similar to those used on contour maps to illustrate elevation.

The numbers that indicate normal annual precipitation in inches are quite high in portions of the extreme Northwest— around 100 inches per year in the mountainous areas separating Seattle and Portland from the Pacific Ocean—but they are dramatically lower in the Southwest: 8 inches along the San Joaquin Valley, 4 inches near Yuma, Arizona, less than 12 inches at Phoenix, about 12 inches at Albuquerque. Then, east of the Front Range of the Rocky Mountains, the numbers increase: 20 inches or so along a line that connects Brownsville and Amarillo in Texas with Dodge City in Kansas and Fargo in North Dakota; 48 inches or more from the Mississippi River through most of the rest of the East (although the totals are nearly double that in parts of the Smokies, where North Carolina, South Carolina, and Georgia meet).

Because of the great variations in precipitation, the Eastern United States traditionally has concerned itself very little with what the bureaucrats call "water resources management," while for Westerners such concern has been almost a fixation and has led to the development of a body of state water law that is about as foreign to the Eastern states as, say, the laws of Islamic religion would be to a Georgia sheriff.

In the East, generally speaking, the states follow a doctrine of water rights known as "riparian"—from the Latin word referring to the sides or banks of a waterway. It means, basically, that anyone who owns property alongside a stream has a right to the water in that stream—a right to look at it, to fish in it, to do nothing wih it, or to use it, provided that use does not conflict with the similar rights of others downstream. Such a doctrine has always fit neatly into the Eastern water situation, in which rivers traditionally have had plenty of water for anyone who wanted it. "Doctrine" is, in fact, almost too important a word to attach to the practice, since there was so much water that Easterners didn't have to worry about rules.

The system in use in the West (in its various forms, since it is administered by the individual states) is generally known as the doctrine of "prior appropriation." A simple explanation is impossible, inasmuch as entire law firms have been founded, and fortunes made and lost, on attempts to explain it. But it might be said that prior appropriation means the person who gets to the stream first has a superior right to the water over those who get there later. "First in time, first in right," is the way the doctrine is often summarized. Appropriative rights may be sold and traded and switched up- and downstream. Usually such rights are administered through the offices of state water engineers (with ultimate settlements of disputes in the state courts), and the quantity of water to be diverted is clearly specified. A claimant who establishes a right to water but who doesn't use it can forfeit his right to it, and so one irony of the western doctrine is that it can encourage waste.

The system grew out of mining, as David Lavender, an educator, explained in 1977 in a book assessing future water needs. When the gold miners invaded California in the middle of the nineteenth century, he wrote, they had no desire for land, but rather for the minerals in it, so laws were drawn up to fit their needs. When all the gold was taken from a particular plot and the miners ceased to use the land, the law specified that their right to use it was terminated. A similar situation existed with the miners' use of water in the West, where, wrote Lavender, "such streams as do exist are perverse, deceptive, and difficult to control. . . . Inevitably, the volume of water in the foothill streams diminished as the dry summer advanced.

No attempt was made, however, to equitably apportion the shrinking supplies among different claimants. Instead it was decreed that whoever first put water to use was entitled to his full quota before later diverters could take a drop." Thus a basis was formed for the doctrine of prior appropriation. The doctrine persists to this day, although it has been modified considerably by some states and will probably be changed a great deal more in the future.

Stephen E. Reynolds, the New Mexico state engineer, is one of the Western state officials who enforce the doctrine. In New Mexico it is set forth by Article XVI, §2, of the state's constitution, which includes this fairly simple statement: "The unappropriated water of every natural stream, perennial or torrential, within the State of New Mexico, is hereby declared to belong to the public and to be subject to appropriation for beneficial use, in accordance with the laws of the state. Priority of appropriation shall give the better right." Beneficial use in New Mexico, said Reynolds not long ago in an interview in his office in Santa Fe, means nothing more than "not wasteful." The state, counties, and municipalities may, however, use condemnation to obtain a water right when the substance is needed for public purposes.

"In New Mexico," said Reynolds, who is a friendly, down-to-earth person with none of the mannerisms, trappings, or vocabulary of bureaucracy, "there is no such thing as an in-stream right. Nobody—the state or anybody—can require that there be a certain minimum flow that stays in the stream for looking at, for fishing, or for any of those environmental things. Now, to people from the East, this is just outrageous; it's just terrible. But, you see, as a practical matter it isn't that bad."

He explained that under the New Mexico rules, the water user who establishes the first claim is fairly close to all-powerful. If he is situated downstream, he can force other users upstream to leave enough water in the stream to meet his needs. If he is situated at the head of the stream, said Reynolds, "he can take his water out and dry the stream up, and the guy who wants to fish downstream is stuck. Now, that sounds horrible, but as a practical matter it doesn't happen. There aren't any storage sites up in those high mountain streams. Because of simple geography, you don't *need* an in-stream right to keep water in the stream. It just takes care of itself."

Was the system he administered, Reynolds was asked, the best possible one for a place such as New Mexico?

"In my opinion, yes," he replied. "There's really no other way to do it in semi-arid land. You can trace it back to the Moors. You can trace it back in New Mexico to the Indians, who, before the Spanish came, generally operated under that same system. Look at it this way: Were it not for the doctrine of prior appropriation, there would have been *no* development out here. Grazing is about what you could have done. People are not going to come into a system like this, a semi-arid system, and spend money developing farms, or any enterprise that depends on water, if the latecomer can come take away the water supply on which his investment is based. So you just simply *had* to have the doctrine of prior appropriation in order to use this country and live in it."

10

If people would have been reluctant to move to the West without a water law that recognized the primacy of the first arrival, they also wanted some assurances that there would be water there in the first place. The federal government provided *that* assurance, and still is providing it, in ways that have infuriated critics of the system and that have profoundly influenced the forms and future of American agriculture.

With the exception of projects initiated by Mormon communities in the middle of the nineteenth century, private attempts at irrigating Western lands met with little success, even though the federal government, after the Civil War, undertook programs encouraging the settlement of arid, uninhabited lands. "Gradually," as a government-written history puts it, "a movement began that stressed federal reclamation as a means of settling the West and strengthening the family farm." That "family farm," with its wholesome connotations, was widely believed to be one of the objectives of Congress in passing the Reclamation Act of 1902 and its later amendments and extensions. Among other things, the act empowered the Secretary of the Interior, in the words of one government summary, to "locate, construct, operate, and maintain works for the storage, diversion, and development of waters for the reclamation of arid and semi-arid lands in the Western States." The agency chosen to do the work was eventually to be known as the Bureau of Reclamation. (In November, 1979, the Bureau's name was changed to Water and Power Resources Service. Interior officials said the renaming reflected changes in the agency's mission. Government offices undergo name changes all the time, to the accompaniment of the usual folderol about new missions, but some of the critics of BuRec, as they like to call it, said they believed the Bureau wanted to obscure the public's recollection that it was the agency that had built the Teton Dam, which collapsed in 1976).

One of the things the 1902 act did was to provide for the construction of water storage and distribution facilities in the sixteen westernmost states (later expanded to seventeen) and for the use of those facilities to irrigate otherwise dry farmland. Dams were built; rivers were diverted; canals were cut through the desert. Today a map of the Bureau's operations (which is a map of just half the nation, since the agency does not operate in the East) shows dozens of artificial lakes, dams, reservoirs, and aqueducts. By late 1979 the Bureau had responsibility for 138 water and power projects, along with 333 reservoirs, and the projects were said to supply the water used by 30 per cent of the population of the West. More than 146,000 farms, covering about 9,000,000 acres, receive irrigation water courtesy of the Bureau. The recipients are supposed to reimburse the government for the costs of the water, but in the past the repayment schemes, which have featured scandalously low interest rates, have drawn great criticism from environmentalists and others who oppose such a distribution of a national resource.

Furthermore, the "family farm" aspect of the 1902 act was quickly scuttled in favor of taxpayer-subsidized irrigation water for corporate agriculture. Under the act, the size of the farm getting the subsidized water was limited to 160 acres for each family member. In addition, each family member could lease another 160 acres nearby. The family had to live within fifty miles of the land it owned. Thus the "family farm" was protected and encouraged by the legislation. There was one major hitch, however: The Bureau of Reclamation never enforced the law. In one case, dealing with the Imperial Valley of California, which started siphoning off irrigation water from the Colorado River before the provisions of the act took hold,

Washington granted a specific exemption from the 160-acre rule (although there are serious questions as to the motives and ethics involved in the exemption). In most of the others, however, the exemption was less formal. The government just winked at the violators. In 1978 a federal task force examined the situation in a section of California and found that both the spirit and the letter of the 1902 law were being violated by means of various devices, including joint mortgage arrangements and trick leasing schemes. Tracts of land averaged 2,200 acres, said the task force. And the residency rules weren't enforced, either.

In the meantime, a lawsuit was brought by those seeking to force the Bureau to pay attention to its own law, and the matter is still before the federal courts. The Carter administration in 1978 suggested that Congress rewrite the acreage provisions to protect the much-discussed family farm, but what Congress came up with seemed more like a revision that would continue to supply irrigation water to corporate farms with subsidies from the federal taxpayer. One California congressman, from a suburban district that has only 1 per cent of its population engaged in farming, called the plan "socialism for the rich" and "the biggest western stage coach robbery of the public since Jesse James." Former Secretary of the Interior Cecil Andrus, who caught a lot of flak as President Carter's chief activist in this and other water reforms that were not wanted by the heavy Western water users, estimated that corporations in California operated farms running to 100,000 acres or more and that they received $150,000,000 worth of water subsidies.

Whatever the politics, economics, and ethics of agricultural water use, it is growing and it is expected to grow, both in the nation and in the world. Farmers now are using irrigation in parts of the country where before they had depended on rainfall, and their motives are quite understandable: They don't like what happens to their income during those years when it doesn't rain. Irrigation is catching on, particularly, in the crescent of Eastern states that sweeps from lower Virginia down through North and South Carolina, Georgia, Florida, Alabama, Mississippi, Lousiana, and part of Arkansas. The Geological Survey estimated in 1975 that 8,900,000 acre feet of water was withdrawn in that region each year to irrigate 5,400,000 acres of farmland.

In addition to the farmers' desire for economic stability, newer, improved machinery has made it possible for one or two people to irrigate large tracts of land at relatively low cost. These include stationary sprinkler systems, as well as the more recent center-pivot apparatus, in which sprinklers resembling huge carnival rides wheel themselves around in 160-acre circles, depositing precisely calculated amounts of artificial rainfall on the crops below. There is drip irrigation, also relatively new, in which emitters on pipes running on or just below the surface of the fields frugally deliver water to each individual plant, rather than to both the plant and all the soil around it. Older techniques include flooding the planted land until the required amount of water has been taken into the soil, and using siphons to carry water from supply canals into channels between furrows of row crops.

Prodigious quantities of water are used for agriculture, most of it in irrigating crops. One calculation, by the University of California in 1979, was that 4,533 gallons of water were required to produce the food that a Californian eats in one day, assuming that the eater consumed 2,500 calories. One grapefruit required 26 gallons of water to produce; 2,607 gallons were needed for a steak. Another computation, also in California, which produces one-quarter of the nation's table food, was that it took up to 13,000,000 gallons of water to grow 10 acres of tomatoes, and 16,000,000 to 23,000,000 gallons to grow 10 acres of rice.

Irrigation usage in the United States in 1975, including Puerto Rico and the U.S. Virgin Islands, was estimated by the Geological Survey at 140,000,000,000 gallons per day. The water was estimated to have been spread on 54,000,000 acres of farmland. The water usage in 1975 was up about 11 per cent over 1970, and the acreage under irrigation had climbed by more than 9 per cent.

Estimates by the United Nations are that about half the world's food production is based on irrigation, with the other half dependent on rain. In 1970, according to the UN, about 494,200,000 acres of land were irrigated worldwide; by 1975 the area had grown to 551,033,000 acres, or about 15 per cent of the world's arable ground, and an additional 123,550,000 acres were expected to be added by 1990. Much of the additional irrigation is expected to be in the developing nations.

The use of water for agricultural irrigation is fraught with problems, not the least of which is that it encourages political boondoggling, expenditure of enormous sums of the taxpayers' money for the benefit of a relative few, and schemes of marginal value to make each and every desert bloom. There are physical problems, as well. Some scientists fear that wholesale withdrawal of river and other forms of runoff water for irrigation purposes will dry up major world streams before they make it to the seas. This could happen, said some participants in a recent world conference on climate, in the rivers feeding the Mediterranean Sea, with the result being that the sea would become more saline. Already withdrawals from the Colorado River, which is born in Rocky Mountain National Park in Colorado, are so great that the river is an intermittent trickle by the time it gets to Baja California and the Gulf of California. "Irrigation consumes nearly the entire flow," states a Geological Survey document. The prevailing attitude about the Colorado is evident in the title of a pamphlet published by the Colorado River Water Users' Association: *The Role of the Colorado River*. The river, it seems, has no existence of its own, but only serves its "users"—plays "roles" in the scenarios they design.

"Applying water to the land is an art," says a Geological Survey document on the subject, "and experience is necessary to do the job well." Too often, such experience is lacking, and irrigators apply either too much or too little water to the soil. Often the error is on the side of too much, and it is an easy error to make as long as the cost of the water to the farmer is held artificially low by federal and state subsidies. Too much irrigation can raise the water table beneath the cropland, resulting in the virtual destruction of the usefulness of the soil by waterlogging. Too little irrigation can contribute to the salinization of the soil.

All water in nature contains at least trace amounts of dissolved salts. When irrigation water is applied to dry lands, however, these salts tend more to be left behind in the upper layers of the soil. They become, quite literally, the "salt of the earth." The concentration of salts increases in the topsoil, and the salts are picked up by the water that percolates down to the aquifers and by the water that runs at or near the surface on its way back to the nearest stream or irrigation ditch (such water is called the "return flow"). "In this way," says a Geological Survey paper on water in California, "both the quantity and quality of water resources are modified. Irrigation, even though it may simulate natural processes, tends to deteriorate the water, and thereby man causes pollution." It is possible for land to be simultaneously damaged by waterlogging and salinization. Malin Falkenmark and Gunnar Lindh, in their survey for the UN Water Conference, wrote that "The frequent occurrence of salinization and waterlogging as a result of irrigation is a major global problem in the agricultural sector. It is now estimated that, on a world basis, between 200,000 and 300,000 hectares of irrigated land [494,200 to 741,300 acres] are lost every year due to salinization and waterlogging." The Swedish authors pointed out that irrigation also facilitates the transmission of waterborne diseases, such as schistosomiasis, in which a worm destroys blood and tissue, and malaria, particularly in tropical and semitropical areas, and that irrigation return flows can carry fertilizers into nearby rivers and lakes, where their constituent nutrients, phosphorus and nitrogen, can cause rapid, widespread growths (called

"blooms") of algae. By the time irrigation water has gotten
to the stage where it may be thought of as return flow, says
the Geological Survey, it has less than half of its original
usable volume "and has little reuse potential. In contrast,
nearly 90 per cent of the water withdrawn for manufacturing
and other industries, such as mining and construction, is returned to water sources for additional use."

Salinization, due in large part to poor drainage, appears to
be threatening California's San Joaquin Valley, according to a
government report on desertification in the United States. (Desertification, said *The Global 2000 Report*, is "a broad, loosely-
defined term encompassing a variety of ecological changes that
render land useless for agriculture or for human habitation.
Deserts rarely spread along well-articulated frontiers; rather,
they pop up in patches where abuse, however unintended,
destroys the thin cover of vegetation and fertile soil and leaves
only sand or inert earth.") The San Joaquin, said the government, is suffering from all the forces that work to produce
desertification: "Poor drainage of irrigated land, overgrazing,
cultivation of highly erodable soils, overdraft of groundwater,
off-road vehicle damage."

It is agriculture's high *consumption* of water that rankles
some critics, who are more likely to use the term "waste" and
whose voices are being heard now, louder than ever before,
in discussions of Western water matters. Not only are they
concerned, or even outraged, by the issues of corporate agriculture and governmental subsidies; they also argue that the
relative cheapness and abundance of water, even in regions
that otherwise would be deserts, has led to agricultural practices that otherwise would never be countenanced. Cotton and
alfalfa are being grown on the desert floor south of Phoenix,
for example. Forage crops are being cultivated in California,
all because the economics of Western water encourage the
profligate use of the precious substance and because the
economics of the federal pork barrel favor—demand—the
continuous construction of dams and ditches to catch every

possible drop of fresh water before it finds its way to the sea and to transport that water to the drier, southern portions of the state, where it may be used to create cropland and to enable Los Angelenos to wash their cars and top off their hot tubs. As an educational film about water problems in California, produced by the state's Water Resources Control Board, explains: "We solve the problem that three-quarters of our natural water runoff occurs north of Sacramento, while 90 per cent of our population lives south of it, by transport." A water-resources map of California that shows all the canals and aqueducts and feeder lines and impoundments (there are several such charts, published by various public and private agencies, for water is of immense importance there) looks almost like the layout of some government-run fish hatchery— the waterways and lakes are all there, but once they stop being mountain streams and ponds they have a *man-made* look about them. It is as if the decision had been made long ago that if the reflection of a mountaintop or a cloud crept into the mirrored surface of a reservoir, or if a stream made a gentle, eccentric meander on its way to deliver irrigation water to valley farmers, that was permissible, but it certainly wasn't necessary, and such behavior surely must not be encouraged.

David F. Abelson is a native Arizonan, now a Californian, who is among the critics of the ever-growing water projects. He is the executive director of the Planning and Conservation League, the oldest environmental lobbying organization in California. Abelson, a curly-haired man in his early thirties, has his offices in Sacramento. He feels distinctly outnumbered in the state capital; the League's fund-raising literature notes that "PCL is one of only three environmental organizations employing a full-time lobbyist on behalf of natural resource conservation and sound land use planning, and the task is a formidable one when you consider that there are over 500 registered lobbyists in Sacramento." The executive director is, himself, something of a cornucopia of information, as a good lobbyist must be, on aspects of his particular cause. He is aware (as are others all over the nation whose work has to do with water matters) that most people simply don't know where water comes from and where it goes. So when a visitor asked him for his assessment of the water situation in California, and particularly the status of agricultural water, Abelson replied with a complete lecture:

"There is plenty of water in California," he began. "In terms of supplies, we've got an annual production in this state on the order of 36,000,000 acre feet a year, which is a trillion gallons of water. The largest single lake in the state is Lake Shasta. It has about 4,500,000 acre feet of storage capacity when it's filled to the brim; you'd have to take that lake and fill it all the way to the top eight times in order to realize what the total water supply of this state is.

"To break it down in terms of where the water comes from: These are round figures. Basically we get on the order of 5,000,000 acre feet a year from either the Colorado River or the Owens Valley, which is basically funneled in to Los Angeles." (Los Angeles began diverting water from the Owens River, 240 miles away, in 1916. The Metropolitan Water District of Southern California, which serves a 5,100-square-mile area in and around Los Angeles, diverts water from the Colorado River, also 240 miles away, and taps supplies in northern California.)

Abelson continued: "We get something on the order of 10,000,000 acre feet a year from various projects, federal and state, that have been built along the Central Valley. They dam and drain the Sierra Nevada streams. There are over 1,200 dams in California today. Twelve *hundred* dams. That's a lot of concrete. We get about 15,000,000 acre feet a year that we pump out of the ground in various parts of the state. So that gets you 30,000,000 acre feet. And then you've got about another 6,000,000 acre feet that comes from small, local water districts and private reservoirs.

"That's kind of the ball park on what our supplies are. About 36,000,000 acre feet a year. Now, to put that in the perspective of the total water that's available in California: Every year, from natural rainfall and precipitation, we get about 200,000,000 acre feet of water falling down on the state. But of that 200,000,000 about 130,000,000 is lost through natural systems that are non-recoverable—principally through natural evapotranspiration in our forests and so on. That leaves us with 70,000,000 acre feet of runoff water, which either re-charges the groundwater basin or runs out to the ocean, taking with it nutrients, restoring the beaches in the southern California area, carrying sediment, providing natural waterways for salmon to spawn in, and what have you.

"Of that 70,000,000 acre feet in this state, we have tapped 36,000,000 acre feet a year. So we've taken over half of all the available water supplies in the state and we've already developed them. The impact on the fisheries, just for one example, has been horrendous. In the Central Valley alone, which was the second-greatest salmon spawning ground in the country, second only to the Columbia River, the salmon have gone into a nose dive because of all the dams and diversions."

Much of the runoff that has not been captured, said Abelson, is carried to the sea by rivers in northern California that are still relatively wild—the Eel, the Smith, and the Klamath among them. Farther south, though, the rivers have been mostly tapped, their waters diverted to the lower part of the state for agricultural and municipal uses.

Abelson's visitor reminded him that he had said California had already developed "over half" of the water that comes into the state. Couldn't it be argued that the amount was "*only* half"?

"Right," he said. "In order to get to that issue, let's talk about what we do with the water that we have. More than 85 per cent, or 32,000,000 acre feet a year, is in agriculture, which is the state's leading industry and which produces revenues in the neighborhood of $10,000,000,000 a year to the state. The remaining 4,000,000 to 5,000,000 acre feet is in the urban sector. It serves residential urban uses—showers, toilets, lawn watering, and so on; it serves municipal uses, for parks, waste-water treatment plants, and the like; and it serves industrial uses for cooling and what have you. So it's a fairly small percentage of our overall water supply that is obviously needed to sustain life in the state of California.

"Let's focus," Abelson continued, "on the agricultural use, because this is really where the biggest problems reside. Of that 32,000,000 acre feet a year that's used in agriculture, more than half—something on the order of 17,500,000 acre feet a year—is used for the production of exceedingly low-value, very water-intensive forage groups: irrigated pasture; alfalfa. You're talking about crops that are basically used to feed cattle. Now, it's important to recognize that this is the most water-intensive crop that you can grow, and we *are* talking about a semi-arid area. Clearly, the single largest user of water is not a food crop in the sense that most people think of it, like tomatoes or lettuce or melons, or a clothing crop such as cotton, but indeed it is feed for cattle."

And most of the cattle that are raised in California are not even born there, said Abelson, but rather are trucked in from Texas and fed on California's natural rangeland and the forage crops that low-cost water produces. Once the cattle are fattened up, he said, they are trucked out of the state for slaughter. "So we bring them up from Texas, feed them here in California, ship them back to the Midwest for slaughter, and then put them back on a truck and ship many of them back out to California to be consumed." In the process, he added, the cattle (or their butchered carcasses) are trucked past millions of acres of prime Midwestern forage land which, for one reason or another, is lying fallow. "So the bottom line," he said, "is that while America has this very cheap, subsidized water in the West—cheap in the sense of the dollar cost to the farmer, but not cheap in the cost to society, either in economic or environmental terms—we cannot competitively use our natural lands that are lying fallow in the Midwest" but do not enjoy taxpayer subsidies.

If the water were used more wisely, said the lobbyist, there would be less reason to worry, as some in California do, that the state was running low, or even "running out" of water. "And," he continued, "the other factor that leads me to the conclusion that we have more than enough water to meet our needs, in any sense of the word 'needs,' is the fact that we are wasting something on the order of at least 4,000,000 acre feet a year. It simply is wasted through inefficient use of the resource."

Some of the waste, said Abelson, has nothing to do with agriculture. He calculated that urban use of water could be cut by as much as 1,000,000 acre feet a year "without any major change in lifestyle" and that another 800,000 acre feet, at least, could be saved by reclaiming waste water from urban centers. But fully 2,000,000 acre feet a year, he said, is wasted by agriculture through "inefficient irrigation practices, both in the way we deliver the water and in the way we apply it." One million acre feet, said Abelson, was lost in evaporation, while another million disappeared as runoff, some of which was "quite brackish in nature" and could be reclaimed and reused, but wasn't.

If California were to change its attitudes about using water, particularly agricultural water, Abelson said, there would be plenty of the stuff to go around, even if the state's population continued its anticipated growth. If conservation and wise use became the rule, he said, Californians would see that "we really do have a tremendously large supply of water in this state. There is plenty of water in California. What there *isn't* plenty of is much incentive to use it wisely. And that is, in short work, where I come down on the issue."

As might be expected, there is some disagreement in California with the sort of analysis made by Abelson and others who share his views. Ronald B. Robie is the director of California's Department of Resources, which oversees the state's water policies, among other things. "Mr. Abelson's objective is to stop building more dams in California," said Robie in an interview not long ago. "And he's relatively new to the water business, and he has oversimplified some of the problems." One of those oversimplifications, said the state official, concerned cattle and forage. To force California farmers to stop growing forage crops because they used a lot of water, said Robie, would involve "a massive amount of social engineering." "My answer to Dave Abelson's theory," he continued, "is that it's a very complicated society, and we should make the most efficient use of water on whatever crops we're growing. What *he* would like to do is just take the equation of water use and reduce it by a big chunk and take that savings and apply it in lieu of building something else. And I think that's unrealistic."

Jack R. Gualco and William I. Du Bois also dispute Abelson's contentions. They are lobbyists in Sacramento for, respectively, the Agricultural Council of California, which includes organizations ranging from the purveyors of Sunkist oranges to the California Fig Institute, and the California Farm Bureau Federation, which is a dues-supported group representing more than 91,000 members. Both men, and particularly Du Bois, are pleasantly argumentative in the manner of state capitol lobbyists the nation over, men who have fought a lot of battles and seen virtually all of them settled by the old-fashioned expedients of politics and economics, which frequently come very close to being the same things.

"Have you made the observation that those people that are the most critical of agriculture are the people who know the least about it?" asked Du Bois when a visitor brought up the subject of the industry's current public image. "They're the furthest removed from knowledge about what the situation really *is* in agriculture. I don't know of any of them that have ever irrigated, themselves, who make those claims." The critics, he said, rarely are willing to carry their analysis all the way from the cornfield into the grocery store, where, they would find, the reforms they urge on agriculture would soon result in higher prices for consumers.

"There's the statement about how, if the water wasn't so cheap, we wouldn't be growing these crops," said Gualco. "That doesn't make any sense. Because there's a demand in the market for what we're growing in California. Rice is a good indication of that." California was, in 1977, the nation's third-ranking producer of rice, raising some 812,400 metric tons of the water-intensive crop. California exports about half of its rice crop, some of it, in fact, to the Orient. "Of course," said Du Bois, "we could raise a lot less food in California, and in the process we would, of course, put a lot of land to waste. And we could feed a lot less people in the process. The value of the farms that remained would probably be greatly enhanced, because people would be bidding for the food. And if that's the way society wants it, that's the way we're going to do it. But I don't think they want it that way, and I think when they find out what that sort of system would result in, the rush will be in the other direction—to try to get some *more* water out there on the farm so that the buyers of food can then be the choosers."

"There's a real void of understanding on the part of a lot of urban residents on how food is produced," said Gualco. "It *doesn't* come from a can. It *isn't* found in a carton. It comes from someplace much more basic than that: It comes from a cow, it comes from a plant. Both of which require great amounts of water."

Everyone familiar with the situation agrees that a major source of the friction over agriculture's use of water is urban growth. In places where water is scarce, particularly in the West, urban residents are quick to accuse agriculture of being wasteful. "There's this real anti-agriculture feeling that's spreading throughout California," said Jack Gualco, "and I think it's because of the changing complexion of the state. It has become overwhelmingly urban, and the pressure to expand

and develop in agricultural areas is putting a lot of pressures on our particular industry here. This is going to be reflected in some of the other states of the Southwest, which, if they haven't felt it already, will eventually feel it as well."

Ronald Robie, in his discussion of the situation, agreed. "California is just too large and too fractionalized as a state," he said. "There is southern California, and there is a desert, and there is the San Joaquin Valley, and there is the Bay area, and the Sacramento area, and then the Sacramento Valley. And in spite of the mobility of people, people tend to be either urban people or non-urban people. I grew up in Oakland, and I had very little appreciation for agriculture. I never went to the Valley. There are people in southern California, many friends of mine, who have never been to San Francisco. California is large, and the political structure is so diverse, that it doesn't have any identity as a state, in my opinion, the way some other states do, where the urban and agricultural people cling together around some kind of common state objective, whatever it may be that they're feeling. You don't have that here. You don't have a feeling of rivalry, of California versus the world. Everybody is separate. And that's why we have trouble in the legislature and why we have trouble with the water policy—because northern Californians point their fingers at southern Californians and say, 'They waste water down there,' and southern Californians point their fingers at northern Californians and say, '*They* waste water.' They *both* do. They all blame agriculture. Agriculture blames the urban areas for being insensitive. Everybody points his finger at everybody else."

11

Growth—one definition of which might be the addition of people, their homes, garages, pets, supermarkets, shopping centers, schools, hospitals, and all their other impedimenta and raiment to the lists of creatures and things that already exist and depend on the planet—has profound effects on water's quality and quantity, and obviously has a lot to do with the current crisis in water. Each new soul that is added to the planet's inventory of human life requires a few extra gallons of the substance each day just in order to stay alive, and for those lucky ones who are allowed, because of nationality or ethnicity, to aspire to lives in which comfort and security play major roles, many more gallons per day must be located, reserved, pumped, cleansed, stored, transported, and (once they have finished with it) cleaned once again before it may be returned to the hydrologic cycle.

The growth in numbers of human beings on Earth has been proceeding in recent years in ways that are somewhat baffling for the demographers, planners, and politicians. Those whose business is population projection, which is surely one of the more uncertain sciences, not long ago were predicting stupendous increases in global numbers (the term they normally employed in describing this was "population explosion") with concomitant famine, starvation, and intense competition for room in and on which to live. Now, however, the world's overall birth rate seems to be slowing, and much of the decline is being attributed to new attitudes toward marriage, birth control, and similar phenomena in the more developed nations. However, three-quarters of the world's population is concentrated in the poorest, least developed nations, and in *those* places the overall population is increasing. And it is in those places, with their need to encourage urban, industrial, and agricultural development, that stronger demands are being placed on water supplies. The world's population, as the eighties began, was believed to be about 4,321,000,000. The U.S. Census Bureau, in an estimate done for *The Global 2000 Report,* projected that the figure would reach 6,350,000,000 by the year 2000, with 90 per cent of the growth occurring in the less developed countries; another, more recent prediction, by the UN, was that the world population would stabilize at 10,500,000,000 by the year 2110. Another way of expressing the sort of growth, and therefore the need, that might be expected is found in a United Nations document on population: ". . . the less developed regions can be expected to have a larger population size by the year 2000 than the world had in 1975." The implications of all this for the availability of food and water are, of course, mind-boggling.

Although "acceleration seems to have given way to deceleration" in global population figures, as the UN document put it, "It still appears certain that world population will more than double in the next century." One reason for this, of course, is that even though people might have fewer babies, there will be more and more people to have babies at all. Another is that people are living longer than their forebears, and so they are eating and drinking more on their passages from the cradle to the grave. Mortality levels in the less developed countries have dropped most spectacularly, according to the UN: "Many of the recent trends in Asia and Latin America, within a decade or two, have led to mortality levels which today's low-mortality populations achieved only after multiple generations of progress." (In the early seventies, the expectation of life at birth for the entire world population was 55.2 years. In the more developed countries, it was 71.1 years, while in the less developed regions it was 52.2 years. The United States' average was 71.3 years, which was almost double that of some of the

African countries; Africa as a whole had an average of 45 years. As high as it was, the mainland United States still had a shorter life expectancy than Puerto Rico, Canada, Japan, Cyprus, Bulgaria, Denmark, Iceland, Ireland, Norway, Sweden, the United Kingdom, Greece, Italy, Spain, Belgium, France, the Netherlands, Switzerland, Australia, and New Zealand.)

Population growth seems to be slowing in the United States, in the meantime, and demographers have been revising their predictions locally as well as globally. Several years ago, for example, the nation's population was said to be headed toward 300,000,000 by the year 2000. More recently the word was that growth would "peak out" at 253,000,000 in the year 2015. No one on the face of the earth, of course, has the slightest idea what events will occur between now and 2000, or now and 2015 (or, for that matter, between now and next month), that could affect, upward or downward, the nation's or the world's actual population trends.

Much more *is* known, to be sure, about the sort of growth that is under way right now, both in the world and in the nation. The less developed nations and regions are already demanding much more water and the means to use it. This has produced some environmental questions that the industrialized nations have found hard to answer.

Enzo Fano, an Italian who studied economic development at Vanderbilt University, is the deputy director of the Division for Natural Resources and Energy of the UN Secretariat's Department for Technical Cooperation for Development, and he had a lot to do with the organization of the 1977 Mar del Plata water conference. Fano recalled, in an interview, that one of the purposes of the conference had been to bring together the richer countries, which spent relatively little of their time and resources worrying about water, with the poorer countries, which had almost an obsession with the topic. "The main thing that we were trying to push through to the developing countries as a concept," said the UN official, "was this: Don't learn from what the developed countries have done, because what they've done is generally bad. By and large, developed countries have got superstructures and encrustations of bureaucratic infighting as a basis for their water resources development. You have different agencies at the national level and at the local level which vie for power and authority in managing water resources. And therefore each one plans on a sectorial basis, whereas in fact what we *really* should be after is planning on a unified basis."

Another problem, said Fano, was that the leaders of some of the developing countries (who now are beginning to exploit their water and other natural resources in the name of development) weren't very favorably impressed by the advice they got from their richer neighbors (who already had exploited theirs) about the need to be good environmentalists. After the UN had held its conference on the environment in 1972, said Fano, the developing countries "were saying that this was a ploy, or a plot, by the developed countries to slow up their progress." The poorer countries responded to urgings of environmental caution, he continued, by saying, " 'We want quite the reverse. We want to invite industry to come in and, as an incentive, we want to be able to tell them that they *don't* have to worry too much about environmental concerns.' Now, of course, some of this is boomeranging because some developing countries are finding that they're getting a lot of pollution in their waters, and so on, because of this very policy."

The 1977 conference on water ended with a number of recommendations, the first of which called for more information on global water issues. It would be safe to say that the conference, and the topics it pursued, did not ignite worldwide fires of emotion over water issues. This was undoubtedly not the fault of the conference or of the UN, but rather a reflection of one of the oldest truisms in the water business: People, and governments, are not interested in water until it starts to run out or until it begins to flood. An aide to a U.S. congressman, who attended the conference, commented afterward that

"It did nothing. It was just another step in the dialogue between North America and South America, between the developed nations and the undeveloped ones. The undeveloped ones asked for a hundred billion for water improvements, and they won't get it."

In the meantime, global development goes on in various forms and often when a price must be paid it is water that pays it. Fox Butterfield, the *New York Times* correspondent in China, reported in the spring of 1980 on the widespread obliteration, in the name of growth, of forests in Heilungkiang Province, the most northern section of China. "Some Chinese scientists believe the destruction of the forests may be responsible for a 50 per cent drop in the province's rainfall since the early 1950s" because they were not there to provide evapotranspiration, Butterfield wrote.

All over the world, rain forests, which provide enormous amounts of moisture to the atmosphere, are endangered by development. Some 40,000 square miles of jungle disappear each year, by one estimate, and scientists are paying especially close attention to the globe's largest such forest, the one that exists alongside the Amazon River, which drains an area 478 times as large as the state of Connecticut.

In the United States, much of the recent development has been in environments that are, in terms of water, among the nation's most fragile. As is well known, recent population growth in the United States has tended away from the older cities, particularly those in the colder regions, and toward the suburbs and smaller cities of the South and Southwest—the much-popularized "Sun Belt." Texas, which once was thought of as a vast geographical cornucopia of prairie, desert, rangeland, mountains, and sagebrush, is now the third most populous state in the nation.

The crisis in world energy supplies has focused the nation's attention on ways to develop energy sources at home —and that means, among other things, mining for coal, uranium, and oil shale in ways that use vast amounts of water, and doing it "at home" in the ecologically vulnerable Mountain States. And where the land is not suitable for strip mining, the federal government itself seems always ready to promote some military construction scheme that will destroy the ecological balance of millions of acres of Western land, along with the scarce water beneath it.

Supplies of water in much of the South have always been considered more than sufficient to meet the region's population and industrial needs, and, although some parts of the region are having quality and quantity problems, water remains high on promoters' lists of inducements to Northern industry and population to abandon the cold winters (and labor unions) and come on down. Development in the South is causing some very serious problems, however. The coastal zone and the mountains, both of which are attractive to resort and recreation enterprises and to builders of second-home and condominium communities, are ecologically very fragile, and the limits of their "carrying capacities" are quickly reached. Anita Parlow, in a report on mountain land development published in 1976 by the Southern Appalachian Ministry in Higher Education, points out that home and resort building in the mountains (a lot of it has occurred in western North Carolina), along with ancillary road building, strips the mountains of their protective vegetation and promotes sedimentation and pollution of streams.

Urban and suburban development has been blamed for contributing largely to the loss of U.S. cropland, at an estimated rate of 3,000,000 acres a year. (The total amount of land used for crops in the nation is said to be 1,700,000,000 acres.) Much of the agricultural land that is turned into housing and shopping centers is situated within the floodplain, or the area that might be inundated by a flooding stream, and that causes problems of its own. Development means more paving, which means less opportunity for rainfall to soak into the earth as it goes through the hydrologic cycle. The precipitation heads instead for the closest available river, which then rises beyond its banks. If there were no development within the floodplain —if humankind had not built expensive and valuable things like supermarkets and homes and hospitals alongside the rivers —there would be no "flood," but rather a predictable and relatively harmless rising of the water. It is like the question whether a tree, falling in the forest, makes any noise if there is no one to hear it: A flood isn't really a flood until man gets into the picture. Because we live in an era in which studious attempts are made to avoid responsibility for our own actions, we have come up with the idea of nationally subsidized "flood insurance" to literally bail out those who put valuable possessions in the floodplain and then feel bad when they are swept away by the perfectly normal forces of nature, augmented by human development. Although a stated purpose of the flood insurance program has been to encourage communities to do better jobs of floodplain planning and zoning, that has not been one of its major accomplishments. As soon as the waters recede, the victims return with more valuable possessions to place in the path of the next flood—western Pennsylvania provides an almost annual reenactment of this ritual—and when a television reporter asks the residents the stock question about why they are building again, the stock answer hardly ever varies: "Because this is our home."

Much of the development that is ill-advised may be attributed to the simple urge, on the part of land speculators, to make a buck. But sometimes government programs that seem obviously "good" have paradoxical effects on the watery environment. The Council on Environmental Quality, in its annual report on the year 1977, noted that "sometimes there have been adverse, unexpected effects from well-meant programs; for example, the urban sprawl created by overambitious sewer projects which drew their inspiration and funds from the federal program to clean up the nation's waters." The sprawl has continued; the first returns from the 1980 Census indicated a trend in population growth toward small towns and rural areas, at the expense of the cities and the older suburbs.

All this has produced what has been called, not altogether correctly, the "growth–no growth" controversy, in which one side, which usually prefers to be known as the "environmentalist" side, accuses the other side of promoting unbridled growth, probably for its own enrichment, regardless of the cost to nature. The pro-growth people, meantime, accuse their foes of wanting to stifle all growth and return the planet to the Stone Age, or at least to a time when reading was done by candlelight and walking was the chief mode of transportation. Each side, of course, has exaggerated the other's aims tremendously.

The issue has been around a long time, but it became most noticeable in the early seventies, as an outgrowth of the book publishing, speech making, and legislation writing that came to be known as the "environmental movement." The environmentalists' side of the argument was expressed back then in a quotation from Barry Commoner, a biologist then at Washington University (and now at Queens College in New York, after an unsuccessful run for the presidency in the 1980 elections): "The environment got here first, and it's up to the economic system to adjust to the environment. Any economic system must be compatible with the environment, or it will not survive." Another interpretation of the growth issue was made later in the decade by California Governor Edmund G. Brown, Jr., as he addressed a Los Angeles conference on the two-year drought that was plaguing his state. Californians and others must learn, he said in a statement that has been repeated many times since, that "this is an era of limits, and there are very hard choices to make."

The other side of the argument, articulated ordinarily by those whose chief identification was with the "business community," might be represented by a 1979 comment from Chauncey Starr, the vice chairman of the Electric Power Research Institute. In a speech that later was printed as part of an elaborate advertisement by the electric industry, Starr took a dig at what he called "paranoid anxieties created by the doomsday syndrome" and then explained why he didn't subscribe to the notion that resources were limited: "History testifies that advances in technology expand the availability of resources. Technology does this by providing increased efficiency in the conversion of resources to human needs, i.e., less is needed to produce more, and in the extraction of traditional resources from the biosphere, as well as by providing methods for the conversion of dormant substances into new resources. So far, we have extracted only a small fraction of the store in the earth's crust." And while the argument over "growth–no growth" has been going on, growth has been proceeding. Some of it has occurred in balance with the environment; much more has not. The "advances in technology" of which Starr spoke have enabled contractors in south Florida to fill in the Everglades with greater efficiency and to build condominiums with greater speed, but similar technology has not been promoted with equal vigor to preserve south Florida's limited supply of potable water. Technology, of a sort, has assisted land speculators in Phoenix in selling enormous stretches of desert to people to live on, but it hasn't helped much with the problem of the land's collapse due to groundwater mining, or even with floods on the Salt River which destroy homes built practically in the riverbed.

12

"Growth" and "development" are terms that may be used in describing diverse regions, states, and communities within the country; three such places are Florida, New Mexico, and Arizona. In the last two states, rapid growth in population and commerce, and its effect on water, is a relatively new phenomenon. In the case of Florida, it is both an old story and a new one, depending on which part of Florida is involved.

At first glance, Florida seems almost to be *made* out of water. The 400-mile-long peninsula juts out into the Atlantic and the Gulf of Mexico with more than 3,000 miles of shoreline. It sits down close to sea level; Florida's highest point is the lowest of all the states, a 345-foot hill that is almost in Alabama. Much of the southern half of the state is literally green, of a shade that usually is described as "lush," owing to the fact that the climate is split, as it is in the tropics, into two seasons, a wet one and a dry one. During the wet period, it is not uncommon for six inches of rain to fall in a given area during a twenty-four-hour period. The state's intimacy with water is reflected in the names of dozens of cities, towns, and communities: Clearwater, Lakeland, Edgewater, and a plethora of place names that contain the word "Springs"—Salt, Orange, Silver, White, Blue, Coral, Crystal, Tarpon, Bonita, Citrus, and Winter Springs, to name a few. There is a lake district that looks almost like a map of Minnesota. Farther south in the center of the state, to the west of Palm Beach and east of Fort Myers, lies Lake Okeechobee, which, at about 700 square miles, is the second-largest body of fresh water wholly within the United States. Okeechobee, which the Indians named "Big Water," is full of catfish and good old Southern boys trying to catch catfish, and is so shallow (its normal maximum depth is about 15 feet) that there are many places where a boater who is out of sight of land could step out of the vessel and walk along beside it.

South of Lake Okeechobee is the river that it feeds, a river that is unlike any other in the world: the Everglades. The Everglades is so different from other ecosystems that there is considerable argument over whether the water in it actually flows at all. Most sentiment, however, is with the assumption that water in the Everglades—part swamp, part tropical jungle, a place of mangroves, cypress heads, wet prairies, hardwood hammocks, and pine ridges—moves very, very slowly along the 110 miles from Lake Okeechobee to the salt water of Florida Bay, the body of water that lies at the foot of the peninsula, behind the Keys and between the Gulf of Mexico and the Atlantic Ocean. In that 110 miles, the gradient of the land drops only about 10 feet. The Everglades, or what is left of it after earlier, and extremely successful, attempts at developing south Florida, is 50 to 70 miles wide. Once it reached all the way from what is now West Palm Beach, on the Atlantic, to the Gulf of Mexico, a distance of close to 150 miles.

As the traveler proceeds south in Florida, and nears the centers of development and habitation that are packed tightly together along the east coast, from West Palm Beach down to Miami, he might become increasingly aware that the surface waters, although they are practically omnipresent, are arranged *precisely*. No longer are they streams that wander over from the Everglades; now they have become *plumbing*, with right-angled turns and long, straight lines, as well as gates and valves. They have become the waterways of development, of growth.

South Florida was recognized as ripe for plundering a long time ago, but it was Hamilton Disston, the hardware king, who is best remembered for destroying the lush, wet environment and replacing it with the wall-to-wall cement and pavement that exist today. Disston's motto, in the 1880s, was "Drain the Everglades" to make way for development, and he was so successful in convincing the politicians and speculators of the efficacy of his dream for Florida that the legislature created, in 1907, something called the Everglades Drainage District, which did a fine job of doing what its name implied.

As the century progressed, south Florida became recognized as one of the nation's true, bona fide environmental disasters. There were few other places in the United States where the term "environment" meant so much—the ripeness of the landscape, the uniqueness of the Everglades, the abundant wildlife and flora, the afternoon thundershowers during the rainy season; the so very obvious *connectedness* of the place with nature. South Florida, along with a small portion of southern Texas that is, fortunately, off the beaten track, is the closest thing there is in the continental United States to the tropical world, with all the sensuality that that implies. It drew people like some mysterious potion, especially during the winter months. And yet, it seemed that, while people went there to enjoy the environment, they locked themselves up inside air-conditioned rental cars and hotels that were among the tackiest imaginable. At Miami Beach the hotels were built along the beach itself, in defiance of the widely known fact that such land is fragile and subject to constant shifting. The promoters called the shifting "beach erosion" (thus firmly placing the blame and responsibility on nature rather than on themselves) and got the Corps of Engineers to take the federal taxpayers' money and invest it in absurd schemes to "nourish" the beaches thus "eroded." Even when a bit of beach was visible in front of the hotels, as at extreme low tide, the tendency was to downplay the shoreline, the most magnificent of nature's creations, in favor of artificial intrusions upon the environment: At Miami Beach in the sixties it was routine for hotel employees, at about dusk, to stroll out of the hotels, past the oceanfront swimming pools (one fresh water and one salt), past the deck chairs and lounges and the other detritus of lethargy, and to walk up to a doorway built in a long, curving, whitewashed wall that separated all this from the ocean itself, and to *lock the door to the beach.*

Long after the engineers and politicians knew better, they poured million-dollar bills into the surf in front of the tacky hotels. In his May, 1977, message to Congress on the environment, President Jimmy Carter spoke of the need for protecting coastal barrier islands, which he called "a fragile buffer between the wetlands and the sea." Two years later, as he started his unsuccessful campaign for a second term, Carter, who badly needed Florida votes, asked Congress for $87,000,000 for public works projects in Florida in fiscal year 1980, of which $2,600,000 would be spent to "nourish" beaches in front of the hotels. At that time the overall Corps of Engineers "nourishment" project, which was budgeted at $40,000,000, was well into its goal of pumping 13,500,000 cubic yards of sand from one place to another.

Elsewhere in south Florida during the heyday of development, split-levels and condominiums were going up faster than the suckers could be lined up to buy them—which was very fast, since there were many refugees from the cold North, especially older ones, who wanted to live in the Florida environment. And with the housing came the shopping centers and airport runways and mortuaries and discount stores and fast-food joints. The Corps of Engineers had not come up with a way to fill in the Atlantic Ocean, so development had to push in the other direction, farther into the Everglades. A lot of flimflammery went on, as it always does when unscrupulous people see an opportunity to make their fortunes quickly in real estate, and a lot of damage occurred. By the sixties, southern Florida was one of those places (Los Angeles was another) that environmentalists urged other places not to be like. "We don't want to be another Florida," they said, in the same way that southern politicians conscious of their race relations and the futility of resisting desegregation, and perhaps even the correctness of integration, would talk of not becoming "another Birmingham."

Several events conspired to disrupt the destructive pattern of development in south Florida, not the least of which was that, in developing as much as it did, the area lost practically all of its visual attractiveness. (Efforts were made to remedy this by producing, as part of the development, entertainment parks that were fantasy worlds and that thus created their own, artificial environments, but the result, which was predictable, was to make the region look more like a carnival midway.) One event, or series of events, was a number of hurricanes that struck central Florida in the twenties and forties, bringing heavy rains that caused serious flooding. The politicians, who had been concentrating on draining the Everglades, now started realizing that the river of grass was important, if not on its own terms, at least as an efficient buffer between storms and other sources of "too much water" and the densely developed coastline. Then in the sixties a drought began, one that lasted until the end of the seventies, and Floridians learned once again that their environment could not be entirely man-made. Some of the politicians and planners started to wonder if the Everglades could not be used to store water during periods of abundance which could be released during periods of dryness. At pretty much the same time, the environmental movement of the late sixties and early seventies was in blossom, in Florida as elsewhere, and the legislature passed a number of strong laws to protect what was left of the state from the sort of development that had been so destructive earlier. Not surprisingly, many of the laws concerned water. An outgrowth of the laws and the awareness that has generated itself in the state—in Florida generally, not just the southern part—has been the establishment of state water management districts. The five districts are laid out not along political boundaries but along natural water basins, so that each of them may respond to local needs and problems.

The district that covers southern Florida—the South Florida Water Management District—watches over some 1,400 miles of canals, which serve as flood controls, as conduits to transport water from Lake Okeechobee to urban consumers, and, because the water they carry seeps into the earth below, as instruments to recharge the groundwater aquifers. The district oversees 1,600 square miles of "conservation areas," the places in the Everglades where excess water is stored. And the agency issues permits to people and corporations who want to obtain water by pumping it out of the aquifer. The system is a combination of the traditional Eastern riparian and Western appropriative water rights, but here the object is not to settle arguments over which private user has first rights to a water supply, but rather to use the supply as a device to maintain some handle on growth.

One of the district agency's missions is to contribute to a statewide reckoning of what the water supply will and should be like in the year 2020. The water projections will be put with other elements, such as transportation and housing, into a comprehensive plan for all facets of Florida life. In getting together some of the components of the plan a few years ago, said Bruce Adams, whose job at the district is "water resource advisor," the agency went before the public with an array of reports, meetings, and workshops and sought the people's reactions and suggestions. "We've got three and a half million people in the district," said Adams, "and about 60 or 65 per cent of them live on the Gold Coast [the highly populated area along the eastern coast]. So we went there first to do our planning effort and to get our public input. We listed fifteen items in the water-use plan as alternatives for water supply for the future. Basically they revolved about a lot of structural measures such as back-pumping—taking urban runoff water and pumping it into storage areas, through our canal system; taking runoff water that now just goes out into the ocean and pumping it down into the ground—that's called deep aquifer storage; taking semi-potable water that's runoff and pumping it down into the Hawthorne or the Floridan Aquifers to create a bubble of fresh water. We even talked with them about things like water importation. Some people are talking about tapping the springs in north Florida and running pipelines to south Florida." Adams paused a moment. "This has a lot of political implications to it, of course," he said.

"Another alternative was desalinization. A lot of people think desalinization is the answer. Well, we can run a line out into the ocean and bring in salt water and desalinize it. But it might cost twelve dollars a thousand gallons. There might be tremendous capital cost to build the plants. Is it energy-efficient? Will the people buy it?

"So we put out all these alternatives, fifteen of them. We included taking anti-transpirants, which are thin oil films which we'd put over large expanses of water storage areas in order to suppress evaporation. Things like this. We put all this out to the public, and we got their response. And the biggest response, the one that 95 per cent of the people had, was that they wanted to get more information about conservation.

"It shocked us. We thought people were going to respond to something more exotic. We didn't even anticipate that conservation would be high on the list, even though *all* the ideas were conservation, in theory. The people were asking, 'What can the individual user do to reduce his consumption to allow for the retention of more water in the natural resource?' "

The South Florida Water Management District's reply was to open the south Florida version of a storefront operation to provide the information that the people needed. The Water Resource Center, as it is called, is situated in an office-shopping complex in Pompano Beach, and it is full of displays that show where south Florida's water comes from, where it goes, and how consumers can waste less of it. There is a device which reclaims as much as 95 per cent of the water used in commercial car washes; and there are controlled-flow shower heads, in-home water purification systems, various pressure regulators, and a variety of toilets. One of them, which requires only two quarts of water per flush, uses air pressure to propel waste down the pipe, while another employs no water at all, but rather uses and reuses mineral oil. There were on display numerous devices (known, in the trade, as "dams") that fit in toilet tanks and reduce the amount of water available for flushing (one is named the "Watergate" and another is called the "Moby Dike"). The manufacturers of many of the items claim for their inventions what must be highly exaggerated savings, in water and in the energy used to heat water—usually on the order of 20 or 30 per cent. (This seems to be the standard claim of *every* manufacturer of devices that are supposed to "save" things, from the spark-plug gizmos for automobiles to storm windows and furnace flue dampers.) Still, the devices are there to be looked at and fiddled with, and the agency staff is on hand to answer questions on such topics as which house and garden plants and trees are most drought-and salt-tolerant.

Both the public and the Water Resource Center staff are interested in devices, some of which are quite simple and inexpensive and which return their investments very quickly, that reduce water pressure as it comes into a home or business, or as it comes out a faucet or shower head. Experts in the field of water conservation agree that these are among the most efficient, as well as painless, methods for reducing waste. When the Resource Center began its operations, it was one of only a few tenants in a new building. Two nights before the center's grand opening, excess pressure in the building's water lines cracked a seal on the center's plumbing. "We came back the next day," said Bruce Adams, "and there must have been five or six thousand gallons of water on the floor. When you're aiming at water conservation and you've got five thousand gallons of it wasted on the floor, you get the wisecracks. The next day we tapped the line and put on a water meter and pressure regulator."

Conservation is not the sole aim of the South Florida Water Management District. The planners know that whatever is done about water in Florida must be done in a many-faceted way, for the problem is many-faceted. As Adams said: "We don't consider conservation as the ultimate answer. We consider it as an immediate answer and as an interim answer and as a long-range planning tool. But it is not *the* answer."

Whether *the* answer, or *the* answers, will be found in south Florida is not yet known. The pressures are great there to let the old-fashioned laws of politics and development provide the answers, in which case Florida is doomed. But there are at least some in the state who are very aware of the problem, and this fact alone gives them an advantage over places—much of the Northeast, the middle Atlantic, the Midwest—where the problem is not being studied much at all, and where shortages of water are thought of as eccentricities of climate, soon to be remedied by a few good thunderstorms. "We don't want to be caught behind the eight ball like California was when their drought came," said Bruce Adams. "Everything they did towards water conservation in California was crisis-related. They had the situation and they hadn't planned for it. Luckily we benefited from their crisis, because we saw what could happen." What he was saying, in essence, was that Florida, which for so many years had served as a textbook example of badly planned development, now didn't want to become "another California."

The state has its work cut out for it. Floridians and their leaders again became painfully aware of the importance of water during the summer of 1981, when the normal rainy season did not materialize. The falling underground water table created a spectacular sinkhole in Winter Park—a 400-foot-wide crater that swallowed buildings, streets, cars, and a swimming pool. And the water level in Lake Okeechobee dropped to a level previously unrecorded by modern society—and one that had not been experienced since modern society started fooling around with the lake and its natural balance in the name of development.

New Mexico knows better about development. The reddish-brown state, which some might think of as "barren" and others as "beautiful," has always known that the water is limited, that the land cannot be exploited for long without disaster. The Anasazi Indians settled around A.D. 500 on land now designated as the Chaco Canyon National Monument, in north-western New Mexico, and lived, at first, a life of lush plenty. They cut wood in the forests to burn and use in construction, and the water nourished their crops. The population grew; soon the forests were gone, clearcut to nothingness. Without the trees, the soil couldn't hold water and so rains and melting snow produced floods that wiped out the canyon's agriculture. Eventually the Anasazis had to leave. They had ruined their land.

Throughout much of their state's later history, New Mexicans have been generally aware of the preciousness of their water supply, and they have protected it as passionately as some Floridians now strive to protect the mangrove and manatee. They know that not much water comes down from the sky—8 inches of precipitation along the lower Rio Grande and San Juan valleys, as much as 30 inches in the mountains— and they have always felt that this awareness, which amounted to a general *acceptance* of the situation, imposed a sort of natural lid on population growth and development. In 1979 the population of the entire state was estimated at only 1,212,000, with about 30 per cent of that in Bernalillo County, where Albuquerque is situated.

The Sun Belt boom has threatened to remove the lid, however, and projections are that population will grow with unaccustomed speed in the near future. Already there are some tensions; travelers with out-of-state license plates, particularly those from the colder regions, are told to "go back where you came from" by locals in Sante Fe shopping-center parking lots, the only apparent reason being that the locals (who might have been strangers themselves only a few years before) resent the possibility of another immigrant.

Abel and Sue Davis were immigrants to Sante Fe themselves about a decade ago, from Chicago, but few think of them as outsiders anymore. Abel Davis was, a year or so ago, the head of the Sante Fe Federation, a coalition of fifteen civic groups that originally was organized to urge the Sante Fe city government to pay more attention to neighborhood problems. Both Davises, when they were asked about water problems in their adopted state, phrased their replies in terms of development.

"We were an agricultural state," said Abel Davis, "and we're making the switch into a real estate state." And that, he said, is going to cause multitudinous problems with water. Not everyone in Sante Fe agreed with that thinking, though, he said. "There are real estate developers with whom I'm friendly, with whom I lunch, who would tell me, 'Abel, it's a waste of time. This is America. We've got ingenuity here. We can figure out a way to get the water if that's all we need. Let's build what the people want. We can always bring the water in. It's no big deal.' They say bringing water to northern New Mexico is just another mechanical facet of the proper development of northern New Mexico. They agree it's a factor, but not to worry about it: Do it. My own inclination is to worry."

So the tendency is to promote development, secure in the belief that a way will be found to produce the water—that, in the words of Chauncey Starr of the Electric Power Research Institute, technology will expand the limits. In New Mexico, particularly, that notion is attractive; mining, one of the state's largest sources of income, has always proceeded under such an assumption.

"That goes way back into history here," said Sue Davis. "Mining's an integral part of the history of this state. It's always been 'This is mining country, and we can't let the newcomers come out here and tell us to be concerned about it.'"

" 'It's my land, and I can do anything I want with it, and who are you to tell me what to do with it?' " said her husband, quoting another manifestation of the historical attitude. "And to some degree, I think it's genuine: 'It's the old West. We can do what we want to do.' The trouble is, it's no longer the old West. It's becoming part of metropolitan United States."

"Boca Raton West," said Sue Davis.

"What Sue's referring to," said Abel Davis, "is that, even though Santa Fe's been attractive to non-New Mexicans for years—to 'foreigners' and even foreigners with *money*—in the last few years the town's been discovered by the Beautiful People. There are some stylish people coming to town. And this, to me, is an essential difference. People for years have found Sante Fe attractive and have said, 'I think I'm going to change *my* way of living, and move to Sante Fe and become a Santa Fean.' What's happened in perhaps the past five years is that people are saying, 'I find Sante Fe attractive; I am going to bring *my* way of living to Sante Fe.' And they're bringing the Gucci loafers and fine linens and all that. And we've got to have all the services that they had in Dallas or New York or Los Angeles. The guy who moved here ten years ago or before, one of the reasons he came here was he didn't *want* all those things. He *had* all those things in New York, but he didn't *want* them here. He wanted to be different from New York. He wanted to be Sante Fe."

Said Sue Davis: "Sante Fe, I think, used to be sort of a *rough* place to live. Bumpy roads and a couple of movie theaters, and there wasn't a whole lot to do. You had to sort of be your own person. I think now that there are many people who want discos and restaurants and more fancy boutiques and more parties. I notice in the mail, we get inundated with invitations for benefits. Hundred dollars per couple, two hundred dollars per couple, this sort of thing. I'm all *for* these things. But somehow before, the stakes weren't quite so high. It's different now."

13

It is fashionable to say that the water is running out in Arizona. Even some Arizonans say it, and it's easy to see why. Sixty per cent of the water that the state uses is pumped from the ground, and it is pumped out at a much greater rate than it is replenished by nature. There is not much precipitation over most of the state anyway, and much of what does fall is consumed in evaporation and transpiration. Tucson, the state's second-largest city, depends entirely on groundwater for its supplies; Pima County, which surrounds Tucson, consumes 4.7 times the dependable supply of water. Statewide, the rate of groundwater depletion has been calculated at 1.7 times the dependable supply. Each year about 2,500,000 acre feet of water, or more than 814,000,000,000 gallons, is overdrafted— "mined." The Geological Survey has reported that a large portion of the Arizona landscape, in a 4,500-square-mile area in Maricopa and Pinal Counties (around Phoenix), has subsided by as much as seven feet in the years between 1952 and 1978, due to agricultural overdraft.

But the water is not running out. All that is missing from Arizona's water supply is the realization that the era of cheap water is over. And part of that realization includes a new assessment of the role of agriculture in a dry state, and part includes taking a sensible look at the issues of growth and development in a rapidly expanding urban area that has been forced to bloom on a desert.

Arizona is the nation's sixth-largest state in area, at 113,909 square miles, but only 18 per cent of the land is held in private ownership. Indian reservations occupy more than a quarter of the terrain, the federal government has 42 per cent, and the state holds most of the rest. The state's population is spread out at the rate of about 16 persons per square mile. (In New York's Manhattan, the figure is 67,808 per square mile.) More than half of Arizona's population, which in 1978 was estimated at 2,449,200, lives in Maricopa County. Much of the remainder resides in Tucson, a city where, according to an assessment made by a *New York Times* reporter in 1979, "with relatively few exceptions, growth at any price seems to be the official civic doctrine." Manufacturing is Arizona's chief producer of wealth, followed by tourism and travel, mining, and, finally, agriculture (including farming, ranching, and cattle feeding). Agriculture uses 89 per cent of the state's water, however; municipal and industrial uses, which include household water, water used in firefighting, and the like, account for 7 per cent, and the mining industry uses less than 3 per cent, with the rest going for power production and evaporation from lakes.

The promoters of the state, and there are many of them, are aggressive in soliciting outside investment and business migration, and they do not hesitate to face the water issue squarely—not a bad idea, inasmuch as practically any potential investor would have heard about the state's water problems, and since it is difficult to hide the fissures of sinking farmland. "True to its reputation, Arizona is an arid state," says an economic profile published by the governor's office and aimed at "business and industry seeking new or more profitable locations." But in an adjoining paragraph the profile boasts that "present Arizona water rates are lower than those of most other areas in the country." The Valley National Bank, which dominates Arizona finance as well as the Phoenix skyline, romances investors with claims of "Abundant sunshine, fertile soil, and a guaranteed supply of irrigation water" as components "in the development of Arizona agriculture into a billion-dollar industry."

Sometimes romance is not enough to dispel outsiders' fears of dying of thirst or from falling into a hole in the dried, cracking earth. The Arizona Water Commission issued a "Position Paper" on "Water for Municipal and Industrial Growth" in June, 1977, that was a clear signal that the state's leaders would not allow the water to run out—unless it was water needed by agriculture. The paper, signed by Wesley E. Steiner, the state water engineer and executive director of the commission, said, in part:

"In recent weeks, eastern investors have pointed to the state's water supply problem as justification for stopping investments in Arizona real estate.

"The fact that we have a water problem is undeniable. Arizonans are consuming water at almost twice the natural replenishment rate. This is possible only through the over-drafting or mining of groundwater reserves. Fortunately, however, the state's ground water reserves are of very great magnitude, sufficient to support growth in most developed areas for a long period of time even though no remedial actions are taken. The state's water problem, then, while serious, is long-term in nature. It is not immediate. It is cause for intelligent planning and corrective action, but not for panic.

"The Arizona Water Commission, the state's official water resource planning agency, is in the process of developing a State Water Management Plan that will define the magnitude of the overdraft problem county by county, establish priorities of use, and serve as a basis for bringing consumption and supply into balance throughout the state. Studies completed to date clearly reveal that Arizonans are attempting to irrigate a much larger agricultural acreage than can be sustained indefinitely without augmentation of the supplies available to the state via weather modification, desalination of sea or geothermal waters, or importations from areas of surplus such as the Columbia River." (This last may have been an example of Arizona's directing its arid wit at Easterners, who, according to the stereotype, don't have the slightest understanding of western geography. Weather modification is an extremely imperfect, potentially dangerous science; desalinization of seawater is very expensive even in states that *aren't* landlocked; and although schemes have been in the works for decades to exploit the Columbia River, or even the waters in the Yukon, and ship them down to the Southwest, they are nowhere near practicability, and the Columbia River remains in the State of Washington, about a thousand miles north of Phoenix.)

The position paper noted that the water commission had been looking into the question of "the state's ability, through reductions in agricultural acreage, to effect and maintain a water balance while meeting future municipal and industrial needs." By this, it meant, as land passes from agricultural use into municipal ownership, the water rights also are transferred. "Our studies indicate that with completion of the Central Arizona Project and retirement of a portion of the existing agricultural acreage," said the paper, "it is possible to effect and to maintain into the indefinite future a balance between water supply and consumption as the state's population and economy continue to expand. The retirement of all agricultural uses in Arizona would permit the support with firm water supplies of a permanent population in excess of 15,000,000, or some seven times the current population. . . . There simply is no water-related basis for a decision to stop all investments in Arizona real estate."

Continued development of Arizona, then—development in terms of population and industry, not in terms of agriculture—could proceed if agriculture gave up its water and if the Central Arizona Project were completed. That last item, known to Arizonans as CAP, for years has been hailed by its promoters as the solution for many, if not all, of Arizona's water problems. Its opponents see it as a whole new problem, all by itself.

The Central Arizona Project has been in the works for decades—as far back as 1918, if one includes discussions about bringing water to the central part of the state from the Colorado River, which cuts through the northwestern quadrant of Arizona and then drops down to form the state's western boundary with California. The Colorado, which has been called the most litigated river in the nation, has always been the object of exploitation by the Western states, and in 1922 it was necessary for them to enter into a compact to apportion the river's water between the states of the upper and lower basins. Another agreement, in 1938, allocated water among Arizona, California, and Nevada. Later, in an international treaty, the United States promised Mexico 1,500,000 acre feet at the southern end of the river. Presently, the sum of the Mexican commitment and the apportionments upstream is considerably greater than the actual flow of the river. On paper, at least, and often in actuality, the Colorado is used up.

When Arizona's plans for a water project reached the serious stage in the forties, and the state started making noises about actually using its apportioned share of the river, California, which *had* been using it, resisted. In 1973, after a dozen years of litigation, the Supreme Court ruled in Arizona's favor. The state immediately went to Congress with a request for authorization and financing of the CAP, got it, and has been proceeding, with the Bureau of Reclamation's help, on the costly project ever since. When it is finished, the project will take water from the Colorado at Lake Havasu and send it, via aqueducts, dams, tunnels, and reservoirs, into the center of the state at Phoenix and then down to Tucson. Because mountains are in the way, pumps will have to lift the water over them, at a considerable expense in energy and pollution from a generating station run by coal. On the Havasu-Phoenix leg alone, the water will have to be lifted 1,200 feet.

The project's backers refer to it, in the language of the water technocracy, as "a multi-purpose water resource development and managment project which will provide nearly 1,000,000 acres of irrigated land with supplemental Colorado River water," and which will "ultimately provide 500,000 acre-feet of municipal and industrial water for the Phoenix and Tucson metropolitan areas and provide substantial benefits from power generation, flood control, outdoor recreation, fish and wildlife conservation, and sediment control." In actuality, the project will change the face of Arizona forevermore by encouraging and subsidizing industrial and population growth. Comparisons with the environmentally destructive suburban mélange of southern California are not out of place.

Although agriculture is universally listed as one of the project's beneficiaries, the only croplands that will be allowed to receive project water will be those that were irrigated during the period 1958–68. And farmers using the water will be required to reduce proportionately their pumping of groundwater. Indian reservations are excluded from these restrictions.

The project's promoters waste no opportunity to herald CAP as the solution to Arizona's overdraft problem. A typical Bureau of Reclamation pitch goes like this: "Constant vigilance in the development and management of water resources has been essential in sustaining a strong economy in central and southern Arizona. For over three decades, central Arizona's natural water supply has been out of balance with total water demands [note that it is nature that is out of balance with human "demands," not the other way around], and the agricultural economy in particular has flourished and declined in direct relationship to the adequacy of water resources. Massive overpumping of ground water reserves has been necessary to balance the yearly supply-demand relationship. The current annual overdraft of the underground basins is over 2,000,000 acre feet. The importation of Colorado River water through construction of the Central Arizona Project will be a giant step toward reducing this annual overdraft, which is causing ground water levels to decline at an average rate of eight to ten feet per year with serious land subsidence occurring in many areas."

And, for those who don't particularly care if desert land planted in cotton or alfalfa cracks and sinks, Congressman Morris K. Udall of Arizona reminded city folk, in a 1977 issue of the *Congressional Record*, that it could happen beneath *their* feet, too: "With continued mining of ground water by the cities . . . it is only a matter of time until the effects of differential subsidence and earth cracking are experienced by urban dwellers." (Differential subsidence occurs when adjacent layers of earth subside independently and at different rates. If urban water pipes, or sewer mains, or electrical conduits run through the earth at that point, they may be sheared by the differential pressures.)

Although it appears that the CAP enjoys widespread acceptability among Arizonans generally, both its proponents and its opponents recognize the constant need to keep "educating" the public about either the project's indispensability or its folly. T. Richard Johnson, of the Central Arizona Project Association, which is made up of bankers, miners, irrigators, and others who, he says, "have a vested interest in water," explained not long ago that "One of our problems with the public is that our in-migration rate is so terrific that every ten years you've got a new set of people to deal with." Inside the cities, he said, these people have little reason to concern themselves with water matters. "When they turn on the faucet, they've always got water. Generally, though, they can see that it's a dry place the minute they get outside the city limits. We need water."

Frank Welsh sees it another way. Welsh, a civil engineer who worked in the mid-sixties for the Corps of Engineers on flood control projects in the East, is now the executive director of Citizens Concerned About the Project, a Phoenix-based group that opposes CAP and that also has "a vested interest in water." To Welsh, a wiry man with intense eyes, the problem is that the Arizona public looks out and sees desert and cactus and assumes that there is no water around. The truth, he said, is that there are boundless quantities of water beneath the desert floor—water that cities and industries can afford to pump out, but that agriculture can't. Until now, agriculture has relied on the cheaper strata of underground water—the water nearest the surface. The Central Arizona Project will further subsidize farming, feels Welsh, with cheap supplies.

"What we're doing is, we're using CAP," he said, "to get public attention to water, so we can straighten out Arizona's water policies for the future. We're using it to point out to Arizonans that they have plenty of water for future growth; that if they are going to build something, it should be economically feasible and environmentally feasible. But our major thrust is the economic, taxpayer approach, to get public attention to it. What I'm finding, both nationally and locally, is that the environmentalists have really picked up on the economic issues. And more power to them."

One of Welsh's friends and colleagues in the effort to stop or trim down the project is an environmentalist who appears to have made the complete conversion to economist. Robert A. Witzeman is a Phoenix anesthetist and conservation chairperson of the Maricopa Audubon Society. He is quite impassioned on the subject of bald eagles, but a lot of his arguments against CAP are purely economic ones.

"Subsidence is a lot of hokum," said Witzeman in an interview. "There's nothing wrong with overdrafting if we just recognize that there are some harmful effects. Most of the time subsidence is used as a scare; they talk about cracks and fissures and they mean nothing. They have no economic consequence at all except to scare people into saying, 'We need the CAP to address our imbalance of water.' It's a bugaboo." What *is* important, said Witzeman, is that the people who use the water should pay its full cost. "As a taxpayer," he said, "I am paying to subsidize the growing of cotton in the West at the expense of cotton growers who are being put out of business in Texas and Louisiana."

To back up their economic arguments, the anti-CAP forces published in 1978 an attack on the project by Thomas M. Power, chairman of the economics department at the University of Montana. In its format, the paper contained no visible direct link with Citizens Concerned About the Project. Its title ran:

AN ECONOMIC ANALYSIS OF THE

CENTRAL ARIZONA PROJECT

U.S. BUREAU OF RECLAMATION

So it would have been easy for a casual reader to conclude, erroneously, that the report was written by the government agency. Among other things, the document said the project would cost taxpayers $5,400,000,000 and would return less than 35 cents on the dollar, and that it is an urban water project disguised as a farm reclamation effort. (CAP proponents generally avoid talking about the cost, but one BuRec estimate was $1,400,000,000, as of January, 1974.) The Arizona Water Commission, which is a guiding force behind the project, responded with its own "review" of the Power paper, by a staff economist, and the result could only be called unenlightening. The economist, Alan P. Kleinman, took issue with, among other things, the Power argument that raising the price of water— rather than going to the extremes CAP proposes to keep it low —would cut demand and help eliminate shortages. (The argument is a well-known one, used often in discussions of global water supply and demand.) Kleinman then accused Power of saying that "if anyone ever imagines there is a need for additional water, all that is required is to raise the price and the shortage will disappear. . . . Thus if the price is high enough, one gallon of water will satisfy the entire state."

Such silliness, which presumably some people will take as solid economic theory, only serves to underscore the seriousness with which the water battle is being fought out in Arizona. Agriculture will almost certainly become the fall guy as new sources of cheap water are tapped; the future in Arizona, almost certainly, belongs to the real estate speculators and the condominium builders who already have spread metropolitan Phoenix so broadly across a broad desert floor that it takes half a day to drive through it.

Phoenix's overdevelopment is also *dangerous*, as many of its residents learned in February of 1980 when the Salt River, which runs through the center of town, flooded for the fourth time in two years. Ordinarily the river is nonexistent; it is commemorated by a dry, dusty wash that curves through the city, spanned by dozens of bridges as well as roadways built directly across the riverbed. Homes and businesses fill the Salt's floodplain, their owners confident that the chances of the Salt's flooding are minuscule.

Everyone thought the river and its neighbor, the Verde, had long since been tamed upstream, as they descended from the high country, by the Salt River Project, one of the first water projects authorized by the 1902 Reclamation Act. The Salt was called a "multi-use" project, one which captured water and sold it to municipalities and to irrigators and which also produced electric power. Dams upstream held the water back and released it as it was needed below in the valley, which Phoenix's boosters refer to as the Valley of the Sun.

A lot of the people in the valley assumed that one of the "multi-use" purposes was flood control, since there were dams up there in the hills, but they learned differently during the floods. (Neither the Salt River Project nor the Bureau of Reclamation, the builder, had claimed much in the way of flood protection, but BuRec never exactly denied that its dams might help. In a 1975 statement of its national mission, in fact, the Bureau said: "Probably the least-heralded feature of many multi-purpose dams and reservoirs is their ability to control flood waters. Virtually all regulating facilities on Bureau of Reclamation projects provide some flood protection, even though they may not have been initially authorized nor de-signed for that purpose.") When the February, 1980, rains came, the project had to release vast quantities of water—some 200,000 cubic feet per second of it—to keep their dams from being demolished. More than two dozen river crossings were wiped out in Phoenix and its environs; hundreds of homes and businesses were damaged; thousands of people were evacuated, and many thousands more found their homes separated from their places of employment by the torrent. The dangers of building on the floodplain, and of the sort of hell-bent develop-ment and growth that encourages such building, were never clearer. And yet the prospects are for more of it.

In the summer of 1980 the Carter administration convinced Arizona politicians that their great dream, the CAP, would suffer Washington-inflicted delays and money troubles unless the state came up with some kind of a comprehensive water plan. The legislature responded with a document that has been called forward-looking and innovative, and which encourages conservation and elimination of the groundwater overdraft, most of it at the expense of agriculture. Municipal growth—the condominiums and subdivisions and shopping centers—is unlikely to be affected.

And so development continues on the floor of the Arizona desert. In 1977 a group of Arizonans called Arizona Tomorrow, Inc., hired the Hudson Institute, of Croton-on-Hudson, New York, to look into the state's future. The result, a slick booklet called *Arizona Tomorrow*, referred to itself as a "framework for speculation on the future of Arizona." It was written by the well-known "futurist" Herman Kahn and Paul Bracken. The report was fulsome in its celebration of growth. What was on the way for Arizona, the authors said, was the discovery by the rest of the world that Arizona's "lifestyle of the future" was "one of the first manifestations, or precursors, of a national and international trend, of a post-industrial marriage between an appealing environment and new technology where lifestyle considerations are the central organizing principle around which society is organized. . . .

"Arizonans will live in this society on their own terms. Desert living with air conditioning, water fountains, and swimming pools; getting back to nature with a motorized houseboat on Lake Powell (itself a man-made lake); hiking in the wilderness; and surfing in man-made ocean waves—all are contemporary examples of this marriage between lifestyle and technology. . . . Arizona may indeed be a development prototype for post-industrial society."

Water would not be a problem, said the report. Questions as to Indian water claims and the most efficient uses of water

were dismissed as "shorter-term tactical problems." In its unrestrained cheerfulness, the report made no mention of the
future of organized crime in Arizona, believed by many to be
already a major force in the state's economy and politics.

What Kahn was projecting, of course, was another Disney
World, a place where the environment would be dismantled
and then rebuilt according to new specifications and out of new
space-age materials, with everything designed by "technology."
It would be the sort of place where one could get back to
nature, but only in a motorized houseboat. A colorful map of
"Projected Regions of Arizona, 2012," which accompanied the
report, depicted the state as all sorted out into regions, as in a
theme park: "Open Zones" lay in the desert between Phoenix
and Tucson; a "Mexican Tier" stretched along the border;
"Colorado River Cities" were sprinkled along the western
boundary; an "Artistic Center" thrived at Sedona; there was a
grand sweep of "Second Homesites-Camping-Hunting"; a
"Northern Wilderness Facade" was erected along the Utah
border. And, finally, there was "The Canyon." There were
apparently no immediate plans to refurbish the Grand Canyon,
to costume it up for the post-industrial marriage, although
Kahn warned that "Major controversy will center around its
future."

In the face of such enthusiasm many Arizonans have
become resigned to what is happening to their habitat, but few
seem to be trying to stop the damage. Congressman Udall, in
that 1977 statement favoring the Central Arizona Project that
was printed in the *Congressional Record*, concluded this way:

"I was born and raised in Arizona. In my youth it was
small in population, isolated, little subject to change. Frankly,
I liked it better that way. But times change and events overtake
us. My state is now the fastest growing in the union; that growth
is accelerating. I wish it were not so; I wish our growth patterns
had given us smaller, more diverse population centers. But
Arizonans can do little to stop the flow of people who seek its

climate and special way of life. We can only try to be far-sighted, to shape as best we may the quality of our environment. Water is life in the desert. We have not always used our water wisely, but we are moving to correct our mistakes."

In December, 1981, meantime, officials in Phoenix analyzed the area's recent, profligate use of water and realized that the city could be headed for a serious shortage during the following summer. The citizens were not immediately informed of these findings: A municipal water official was quoted as saying that "There was concern that the supply problem might be capitalized on by other cities competing with Phoenix in terms of growth." Economic growth—at the expense even of the water that facilitates growth of any sort—seemed to be the only thing the operators of Phoenix cared about.

14

The water problems that are associated with too much development or growth, or growth that comes too quickly or is poorly directed, are not limited to places that are newly settled. The older urban centers have multitudinous worries, as well. In many of them, particularly those in the Northeastern part of the nation, the systems that were built close to a century ago for getting and distributing water and for carrying off wastes are collapsing. And in several metropolitan areas with established cities at their centers, growth has forced a search for new and more dependable water supplies and increased competition for the water that is presently available. The term for all this, in the language of the city water managers, is the "urban infrastructure" crisis.

One reason the crisis exists, in the first place, is that the pipes and tunnels and mains that serve a city are truly out of sight, and therefore they may easily be kept out of mind, especially when financially troubled cities face so many other, and more visible, problems. So it should not be surprising that cities have neglected to perform routine maintenance, repairs, and replacement on the systems that are so very basic to their citizens' livelihood and welfare. There was always some reason why the pipes that were laid at the beginning of the century, and that had life expectancies of fifty or seventy-five years, could not be attended to. John Herbers, writing about the crumbling infrastructure in *The New York Times* in the late seventies, noted: "In the 1930s, when modernization should have started, the Depression struck. In the 1940s there was World War II. In the 1950s the cities began developing financial trouble as the white middle-class started moving to the suburbs. In the 1960s the demands were for solutions to social problems, and in this decade the emphasis has been on the employment of the poor and on public works projects usually unrelated to the infrastructure."

As a result of all this, Boston was found to be losing 78,000,000 gallons a day, or about half of its water supply, from leaking and broken pipes. New York City's losses have been estimated at from 70,800,000 to as much as 200,000,000 gallons a day. Even a relatively young city such as Houston has been found to be losing 20 to 30 per cent of its water—another 70,000,000 or so gallons per day.

And there are other problems. As was noted earlier, engineers have sought to line water pipes with vinyl in order to reduce the chance of asbestos contamination, only to discover that the toxic substance TCE, a solvent used in installing the liner, has been turning up in drinking water sent through the pipes.

In 1976, state and federal scientists accidentally discovered elevated levels of lead, a poisonous element, in the blood of residents of Bennington, Vermont. The metal was traced to century-old lead water pipes. The element had entered the drinking water, it seemed, starting in 1975 when Bennington switched to a supply of softer water, which corroded the pipes and released the lead. Frank Velkas, a Bennington psychologist, pursued the problem and was surprised to find that, in his words, most public officials wanted to sweep it under the rug. The situation changed some in 1977, when the Environmental Protection Agency found Bennington's water in violation of federal standards and gave the city a $225,000 grant to remedy the situation.

Another problem plaguing older cities in the East, the Great Lakes region, and at some points along the West Coast is "combined sewer overflows." In these cities, storm water and sewage are carried off by the same pipes; in the event of a heavy rainfall, the sewage treatment plants cannot handle the combined flow, and much of it—including sewage—bypasses treatment and heads into the nearest river or estuary. In Chicago, for one example, the treatment plants are overwhelmed as many as a hundred times a year. A routine result is the flooding of some residents' basements with storm water and raw sewage. Even in newer communities, such as those that grew on Long Island and in northern New Jersey after World War II, bad planning and unregulated development result in home flooding after almost every hard rain. In Long Island's Suffolk County, many of the homes were built in the late sixties when a boom in construction coincided with a drought. Consequently the homes were built on wetlands that were temporarily dry, a fact that the owners quickly appreciated when the drought ended and the water table returned to its normal level, flooding basements and damaging foundations. One proposed solution has been for the residents to move furnaces, boilers, and the like to the upper floors of their homes and fill in their basements with sand.

A further complication in the infrastructure on Long Island and other suburban-urban places is caused by corruption, which seems a not uncommon ingredient of the water distribution and collection business. Water, it appears, not only is essential to human life, but also provides high-grade nourishment for criminals. (There was even a motion picture, the very popular *Chinatown*, made about water politics and corruption in Los Angeles.) Residents of Suffolk County not only have had to cope with flooded basements; they also are insecure in the knowledge that a $1,200,000,000 sewer project that is supposed to serve 400,000 of them was shot through with what investigators termed kickbacks, payoffs, and shoddy workmanship, and what a grand jury called (without naming names) deceitful efforts at "strengthening political power and, in some cases, establishing private fortunes." In October, 1981, a federal jury on Long Island convicted an engineering firm, its principal partner, and an attorney for the firm on charges that they participated in a $900,000 bribery scheme that concerned four federally backed sewer construction projects in three states. One of the projects was in Suffolk County. A few months later, the design engineer for the firm was sentenced to 12 years in prison and was fined $85,000. He obtained contracts worth nearly $70 million, the government had argued, by arranging for bribes to be paid to government officials and politicians.

Sewage treatment projects also present unbounded playgrounds for technocrats and builders. The Environmental Protection Agency has a construction grant program for advanced sewage treatment that is expected to cost $106,000,000,000 by the time it is completed; the effort is routinely referred to as the largest public works project in the history of the world. A House Appropriations Committee investigation of the program in 1978 revealed widespread examples of failure, particularly at EPA's flagship project, the much-publicized Lake Tahoe plant, on the California-Nevada border, and recommended that no more money be spent on it. EPA backed an advanced treatment plant at Greenville, Maine, which had a population of 1,900, to keep waste water from tainting Moosehead Lake. The $4,000,000 project was badly designed, suffered from operational problems, and ended up costing the residents $125,000 in annual operation and maintenance, four and one-half times more than the original estimate. The town abandoned the costly plant. A report from the Appropriations Committee's investigations staff concluded: "Thus, the federal government has expended over $6,000,000 for waste water treatment with little or no assurance that the quality of the receiving waters will be improved commensurately." The same investigators found flagrant examples of what in the trade is called "gold plating"—the construction of "elaborate, ornamental, and costly aesthetic features which do not contribute to the functional use of a treatment plant." The administration and visitor center building of the sewage plant in Durham, Oregon, said the investigators, was "by far the most outstanding dwelling in the area." In Philipsburg, Pennsylvania, they discovered a $7,000 flagpole, along with a sign, identifying the facility, that cost $5,000. Another audit, a 1976 General Accounting Office survey of twenty-six advanced treatment plants, determined that "most were built without a thorough analysis of whether they were needed or, in fact, what their impact on water quality would be," according to the Council on Environmental Quality.

Not all the efforts at coping with the water infrastructure crisis are corrupt or even inept, but many of them are immense, simply because the plumbing has been allowed to deteriorate for so many years. Chicago's plans for dealing with the problem of combined storm water and sewer runoff are not only immense to the point of being outlandish, but also intensely controversial—mostly on economic grounds.

Chicago's TARP, which stands for Tunnel and Reservoir Plan, would, when complete, burrow three tunnels, 20 to 30 feet in diameter, for 132 miles under the city. The tunnels, along with surface reservoirs, would be used to store as much as 44,000,000,000 gallons of excess water during storms. After the storms the water would be pumped back to the surface— at considerable expense for electrical energy—and then processed through the city's treatment plants. In the early seventies, when TARP was initiated, the cost was expected to be $1,200,000,000. Later estimates put it at more than $11,000,000,000, and critics were fond of saying that another Panama Canal could be built for about half that. The expense of the scheme, which was dreamed up by the Corps of Engineers as a model for dealing with the urban runoff problem, finally caused its halt. An EPA restudy is said to be proceeding. Digging proceeds, too, on portions of the tunnels for which contracts have been let, but when that is finished it is doubtful that the project will continue. Chicagoans will be left, meantime, with several dozen miles of deep tunnels that go nowhere. With some imaginative entrepreneurship, the city could become the mushroom-growing capital of the Midwest.

New York City's water problems are abundant, and one reason, as with many of the city's troubles, is sheer huge numbers. The city's residents, along with businesses, governmental agencies, and leaky pipes, consumed an average daily quantity of 1,419,000,000 gallons of water in recent years, while another 103,000,000 gallons a day were used, as provided for under state law, by upstate communities through which the city's complex system of aqueducts and reservoirs runs. The total withdrawal, then, was 1,522,000,000 gallons a day, or some 555,000,000,000 gallons a year. New York City's system has what the engineers call a "safe, dependable yield" of 1,290,000,000 gallons per day during normal conditions, which means that withdrawals exceeed safe yield by 232,-000,000 gallons per day, or close to 85,000,000,000 gallons a year. (That figure was reduced during 1981 as a result of conservation measures undertaken by industries and private citizens in response to the shortage that started in the summer of 1980.)

There has always been an assumption, among those who are knowledgeable about the city's water supply, that the vast majority of the population is *not* knowledgeable—that New Yorkers know as little about where their water comes from as they do about the origins of milk, pinto beans, and other products of the bucolic world to the west of the Hudson or to the north of Yonkers Raceway. There may be some justification for this assumption, at least as it applies to water; an unscientific survey, conducted among a few dozen of the city's residents in recent years, showed that only a few knew that the city's water came from mountain reservoirs upstate and that relatively little was done to the water, in the way of treatment, between the time it fell as rain and snow in the Catskills and on the Croton watershed in Westchester and Putnam counties and the time it flowed out of a faucet in New York City. (The survey was undertaken before the city's 1980 discovery that it had entered a period of water shortage. Presumably the shortage and resulting publicity have made more citizens aware of their water's sources.) Some of those questioned said they believed their water came from the Hudson, and some the Delaware. The latter is partially correct, for the city does obtain some of its water from the headwaters of the Delaware, on the western slopes of the Catskills, but the difference between that water and the Delaware water that is consumed by, say, Philadelphians, after it has served as a sewer and diluting basin for much of New York State and New Jersey, is like the difference between filet mignon and Hamburger Helper.

Many people assume that New York City's water is "bad," basing their assumption on the idea that if it is purveyed by the City of New York, there must be something wrong with it. A city that does such an awful job of patching potholes, catching criminals, educating its children, maintaining its parks, picking up garbage, and changing burnt-out streetlight bulbs (it can take as much as half a year), they reason, certainly hasn't figured out how to get clean, tasty water into a pipe. A television performer, Tom Brokaw of the National Broadcasting Company's Today show, shared such an assumption with his audience in April, 1979, when he explained to a national audience why one of his guests would not drink coffee but nevertheless was consuming something from a cup. "That's not coffee in that cup," Brokaw was quoted as saying; "that's New York City tap water. It's probably more dangerous than a cup of caffeine."

The performer was wrong, and those others who assume that the city's water is by definition bad are wrong, too, or at least they have been up until the present. New York City has been singularly blessed in the high quality of its drinking water, and the blessing has come not from some benevolent Presence that looks out for the city's fortunes, but from the fortunate fact that New York has had a series of water managers—most of them were professional water engineers, but all of them by the nature of their jobs had to be politicians as well—who approached their work with a lot more foresight and concern for future populations than did run-of-the-mill bureaucrats and agency heads. It is because of them that New Yorkers until now have not had to drink water from the Hudson River—although current conditions make that an imminent and horrible possibility—but rather enjoy a drinking water (the temptation is great to call it "table water," in the snooty manner of the bottled-water promoters) that comes, literally, when all is working properly, from cold, clear, protected Catskill streams, fast-moving and full of the sort of trout that attract fly-fishers. Few cities in the nation, or the world, are blessed with water so clean that trout choose to live in it.

The city's water, or most of it, seeps and drips and tumbles and gushes down the mountains in the near-wilderness of the Catskills Forest Preserve. It starts at the highest elevations with the tiniest of trickles, some of them so seemingly insignificant that they can be covered by a rock or a few autumn leaves or a water-loving plant. Some, like the spring that does such a splendid job of appeasing the thirst of hikers doing the more difficult ascent of Slide Mountain, the tallest peak in the Catskills, fairly explode from the side of the mountain. The trickles gather themselves into hundreds of brooks, slender as saplings at first and then, when two have joined and then added one or two or three more at the junctions of the mountain hollows, growing into full-sized streams.

In the spring of the year, following a winter of normal Catskill snowfall, the streams are regular torrents, cascading their almost frozen waters over worn, smooth rocks and moving clearly and noisily and with immense strength through pebble-bottomed pools where the trout have learned to hang suspended in the current, almost invisible. It is in these springtimes that the temporary waterways, the perennials, appear. They exist only to carry off the extra-heavy flow of the spring melt, and so they cannot afford the luxury of meandering or providing pools for trout. The perennials come straight down the crease where two mountains join, and when there is snow melting above they bring the water down in a hurry, and when the late summer comes they bring down nothing at all. They have dried up by then, and there are only beds of smoothed cobbles to show where they have run, and where they will more than likely run next time.

The streams that come down from the Catskills, both perennial and annual, *are* the Catskills, just as much as any mountain summit or far-off vista, for the region is not made up of true mountains at all, but rather of a plateau that has been eroded differentially over a great period of time by water—by the ancestors of the very streams that bring New York City its drinking water today. The water-bearing process is repeated all over the Catskills, wherever the topography and gravity allow it, and at the lowest elevations the streams join full-fledged creeks that collect all the mountain water. The city has successfully laid claim to some of those creeks, along with a similar watershed in Westchester and Putnam Counties, and has built reservoirs on them to store their product, and that is the city's drinking water supply.

In the watersheds, or drainage areas, of the Schoharie and Esopus Creeks, the city collects water in a reservoir and then sends it through a tunnel that is a little more than 18 miles long into the Esopus, a fly-fisherman's paradise. The Esopus empties several miles farther on into the Ashokan Reservoir, a huge lake which is capable of impounding 128,000,000,000 gallons of water. Water leaving the Ashokan enters a 92-mile-long aqueduct that takes the water down toward the city. The Catskill system has what the city calls a safe, dependable yield of 470,000,000 gallons a day.

The Croton system is the city's oldest, opened in 1842 when New York City meant just Manhattan. It comprises a dozen reservoirs and four "controlled lakes" in Westchester and Putnam Counties, and has a safe yield of 240,000,000 gallons a day. The newest supply comes from the Delaware system, which has a safe yield of about 580,000,000 gallons a day.

Water from the watershed of the Delaware and Hudson rivers is collected in a series of reservoirs and routed to the city via an 85-mile-long aqueduct. Both the Delaware and Catskill aqueducts pass beneath the Hudson River, and the Catskill crossing, an enormous siphon through deep rock, 1,114 feet below sea level near the town of Cornwall, is generally considered an engineering marvel. The Hudson itself, which is not only saline during much of its lower stretches but also laced with toxic chemicals, some of which are believed to cause cancer, is not ordinarily used for city drinking water, although an emergency pumping station was built about 50 miles upstream during a dry spell in 1949 and 1950. The Chelsea Pumping Station, as it is known, was dismantled in 1958, but when the drought of the mid-sixties came, it was rebuilt and it put about 70,000,000 gallons a day into the New York City system. When that drought ended, the station was deactivated and "mothballed." As the possibility of another period of shortage loomed over the metropolitan region in the summer and fall of 1980 and then became more serious in 1981, the city and state health officials began studying the feasibility of reopening the plant. There was one suggestion that water from the Hudson could be mixed with what was left of the city's regular supply, in a ratio of one part Hudson to four parts clean, after the Hudson water had received heavy treatment. The deliberations this time were tempered by a great deal more knowledge about what humans had done to the river; toxic substances were not much a part of the vocabulary back in the sixties.

Altogether, the upstate reservoirs are capable of storing 550,000,000,000 gallons of water. Little must be done to the substance as it moves through the system; New York's water is so clean that it does not require filtration (although large-mesh screens are used at the reservoirs to keep out the trout).

Chlorine, a disinfectant, is added in very small quantities in order to achieve a solution that averages, at the household tap, between .05 and 1 milligram of chlorine per liter of water.

(A solution of milligrams per liter is comparable to parts per million. One way to think of parts per million is to consider the relationship between one inch and a little more than fifteen and three-quarter miles.) The amount of chlorine added varies seasonally, with more of it being required during the warmer summer months. Two other chemicals, aluminum sulfate to settle out particles of foreign matter and copper sulfate to control algae growth, are also added in varying quantities, and sometimes not at all, depending on the time of the year. Fluoride, which helps to prevent tooth decay, is added to New York City's water at the rate of a little less than one part per million, along with a bit of caustic soda, an alkali, to restore the water's pH to its normal rating of around 7, which is a neutral balance between acidness and alkalinity. The water is in a state that is remarkably close to "natural" when it comes down the aqueducts, runs through the final reservoirs in the Bronx and Central Park, and enters the city's distribution system. *That* system starts out with two large tunnels, along with a smaller one to carry water from Brooklyn to Staten Island, and then breaks down into mains and pipes that deliver the water to individual homes and businesses. (Another, private system, the Jamaica Water Supply Company, provides about 60,000,000 gallons a day from wells to some residents of Queens.) There are believed to be 6,141 miles of water pipes under the city's streets, along with something like 170,000 valves and 103,000 fire hydrants. The final distribution system is almost an urban mirror image of the system by which the water is collected in the mountains in the first place, with tunnels giving way to mains, and mains branching off into pipes, and pipes leading into kitchen faucets. The entire system, with minor exceptions, runs on gravity. The trickles and seeps and the gushing spring on the eastern side of Slide Mountain are more than 4,000 feet above sea level, and their water moves by gravity all the way to the city, which is almost at sea level. The final network of mains is divided, in fact, into zones, which do not follow political, neighborhood, precinct, or borough boundaries at all, but which rather are laid out according to their elevation in what must be one of the very few concessions the big city makes to geography, to topography, and to the natural world.

15

The water may be amazingly close to purity when it gets to the faucet, but it is not clean at all when New York's 7,105,608 or so residents finish using it. By then it is contaminated not only with fecal matter but also with all sorts of heavy metals and chemicals, both organic and synthetic, as well as pathogens and viruses that are just as deadly as any chemical on the toxic substances list. Virtually all of the contaminated water goes down the same drain, and that drain empties part of its burden into thirteen treatment plants that process 1,100,000,000 gallons of waste each day; another 290,000,000 gallons a day flow directly into the Hudson and East Rivers. New York City suffers, along with Chicago and many other older urban centers, from the problems of combined storm and sanitary sewers; here, about 70 per cent of the city's 6,500 miles of sewers are of the "combined" type.

The combined sewers are a relatively minor part of the city's water problems. The deterioration of New York's infrastructure is well advanced, and the blame for this is usually laid on the city's financial problems. The decisions by the city's leaders to forgo any capital improvement projects between 1975 and 1978 may have given the appearance of saving some money at the time, but they only put off—and made much more expensive—the day when the work of replacement and reconstruction had to be done. Because of the lack of both money and leadership, huge sections of the city's infrastructure have simply been allowed to collapse—the failure of the elevated West Side Highway in December, 1973, was a visible, aboveground manifestation of the sort of decay that has been allowed, and even encouraged by the city's policies, to continue at all levels of the city's physical plant.

Between 1955 and 1978, there were 2,500 water main breaks in Manhattan alone. Surveys showed, to the surprise of many, that it was not so much the advanced age of the pipes that was causing their failure as it was the fact that they were being pounded to pieces by traffic and construction overhead. There are more water pipe breaks per mile, for example, on Manhattan's *avenues*—the more heavily used streets that run roughly north and south—than there are on the cross streets, which carry more local traffic. A 1980 survey by the federal government concluded that $90,500,000 should be spent during the following ten years to replace the borough's most damaged mains. Proper maintenance has been lacking, too, on some of the city's upstate reservoirs; in 1978 one of the impoundments in Putnam County had to be drained because its dam was close to giving way.

Although lack of money is usually blamed by the politicians for the collapses and near-collapses—lack of money with which to purchase new pipes and to hire contractors to lay it and to pay city employees to perform the routine maintenance—that is not the only reason that the situation is so desperate. There is a great lack of inclination, as well, on the part of the politicians themselves and the city's employees to do the work that should be done. The work doesn't get done even when there *is* money with which to do it. A state audit of the city's Bureau of Sewers in 1980 showed that low productivity and oversized work crews cost the city at least $2,800,000 a year. The Bureau, which is supposed to oversee some 6,500 miles of sewers, 125,000 catch basins, and 225,000 manholes, had a staff of 680 and spent about $10,000,000 a year in salaries alone, and yet it managed to accomplish amazingly little. The catch basins, which are supposed to keep street debris from entering the sewer system, are each cleaned on the average of one time per four years, according to a state legislator; the city often takes several months to respond to complaints about clogged basins, he said.

Sometimes the city goes to elaborate and costly lengths to *not* stop underground leaks. In at least one subway station a complex system of metal gutters has been fabricated and installed along the ceilings to catch water descending from above and to carry it off to someplace else. Even at ground level, the people nominally in charge of the infrastructure seem incapable of coping with it. A broken fire hydrant started pouring water into the streets of the Bushwick section of Brooklyn in June of 1978, but the city's Department of Environmental Protection did nothing about it, despite citizens' complaints (except to send repair crews which did nothing), until one month later, when Mayor Edward Koch personally complained about the leak. If the hydrant was running wide open, as it quite likely was, that means approximately 42,000,000 gallons of clean, sweet drinking water were wasted due to bureaucratic and political incompetence. The City Comptroller's office issued a report that summer saying that "Normal maintenance" on the city's infrastructure "has been almost nonexistent," and the City Planning Commission concluded that "We are losing the battle to keep up the city's lifelines." Revelations of waste and inefficiency in New York City government are about as routine as are the citizens' discoveries that the subway system has progressed another notch toward becoming the world's longest cesspool, but in the case of water supply they took on new meaning in 1980 and 1981, when it became clear that all that high-quality water that the city government was allowing to be wasted was not going to be magically, effortlessly replaced on the other end of the pipeline. Even when the seriousness of the shortage was clearly evident, the city moved in only the most sluggish ways to stop the more flagrant leaks and to inform its citizens and educate them about the possible consequences of continued waste.

Almost every summer, when a period of particularly hot
weather descends on the city, children and adults open
thousands of sidewalk hydrants, which are supposed to serve
the fire department, and turn them into urban cooling devices.
The hydrants are relatively easy to open, with wrenches that
are larger and heavier than those found in most home tool-
boxes, but nevertheless easily obtainable. A fully open hydrant,
according to the New York City Fire Department, releases
1,400,000 gallons of water a day, or almost 1,000 gallons a
minute. The city encourages its citizens to use sprinkler caps
on the hydrants. These perforated devices turn the hydrant's
high-pressure stream into a finer, lower-pressure spray, thereby
reducing considerably the amount of water used. But in most
cases the caps are ignored. Quite often, when the users have
finished their play, they simply leave the hydrants running,
as do many of those who use the hydrants for another purpose
—washing their automobiles. This has the effect not only of
wasting some of the highest-quality drinking water in America
but also of lowering dramatically the water pressure in much
of the city, and the fire department complains that its ability
to cope with fires is threatened. The city then usually declares
some sort of a water pressure emergency, ordering residents
not to wash cars or water their lawns. What the city *cannot*
do, apparently, is cause its own employees to close the hydrants, many of which may be observed each year running well
into the winter, when they freeze. "The fire department, which
stands to gain most if they're closed, refuses in most cases to
close them," said a city official who asked to remain anony-
mous. As he spoke, the city was undergoing its annual water
pressure emergency, this one for the summer of 1980. Citizens
were being told, through that summer, that they would be
found guilty of breaking the law if they watered their backyard gardens, but others were washing their cars and taking
outdoor shower baths and leaving the hydrants open when
they finished, and nothing was being done about *them.* In no
case was the city seeking to explain the possible results of

water waste, although it was becoming clear that the upstate reservoirs were not in good shape and that a real shortage might be in the works. "We give each police precinct a wrench for closing the hydrants," said the city official, "but they all disappear. I think they sell them." Trying to get the uniformed city work force to do such simple, but potentially lifesaving work, he said, was "about like asking them to work overtime without pay. It's a union issue, and the city isn't willing to tackle it." Asked why not, he said, " 'Fear' is one way you can put it. The city is afraid of them. They're a law until themselves."

More recently, the city has at least been *talking* about tackling some of the problems that lie beneath its streets. The volume of talk has, in fact, been in reverse proportion to the volume of the reservoirs. Capital spending is up, and there is a push on to seek some sort of financial aid from Congress for a third water tunnel. The two that are now in operation, carrying water from its final collection point in the Bronx into the boroughs, have run continuously since they were built in 1917 and 1936, respectively. Neither has been inspected from the inside; if the tunnels, or one of them, had to be closed down for repairs, according to municipal officials, New York City would be thrust into a major calamity. Rationing would be necessary, and some lower-priority users of water would find their pipes dry. Mayor Koch, in testimony to members of the House of Representatives subcommittee on water resources as they gathered in New York in April, 1979, to hear the city's pitch for a federal loan for the third tunnel, made the point that a water catastrophe in New York would automatically be a water catastrophe for the nation. "I am proud to note," the mayor said, "that New York City is the financial and communications capital of the world, one of its leading cultural centers, the hub of the national fashion industry, and, in short, an urban center upon which many national and international industries, as well as smaller urban communities, depend. If a water tunnel failure were to impose the requirement of water use only to the level necessary to sustain life, all of these cultural and commercial enterprises would grind to a halt, with rather disastrous implications for our national economy. New York City and, in turn, many of the communities dependent on it, would slowly die of thirst—with water but a tunnel away. It is hard to conceive of any American who would not be negatively affected by such an event."

Not everyone is as openly enamored of the third tunnel project, and it is difficult to determine how much the tunnel is needed to provide jobs for workers friendly to politicians and how much it is really necessary to ensure an uninterrupted supply of clean water. The New York City Planning Commission estimated before the 1980–81 shortage began that if elementary steps were taken toward conserving water, such as using fixtures that control volume and flow, the city could save 30,000,000 to 50,000,000 gallons a day by the year 2000. The commission, in its statement of capital needs for 1980, asserted that "before any major expenditures on increasing water supply are considered, *a serious attempt should be made to decrease water consumption through conservation and leakage detection.* There are less costly ways to protect the City against severe water shortages." (Emphasis in the original.)

A third tunnel would have one undeniable advantage: It would permit the city to inspect and repair the other two, as well as ensure a supply of water in the event of a collapse or some other disaster. Work on such a tunnel, a 13.7-mile-long, 24-foot-diameter tube through rock, began in 1969 but stopped abruptly five years later when a contractor defaulted. So far, construction has claimed the lives of twenty-two persons and has devoured $360,000,000, according to one estimate. Another $500,000,000 is needed to finish just the first phase of the project, plus a billion dollars each for Phases Two, Three, and Four. It costs $10,000,000 a year for security and maintenance just to protect the work that has been done on a tunnel that goes nowhere and that serves, as clearly as anything, to symbolize City Hall's lack of interest in the issue of water.

In the meantime, the city suffered mild effects of a reduced rainfall through the summer and early fall of 1980. When the shortage continued into the early months of 1981, the situation clearly became a serious one. It also tended to reveal a number of things about New York City, its administration, and its citizens, and the relationships of all these with water. For one thing, it seemed that the city administration—specifically the mayor's office and the Department of Environmental Protection, which is responsible for overseeing various forms of pollution, for disposing of waste, and for providing a plentiful supply of potable water—waited as long as possible before impressing upon the public, through publicity campaigns and official proclamations, the fact that the shortage was serious and bona fide. A result of this was that much time, which could have been used in conservation of water by citizens, was lost—and, with it, a great deal of water. (Indeed, once the campaign *did* start, the citizenry responded enthusiastically.) Another revelation was that observers of the shortage as it developed in the city—and these included the media and the city administration itself—tended to view the situation as one which involved only two key elements: a lower-than-normal amount of rainfall and citizens' extravagant use of water. The villains in the crisis seemed to be nature, which didn't provide enough water, and individual New Yorkers, who flushed too many toilets and brushed too many teeth. The observers almost universally overlooked the fact that a great portion of the waste—perhaps the greatest portion—was due to the policies of the city itself, and that the city was inordinately slow in attempting to amend those policies. This left the very important question of whether, once rains returned and the shortage reached what could be a temporary end, the people who run the city would have learned the lessons they must learn if future shortages, and perhaps real water supply catastrophes, are to be avoided in the nation's largest city.

The city had begun the summer of 1980 with its reservoirs

full of water—enough of the stuff so that New York could use an average of 1,500,000,000 gallons a day, which is plenty, for the next full year even if no precipitation were to fall. It was a hot summer, though, and use was sometimes as high as 2,300,000,000 gallons a day. (The National Weather Service reported that it was the driest summer on record, then discovered that its methodology was all wrong and admitted that 1980 actually was much wetter than it had said.) Hydrants ran throughout the summer, as usual, contributing mightily to the high usage statistics. By October 1, the reservoirs were at about 56 per cent of their capacity; the city's DEP called this in the "low range of normal."

Half a month later, little rain had fallen and little effort had been made to close the hydrants. The city declared a "drought watch," which meant that it was keeping an eye on the situation. It was about then that water supply systems in northern New Jersey were running into serious trouble and the communities served by the Delaware River Basin Commission, an interstate agency, began paying close attention to the flows in the Delaware River, which are affected by New York City's withdrawals from the stream's headwaters. In late October, the city announced that it had begun looking for underground leaks in its water mains. It was the first time New York had taken such action in years, and the results were immediate. The leaks, which had been going on for unknown periods of time, were pouring millions of gallons of potable water from the Catskills into the ground and gutters of the city each day. By October 23, DEP announced also that it had closed 1,000 open hydrants, but that "hundreds" of them were immediately reopened. (Numbers bandied about during the shortage were even less reliable than most water statistics. But if it could be assumed that those "1,000" hydrants had been running at even half strength, and that they had run for 100 days before being closed—which is certainly an underestimate—they alone would account during that period for the waste of 70,000,000,000 gallons of water, or enough to meet all the city's needs for more than a month and a half.) On that same date, DEP reported that the reservoirs were at 46 per cent of their capacity and that long-range weather forecasts showed "minimal chances for appreciable amounts of rainfall in the near future."

In early November the "drought watch" was upgraded to a "drought warning," and the city started hiring a crew of twenty-eight laborers and supervisors to look for leaks. The reservoirs continued falling, but so did the city's consumption of water. By late in the month, it was down to 1,380,000,000 gallons a day from the usual 1,522,000,000—a saving of more than 9 per cent. Francis X. McArdle, who at that time was the city's commissioner of environmental protection, seemed to be stepping up his department's campaign to educate the citizenry. "Prospects of entering a drought emergency increase every day," he said. "I don't know how much longer we can hold the line unless we get some rainfall and people start conserving water on a more sustained basis. At the moment, we have only a 110- to 115-day supply of water." Mayor Koch asked restaurants to serve water to their diners only upon request. The media, which had been preoccupied with the presidential election, with the transition to the new Reagan White House, and with negotiations for the release of the American diplomatic hostages from Iran, now seemed to be paying a bit more attention to the situation. The *Daily News* started running readers' tips on how to save water; many of them were silly or stupid, such as suggestions that New Yorkers brush their teeth in gin. Very little attention was paid to the enormous amounts of water that were still being wasted from open hydrants, main leaks, and open pipes in abandoned buildings that had been vandalized, some 6,000 of which were owned by the city itself. There were occasional heavy local rainfalls, too, which were believed by some officials to make far too many citizens feel that the need to conserve was over.

In early December, the city began an effort to involve children in its conservation campaign. Mayor Koch, who is thought by some of his critics to act rather childish anyway, had great success in deputizing schoolchildren as water savers and in getting them to recite conservation slogans. There was some talk of what might have to be done if the shortage became critical, and speculation naturally turned to the Hudson River, which flows smack-dab next to the city on its way to the sea. The *Times* quoted "city officials" as saying that the Hudson was "too polluted with organic and potentially cancer-causing chemicals to treat and use" for drinking water. Similarly, little serious attention was being paid to the enormous Brooklyn-Queens Aquifer, which underlies portions of two of the city's boroughs, and which in years previous had provided potable water for thousands of residents who patronized private water companies. As in the case of the Hudson, many experts assumed that the groundwater under Brooklyn and Queens was now too badly contaminated to risk using. So New York City was virtually surrounded, during its newest water shortage, by water that it could not wisely use because society had ruined it. By Christmas of 1980, the upstate reservoirs were at about 38 percent of capacity and daily consumption was down by 192,000,000 gallons to 1,330,000,000 gallons.

But not enough precipitation fell, and as the new year began, the seriousness of the situation became more apparent. The City Council voted, 37 to 1, to increase the penalty for unlawful use of fire hydrants. The city took its first substantial steps toward dealing with leaks, which, it now acknowledged, were costing the supply system about 100,000,000 gallons a day. An electric leak detector was purchased; there was talk about repairing broken hydrants; the city advertised for bids from plumbers to shut off the water in its 6,000 vacant buildings. These actions came almost three months after the "drought watch" had been announced, and years after they should have been implemented. (An article on leaks in the *Journal* of the American Water Works Association for February, 1979, noted that "Water utility managers are realizing that unaccounted-for water is a measure not only of the physical condition of the system, but also of the distribution system's management." A survey of leak-detection devices patented between 1935 and 1976 showed that "presently used sonic techniques and the use of tracer gases will locate most leaks." And the article concluded that the sort of water leakage that afflicted urban systems "can no longer be tolerated.") But at least New York's actions showed that the city had finally become aware of the need to plug its leaks. Still, it was difficult to translate the paperwork and press releases into action. A water main broke in Brooklyn in early January and poured water into the frozen streets for two weeks. And a newspaper reported that inspectors were still finding at least 100 open hydrants each day, even in subfreezing weather.

On January 19, 1981, with the reservoirs standing at 32 per cent of their capacity, Mayor Koch declared a "drought emergency" and listed the steps that the city would have to take if the situation continued worsening. If consumption did not eventually decline to 1,250,000,000 gallons a day, mandatory conservation measures would be invoked. These included prohibitions against using hoses or sprinklers to water lawns, filling private swimming pools, and using hydrants even if equipped with spray caps. If the crisis got even worse, city water pressure would be reduced, water-saving devices would become mandatory in homes, industrial and commercial users would be required to save water, the use of air conditioners would be restricted, and the Chelsea pumping station would start injecting treated Hudson River water into the city's pipes. Apparently those unnamed "city officials" had overcome their objections to the Hudson water. If the city got down to a very few days' supply of water, Commissioner McArdle said during the winter, an even more drastic step might be taken: The city would bottle what good water was left and give it away to its citizens, a few quarts each day, and non-potable "gray" water, such as that from tainted aquifers and streams, would be run through the mains for use in clothes washing and the like, but not for drinking. Cleaning the "gray" water out of the mains and domestic pipes once the crisis was over would be a tremendous job, and one that McArdle said he didn't even want to think about, but one that he said he *would* consider if he eventually was forced to.

Although the reservoir levels continued to decline in January, so did consumption, and the outlook for the city improved considerably—even more when heavy rainstorms arrived in February. Mayor Koch, commenting on the situation in Greenwich, Connecticut, where the shortage was much more serious and where conservation had become a central part of life, implied that residents of that town were identifiable by their smell—a crudeness that was not out of character for the mayor but one which cast doubt on his understanding of the seriousness of the emergency. There was some talk about requiring the installation of water meters in residential buildings, but it went nowhere, largely because of the opposition of the real estate interests who wield much influence in City Hall. (Unlike many cities, New York does not require residential users to pay for water according to the amounts they use. Such consumers may choose, and most do, to pay a flat annual rate that is based on building frontage, number of water-using appliances, and other factors. Thus there is no incentive to conserve water, and much is wasted. A Geological Survey report says that American families paying a flat rate for their water consume twice as much, on the average, as those with meters. As for water that *is* metered in New York City, primarily in businesses and industries, an estimated $8,000,000 a year in revenues, and countless millions of gallons of water, are lost annually because of faulty meters. Water that is metered and that is sold for domestic use in the city cost $701 per 1,000,000 gallons in 1982.)

There the situation stood at late winter, with the population fully awakened to the need for conservation and the city at least beginning to awaken to the need for repairing an infrastructure that was still wasting, by the city's own count,

36,500,000,000 gallons of water a year. The rule still seemed to be concentrating on the quarts used during tooth brushing and ignoring the millions of gallons gushing from open hydrants and underground leaks.

This has become a typical reaction of those in power in government, and particularly those in power in New York City's government: to dodge the responsibility for solving the city's problems and to attempt to pin that responsibility on the citizens, while at the same time employing vast numbers of people on its payroll who are *supposed* to be solving those very problems but who aren't. In other words, the taxpayers are made to pay twice. This evasion manifests itself in almost every area of municipal life. There are great numbers of police officers on the city's payroll, and they are paid handsomely, but the list of jobs they refuse to perform with any regularity, such as directing traffic, ticketing parking violators, and seriously pursuing any but the more celebrated crimes, grows every year, and so the citizens must shell out more—to hire *other* employees for directing traffic, to replace stolen automobiles and television sets, to replenish their funds after muggings, to install alarm systems, and to pay the salaries of rent-a-cops in virtually every retail store and office building— while still paying the police officers' salaries. The city employs a large staff of well-paid people to sweep and clean the gutters of its streets, but they do not do the job well or, in many instances, at all. (In one case, in Brooklyn, the men who are supposed to repair mechanical sweepers may be observed working, instead, on their own automobiles.) So the city recently passed a law requiring property owners to clean the gutters in front of their property—not a bad idea, really, except for the fact that the people who are paid to clean the gutters don't, and are seemingly immune to firing or any other form of discipline.

Similarly, until its water crisis of 1980–81 the city ignored its role in repairing the pipes and closing the hydrants, and concentrated instead on pushing for a new water tunnel and on blaming restaurant diners for drinking water.

Commissioner McArdle argued, as might be expected, that the city *had* reacted to the shortage in the proper ways and that it was learning a great deal from the crisis that it would use long after the shortage is over. Already, the commissioner said in an interview in February, 1981, about a month after the emergency had been declared, the experts had learned a lot about how to market a water shortage to the public. (He did not, however, comment on the city's own role in the conservation effort until he was asked about it.) "We are now perhaps much more aware intellectually than we were before," he said, "that you can change basic behavior patterns. But you've got to work at doing it. If we have learned anything, it's that we need to change fundamental behavior patterns—and it's not something that you do and then don't continue working on. It's a *process*. We will learn from this drought. And I would hope that one of the things we'll learn is that when the drought is over, you don't stop."

McArdle defended his agency's timing in cultivating the public's attention by noting that city officials had declared an emergency in the early stages of the mid-sixties drought, had had to call it off when some rains came, and then faced the difficult task of convincing the citizens, when dryness returned, that they were telling the truth. And one reason the city waited until the late fall of 1980 to begin searching for leaks and closing hydrants, he said, was money. "The city has not had the resources," McArdle said. The physical nature of the system was a factor, too: "It's all gravity. And during a fiscal crisis, which coincided with a time when the reservoirs were spilling over, there was nothing compelling the city to save the water. Say I'm losing it in a street leak in Brooklyn. It goes into a storm sewer and it's not hurting anybody. It's going to drain into the Hudson. It would have gone into the Hudson anyway, or the Delaware. It's going into the cycle someplace. And what's my interest in spending a dollar to stop that leak as opposed to hiring a policeman? Sure as hell the *public* is more interested in having a policeman hired than they are in having that leak fixed—if there is no drought.

"Now there is a drought. And we have to shift the mode of operation, to control the things that were not controlled during the fiscal crisis. Now we have to control it. Did we wait too long? I don't think so."

The problem of open hydrants during the summer of 1981, McArdle said, would be dealt with partly through new technology—devices that would make it more difficult for unauthorized people to open the hydrants. McArdle's agency would be working more closely with community and neighborhood groups to control the hydrants, he said, and there would be enforcement of the law against misuse of the devices. "I would expect that one of the things that is most the bane of our existence, which is car washing," said the commissioner, "is basically going to disappear because people will be paying a hundred bucks a car wash. It's going to be pretty expensive if they are caught washing cars on the streets of the city of New York."

The city's plans sounded tough and uncompromising and not at all unwarranted for dealing with a crisis in which the availability of drinking water was very much in jeopardy. But what New York City *says* frequently outshines what it is prepared to really *do*, and a reasonably skeptical New Yorker might suspect that, as the city's water emergency grew through the normally damp months of late winter, a few soaking rainstorms would divert the city's attention away from the difficult problems of conservation, leaky pipes, and open hydrants, and back to the seemingly more pressing matters of crime, street filth, economic issues, and the ghastly decline of the subway system. One city official, who preferred not to be named, expressed fears about what the summer could bring, and added: "At what point do you make a political decision, when it's 100 degrees Fahrenheit, to leave the hydrants open because you want to prevent a riot? Do you save water, or do you save people's lives? That's a very hard political decision that has to be made this summer."

As it turned out, the hard political decision was not made, and few, if any, New Yorkers paid hundred-dollar fines for wasting water. The upstate reservoirs received enough runoff to forestall a very dry summer, and citizens and industries undertook conservation efforts that produced good results. Daily consumption dropped to around 1,222,000,000 gallons a day, an impressive decline from the standard 1,522,000,000 gallons. (The truly heavy users, a look at the records revealed, were not those individual bathers, tooth brushers, and restaurant patrons at whom the conservation campaigns had been aimed, but government, office buildings, hospitals, colleges, some manufacturing plants, and, most especially, the electric-and-gas utility, Consolidated Edison.)

There was scant evidence that the city government itself wanted to aggressively pursue a summer program of education about the true nature of the shortage, or one of punishment for those who deliberately wasted the precious resource. Car washers opened hydrants as usual; perhaps other citizens and some city employees (notably firemen) were quicker than usual to close them when the wasters had gone. On the whole, it appeared that City Hall had simply lost interest in the emergency. The situation was not unlike others that come up periodically in New York: The city announces a crackdown on motorists who double-park, or who toot their horns unnecessarily, or who create traffic jams in intersections. The mayor shows up, surrounded by his coterie of amused reporters and television newsreaders; some poor unsuspecting sap is given a ticket and immortalized for a few moments on the evening news; the campaign lasts less than two weeks; and then everything returns to normal. That was the way the government of New York City reacted to the water shortage of 1981, despite its seriousness.

Privately, the city was gloomy about the future. One water

supply official said in early May, 1981, that the city had a secret long-range forecast that by the following New Year's Eve its reservoirs would be down to 16 per cent of their capacity—a projection that, if it had come true, would have meant severe rationing and other emergency measures.

One of New York's neighbors across the Hudson, Newark, had a rougher time. Early in June, 1981, persons referred to as "vandals" opened a valve on an aqueduct that transported water from reservoirs to the city, setting off a chain reaction that resulted in the bursting of two pipelines. Newark was cut off from its major supply of water. The link was repaired hurriedly, and citizens responded well to the crisis by conserving what water was left. Then reporters discovered that the man appointed by the mayor and paid $24,255 a year to serve as "chief of security" for the reservoir system actually lived in Florida and hadn't even visited the system in months.

By the end of 1981 it was obvious that New York's shortage, and the city's interest in it, had just petered out. It helped that fall and early-winter rains and snow had brought the reservoir levels closer to normal, but the major factor seemed to be the cost of conservation. On January 19, 1982, one year after declaring a "drought emergency," Mayor Koch reduced the status of the problem to "drought warning." Michael Goodwin, writing in *The New York Times*, pointed out that the downgrading meant the city no longer needed the employees it had hired to oversee the emergency. Goodwin quoted the city's budget director as saying the city could save itself about $6,000,000 "by declaring victory in the drought."

Victory was therefore declared, and New York City's mostly man-made water shortage receded from the citizens' consciousness. It will almost certainly be recalled again someday when another predictable variation in rainfall patterns combines with the city's profligate use and waste of water to push the problem to the top of the list of crises that confront New York and that New York remains incapable of dealing with.

As is the case with most of the issues facing water today, the quality of governmental leadership in responding to questions such as those facing New York is at least as valuable as tunnel digging and hardware purchases. Nelson Manfred Blake, a professor at Syracuse University, in 1956 wrote a book, *Water for the Cities*, that is on practically every urban hydrologist's shelf. Blake related the history of water supply systems in New York, Philadelphia, Boston, and Baltimore, and he ended up on a note of pessimism. "No one with faith in the problem-solving genius of modern science," he wrote, "doubts that a solution will be found" to water problems (which, at the time of Blake's writing, were generally considered to be problems of quantity). "But the history of the urban water supply problem suggests that something else will be necessary. Science can solve the technical problems, but will municipal statesmanship show itself capable of intelligent planning?" The unfortunate answer, a quarter of a century later, is *not yet*.

The issues of development and growth are multitudinous, are related to all facets of water quality and quantity, and are intertwined with virtually all the other components of the current water crisis. Hydroelectric power, for one example, might be thought of as one of the least harmful manifestations of growth. Growth, in population and therefore in everything a population needs, means more electric power. One relatively cheap way to obtain electricity is through hydropower—using flowing water to turn blades, on an ancient waterwheel or a modern turbine, to generate the current. Hydro provides about 15 per cent of the electric power production in the United States, 50 per cent in Japan, and as much as 90 per cent in some other countries, notably Canada and Norway. With the cost of energy up, and with the future of atomic power somewhat in jeopardy, hydro is likely to become a much more attractive source. But hydro has problems, too. Dams and reservoirs must be built, and such facilities collect silt, drive people off their land, and ruin nature. As in the urban infra-structure crisis, too often the perceived solution is to build more things, rather than to make more effective use of what we already have.

Growth means controversy and tension, particularly when the community that is growing feels that it doesn't have enough water. All too frequently, the "solution" involves taking the water that is needed from a neighbor. The section of coastal Virginia that is known as Tidewater—Norfolk, Portsmouth, Hampton, and the newer "suburban cities" of Virginia Beach and Suffolk—not long ago found itself in the midst of a water crisis of its own. Rapid growth, particularly in the newer communities that make up the region, is outstripping the availability of potable water. So the Corps of Engineers, that faithful friend of growth-at-any-cost, was called in to provide a solution. The answer was an easy one: Take the water, 240,000,000 gallons a day of it, from Lake Gaston in North Carolina and pump it 50 or so miles east to satisfy Tidewater's projected thirst. The scheme outraged North Carolinians, and their governor pledged to use "every lawful means at our disposal" to fight it.

Farther south, in the Florida Keys, the availability of water, or lack thereof, has figured in a controversy over whether growth should be encouraged on the slender, fragile, hundred-mile-long string of islands that march off toward the Caribbean.

Keys residents obtained their drinking water from the sky, catching rainwater in cisterns, until World War II, when the Navy, which opened a base in Key West, at the end of the populated Keys, ran a thin-walled, aluminum pipe out from the mainland. It was 18 inches in diameter and it was not considered a permanent installation. It *became* one, however; though the pipe was battered and worn to the extent that it has been called a "hundred-mile-long leak," it has provided most of the drinking water for the Keys' growing population of residents and tourists. In the late seventies, the Farmer's

Home Administration offered the pipeline's operators a loan, at attractive rates, so they might replace it. The operators, naturally, planned to build a new pipe with a greater capacity. The controversy that followed was almost a textbook example of the argument over whether water should be used as a control on growth. William Westray, a retired naval commander who settled in Key West at the end of World War II, was one of the opponents of the new, larger pipe. Build it, he said one day in 1979, a few days before the residents of the Keys voted on the issue, and you are automatically promoting growth—and growth of the wrong kind, by which he meant condominiums and second homes. "All they have to do," he said, "is put the line in and say, 'Come and get it', and the realtors'll do the rest. What does this do to a place where the situation's already critical in terms of schools, picking up waste, and other community services? We're scared to death about what unlimited supplies of water will do. Water becomes a catalyst promoting development, financed from outside, which produces a net decrease in the area's well-being because it places demands on services but takes money out. Rapid development will just destroy the quality of life here, and that will be irreversible. Once destroyed, it's gone. Look at our air, our water, our reefs, our land. Pollute them and they're gone. The better fish will disappear, and then the higher forms of animal. The eagle, and the osprey; they will leave. These will be the signals of overstress."

The referendum passed, and construction on a new pipe got under way toward the end of 1980. Its operators, the South Florida Water Management District, have rejected the notion that government, which can control growth very strictly, if it wants to, with its zoning power, has any business either promoting or retarding growth by turning the handle of the water faucet. And each year, more people descend on the Keys, and the eagles and the ospreys become harder and harder to find.

It is clearly not a matter of the water's running out. It *is* a matter of something a bit more subtle: No longer will we be able to count on a guaranteed supply of water of unlimited quantity, and of high quality, at a price that is very close to scot-free. No longer can we build houses, factories, toxic waste dumps, and cities wherever we want them, confident that if the water isn't immediately available we can just pipe it in from somewhere else. And no longer can we continue to "solve" our water problems by merely finding new sources to exploit, new streams to dam. *The Global 2000 Report* paints a fairly bleak picture of the world that is just around the corner: "Water shortages will become more frequent, and their effects will be more widespread and more severe. The availability of water will become an even more binding constraint on the location of economic development. The notion of water as a free good, available in essentially limitless quantities, will have disappeared throughout much of the world."

Residents of the Western United States have had more time and inclination than most to reflect on the future of water. The Eastern states could profit by what they have learned. Colorado Governor Richard D. Lamm, in a collection of writings on water published in 1977, wrote: "The whole question of how we manage Colorado's remaining water is now of vital importance, perhaps of greater importance than the traditional question of how we can develop additional water. In short, the only water available in Colorado is the water we now have. . . . the challenge will be to manage the use of our remaining water without destroying the quality of life in the state."

Westerners also have been able to predict, with what is likely to be some accuracy, the future of the growth and development issue. Agriculture's traditional free hand with water will be seriously challenged, they say, by urban users.

"Ultimately the percentage of urban water will grow," said Ronald Robie, California's water resources director. "And the agricultural water supply will remain fairly static. What I think is going to happen is agriculture is not going to be able to expand in California in terms of sheer geography. But they're going to become more efficient within the existing land, and they're going to be growing different crops."

And the Westerners have been able to sense, as well, what Robie called "the battle of the next decade"—the realization by the East that its water systems are wearing out and that region's subsequent demands that the rotting infrastructure be replaced not by local initiative but by the federal government. The feds have spent billions to subsidize cheap water in the West; now, is it not fair for the East to ask for the same? "It's already obvious," said Ronald Robie, "that the Eastern states have decided they want to get some of the pie that's now going to reclamation projects in the West. And my prediction would be that they are going to be successful."

An effort—though not the most spirited one in the world —has already begun. The National League of Cities held a conference in 1978 on water matters, and the overriding emphasis of the meeting was on figuring out ways cities could get a piece of the pie. Senators Daniel P. Moynihan of New York and Pete V. Domenici of New Mexico introduced legislation which would require federal water funds to be distributed to the states according to a formula, rather than on a project-by-project basis. The bill, which its backers said would more than double the Northeast's 6 per cent share of the funds, failed to get subcommittee approval.

And Northeastern politicians are learning how to remind the keepers of the federal ledger books that they, too, need water money. When New York's Mayor Koch, a former representative himself, was welcoming members of Congress to a tour of the incomplete third water tunnel, which the city has financed itself so far, and for which the city now wants a federal loan, he reminded them: ". . . we are not requesting anything more than what the Congress has done in the past for other communities needing fiscal support for water resource development. As a member of Congress I often voted for appropriations to help develop water supply and distribution systems for drought-stricken or arid and underdeveloped regions of the United States. I did so because I recognize that my responsibility as a national legislator required I eschew the parochial view and perceive the national interest. I am proud of those votes, as an American and as a U.S. representative, because just as surely as I believe much of this country depends on New York, so do I believe that New York depends on this country."

16

Industry's treatment of water has been scandalous and, all too frequently, immoral. Those firms that have abused the essential substance of human life—and there have been very, very many of them—have willingly and knowingly taken the most dangerous concoctions that their chemists have perfected and they have used them in one or another process and then they have taken the leftovers and routinely dumped them into rivers and into the aquifers, and thus into humans' drinking water supplies and their bodies and, it is quite likely, into the lives of their unborn children. Some of these industries and their hired hands—the truckmen who come at night to haul the poisons away—have then conspired to keep the public from knowing what they have done.

These actions, which more law-abiding citizens might consider not only disgraceful but also risky, have paid off handsomely. Rarely have governmental agencies imposed strict punishment on corporations or their officials who consistently engage in these acts. Rather, the attitude in government seems to be that whatever industry does in order to make money is, by definition, acceptable. It is a time-honored attitude, of course; the man who robs a bank of $1,000 has always been more likely to be shot to death or sent to prison than a corporate officer who steals $1,000,000 from the public or the government. The severity of the punishment is inversely proportional to the reflectivity of the collar of the thief. But we are talking about *water* here, not dollar bills or securities. An individual who knowingly and deliberately poisoned a neighbor's well would be sent to prison in most of the jurisdictions of this nation; in some places there would be talk of stringing him up on the spot. But industry, when it poisons us, seems immune to any sort of meaningful punishment.

Water is very attractive to industry for two basic reasons: It is sufficient as a solvent, and it is literally cheaper than dirt. Malin Falkenmark and Gunnar Lindh, in their book that was published in connection with the United Nations' 1977 Water Conference, point out that "Water has a far greater dissolving power than any other substance, and therefore plays an important part in chemical industries, all the more so as it is cheap." Often the cheapness is made possible, as it is in the American West, by taxpayer subsidies, and globally it remains relatively inexpensive as well. A UN document has found that the cost of water is a very small part of overall industrial expenses around the world; for the five most important water-using industries, says the UN, "water may represent from 0.005 to 2.58 per cent of total manufacturing costs, and rarely exceeds 1 per cent." And as another document, the Arizona State Water Plan, puts it: "Industry will use water instead of capital, labor, or some other input as long as it is more profitable and a substitution is not forced upon it by society."

In the presence of such profitability and the absence of forced substitutions, industry proceeds, then, to use copious amounts of water. The Geological Survey has calculated that it takes about 16.5 gallons of water to manufacture a twelve-ounce soft-drink can. Industry's major uses for the substance include cooling, processing, water for boiling, and on-plant uses such as air conditioning, drinking water for employees, and cleaning. Cooling accounts for 60 to 80 per cent of the water withdrawn by industry. It is not unusual to see that different manufacturers of the same products use greatly varying amounts of water; usually this is a reflection of the fact that some manufacturers recover and recycle their water and others don't. Industry's enthusiasm for recycling, as might be expected, is directly related to the cost of the water.

Only a few industries account for the great proportion of

water use, according to the UN. The chief users are the manufacturers of primary metals, chemical products, refined petroleum, pulp and paper products, and processed foods. The Geological Survey has estimated that it takes 32,000 gallons of water to make a ton of finished steel, and 10 gallons of water to make one gallon of gasoline. Other estimates were compiled by the UN in 1969 and published six years later in *Water Resources of the World: Selected Statistics*, by Fritz van der Leeden. It requires from about 550 to 1,100 gallons of water to make a ton of bread; 6,350 gallons to can a ton of fruits, vegetables, and juices; more than 6,000 gallons to process a ton of meat; 7 gallons to prepare a chicken; 20 gallons to prepare a turkey; close to 800 gallons to produce 264 gallons of milk; 1,600 gallons to process a ton of sugar beets. The industry average for the water used to make a ton of pulp and paper in the United States was 62,350 gallons, while in France it was under 40,000 gallons. A ton of rayon required from 264,000 to 528,000 gallons to produce in Finland, and an automobile manufactured in the United States required more than 10,000 gallons. In many of the categories listed, water usage in the United States was considerably higher than in other countries. In Israel, particularly, where water is universally recognized as a precious material, industry manages consistently to get by on much less than its American counterparts.

The American chemical industry frequently makes the point that, while it and other elements of industry are prime users of water, they return most of it to the environment. "Industry manipulates very large amounts of water," says the American Chemical Society in *Cleaning Our Environment: A Chemical Perspective*, "but returns almost all of it to receiving waters. Of the 15,500,000,000,000 gallons that manufacturers withdrew in 1968, some 92 per cent was discharged and only 8 per cent was evaporated, incorporated into products, or otherwise consumed (made unavailable for reuse)." The problem with this, of course, is the condition of the water when industry "returns almost all of it" to those "receiving waters."

The Chemical Society adds that two pressures are now being exerted on industry—the increasing cost of water and the growing urgings of the rest of society to avoid contaminating it—and that "Industry has reacted to these economic incentives basically by raising the recycle ratio—the number of times each gallon of water is 'used' between intake and discharge."

The changes brought about by those pressures have been slow and undramatic, however, and many experts insist that they will have to be speeded up if the world water crisis is to be dealt with properly. Falkenmark and Lindh have written: "To avoid the gradual development of a pollution disaster during the next few decades, there is no choice but to implement a completely different water policy, above all in industry. . . . considerable changes will have to be made to current water policy if we are to avoid being 'swamped' in the rising tide of waste water. Treatment will not get us very far. If a concentration of pollutants in waste water is cut to a third at the same time as the volume of waste water is trebled, the amount of pollution carried by the water will remain the same. Industry must, therefore, reduce its water demand by means of alternative technology. Dry manufacturing processes will have to be used more frequently. Indispensable water must be recycled, and water which cannot be recycled must undergo advanced purification before being returned to rivers."

If American industry has begun to treat water a little differently, then the reason, by industry's own account, is strictly economic. When water starts costing more, industry exhibits its well-known genius for ingenuity and imagination by inventing ways to recycle the water it has—but not until water starts costing more. When laws and regulations, or perhaps public outrage, make it economically feasible for industry to return water to the environment in something other than a toxic condition, the well-known genius comes into play again—but not until the profit motive makes it worthwhile. All this, say some, is little more than the American Way: the same body of largely unwritten economic law that governs the way banks treat their depositors, television networks treat their viewers, department stores handle their customers—deplorable, perhaps; maybe unconscionable; but certainly not something to be amazed at. There is, however, in the case of water, the all-important, unforgettable addition: Water, in sufficient volume and quality, is absolutely essential for life.

The worst side of industry has been presented in the toxic waste scandal. Governor Brendan Byrne of New Jersey, touring the site of the spring, 1980, explosions and fire at the Chemical Control dump in Elizabeth, was quoted as saying, "If there is one message that comes out of a day like today it is that government indeed cannot trust private industry to dispose correctly of its toxic wastes." Actually, some of Governor Byrne's own appointees had received that message—specifically in connection with the Elizabeth site—not on that day but a long time before, but had chosen to trust industry to clean up its own mess, with disastrous consequences. One reason why government seems unlikely to require industry to clean up after itself, even if it has decided industry is untrustworthy, was given in mid-1980 by a New York state legislator, Joseph T. Pillitere, who represented the Love Canal district. His fellow legislators had failed to enact laws holding industry accountable for its poisonous wastes, said Pillitere, because the business lobby is "a fourth arm of government."

Part of the chemical lobby—the best-known firms, the ones that have the most to gain from peaceful relations with the general public—did not engage in an all-out assault on the Superfund bills as they made their way through Congress in the fall of 1980. But there was powerful lobbying nonetheless, and the outcome was a mixed piece of legislation: a fund totaling $1,600,000,000 for the cleaning up of toxic waste dumps, of which $1,380,000,000 would come from excise taxes on chemicals and the remainder from general government revenues, and with no provision for compensation to those whose health or property have been damaged by toxic wastes. While outfits such as Du Pont had seen that such a law was inevitable, and had urged the enactment of compromise legislation, others—represented by the Chemical Manufacturers' Association—lobbied hard against any legislation. And a third segment of the industry apparently felt that Congress was not a proper forum for a discussion of toxic wastes at all; in the weeks before the federal Resource Conservation and Recovery Act took effect in November, 1980, requiring stricter record keeping on chemical wastes, thousands of tons of illegal poisons were said by EPA to be hurriedly dumped in municipal sewer systems, on vacant lots, and alongside roadways.

The chemical industry in general, meantime, seems to cling to a couple of arguments that once may have soothed an anxious public but that seem somewhat less convincing in the days of dioxin, PCBs, and Kepone. One of those arguments, as expressed in a pamphlet that the Monsanto Company sends to members of the public who respond to a magazine advertisement, is the old "Chemicals-are-all-around-us" notion. "Absolute safety is impossible," says the pamphlet. "If we were to eliminate every substance that might be hazardous under any circumstances, there would be no world. If we tried to eliminate risk entirely, literally nothing could be considered free from the potential to cause harm—not even our own bodies, which contain billions of bacteria and viruses with the potential to cause illness or death." The other argument, not as simplistic but nevertheless wearing a bit thin, is an offshoot of the "If-we-can-put-a-man-on-the-moon-we-can-do-anything, provided-we-have-enough-money" routine. "Many of the difficulties in conserving the environment are inherent, of course, in the size and complexity of the task," says the American Chemical Society in its book on the environment. "They can be resolved, given the time, the will, and the money."

The event that made arguments such as these so suddenly shallow was the horror of Love Canal, a neighborhood in overindustrialized upstate New York. The canal was part of a scheme, hatched in 1892 by a man named Love, to generate electricity by connecting the upper and lower stretches of the

Niagara River. The scheme failed, and the uncompleted canal was still there in 1947, when the Hooker Chemical and Plastics Corporation (as it was then called) bought part of the site for use as a dump for its wastes. The canal had a relatively impervious clay bottom, and so it was presumed to be adequate for Hooker's plans. The toxic wastes were dumped in, some in the ubiquitous fifty-five-gallon drums, and sealed over with clay. There is considerable speculation that the federal government used the site, as well, for toxic wastes from an army installation. There is no indication that any of this was at variance with what at that time constituted standard industry procedure for dealing with unwanted chemical wastes.

In 1953 Hooker sold the site to the Niagara Falls Board of Education for one dollar. (As a Hooker executive put it later in congressional testimony, Hooker had told the school board "of the chemicals that were disposed of in the canal site and warned them against any construction activity of any kind going on at that disposal site. The board of education, however, insisted upon the acquisition of that property for the construction of a school.")

The chemical firm included in the deed to the land the statement that it had advised the school board that the canal had been "filled, in whole or in part, to the present grade level thereof with waste products resulting from the manufacturing of chemicals by the grantor [Hooker] . . . and the grantee assumes all risk and liability incident to the use thereof. It is, therefore, understood and agreed that . . . no claim, suit, action or demand of any nature whatsoever shall ever be made by the grantee . . . against the grantor . . . for injury to a person or persons, including death resulting therefrom or loss of [*sic*] damage to property caused by, in connection with, or by reason of the presence of said industrial wastes." There was the further agreement that each future change of the land's ownership would be subject to the same warnings and conditions.

The school board, for reasons that have never been made clear, proceeded to build an elementary school and playing field on the land and to provide lots for modest homes. It was not until 1976 that the poisons contained in the covered-over canal made their presence known to the public in a dramatic way. As a report of the Council on Environmental Quality put it:

"Chemicals had appeared sporadically on the surface of the canal for years. In 1976, after six years of unusually heavy rains and snow, the chemicals began seeping into basements. Rain had filled the canal and was prevented by the canal's clay bed and banks from percolating deeper. The canal overflowed. Chemicals that had leaked from the now decayed drums entered the environment." Once the water had brought the chemicals to the surface, children and dogs playing above the canal were burned by them. There were reports of people's shoe soles' being eaten through. The roots of trees were dissolved by the chemicals. Residents of the area began reporting abnormal rates of miscarriages, birth defects, and cancer (although scientific evidence on the incidence of the last disease is not conclusive).

Eighty-two chemical compounds were identified at the site, said the Council, of which eleven were said to have been known or suspected carcinogens. One of them, trichlorophenol, is one of the scarier compounds recently unleashed on the environment; about 200 tons of it are believed to have been buried at Love Canal, and another 3,300 tons at another, nearby Hooker landfill in Hyde Park. Trichlorophenol contains dioxin, a chemical which tests on animals have shown to be "100 times as deadly as strychnine," according to the Council. Dioxin, says the agency, has "the potential for causing miscarriages, birth defects, and other adverse reproductive effects," and research has shown it to be "one of the most toxic substances ever studied." The Hooker Chemical Corporation is accused of dumping trichlorophenol, and other chemicals like it, into the ground in a populated area, next to a river.

Hooker has not been alone in pouring poisons into the ground, of course, either in the nation or even in Niagara

County, New York. The Love Canal site was just one of thirty-eight industrial waste landfills known to be in the county at the time. But Hooker was responsible for at least three of those sites and for millions of pounds of industrial chemical wastes in them. Hooker's own Niagara Falls manufacturing plant has been the subject of concern as well. In 1979 an internal company report, written four years previously, found its way into the hands of the press; it revealed that discharges of toxic substances into the air and sewers were regular occurrences at the plant. And Hooker refused to cooperate when its workers' union sought to conduct a health survey to determine the reasons for higher than normal rates of cancers and skin diseases among its employees, along with higher rates of miscarriage for their wives.

All of this has caused great quantities of criticism—not to mention lawsuits—to be heaped upon Hooker and upon its parent company, Occidental Petroleum Corporation, which acquired it in 1968. But Hooker and Occidental have always seemed not to be overly perturbed by all the fuss. An Occidental annual report referred to Love Canal as "that difficult situation." And Hooker President Donald Baeder, in a letter to *The New York Times* in the summer of 1979, wrote that "our disposal practices at the Love Canal in the Fifties . . . were considered 'state-of-the-art' at the time," and that "we believe our current waste disposal practices and our new management's attitude toward environmental responsibility are at least as good as anyone else's in industry"—a disconcerting suggestion indeed. But even if the physical practices of the recent past—throwing poisons in thin-walled metal drums into holes in the ground—were the best that American industry could come up with, what of the *responsibility* of it all? What were the moral implications of turning over a poisonous dump to people who wanted to build a school on it?

Hooker's reply to that question, issued in 1978 as the Love Canal tragedy was unfolding, was to point out that it had informed the school board about the chemicals. "Because we were concerned about the future use of the property," said a company statement reported in the press in August, 1978, "we warned the Board of Education before the property was deeded over to them that it had been a dumping site for waste products resulting from the manufacture of chemicals. The Board of Education acknowledged the situation contractually and agreed to make no claims against Hooker arising from future use. Hooker does not believe it has any legal obligations or responsibility for the situation that has evolved completely outside its control. However, as a responsible corporate citizen of the Niagara area, it is lending its technical skills to the agencies to help correct this situation."

There are some—many—who would question Hooker's description of itself as a "responsible corporate citizen." The subcommittee on oversight and investigations of the House Committee on Interstate and Foreign Commerce held hearings in 1979 and concluded, in a report on hazardous waste disposal, that "Hooker Chemical was aware at least as early as 1958 that children were experiencing chemical burns from substances percolating up from the Love Canal dump site, yet took no action to inform local residents of the potential hazards." The report recalled the following amazing exchange during the hearings between Representative Albert Gore and Jay Wilkenfeld, who had been a Hooker executive in charge of "quality control" and "services in the environmental area," as he put it:

GORE: Twenty-one years ago when this incident occurred with the children being burned, did the company warn only the school board or did you take any steps to alert the people who lived there?

WILKENFELD: It was my understanding that the people who lived in the area knew that this was a former chemical dump and that these materials were hazardous and that the children should not get in there.

As a matter of fact, on these occasions when children would get into material like that, they quite frequently would call our plant dispensary to get information from the nurse on treatment of irritation from the chemicals.

GORE: Did you tell them not to play in the area?

WILKENFELD: I can't say what the nurse's response was.

GORE: Did you take any steps to inform the people who lived adjacent to the Love Canal dump site to inform them of what kinds of chemicals were in the dump site and what the hazards to their health were?

WILKENFELD: No, we did not.

GORE: Why not?

WILKENFELD: We did not feel that we could do this without incurring substantial liabilities for implying that the current owners of the property were doing an inadequate care on the property.

Gore recapitulated what the Hooker executive had said and then asked:

GORE: That seems like it sure does slight the people who were exposed to the health hazard. If you were worried about that, did that also make you think that maybe the school board would be less than candid in passing on your warnings to the people who lived there?

WILKENFELD: I can't speak for the school board.

And later:

GORE: You would have known if the school board passed on any kind of warning to the people who lived adjacent to the canal, wouldn't you?

WILKENFELD: Not necessarily.

GORE: If they had done an effective job, you would have.

WILKENFELD: I might have known; I might not have. It depends on how they did it.

GORE: Did you ever receive any reports back that they did pass a warning on to the people?

WILKENFELD: No.

GORE: Did that make you wonder whether or not further

steps ought to be taken to warn the people who lived in the area of the hazards they faced?

WILKENFELD: If I did—and I don't recall at this time—I didn't do anything about it at that time.

Wilkenfeld went on to become the director of health and environment at Occidental Petroleum.

The congressional subcommittee report notes that Hooker showed a similar lack of concern about another of its dump sites, the one at 102nd Street in Niagara Falls. Says the report: "A 1972 internal Hooker memo suggests three possible uses for that site: sale to the city of Niagara Falls; sale or lease to private interests for development (the land had been zoned as multiple family residential); or use by Hooker as a warehouse. Another memo suggested that the City of Niagara Falls might want to buy the land for park and recreational facilities."

Hooker's own brand of responsible corporate citizenship has extended to other parts of the nation as well. A federal document released in 1980 stated that Occidental Chemical Company, a subsidiary of Hooker, and its predecessors at an industrial site in Lathrop, California, "have dumped chemical and radiological wastes into unlined ponds, a lined pond, ditches, and other disposal areas at the Lathrop facility. The liquid and solid wastes from the manufacture of pesticides and fertilizer products at the plant have percolated downward through the soil, causing pollution and contamination of the underlying shallow ground water. This shallow ground water, the top layer of which lies approximately seven to 25 feet from the surface, generally migrates in a north-northwesterly direction from the Lathrop facility toward the cities of Stockton and Lathrop. Polluted ground water from the facility's disposal area, in the course of migration, has reached ground water that is the source of drinking water for the Lathrop County Water District, whose wells are located 1.5 miles from the facility and service more than 3,000 persons. In addition, other local domestic and public water supplies within the district have been affected . . ."

A good deal of information about Hooker's internal operations found its way into the public realm during a corporate takeover attempt in 1978, in which Occidental Petroleum sought unsuccessfully to gain control of the Mead Paper Corporation. One of those revelations, according to the House oversight and investigations subcommittee, was that the managers of the Lathrop plant knew for almost four years that the illegally dumped pesticides were poisoning wells. One such document, written by the plant's chief environmental engineer to other officials, was quoted by the subcommittee as having said: "Our neighbors are concerned about the quality of water from their wells. Recently water from our waste pond percolated into our neighbor's field. His dog got in it, licked himself, and died. Our laboratory records indicate that we are slowly contaminating all wells in our area and two of our own wells are contaminated to the point of being toxic to animals or humans. THIS IS A TIME BOMB THAT WE MUST DE-FUSE."

Other internal memoranda from the Lathrop plant offered similar challenges to the idea of Occidental-Hooker as a corporate good neighbor who was just bumbling along in a sea of naïveté. "The attached well data," wrote the engineer in an April, 1977, memo released by the subcommittee, "shows that we have destroyed the usability of several wells in our area. . . . The basic decision is this[:] Do we correct the situation before we have a problem, or do we hold off until action is taken against us[?] . . . In the past I have sent a report monthly to the [state] Water Quality Control Board which gives our discharge to the waste water leach pond. This report does not consider the chemicals leached from our gyp [apparently gypsum] ponds and ditches or the chemicals discharged from Ag Chem. I don't believe the Water Quality Control Board is even aware that we process Pesticides. Since this report isn't exactly accurate even though the inaccuracy is due to omission rather than outright falsehood, I don't really feel comfortable in signing it. However, I don't think it would be wise to explain the discrepancy to the state at this time."

And, in another memo, which raised the possibility that the Lathrop wing of Hooker Chemical may not have been totally devoted to the "state-of-the-art" in environmental matters: "Most other organizations involved in pesticide handling have spent millions to solve their problems. No outsiders actually know what we do and there has been no government pressure on us, so we have held back trying to find out what to do within [sic] funds we have available."

The authenticity of the memoranda has not been questioned. The Lathrop plant's environmental engineer conveyed a sense of real anxiety about what he felt the company might be doing to the water table. This seemed to be in strange contrast to Hooker's official comments on the matter. In one of them, a Hooker spokesman was quoted by *The New York Times* as referring to the memo about well contamination, when he was asked about it, as "conjecture." And a *Wall Street Journal* article on Hooker attempts at rehabilitating its image quoted a corporate spokesman as saying, "The contaminated wells at Lathrop were for irrigation, not drinking water," as if that mattered very much, and that "the company took corrective action as soon as it discovered the problem."

A regional director of New York State's Department of Environmental Conservation accused Hooker in 1979 of dumping toxic wastes illegally into Long Island landfills on more than 400 occasions. Then, Donald J. Middleton told the press, Hooker's staff gave the state an explanation of what it had done that was at variance with information in the company's own documents (unearthed, again, in the Mead Paper controversy). And a private group has supplied horrifying details on Hooker's Long Island actions. The group is the Toxic Chemicals Project of the New York Public Interest Research Group, a not-for-profit research and advocacy organization made up largely of college students. In *Toxics on Tap*, a damning volume on what is happening to drinking water on Long Island, the group identified Hooker's Hicksville plant as "the largest known source of toxic organic chemical ground water contamination on Long Island." Hooker, said the researchers, got rid of much of its hazardous waste in local landfills and buried the rest on its own site. In one case, an entire trailer truck that was thickly encrusted with chemicals was buried at the plant. In others, an estimated 38,000,000 gallons of "heavily polluted waste water [was] recharged directly into the aquifer system below the plant site." Said the report: "Some of the deadliest and most non-biodegradable compounds known to science have been discharged directly into the aquifer system" beneath Long Island. In 1979, when a House committee was holding hearings on toxic wastes, Representative Norman F. Lent of Long Island asked Bruce Davis, Hooker's executive vice-president, about reports that Hooker's plant there had "for 19 years pumped 2,000,000 gallons annually of waste, containing a known cancer-causing agent, into the ground water recharge basins." He added: "We may never know how much of that carcinogen in some 38,000,000 gallons of waste trickled down through the soil into the aquifer on which some 3,000,000 Long Island residents depend for their drinking water."

There was some hemming and hawing about how much information Davis had about his company's operation on Long Island, and the congressman came back with a question that was half-statement: "You do know that the chemical waste from that plant was discharged into the ground water recharge basin." To which the Hooker executive replied:

"It went into a sand sump which went down into the general aquifer system in Long Island. There was no sewer system there."

Representative Lent said: "And the soil of Long Island is conducive to the seepage through the sand and directly into the aquifer upon which some 3,000,000 people rely for their drinking water. You are aware of that?"

Davis: "Yes, sir."

More than two years after the state made its accusations against Hooker, a satisfactory conclusion to the Long Island situation still had not been reached. Frances Cerra, writing in *The New York Times* in December, 1981, quoted Donald Middleton as saying his attempts to negotiate with Hooker had been "fruitless." Middleton further said that after "going around and around with them, I became convinced that they deal in rhetoric." Hopes that policy makers in state government might employ aggressive means to bring action against Hooker seemed equally fruitless. Hooker, meantime, continued to insist that it had not broken any laws, and tests in some sections showed that chemicals have entered the groundwater supply.

In the summer of 1978, Michigan's Department of Natural Resources accused Hooker of having contaminated groundwater and wells around its Montague plant near Lake Michigan. The state said the contaminants included a chemical known as C-56, or hexachlorocyclopentadiene, which is used in pesticides, along with others, such as mirex, chloroform, carbon tetrachloride, and other chlorinated hydrocarbons. A plume of contamination extended 2,000 feet wide and one mile long through the earth from an open field behind the plant, where the company began storing drums of chemicals in 1957, to White Lake. Along the way it ruined numerous wells. The Associated Press reported that Hooker was supplying bottled water to some of its victims, and quoted one woman as saying, "Hooker said they'd give us city water from Montague if we'd sign a release that we and our children wouldn't prosecute them for any health problems later. We refuse to sign." The woman said she was so angry that she and her neighbors were "about ready to threaten to drink the water and then sue them."

The State of Michigan moved much more quickly and effectively against Hooker than had New York State officials, and in October, 1979, the firm and the state reached a court-supervised settlement. Under the agreement, Hooker will clean up the site, the ground water, and the contaminated wells, will monitor the future condition of the water, will supply residents with non-poisonous water, and will pay the state its costs and a $1,000,000 penalty.

And Hooker has managed to foul one of the finest rivers in the nation, the Suwannee.

The firm's phosphorus plant in White Springs, Florida, had been found guilty in 1978 of polluting the air with fluoride. But internal records—again, they came out of the Mead-Occidental takeover fight—showed much more. Donald G. McNeil, Jr., writing in *The New York Times* in August, 1979, reported that documents showed that the plant "had far more violations than the authorities suspected and that the company's top echelon knew and approved of the local manager's violating the plant's emissions permit." Included in the previously unknown violations were releases into the Suwannee of phosphate and fluoride and of phosphate slurry, which creates a river-bottom slime that kills aquatic life. Hooker president Baeder's version is that when top management "learned of this situation," it shut down the process and reported the trouble to state and federal authorities.

Through all of these revelations, Hooker maintained its posture of responsible corporate citizenship, and its public relations staff routinely expressed shock and outrage at subsequent accusations. One glimpse of the firm's way of doing things, and of the image it somehow thought it could still cling to, was gained inadvertently in the spring of 1979. The author of this book had published an article in *Penthouse* magazine on the ways in which Northern-based industry was harming the environment and people of the South, and in the process I referred both to the fact that phosphate strip mining caused numerous problems and to the fact that one of its chief practitioners was Hooker. *Penthouse* soon received a letter-to-the-editor from one D. L. Wood, of Houston, taking me to task for the article and, particularly, for the section on phosphate mining. I "would do well," wrote Wood, "to visit Hooker Chemical's Phosphate mining operation near White Springs,

Florida. To learn what can be done when a company is responsible and concerned about ecology. Hooker's reclamation project has provided recreation areas for local residents and pasture lands. Water pollution is another concern of Hooker. The famed Suwanee [*sic*] River flows near a portion of the mining operation and chemical complex, yet, it is clear and abounds with wild life."

Wood's letter sounded like a wide-open commercial for Hooker and its White Springs operation (which Florida's secretary of environmental regulation had called, a few months before, "the most serious and most deliberate violation of environmental laws in Florida"), and so I wondered who D. L. Wood was. The return address on his letter was obviously a residence. On a hunch, I placed a person-to-person call to "D. L. Wood" at Hooker Chemical Corporation in Houston. A surprised D. L. Wood, who is a credit manager for Hooker, came on the line.

17

Hooker Chemical is not the only business in the nation that has been accused of abusing the water supply. Just as it is dangerous to assume that Love Canal was an isolated event, it would be foolhardy to think that all the problems are being caused by a handful of irresponsible corporations. One of the more unfortunate truths of our recent history is that the president of Hooker Chemical was correct when he said that his firm's procedures in dealing with toxic wastes were in keeping with the "state-of-the-art." Some businesses, to be sure, have been conscientious and respectful of the environment. But the art as it has been practiced by much of American industry has been surrealistic in its treatment of water. Hooker's is just one of the names that have popped up with some regularity. Many of the others are quite well known: Quite a few of them are found regularly on *Fortune* magazine's annual list of the nation's 500 largest corporations, and some are veritable household words.

The Velsicol Chemical Company has been involved, or accused of involvement, in water-related problems in several parts of the nation, most notably western Tennessee. In mid-1978 in Memphis, according to a government report, "a mixture of chemicals," including one used in making the pesticide endrin, was discharged into the municipal water treatment plant, and was believed to have been responsible for making several city workers sick. "The source was believed to be Velsicol Chemical Company," said the government document. In the following year Velsicol signed a consent decree in which it promised "to attempt to bring its operations into full compliance with environmental regulations," according to the report.

Velsicol used a rural landfill in Hardeman County, Tennessee, from 1964 to 1972 to bury 300,000 drums filled with the residues of pesticide production, according to the Council on Environmental Quality. Forty families nearby "drank from wells polluted with such pesticides as endrin, dieldrin, aldrin, and heptachlor," said the council. A Senate report said the Geological Survey had found stream pollution and "contamination of the underground aquifer. In addition, contaminants seem to be moving toward wells of nearby residents. Some of the leachate compounds are estimated to be migrating at a minimum rate of 80 feet per year in the water table zone." Studies in the area, said the report, "have shown an abnormal incidence of liver disorders." Residents filed a class action suit against the manufacturer, which started providing forty families with potable water brought in by truck.

The Olin Corporation specializes in chemicals, papers, metals, firearms, and, it would seem, water pollution. The federal government took Olin and three of its former officials to court on charges that they had concealed the company's dumping of 38 tons of mercury into the Niagara River in New York (not far, as it turned out, from Love Canal) between 1970 and 1977. Mercury, which enters the bodies of fish in the waters in which it is dumped, can cause nervous system and reproductive difficulties in humans eating those fish.

According to the government, which won its case, Olin and its officials dumped far more than the allowed limits of mercury into the water and then misled EPA about the amounts. *The New York Times* quoted the corporation as saying, when the charges were filed, that "no one else was involved except a few individuals in the Niagara Falls plant. In these circumstances, we feel charges against Olin are unwarranted and unfair." The firm further said that when corporate officials learned of the dumping, they notified EPA and undertook emergency repairs on their own.

All of which sounds fine, unless one is aware of the fact that the "few individuals" in question were Olin's plant manager, production manager, and plant chemist. The former officials and the corporation itself were found guilty of filing false reports, and in December of 1979 the sentences came down: probation and $2,000 fines for the employees and a $70,000 fine for Olin. The corporate fine was the maximum permissible under the law, and the federal judge who levied it acknowledged that it was just "a slap on the wrist" for the huge corporation. Olin has also been named by a Senate document as the firm that was believed to be the source of mercury contamination in the North Holston River in Virginia and one of those believed to have contributed mercury to several waterways in Alabama.

E. I. du Pont de Nemours, one of the nation's more respectable chemical manufacturers, was listed in that same Senate report as the firm that was believed to have been responsible for the mercury contamination of 130 miles of the south fork of the Shenandoah River below Waynesboro, Virginia. Mercury had been used in Du Pont's synthetic fiber plant between 1929 and 1950. In 1982 a company spokesman said recent tests showed the metal was still in the river sediment.

The spectacular sea of toxic wastes at and around and in the drinking water of Woburn, Massachusetts, is partly the legacy of chemical companies with respected names. Members of the New Jersey Public Interest Research Group who walk along streams looking for industrial polluters (they call themselves "streamwalkers") found 106 discharge pipes leading into five miles of Deepavaal Brook in industrialized Essex County.

One of the most disgraceful chapters in American industrial history was written by the Reserve Mining Company, a joint subsidiary of Armco Steel and Republic Steel which supplies the parent companies with a form of iron ore, called taconite, which it mines on the Western shore of Lake Superior at Silver Bay, Minnesota.

For almost twenty-five years, Reserve discharged 67,000 tons of the leftover debris of mining (called tailings) *each day* into Lake Superior, a body of water that was otherwise so clean that communities obtained their drinking water directly from it, without filtration. That is more than a trillion pounds of tailings. What did they contain? Nickel, copper, zinc, lead, chromium, phosphorus, manganese, silica, arsenic, and iron. And asbestos. Asbestos-like fibers turned up in drinking water in nearby Duluth and other communities. Asbestos, when inhaled, is known to cause cancer. Scientists are uncertain about the dangers of ingested asbestos. Since 1972, government agencies and environmentalists tried to stop Reserve's discharge, but it was not until March, 1980, that they succeeded. Even when the dumping was stopped, there remained the problem of the billions of tons of poisons that remained in the water and in the bodies of those who depended on it for life. The problem was dealt with, if not completely solved, in a federal court settlement announced in April, 1982. A suit against Reserve by federal and state agencies was dismissed, and the company agreed to pay the cost of filtering drinking water, estimated at $1.84 million, for Duluth and three other towns.

Students from Case Western Reserve who patrolled Ohio's Cuyahoga River at night said they found the Sherwin-Williams paint company discharging its waste in such concentrations that the students' boat changed color after four days in the river, according to a United Press International story. The State of Ohio obtained a temporary restraining order against the company, but a lawsuit seeking damages was later dismissed. The *Sierra Club Bulletin* charged in an article that a Westinghouse Electric Corporation manufacturing plant in Bloomington, Indiana, "has been identified as the primary source of the polychlorinated biphenyls . . . that have contaminated water, land, agricultural produce, sewage facilities and people in and around the southern Indiana city of 65,000." For twenty years, the General Electric Corporation dumped an estimated

1,500,000 pounds of PCBs into the Hudson River north of Albany, New York. PCBs are believed to produce cancer in laboratory animals and are known to cause hair loss, skin lesions, liver changes, and reproductive problems in primates.

The federal government's lawsuits against the users of two hazardous-waste dumps in southern Louisiana listed such household names as U.S. Steel, Uniroyal, Dow, Shell, Exxon, and Allied Chemical. For that last corporation, problems with hazardous waste and the water supply were not exactly new. Allied Chemical was found guilty on federal criminal charges in connection with the poisoning of Virginia's James River and of numerous residents of the town of Hopewell, where Allied had a factory.

Kit Weigel pronounces it HOPE-wul, the way the Virginians do, even though she's originally from Augusta, Georgia. She lives on a nice residential street in Hopewell with her husband and child. Formerly the reporter for *The Hopewell News*, Weigel does freelance writing and editing now. She is something of a booster of Hopewell, and in that connection has become something of a historian as well. It does not take a historian to know that no matter what else may have happened in Hopewell's history—and quite a bit has—the city is going to be remembered most of all for the Kepone incident.

Hopewell, which sits squarely beside the James, about eighty miles upstream from the Chesapeake Bay, was settled by the British in 1613. Largely because of its location on a broad, navigable river, the town was attractive to industry. Du Pont arrived in the early 1900s to build a dynamite plant, which prospered during World War II, attracting workers of many nationalities. Although Hopewell had many of the characteristics of a hell-for-leather boom town ("a Wild West town," says Kit Weigel, "where they talked about having to strap on your six-shooter before going out at night"), it was also very much a company town, and very much under the control of a physician, D. Lane Elder, who blended city politics and corporate power expertly and who also was the company doctor for most of the industries. Elder (who is now dead) was "handsome, charismatic, athletic, loved by a lot of people, hated by a minority because of the way he used power," says Weigel. "He saw the future of the city as being with industry."

The physician and Du Pont sought other industries to share in Hopewell's future, and several of them came to partake of the excellent transportation facilities, the abundant water for processing and for shipping, the "reasonable" labor pool, and the almost worshipful attitude of local and state government toward industry, a characteristic that the State of Virginia displays to this day. A firm named Tubize came to make rayon, although it closed later because of labor problems. There was a paper mill, and an outfit named Atmospheric Nitrogen, which manufactured the liquid base from which nylon is spun. Atmospheric Nitrogen later became known as Allied Chemical. As Allied, it opened several other divisions, including one that made agricultural chemicals—pesticides and herbicides. One of those chemicals was Kepone.

Kepone is $C_{10}Cl_{10}O$, a chlorinated hydrocarbon which is used as an ant and roach poison. It is related to such other chemicals as DDT, aldrin, and dieldrin, all of which have been restricted in use by the federal government. Kepone is not soluble in water. Allied Chemical developed the chemical in the 1950s and registered it as a pesticide with the U.S. Department of Agriculture in 1959. In an assessment of Kepone's toxicity, Allied noted that it caused "DDT-like tremors." Later it was found to cause sterility in people who handled it, along with apparent brain and liver damage, slurred speech, loss of memory, and twitching of the eyes. The National Cancer Institute reported that Kepone caused cancer in test animals. From 1966 until 1973, the Allied Chemical Company poured this poison, along with other chemicals, into the James River at Hopewell, thus damaging the river and part of Chesapeake Bay, one of the most valuable estuaries on the planet.

In 1973 Allied subcontracted the manufacture of Kepone

to the Life Science Products Company. Life Science was virtually an Allied subsidiary; it operated out of a converted gasoline station in Hopewell, making the poison from raw materials supplied by Allied and selling the end product, 400,000 to 1,500,000 pounds of it a year, exclusively to Allied. Life Science was run by two former Allied employees; one had been the plant manager of the agricultural chemicals division, and the other had been a research chemist. They pumped *their* Kepone-laced leftovers not directly into the James, but into Hopewell's waste-water treatment plant, where the poison killed the bacterial "digesters" that are necessary in the treatment of sewage. Although both the city and the state realized that something was wrong, and knew what was causing the problem, they did little about it; Kepone, in the meantime, found its way into the river through the city's pipes.

In July of 1975, a private physician tested the blood of a patient who worked at Life Science and who was complaining of trembling and weight loss. (According to Kit Weigel, the worker had previously seen doctors who were under contract to Life Science, and they had treated his "nervousness" with a prescription for tranquilizers.) The amount of Kepone in the worker's blood, said Weigel, "was unbelievably high. The people who tested it thought they had a contaminated sample; they thought some Kepone had been sprinkled in the test tube before it was sent to them. The concentration was that high." Soon afterward, Life Science was shut down, the state closed the river to fishing and shellfishing, about eighty other workers were diagnosed as suffering from Kepone poisoning, and the slow machinery of government started to work. In the town, said Kit Weigel later, there was a mixture of feelings. "Some people were angry at Allied," she said. "Some people were angry at Life Science. Some people were angry at the workers for being sick. It was: 'If they hadn't gotten sick, none of this would have happened.' 'If they had used their safety equipment right . . .' 'If So-and-so hadn't been such a drunk so much

Kepone wouldn't have gotten into his bloodstream.' Which is true. Alcohol consumption increases the amount that enters your bloodstream."

In May, 1976, federal indictments were handed down on 1,096 criminal counts against Allied Chemical, Life Science, and the City of Hopewell. The city pleaded *nolo contendere* and was fined $10,000 and placed on probation for five years. The two Life Science operators, who also pleaded *nolo contendere*, were fined $25,000 each and placed on five years' probation. And Allied, which also chose not to contest the charges, was fined the maximum—$13,240,000—by district Judge Robert R. Merhige, Jr., who said, at the sentencing, that he didn't buy Allied's contention that "this was all done innocently. I think it was done as a business necessity, to save money." The fine was believed to be a record in such cases. Later Allied, following a suggestion by the judge, had the penalty reduced by about $8,000,000 by donating that amount to a newly formed state environmental endowment. The contribution was tax-deductible.

As is usually the case when a big corporation gets caught at something, Allied sought to dilute the blame and minimize its responsibility. When the trial was over, John T. Connor, then the chairman of Allied, issued a statement referring to the "succession of errors in which many persons and organizations, both public and private, have played a part and must share responsibility." Connor's euphemism for Allied's own practice of dumping poison into the river was "discharging into the James River products not adequately covered by permits." And, in a supreme display of brazenness, he added: "We would like to point out that of the 940 counts in this indictment, only 312 involved Kepone and 628 covered two other chemicals . . . which are biodegradable and of comparably low toxicity." (When this quotation was relayed to William B. Cummings, the United States attorney who had prosecuted the cases, his reply was: "Comparable to what? To Kepone? To clean water?") As is obligatory in those moments when a big firm is finally caught in illegal acts, Connor referred to Allied Chemical's role as that of "a good corporate citizen."

By the time the good citizen's 1976 annual report came out, Allied Chemical's campaign to rehabilitate the responsibility for what it had done, and people's memories of what had happened, was well under way. Kepone, said the report, "was a product manufactured for us under contract by a small independent chemical firm, the Life Science Products Company." And, the reader of the annual report might conclude, it wasn't *Kepone* that messed up the river, but rather a politician: One of the civil suits growing out of the mess, said the annual report, was brought "by watermen whose livelihood was impaired when Virginia Governor Mills E. Godwin, Jr., closed the James River to fishing." The document repeatedly referred to Allied's own discharges of Kepone, without naming it, as "chemical wastes" that hadn't been "adequately covered by permits." The report seemed to be studiously avoiding any connection of its own name with that of Kepone, although it had been convicted of putting Kepone into the river.

The chemical company did announce new efforts to be more careful about pollution and worker safety—efforts that really amount to little more than setting out to do what any American industry, and particularly any American *chemical* industry, should have been doing all along, but which virtually none have. This (coupled, no doubt, with a press and public gullible enough to believe what they read in corporate annual reports) has reaped Allied a bonus of favorable publicity in the years since Kepone convictions—perhaps, even, $4,000,000 worth of it.

The Wall Street Journal did a five-years-later story on Kepone in 1980 which neglected to point out the fact that the poison had been dumped in the river by Allied as well as Life Science. *The New York Times* did a story on Allied's promise to comply with the law and on EPA's glowing comments on the firm's newfound environmental conscience. This was followed by a *Times* editorial titled "Praise for an Ex-Polluter" which spoke of "an impressive corporate turnabout." The most fulsome praise came from *Fortune* magazine, which produced an article so amorous (as well as erroneous) as to be embarrassing. Allied, in fact, distributes reprints of the piece. The magazine said Allied (which was 69th on its 1980 list of top corporations) had "innocently blundered into trouble when it contracted out the production of a chemical called Kepone," and had been "a victim of bad luck," one manifestation of which was being hailed into the court of a "judicial activist" (Judge Merhige, *Fortune* noted, actually had the audacity to write a decision ordering the desegregation of the schools in the Richmond area). In a crowning burst of really bad taste, the article then referred to Kepone as "the biggest windfall to hit Virginia's legal industry since personal-injury suits were invented." What *Fortune* meant was that some of the people who had been poisoned—who had suffered memory loss, twitching, sterility—and some of those whose livelihoods had been destroyed by the poisons, had actually descended so low as to hire lawyers to help them sue Life Science and this "good corporate citizen" which had pleaded *nolo contendere* to *only* 312 indictments charging the illegal dumping of ant and roach poison into a river.

18

The deliberate piping of poisons into a public body of water is, without doubt, one of the more dramatic atrocities committed by industry against Earth's environment and its citizens. But probably the greatest and most widespread abuse of our water by industry is in the more traditional areas, the ones we have always known a great deal about, the ones for which we have had the solutions for decades. The knowledge and technology are there, but our ability to apply them has been increasingly frustrated by industry's own peculiar ways of doing things and by our governments' apparent unwillingness to intervene on behalf of the planet, not to mention the taxpayers.

Agriculture is an industry, of course, as are the construction and financing that go into residential development, and it is when these are operated primarily as *industries*—that is, with unswerving faithfulness to the "bottom line"—that they inflict the most harm on nature and, especially, on water. There are several other areas, as well, in which industry is contributing abundantly to the present crisis in water.

Acid rain is one of them. It is a direct product of industrial and population growth.

When normal evapotranspiration occurs, the water that is released is relatively pure. But once it reaches the atmosphere, the water condenses on solid particles that are there. Historically, this has resulted in a watery solution that would eventually fall, as rain or snow, and would be slightly acetic. (The acidity of a solution, or its pH value, is a measure of the presence in it of hydrogen ions, and is expressed on a scale of from 0 to 14. A solution that is neutral is said to have a pH of 7, while anything below 7 is considered acetic and anything above 7 is alkaline. Milk, pure water, and blood have pH values of around 7; sauerkraut and orange juice are a little below 4; milk of magnesia has a pH of more than 10. The scale is logarithmic, so that a change in acidity from, say, 5 to 4 represents a tenfold increase.) Precipitation classically has been assumed to have a pH of something like 5.6; rain which fell before the Industrial Revolution and then was locked into glaciers has been lately measured at above pH 5, according to a 1979 article in *Scientific American*.

More recently, however, the combustion of fossil fuels has introduced enormous quantities of contaminants into the atmosphere, notably sulfur and nitrogen oxides. One estimate is that the United States and Canada discharge 50,000,000 tons of these oxides into the air each year. These are converted into sulfuric and nitric acids in conjunction with the atmospheric water, and when the resulting precipitation has a pH of below 5.6, it is called "acid rain." Contamination of the atmosphere has proceeded to such a degree that precipitation over much of the Eastern United States, southeastern Canada, and Western Europe now averages from 4 to 4.5 in pH. As early as 1974, a storm over Scotland released rain with a pH of 2.4, which means it was about as acetic as lemon juice.

It is one of the several ironies of our stumbling attempts at environmental self-education that efforts to control aerial pollution have helped acid rain to become a worldwide, rather than a purely local, problem. Industrial smokestacks have been built taller and taller, in order to minimize local pollution, but an apparent result of this has been to lift the contaminants higher into the sky, where they are caught by prevailing winds and carried for great distances before they fall as precipitation. A Canadian minister of the environment has estimated that half of his country's acid rain comes from coal-powered plants in the United States. But smokestacks more than 1,000 feet tall at the huge copper and nickel smelting plant in Sudbury, Ontario, are believed to be the source of acid rain that has wiped out aquatic life in much of New York State's Adirondacks, where rainfall with a pH as low as 2.1 has been measured. Both Canada and the United States are thought to be contributing acids to the rainfall of Western Europe.

The technology exists to reduce the discharges of sulfur and nitrogen oxides; smokestack "scrubbers" can remove much of the sulfur before it gets into the air. Scrubbers are expensive, however, and industry does not want to install them.

Scientists are only now starting to probe the effects of acid rain. It is known that the phenomenon renders lakes and streams sterile, and that growing vegetation, including forests, can be damaged by it. Acid rain falling on drinking water reservoirs lowers the water's quality in a number of ways. The direct effects on humans are less clearly understood. President Carter, referring to acid rain as one of the more pressing environmental problems facing the nation, in 1979 announced a ten-year study of it, with $100,000,000 set aside for research. Not long afterward the Environmental Protection Agency referred to acid rain as possibly "one of the most significant environmental problems of the coming decade." Lobbyists for the electric power industry, whose smokestacks produce the majority of the pollutants that could cause acid rain, have argued, somewhat weakly, that the case hasn't really been proven. They quote a research report, commissioned by them, that says "it is difficult to show that acid rain has caused significant damage to the environment in the U.S."

Equally strange-sounding has been a "solution" to the problem that was proposed by some Cornell University scientists. They are using a healthy sum of the taxpayers' money to try to develop a strain of brook trout that will be resistant to acid rain. This example of society's unwillingness to eliminate the cause of a serious problem, preferring to tinker around with the symptoms, led a Canadian zoologist to ask, "Would we breed a gas-resistant canary for miners?"

Given the present climate, it would not be surprising to find that some government agency *was* supporting research into "gas-resistant canary management techniques." Until Carter's 1979 announcement, the federal government had been particularly unwilling to tackle the problem of acid rain at the same time that it was promoting the burning of fuels, in the name of "energy independence," that are even higher in sulfur content. An official of EPA was quoted in October, 1979, as saying the acid rain situation would get worse before it got better, and that it would require "some fairly heroic measures." The most courageous, although the official didn't say so, would be those involved in getting EPA to protect the environment. Half a year later the official's boss, EPA Administrator Douglas Costle, revealed that the administration was not yet ready to be heroic. Not enough was known about acid rain, said Costle, "But we know enough about it to know we have to start to do something about it this year." He added, however, that "in an election year it is best to keep your head down" and not undertake any new regulatory programs. And so the problem of acid rain goes on. The Reagan administration has continued the program at its original funding levels, but has telescoped the total time involved to five to seven years.

Publicly owned land in the United States is fast becoming an industry. The land is there, in almost unbelievable abundance; it is often "barren" (meaning it has no homes or shopping centers on it yet); it has few advocates who are sufficiently organized or articulate or well armed financially to protect it; it "belongs" to the people of America, which means government agencies are in charge of protecting it, which means that its minerals and other resources can be stolen with relative ease and with virtually no risk of punishment. Public land also is concentrated in the drier parts of the nation, and so whenever its status is changed—to allow for logging, mining, or other forms of development—the delicate water balance is altered, always for the worse. In addition, there are woodlands, many square miles of which are contained in a nationwide system of government-protected National Forests, where they are supposed to be "managed" in a way that provides for a multiplicity of uses—logging and recreation being two of the most prominent. When they are "managed" properly, the forests control erosion of the land and clogging of the streams with silt and debris, as well as contribute to the evapotranspiration portion of the hydrologic cycle. Industry prefers, however, to "manage" forests in the manner that makes the bottom line look best, and that is by clearcutting them—chopping down all the trees in a given area and hauling them away. And the U.S. Forest Service, a division of the Department of Agriculture, has functioned consistently, through all sorts of White House administrations, as a veritable agent for the forest industry, encouraging clearcutting and pretty much anything else the clearcutters would like to do.

Private industry's passionate pursuit of the bottom line has done much to harm the land and the water that runs through and beneath it, but the biggest single abuser of the land is probably the United States itself. With a brand of arrogance that seems uniquely characteristic of bureaucracy, the government delights in violating the environmental rules that it seeks to impose on everyone else; like policemen who steal, there is the security of knowing that you aren't likely to get caught or, if you are, that nothing much will happen. The Council on Environmental Quality reported in December, 1978, that while 87 per cent of the major industrial discharges of pollutants had met the federally imposed deadline to stop their polluting, only 66 per cent of the 228 major *federal* dischargers had complied.

Mining is another aspect of industry that has profound effects on the land, both publicly and privately owned, and on the water that flows through it. Mining has gone on for thousands of years, of course, and it is no news that much of it has been done at the expense of the environment. But two recent trends have conspired to make it even more likely that this particular form of industry will do grave and lasting harm to our supplies of water. One of them is the crisis in cheap energy.

A potential alternative to expensive oil, nuclear energy, is experiencing hard times currently, due largely to the public awareness that the people who are in charge of it are not competent to be in charge of it, along with the fact that we have no idea how to properly deal with the terribly dangerous leftovers of nuclear fission. Coal is a much more likely target, and American industry wants to go after it. Industry has government's blessing and, in some cases, assistance.

Coal is not the only substance that has once more become attractive to industry. As the price of everything has gone up, some other minerals and metals that were bypassed over the past several decades have become interesting again—have become worth the exploiters' time and effort. And that fact coincides with the second trend that threatens the future of water: There are new, "modern" methods of extraction, and almost all of them appear to place the water supply in greater jeopardy.

Much of the renewed interest in beneath-the-ground substances is focussed on the West, where deep-tunnel mining is not ordinarily practiced. Strip mining (or what industry calls "surface mining") is the preferred way to get the material, and strip mining poses numerous threats to the environment. And some of the exploitation is aimed at recovering minerals (such as copper and gold) in places where they once were found in abundance, and mined by conventional methods, and where the mining then ceased. It stopped several decades ago because the operators believed they had reached the limits of commercial feasibility. But now, with the substances worth more, the rules of commercial feasibility have changed. It now is economically worthwhile for miners to go after quantities of minerals that they once had considered to be too small. Unfortunately, they are using new techniques that may be more efficient for them but which may do serious harm to the water. Often these techniques call for using leaching processes in which acids are poured onto the ground and allowed to drift down through the minerals and then are collected at some lower point. What this can do to the aquifers is the subject of some controversy, especially in the more arid Western states where the poisoning of water has traditionally been frowned upon.

Industry, of course, does not take such a negative view of the new mining prospects. The demand for more minerals is but a reflection, in industry's view, of an advancing civilization. A basic-level publication of the American Mining Congress, titled *What Mining Means to Americans*, notes with some pride that the United States has only 5 per cent of the world's population and 7 per cent of its land area, but that it "consumes about a quarter of the entire globe's mineral production. As population increases, technology advances and the standard of living continues to climb, demand for the earth's resources will inexorably grow. Indeed, it is now necessary to produce 40,000 pounds of new minerals *each* year for *each* American and to generate energy equal to having 300 people working around the clock for *each* of us." (Emphasis is in the original.) The mining organization deals very quickly with such issues as mining's potential for environmental damage and mining's lust for public lands. "It's wise to remember that Nature itself is a notorious polluter through the havoc of earthquakes and forest fires, tornadoes and tidal waves, dust storms and droughts, floods and volcanoes," says the report. And: "Much untapped potential lies beneath public lands, primarily in the West. Yet governmental policies have been foreclosing more and more of these lands to minerals exploration and development. . . . Mining could be allowed on public lands and still leave the overwhelming share of them free for preservation of wilderness, wildlife, scenic beauty and recreational opportunities. Otherwise, the country runs the risk of having its minerals supplies shut off abroad and locked up at home."

It is, however, not only nature who is a "notorious polluter." Mining does its bit, stripping the earth bare, slicing off tops of mountains and pushing them down into the valleys, dumping acids into the streams and aquifers. Petroleum exploration is not ordinarily thought of as a threat to water except when tankers produce oil spills, but it is. A common by-product of petroleum when it is mined from the earth is water—a briny solution from the deep aquifers that is considered by the industry to be a troublesome side effect. (A recent magazine advertisement by Texaco, in which the oil company sought to explain why its products cost so much more than they used to, makes the point that "We've got to pump up 5 barrels of expensive water to get you 1 barrel of oil.") Traditionally the producers have dealt with the problem of brine by dumping it onto the ground, where it leaches back down to the upper aquifers and, in some cases, into people's wells. An example of this was uncovered in the late sixties in Miller County, Arkansas, when a farmer complained of salty water in his well. The problem was traced to an oil-field brine-disposal area nearby; about one square mile of the shallow aquifer had been contaminated. A government report on the matter commented that "Consideration was given to several renovation methods," but "All were rejected because of cost. An estimated 250 years will be necessary for natural flushing to restore the affected aquifer."

Two of the innovative processes being promoted now as potential, partial solutions to the energy crisis are coal gasification and the use of oil shale. In the former, deep deposits of coal are burned beneath the earth, cooking out a gas that is a mixture of carbon monoxide and hydrogen which, when mixed with water, becomes a flammable gas. The process may cause problems with land subsidence and pollution of both ground and surface water. In addition, the Department of Energy has noted, gasification produces carcinogenic compounds and toxic metals.

Oil shale (the product sometimes is called "shale oil" as well) has been around for a long time—since the Middle Ages, by one account—but industry lost interest in it after the cheaper petroleum was discovered in large quantities beneath the earth. The shale itself is a very fine-grained sedimentary rock which evolved from layers of organic matter at the bottoms of ancient bodies of water. Each ton of the rock contains anywhere from 10 to 140 gallons of oil—most of it runs between 25 and 60 gallons per ton, according to the Geological Survey—and the oil may be extracted by a heating process, performed either underground or above. The potential for oil shale, both as a source of energy and as a source of wealth for its processors, is generally considered to be great. If commercially feasible ways can be found to extract the oil from the rock, said the Geological Survey in 1977, "the supply of oil from shale will be enormous."

Since the government issued that forecast, oil shale production has come closer to feasibility, and the dangers to the environment have similarly increased. Oil shale recovery calls, in some cases, for strip mining; in others, explosions are detonated underground. Vast quantities of water will be needed to produce the oil, and the process is expected to increase the salinity of water already present. A 1974 U.S. Water Resources Council report, *Water for Energy Self-Sufficiency*, warned that "even with tight controls to avoid or minimize water contamination, the long-term effects of [shale oil] industrialization would result in a decline in water quality." In assessing the quantity demands, the Council referred to a Department of the Interior study that "assumed that, over time, ground water supplies will become depleted and increasing amounts of surface water will need to be used until eventually the full requirement, limited by supplies available, might be obtained from surface sources."

One representative of the energy industry is already thinking about where to get that extra water. Exxon's proposal is that water be diverted from the Missouri River to the shale-mining sites. As if that were not enough to worry those who respect the environment, Occidental Petroleum has become heavily involved in oil shale exploitation in Colorado.

An even more dangerous effort has been the coal slurry pipeline project. This scheme would take coal in the places where it can be strip-mined—again, the fragile lands of the West are mentioned—and transport it to the more densely populated places where it could be used. This would be accomplished by pulverizing it, mixing it with prodigious amounts of water, and sending the resulting slurry through pipelines. The Council on Environmental Quality, commenting on this late in 1979, said: "The principal environmental concern about slurry pipelines is their need for continual supplies of large amounts of water. In the West, where coal is abundant and water is scarce and highly valuable, the demand of a slurry pipeline for water could be a very serious problem. A pipeline transporting 30,000,000 tons of coal a year, for instance, would require about 10,000 to 20,000 acre feet of water each year. This is enough water to irrigate roughly 5,000 to 10,000 acres of farmland a year."

For a while the push toward oil shale and coal slurry had the force of the United States government behind it—Jimmy Carter even wanted to give the slurry pipeline companies the power to take people's land away from them—but more recently it has slowed down because, of all things, of the Reagan administration. In seeking to pare down the federal budget, Reagan sought deep cuts in the alternate-fuels funds that industry was counting on to subsidize its exploration and experimentation. With prospects of less of the taxpayers' money in their pockets, some of the energy companies lost much of their interest.

As noted earlier, not all the miners' attention is devoted to materials that produce energy. The ocean bottom has emerged as a prime candidate for exploitation of minerals and metals, and on land there is great interest in mining phosphate—a substance that is essential to human life. It and potassium and nitrogen form the great triumvirate of soil nutrients; without them, agricultural yields are certain to be low. The only known source of phosphorus is phosphate rock, which generally occurs in sedimentary deposits originating with the sea. Some 84 per cent of the nation's marketable phosphate rock comes from central and northern Florida and coastal North Carolina.

Phosphate rock classically is strip-mined. In Florida, it lies beneath a layer of soil (miners refer to this obstacle as "over-burden") that averages 20 feet in thickness. In North Carolina, enormous machines called draglines must remove about 90 feet of sandy coastal soil before they hit pay dirt. Until fairly recently, when public and governmental pressures caused a change, the ravaged open pits remained after the dragline had moved on, just as they did in the Southern mountains after the coal had been stripped away. By one estimate, 130,000 acres of land have been stripped in Florida.

The environmental and other problems that are caused by the mining and processing of phosphate are enormous, even when stacked up against the undisputed value of the mineral. Strip mining itself is bad enough, but there's plenty to worry about after the white mineral is wrenched from the earth and processed into forms that are more efficiently used in agriculture. The processing involves some unwanted side effects, among them an impure gypsum with few uses and a gelatinous slime which the industry prefers to think of as "waste phosphetic clays" and which the U.S. Bureau of Mines refers to as a "difficult-to-dispose-of waste material." The gypsum is piled into snow-white mountains beside the mines, and the slime is impounded in human-made lakes.

Southern phosphate mines use vast quantities of electricity to drive the giant draglines, and they gulp copious amounts of water. Texasgulf, Incorporated, which refers to itself as part of "the natural resources industry," and which is known as Tg, owns and leases some 35,000 acres near Aurora, North Carolina, next to the rich and irreplaceable Pamlico Sound. Since 1963, Tg has been going after an estimated 1,200,000,000 tons of phosphate at Aurora, most recently with a fleet of draglines that look like something out of a space-exploration movie. The largest of these machines weighs 4,435 tons; on each pass its bucket picks up enough payload to fill a two-car garage. The scene is breathtakingly ugly. Company officials are not reluctant to remind the awed spectator of phosphate's importance to human life. "It's not a question of whether you want phosphate mining or not," one of them said not long ago while showing a visitor around the pit. "You've got to have it if you want to eat. There's no substitute for it."

Water is important to human life as well, and the Aurora mine pumps 67,000,000 gallons of it out of the ground each day in order to relieve pressure on the aquifer so that the pit, which reaches down below sea level, may remain relatively dry. This has the additional effect of reducing the pressure in the wells of most of Tg's neighbors, many of them farm families. Tg has accepted the responsibility for this, and has replaced more than 900 pumps for nearby residents since operations began.

There is a great deal more concern about the effects of phosphate mining on the Floridan Aquifer in Florida, where population and industrial growth have strained the groundwater system to close to its capacity. And there is the additional threat that is posed by the lakes of colloidal slimes. In Florida, the slimes are usually impounded within dikes, and the dikes frequently leak and break. The slimes are not chemically poisonous, according to Gene McNeill, an expert with the EPA in Atlanta, but when they cascade down a waterway "They coat everything that's in their path and kill that way—fish, wildlife, vegetable life, you name it. It has been estimated that it takes three years for a place to recover from one of these breaks." The Peace River, which flows into the Gulf of Mexico south of Sarasota, has been hit by at least a score of slime floods. One of them, in 1971, released an estimated 1,000,000,000 gallons into the river. The slimes had been impounded by the Cities Service Oil Company.

Florida has a law requiring the reclamation of strip mines, but, as one official of the state's Department of Environmental Regulation, John Bennett, put it: " 'Reclaimed' means different things to different people. You can fill a pit with water and call it a lake. . . . Some of them put signs on the dams around the slime ponds that say 'Reclamation Project.' It looks good from the road, but on the other side it's just a slime pond."

There is, furthermore, radioactive material in Florida's phosphate deposits—from 0.1 to 0.4 pound of it per ton. And radiation is a special problem on Florida land that has been mined and then "reclaimed," according to studies conducted by Florida and EPA scientists. One of those studies reported that reclaimed areas had radiation levels higher than those set by the Surgeon General. And an amazing document from EPA in 1976 reported a link among phosphate mining, radiation, lung cancer, and Florida architecture.

Central Florida houses typically are built on concrete slabs poured directly on the ground. Where homes have been constructed on reclaimed phosphate-mine land, a radioactive gas known as radon 222, a descendant of decaying uranium, bubbles up through the soil which has been stirred by the "reclamation" process. It enters the homes and lungs of the residents.

"Radon is known to cause cancer," said Gene McNeill. "Living in one of those places is just like being in a uranium mine." One solution that has been proposed is to improve ventilation by constructing crawl spaces between the houses' foundations and their living surfaces. EPA has estimated that Floridians who wanted to reduce their exposure to radiation by 40 to 80 per cent could do so, but that the modifications would add from $450 to $5,250 to the cost of each new home over the life of the mortgage.

19

There are some notable exceptions, of course, but politicians in general may be said to exist in utter awe of industry, and the more exploitative the industry, the greater the sense of awe. The politicians proceed not from the assumption that the environment comes first and that whatever industry does must conform to that, but rather from the assumption that industry's desires are paramount and the environment must accommodate itself. It is a devilishly shortsighted view of life, one that freely sells out the future of the whole human race for the present benefits of a few influential people. Politicians specialize in such thinking.

Governor Wendell R. Anderson of Minnesota proposed in 1976 not only that the Reserve Mining Company be permitted to continue dumping its poisons into Lake Superior for two and a half more years, but that the polluter also receive $70,000,000 in federal aid. The governor's plan was billed as a "compromise" because it would require that Reserve build a new, court-ordered disposal site farther inland than it wanted to. In New York, a state commissioner of environmental development who seriously pursued General Electric for its dumping of PCBs into the Hudson River was forced to resign by Governor Hugh Carey, whose capacity for astonishing his constituents reached a peak when he volunteered to drink a glassful of PCBs to demonstrate the safety of a state office building that was contaminated with the poisons. The commissioners' successor then negotiated a deal with GE in which the polluter agreed to pay $3,000,000 toward cleaning the river and $1,000,000 for research, while the state kicked in $3,000,000 in taxpayers' contributions. Part of the scheme was that GE (which, some sources said, was threatening to leave New York if the state demanded too much in the way of restitution) would bear no official blame for what it had done. (The state has not accepted the responsibility for *its* actions in allowing GE to discharge some of the poisons.) Carey called this irresponsible compromise "an excellent example of ways that industry and the state can work together to solve complex social and environmental problems." By the end of the seventies the estimates were that it would take $30,000,000 to $150,000,000 to scour the PCBs from just one short stretch of the Hudson. The state spent all of the $7,000,000 from the GE settlement on research and bureaucrats' salaries, and not a penny of it went for cleaning up the poisons.

President Carter relaxed pollution rules for Ohio to allow two Cleveland power plants to burn low-grade coal and, therefore, to produce more acid rain; his alibi was saving jobs in the states' high-sulfur coal mines. The President did not discuss publicly how many jobs might have been provided if the power plants had been ordered to install scrubbers on their smokestacks, or how many jobs, and lives, might be lost as a result of the increased pollution. In the summer of 1979 EPA announced that it was relaxing its water pollution controls for hundreds of business firms, saving them an estimated $200,000,000 in expenses. By this time, it was practically impossible for an inquisitive outsider to tell whether such a move —although surely it was politically motivated—was good or bad. The top officials of EPA had done such a poor job of pursuing their missions that it could not be automatically assumed that a reduction in the number or severity of regulations (while clearly to the advantage of industry) was necessarily bad for the environment. It was like EPA's handling of the scientific inquiries into the victims of Love Canal—so badly managed and so obviously politically motivated at the agency level as to cause far more harm than good. EPA had begun to resemble OSHA, the Occupational Safety and Health

Administration, which in its early days wrote so many imbecilic rules in the name of safety and employee protection that an observer had to wonder if there were not a deliberate inside effort to sabotage the agency's mission. Thus when U.S. Steel, a classic polluter of the first order, says, as it did in August, 1980, that meeting EPA's regulations at one of its plants in Utah would require its closing, and that the water it discharges into a lake is cleaner than the lake itself, the observer must conclude that the company may very well be telling the truth and that EPA's version may be false. By the end of 1980, EPA had lost much, if not most, of its credibility with industry, with environmentalists, and with many of its own more dedicated employees, particularly those in the regional offices around the country.

The effect of all this confusion has been a far-ranging, multifaceted attack on the laws, rules, and regulations that have been written in recent years to protect the environment— a war on the very environmental frame of mind that has possessed this nation since the early sixties. There are numerous efforts, concerted and informal, to repeal much of the environmental progress that has been made. Industry has always been in the vanguard of such attacks, and one of its favorite tactics has been the "cost-benefit' (or "benefit-cost"; the terms seem to be interchangeable) argument. Cost-benefit analysis, which is widely practiced by government, which refers to it as "CBA," is the ratio of a proposed project's or policy's costs to its benefits. The course of action generally is considered a "good" one if the benefits outweigh the costs. In theory, CBA would seem to be a scientific, emotion-free way of weighing the inevitable trade-offs that are necessary in such issues as whether to build a hydroelectric dam, or how to subsidize irrigated farmland, or, even, how great a quantity of toxic substances to allow in drinking water. (There are actually scientists at work debating the value of human life vis-à-vis, as they say, the benefits to society to be gained from such things as insecticides and PCBs.)

In reality, CBA has become a tool whereby economists find employment at government expense, whereby politicians receive impressive reports and analyses that bolster their previously formed opinions, and whereby those who want to manufacture dams, irrigation projects, and poisonous chemicals can justify their continued efforts in those fields. The great danger of CBA, according to some who have studied the phenomenon, is that it is an unreliable, unscientific representation of "facts"—including those that are expected to exist in the wholly unpredictable future—that almost always is presented and treated as if it *were* reliable and scientific. Even when honest, responsible scientists and other practitioners of this form of analysis state clearly that their projections are subject to all sorts of forces that are beyond their control, and that therefore their usefulness is severely limited, such warnings are often brushed aside by the policy makers who either don't understand the scientific method or who don't care about it. Cost-benefit analysis, as it is normally applied by Washington technocrats, and especially as it is applied by them to water projects, is about as faithful to the truth as palm reading.

Millions of Americans have not received this message, however, and they remain impressed by "scientific" proclamations from people with capital letters after their names. Industry, to be sure, is a big fan of cost-benefit analysis, simply because it works so clearly in industry's favor: It is so difficult to assign values to things like rivers and aquifers and human life and so easy to assign values to things like jobs and metric tons of ant poison. "We believe that the time has come," said Allied Chemical of Kepone fame, in its 1977 annual report to stockholders, "to adopt a very cautious approach to environmental regulations, weighing the expected benefits of each proposed new rule against its true economic cost. Existing regulations have inflated industry's costs so heavily that American companies are finding it increasingly difficult to compete with foreign manufacturers. If this trend continues, our economy is bound to be affected adversely, and all Americans will suffer."

"The economy is part of nature, too, really," said Peter Steen, the president of the Inspiration Consolidated Copper Company, not long ago. Steen's firm, which has headquarters in Phoenix, Arizona, strip-mines for copper in the Globe and Miami communities of Arizona. Steen has spoken out in opposition to what he calls unnecessary government regulation. He was asked in an interview if, in the absence of such regulation, he would expect his corporation to regulate itself.

"I certainly would," he replied. "I would make sure that we are not doing anything that's going to be harmful to the water or to the land. Our big kick is not whether we feel it's necessary to do anything or not. Our big kick is that the standards that are being set, and the regulations that are being promulgated, are far too stringent and unnecessary. They're not based on scientific facts. They're just taking arbitrary figures and arbitrary numbers and putting them in. We have to realize that the people in the U.S., and in any country, for that matter, can't exist without a sound economy. We can't all go back to the trees and exist off the land."

Government has been listening to such complaints as these all along, and a clear effort was mounted toward the end of the Carter administration to repeal and reduce much of the regulatory process that restrained industry from exploiting the environment in its old-fashioned, wholesale manner. (The Carter people, of course, put it in terms of "streamlining" the process in ways that wouldn't harm the environment.) But really traumatic, shocking changes came when the new administration of Ronald Reagan hit its stride. Environmentalists were almost universally horrified at the prospect of Reagan as President; there seemed to be some consensus that the man simply was not intellectually capable of understanding environmental issues. (When he was governor of California, he announced that 80 per cent of the nitrogen oxide pollution in the air was caused by vegetation, leading his critics to accuse

him of "blaming trees for smog." Reagan's most infantile statement so far is probably his 1966 comment: "A tree is a tree.
How many more do you need to look at?") A matter with
possibly even more serious implications than Reagan himself
was his selection of advisors and cabinet officers, none of
whom seemed in sympathy with trees, streams, deserts, mountains, or any other physical components of the planet, except
as they exist in order to be chopped, diverted, impounded,
irrigated, and mined. During Reagan's run for the presidency,
there was no environmental specialist working in the campaign. A staff member, asked by a reporter about all this, was
quoted as saying: "The federal government has lost its sense
of balance in this area. To achieve a sound environmental
policy, we should reexamine every regulatory requirement with
a commitment to simplify and streamline the process. Moreover, we should return to the states the primary responsibility
for environmental regulation."

Many of the observers of the political scene who were
sympathetic to environmental causes were heard to say, as
the new administration moved into Washington, that regardless
of its attitudes toward environmental issues, nothing truly *bad*
could happen. The achievements of what now was being called
"the environmental decade"—a bona fide era characterized by
awesome elevations of our consciousness about ecology and by
the equally impressive passage of legislation favorable to the
environment—were too deeply etched into our society to
admit repeal or undoing. There might be skirmishes, the observers said, but there would be no need for any more wars.

By the time the Reagan administration had completed its
first full year in office, however, it looked very much as if
repeal of the environmental era not only was a possibility but
might even be quite likely. Aided immeasurably by a Democratic opposition in and out of Congress that seemed at times
to be nonexistent and at other times uncertain of its obligation,
the President and the men who appeared to be formulating his
policies for him moved on a dozen fronts to undo not only the

environmental progress but also much of *everything* that had
been done before. The nation's economic structure, the status
of the poor, nuclear power, America's commitments to nutrition, civil rights, civil liberties, job safety, education, freedom
of information, and even the credibility of the Voice of
America—all these underwent massive changes, or attempted
massive changes, and all the changes were from the direction
of left or center to right. And among the programs that were
most savagely attacked were those dealing with the environment, and particularly those that had sought to protect or
preserve the environment by imposing some restraints on
industry.

The attacks on all these fronts were facilitated by the
fact that government in the recent past truly *had* imposed a lot
of useless, or needless, or stupid regulations on Americans'
lives and livelihoods, and that the bureaucracy *had* become
arrogant and officious past the point of toleration. If this had
not happened, Reagan might not have been elected in the
first place. But once he was, he wasted no time sharpening
his assault, and the assault was not on just the stupid regulations but on the idea of regulation in general.

The administration toyed for a while with the idea of
abolishing the Council on Environmental Quality, then settled
on cutting its staff from 50 to 16 and installing a new chairman
who pledged to communicate better with the business sector.
Reagan proposed cutting the budget of the U.S. Water Resources Council to zero. For the head of its Forest Service, the
administration chose a man who had been the chief lawyer for
the Louisiana-Pacific Corporation, the chief "harvester" of
timber from the national forests.

In the area of pollution, Reagan and his advisors showed
near-total subservience to industry. They sought to cut the
heart out of the Clean Air Act, and they started figuring out
ways to remove the federal government from the job of protecting wetlands. The Environmental Protection Agency, as

unresponsive as it already had become to its real mission, started developing into a real enemy of the environment.

Reagan's choice to run the EPA, Anne M. Gorsuch, was a former Colorado legislator who once had been quoted as saying that toxic wastes should be a responsibility of counties, rather than federal or state governments. After she settled into her new job, she demonstrated that her position had not changed all that much. At the top of her list of priorities, she said at one point, was the need for balancing environmental protection with energy and economic considerations.

Gorsuch soon showed what she meant by that. Enforcement of laws and regulations already on the books was de-emphasized by EPA, and both the administrator and her boss favored budget cuts for the agency so severe that environmentalists said EPA would be incapable of doing its job. Gorsuch's appointments reflected her philosophy with great clarity: Her general counsel was a lawyer for Exxon; associate administrators included lawyers who had worked for firms representing Dow Chemical and General Motors; her special assistant for hazardous waste had been a lawyer for the Adolph Coors Company, the enterprise of the right-wing Colorado brewer. Her chief of staff had been a lobbyist for the Johns-Manville Corporation, the asbestos manufacturer, and before that he had lobbied for the American Paper Institute. All that was missing was someone from Hooker Chemical.

One indication of the administration's attitude came early in 1982, when Reagan announced his intention to nominate, as head of the EPA program to implement the Superfund operation, the former director of communications for Aerojet-General Corporation. The corporation's own dump in Rancho Cordova, California, was on EPA's list of high-priority toxic waste sites.

EPA, in the meantime, tried to repeal its own rules to allow liquid toxic wastes in metal drums—the same sort of containers that deteriorate and spill their contents into the aquifers—to be buried in landfills. Its rationale, said the agency, was its belief "that the current prohibition is too extreme for real-world application."

And a congressional subcommittee learned that EPA officials had been holding private meetings with representatives of the chemical industry to discuss substances produced by the industry that the government agency is supposed to regulate. One environmental group, which was not invited to or informed of the meetings, complained that "the regulated industry is playing a predominant role in the effort to develop exemptions" to the toxic chemicals regulatory act "and to find ways around the requirements of the statute."

In late spring, 1981, the new EPA ordered its regional offices to stop requiring the cleanup of hazardous waste sites without first obtaining permission from the Washington office; then the Washington office started denying permission. A few weeks later EPA made it easier for industry to dispose of some mining and energy-production wastes in wells. In October of 1981, Philip Shabecoff of *The New York Times* reported that since the Reagan administration had come into power, the number of enforcement cases referred by EPA to the Justice Department for action had "slowed to a trickle." Shabecoff quoted an EPA spokesman as saying the agency wanted to encourage voluntary cleanup of hazardous waste sites. "This administration believes in a nonconfrontational mode," said the official, referring to cases involving the poisoning of Americans' drinking water. Later in October, EPA released a list of 115 hazardous waste sites that it called the worst in the nation—their proximity to drinking-water supplies was a major criterion—and that thus qualified for possible further action under the Superfund legislation.

But there was not the shadow of a certainty that the Environmental Protection Agency under Reagan would actually, actively pursue the operators of any of those sites, or that it would institute aggressive programs of cleaning them up, as the Superfund law specified. The tendency at EPA, it became increasingly clear, was to remain in the "nonconfrontational mode," even when human life was at stake and even as poisons seeped toward and into the aquifers that, once ruined, nobody knows how to repair.

The situation deteriorated further in February, 1982, when EPA announced the formation of a "task force" to accelerate the cleanup of hazardous waste sites. Such a "task force" was not really needed, since the agency already possessed the power to do the job; and, a closer examination of the "task force's" task revealed, its work would consist largely of writing polite letters to operators of dumps asking if they'd mind cleaning them up—and all of this would take place years after the operators, bureaucrats, and everyone else had been apprised and reapprised of the dangers the sites posed.

On the night that the "task force" announcement was made, an official of EPA and several experts gathered on public television's *MacNeil-Lehrer Report* to discuss the issue. Anthony Roisman, a toxic waste litigator at the Justice Department who had recently resigned because EPA had stopped sending him cases to prosecute, commented on the day's announcement: "I don't think there's any comparison between a letter-writing campaign, which is what EPA announced today, and an enforcement program."

William Sullivan, the head of the Reagan EPA's enforcement operation, replied that issuing the letters was a necessary first step in the enforcement process. Just give us some time, he said, and we'll outshine all the effort that's gone before. Responded Roisman:

"In Washington the regulated community's lawyers are telling the lawyers at the Justice Department and at EPA that they have a free pass. If they want to get something at EPA, they go and see the administrator, the deputy administrator, or Mr. Sullivan, and they won't get sued. That's what's happening." Sullivan denied the accusation. And the poisons seeped closer to the aquifers.

❖   ❖   ❖

Reagan's actions in appointing the sort of people he did to handle the nation's environmental problems, along with the crushing inaction that typified agencies such as EPA in their first year, served better than any other barometer to demonstrate the new administration's feelings about issues of land, air, and water. But with the appointment of James Watt as their Secretary of the Interior, Reagan and his advisors executed a masterstroke of communication. They were able to convey in one giant, simultaneous insult both their contempt for the natural world and their fawning allegiance to big, exploitative business.

Watt was an ex-bureaucrat, having worked in Interior before, for part of the time as the assistant secretary who oversees the work of the Bureau of Reclamation. But most recently he had been the president and chief legal officer of the Denver-based Mountain States Legal Foundation, a conservative organization that describes itself as "a non-profit public interest law center dedicated to bringing a balance to the courts in the defense of individual liberty and the private enterprise system." The foundation did not like to list the names of its contributors, but one of its early backers was Joseph Coors, of the brewery family, and there were several reports that mining and drilling interests were among the others. Ron Wolf, writing in *Rocky Mountain Magazine* about the new Secretary of the Interior, said his foundation had "picked up the reputation of being anticonsumer, antifeminist, antigovernment, antiblack, and, above all, antienvironmentalist."

Watt's stated position on environmental issues, after his appointment, was a relatively simple one: America needs a program for "developing and utilizing the tremendous energy resources our nation possesses." The program, he has said, should be an environmentally sound one. Unless such a program is started now, unduly restrictive environmental regulations will keep the resources from being developed, and pressures will grow. Eventually the nation will find itself in a crisis, and the only solution possible then will be a crash program of development that would do real environmental harm. All he wants, says Watt, is to restore the balance between environment and development.

All of which sounds as if it might have a grain or two of truth in it, until one examines the list of things Watt favored in his first year in office. He said he wanted the nation to provide less money to help states and cities buy land for parks; he advocated ending federal land acquisition for the National Park System; he spoke in favor of (and later seemed to deny it) ending National Park involvement in urban recreation lands; he favored permitting gas and oil exploration on public lands, some of which were being studied for possible designation as wilderness areas; he approved of giving "the corporate sector the opportunity to explore the mineral potential on public lands"; he wanted to soften strip-mining regulations and return most of the regulatory power to the states (which have allowed and encouraged strip mining to get to the atrocious point it's at now); he wanted to expand offshore oil and gas drilling.

Watt's own appointments, like Reagan's, were sure tip-offs of his commitment to the environmental side of his proposed balancing act. They included lobbyists for and executives of the electric power industry, assorted lawyers and bureaucrats, and an ex-lobbyist for paper companies. Watt's choice to head the Office of Surface Mining, James R. Harris, was a former superintendent in a strip mine. Andy Paszlor, writing in *The Wall Street Journal*, reported that Harris, an Indiana legislator, had benefited from land deals with big coal producers. The deals, reported Paszlor, were "potentially worth millions of dollars" and were arranged while Harris was chairing the legislature's committee that oversees strip-mining laws and legislation.

Watt quickly became one of the handful of Reagan administration officials who were considered "controversial" and "newsworthy" and always to be relied on for a provocative quote. He seemed to be sort of a double reincarnation of Spiro Agnew and Martha Mitchell, although he lacked their sense of humor. It was obvious, in his public statements and appearances before congressional committees, that he felt a religious zeal toward "preserving" the environment by "developing" it. The natural world, he told one committee, is a "resource base," and the Secretary of the Interior was its "guardian." "We have to get to those resources and develop them," he added.

The federal role in matters of groundwater, he said in answer to a congressman's question, should be "Little, if any." And, in another statement, he was quoted as saying: "We're running the parks under outmoded concepts. We can learn a great deal from Walt Disney's crowd management principles." And: "I don't like to paddle, and I don't like to walk."

Watt apparently hated environmentalists (and he seemed to receive real pleasure in making them, or any of his other critics, angry). In a speech he gave while at the Mountain States Legal Foundation, Watt said: "Today, there is a new political force in the land—a small group of extremists who don't concern themselves with balanced perspective or improvement in the quality of life for mankind. They are called the environmentalists. . . . Today, the extremists—the environmentalists—are opposed to and are fighting this needed orderly development [of Western natural resources]. I fear that our states may be ravaged as a result of the actions of the environmentalists—the greatest threat to the ecology of the West." And, with just a brushstroke of McCarthyism, Watt wondered out loud about "the real motive of these extreme environmentalists." Was it, he wondered, "to weaken America?"

"My responsibility," Watt told a reporter for *The Wall Street Journal* after he had been appointed the guardian of the resource base, "is to follow the Scriptures, which call upon us to occupy the land until Jesus returns."

This raises the question of what Jesus' reaction will be when He sees the public's land littered with the logical outcome of James Watt's philosophy: the strip mines, off-road vehicles, snowmobiles, oil and gas drilling rigs, ghastly water projects, the corpses of extinct species, and the pitiful, naked stumps of clearcut forests. Jesus, it is written, spent more than a month of meditation in the wilderness before Watt became its guardian, and probably has a good idea of what one should look like.

Even a national administration bent on repealing the environmental progress of two decades could not realize that unworthy goal if proper leadership at the local level existed to protect the streams, lakes, aquifers, and the rest of the systems that keep us alive. But such leadership is hard to find. Too often it is just a reflection of the sort of misplaced local boosterism that excuses the environmental excesses, the aerial stench and the watery discharges, of the factory in Savannah that makes paper bags by referring to the plant's disgusting presence as "the sweet smell of money." And too often it is just a reflection of the sort of attitude that so frequently gets rewarded by election to office—as in the statement of Massachusetts Congressman Edward P. Boland, during hearings on attempts to clean up rivers: "But there have to be trade-offs here, too. At some point in time we must consider what the cost really is and whether we can actually stand it; whether business can stand it, and whether it is really worth it." Or the comment by Senator John Heinz of Pennsylvania—the state that, next to New Jersey, most closely resembles an environmental Dresden—that acid rain's a problem, and that Pennsylvania seems to get more than its share of it, but that Pennsylvania also produces a lot of the coal that is believed to produce the acid rain, and so he would hope that "we do not place an unreasonable burden on those industries whose continued vitality is crucial to meeting the nation's energy needs." Virtually every poll that is taken of Americans on the subject shows an overwhelming sentiment toward environmental protection, even at the cost of some of the luxuries the public has been urged to take for granted. But the politicians and technocrats do not listen.

In such an atmosphere, the situation—and the quality of the water—can only deteriorate. Strip miners are already lusting after Minnesota's Boundary Waters Canoe Area, one of the last pristine places left in the lower forty-eight, and Exxon wanted to strip the Grand Canyon for uranium but changed its mind only when its preliminary exploration was unsuccessful.

Not only does industry want public lands; it also wants public money to do its prospecting. Occidental Petroleum, the parent company of Hooker Chemical, of Love Canal, Lathrop, Long Island, Montague, and Suwannee River fame, has been in considerable trouble with the law, not all of it for environmental reasons. Occidental, wrote Judith Miller in *The New York Times*, "is believed to be the only company among the nation's 500 largest to have been formally investigated" by the Securities and Exchange Commission "four times in the last 10 years."

Armand Hammer, the head of Occidental, generally gets soft or even admiring treatment in the press because he doesn't fit into the dull, boring mold of the stereotypical chief executive officer. He is, for example, a big collector of art. (The custodians of the public prints seemed to miss the irony involved when Hammer, the ultimate head of the company that has been accused of contaminating wells and water supplies across the entire nation, spent $5,126,000 in a December, 1980, auction for the Leonardo da Vinci notebook titled "Of the Nature, Weight, and Movement of Water.") Hammer also is a big patron of the political arts. In 1975 he pleaded guilty in federal court to a charge of making illegal contributions of $54,000, in others' names, to Richard Nixon's 1972 presidential campaign.

Occidental paid no federal income tax in 1978. But freedom from taxes, frequent violations of the law, and an inclina-

tion to conduct its business any way it sees fit, environment or
no environment, have not been enough. Occidental must also
receive taxpayers' money for its good works. The Department
of Energy agreed to kick in more than half the expenses of
Occidental's oil shale project, which has been estimated to
cost $1,000,000,000. (Occidental refers to this as "a cost-
sharing cooperative arrangement.")

Occidental has another "cooperative" arrangement, of
sorts, at Love Canal. In January of 1980, New York State
Comptroller Edward V. Regan approved a loan to Hooker
Chemical of $13,200,000 in money he controls. It seems that
Hooker wanted to build a regional headquarters in Niagara
Falls (perhaps as a monument to the tragedy at Love Canal?).
Regan said he did have some reservations at first about
Hooker's "social responsibility" but that in the end he decided
that subsidizing Hooker's construction project was "in the
public interest" and "absolutely vital" to the Niagara Falls
economy, which, like many of the people whose lives have
been forever twisted by what Hooker Chemical has done, has
been severely depressed.

20

American industry, it may easily be concluded, is virtually immune to serious regulation and control when it comes to exploiting the environment, as well as to punishment when its exploitation violates the law. But industry does not always have its way with the environment. Even Occidental Petroleum lost out in Cerrillos, New Mexico.

Cerrillos is what some might call a beautiful little village, situated about two-thirds of the way from Albuquerque to Santa Fe. It is on the back road, well off the interstate. The village is a dusty collection of frame and adobe dwellings, unpaved streets, and a few business places, and it is because of its unpretentiousness that only *some* might pronounce it beautiful. As with much of the Southwest, one either likes it a lot or doesn't like it at all. The town is properly known as Los Cerrillos, which means "Little Hills"; this is the name, too, for the rocky outcroppings that rise on the village's north side. Up beyond Santa Fe, twenty-three miles to the north, the Sangre de Cristo mountain range marks the beginning of the end of the southern extremes of the Rocky Mountains. Thirty-nine miles to the south, near Albuquerque, the Rockies expire in the Sandia Mountains. In between there are Los Cerrillos. On a clear day—and there are many such days in this mile-high terrain—one can see all three sets of mountains, along with a fourth clump of hills, the Ortiz Mountains, just to the south of Cerrillos. To the first-time visitor, all the mountains may look alike, but to the student of this land, a combination of high plains and desert, each is individual.

The visitor, if he or she is from the East, also might pronounce the land around Cerrillos "barren." The soil is sandy and dry, and it encourages little in the way of vegetation. In the bottoms, willows and cottonwoods search ravenously for scarce moisture; elsewhere there is juniper and piñon and desert-type grasses, along with rabbit brush, Apache plume, and saltbush. All of nature's populations that choose to live here do so, but there is not much congregating; the natural scarcity of water sees to that. Human habitations, too, are few and far between, and the rest of the living creatures—rodents, coyotes, foxes, mule deer, the many sorts of lizards, golden eagles, the occasional bobcat—ration the life-sustaining substances that are available. The relative lack of water is the most obvious fact of life. There are sharply eroded, sandy-bottomed gullies, called arroyos in the West, that remain dry most of the year but that turn into channels of fast-moving torrents during the rainy season, from June until September, when most of the region's yearly average of 10 inches of rain falls. The village is built beside one of those arroyos, the Rio Galisteo, which drains, when it is running, into the Rio Grande about ten miles to the west.

Cerrillos and its environs have attracted miners for a very long time. Pueblo potters apparently dug lead from the ground there to use in their paint. Later, turquoise was extracted from the earth and the blue stones played important parts in the prehistoric Indian economy. Francisco Vásquez de Coronado, the Spanish explorer, came up the Rio Grande in the 1540s and turned east on the Rio Galisteo, searching for precious metals. The Indians, who did not want the outsiders to exploit what they considered their birthright, hid the entrances to their turquoise and lead mines and provided guides who eventually led the explorers off to Kansas. The whites did not stay away long, however; later expeditions were aimed not at minerals but at the Indians' souls, and many of those who resisted conversion by the missionaries of peace and brotherhood were murdered by them, while the rest were turned into slaves. Little by little, the white man took over, and by the time gold was discovered in the Ortiz Mountains, in 1828, there were plenty of whites there to prospect for it. Within sixty-five years mining was the way of life in the area, with coal, zinc, lead, silver, gold, and copper staple items in Cerrillos' life. Gradually the mines petered out—or, more correctly, it became financially unfeasible to continue searching for the quantities of minerals and metals that remained—and Cerrillos lapsed into a sort of sluggish, unpaved, unpainted existence. The town's population, which had risen to nearly 700 during the mining boom, stabilized at around 230, with most of the residents commuting to jobs elsewhere and few of them able to exhibit any visible signs of wealth. The single most important community institution in Cerrillos was, and still is, the Turquoise Trail Volunteer Fire Department—important because the region's dryness, and the frame construction of most of its habitations, makes fire a major danger.

During the late sixties and early seventies Cerrillos was discovered by some members of that young generation of Americans who were called "hippies," many of whom were artistically inclined in one way or another. Those who painted and sculptured were particularly drawn to the place—New Mexico has always attracted such artists. Some were dropouts who seemed not inclined to support themselves in any way, while others were dedicated craftsmen and craftswomen. The residents who were of Spanish background, who made up about two-thirds of Cerrillos's population, soon learned to distinguish between the two categories of newcomers. Cerrillos was attractive to others, as well: In 1970 a couple arrived who were quite un-hippie in their demeanor. The man was Brigadier General Samuel McC. Goodwin, United States Army, retired, a West Pointer with a distinguished record that included serving as a horse cavalryman, duty in George Patton's Army, then Berlin, Korea, the Pentagon, and assignments to the Army and National War Colleges. General Goodwin and his wife, Kiki, purchased a piece of land near Cerrillos which they named Crossed Sabres Ranch. When Goodwin would go into Cerrillos to pick up the mail, at a tiny post office amongst the few dwellings, he could be spotted a mile away as a military man, just from his erect posture and purposeful bearing. He was obviously not given to slouching, either physically or in his thinking. He and his wife chose Cerrillos for their retirement in a methodical manner; as he put it not long ago, in an interview at his ranch: "After thirty-five years of service to our great country, Mrs. Goodwin and I made a reconnaissance of six or eight places in this land, and northern New Mexico was one, and we found here what we thought we were looking for; and the setting is part of the culmination of those dreams and ambitions and, we think, the rewards of all the effort and time and energy we devoted to serving the country." Asked what they had found, he thought a moment and replied: "Well, I think first it's the environment. I'm healthier and feel better toward myself and my fellow men at the altitudes above four or five thousand feet. It's almost six thousand right here. It's the openness, the spaciousness, the dispersion of people and houses. And we're out here in the country, twenty-five miles from Santa Fe, because I don't *want* my neighbors to look in my windows and vice versa. I want the freedom to do and go and come according to *my* particular desires and choosings. Yet I want the proximity of that delightful little minuscule cosmopolitan area of Santa Fe, with its cultural advantages, its good restaurants, theater, music, and people."

Goodwin was, to be sure, the only brigadier general in Cerrillos, or even for miles around, but his feelings about the place were fairly typical of all those who had come to Cerrillos in recent years, and probably typical of those, less affluent, who had been there all along. They were examples of those whom Abel Davis, the head of the Santa Fe Federation, had identified as the newcomers who came to the area, liked what they saw, and decided to move there on the land's, rather than their own, terms. Cerrillos's "own terms" included, for most of those who chose to live there, a special way of looking at water.

The dryness of the place, as elsewhere in much of the Southwest, was the single most important constraint on anything that goes by the name of "development" or "growth," be it industrial or residential. Water in and around Cerrillos comes, for a few, from wells; from springs on which humans have depended since Indian times; and from a rickety water system built in the 1890s by the Atchison, Topeka and Santa Fe Railroad, whose tracks pass alongside the town. A small dam two and a half miles from Cerrillos traps water from a spring; from there a pipe delivers about 150 gallons of water a minute to the town. About half of the water is lost because of leaks in the delivery system, and so the Cerrillos system has, in its way, a lot in common with the water systems of New York City and the Florida Keys. Some residents have in-the-house connections to the line that comes down from the reservoir, while others must bring drums and jugs to the system's central point to fill with water. It does not take long for a stranger in Cerrillos to appreciate the importance of water there. A visitor a few years ago was talking to Ross Lockridge, Annie Murray, and Dierdre Hazelrigg, who were among the artists who have settled in and around Cerrillos, and Hazelrigg asked if he'd like a cup of tea. The tea-making ceremony, it developed, included the hostess's hoisting a five-gallon jerry can of water up to the kitchen sink (a sink that had a drain but no faucets) and carefully pouring the liquid into the kettle.

Hoisting the jerry cans is a chore, as is hauling them into town, or to a friend's place in Santa Fe, once a week for refilling. But Dierdre Hazelrigg and the other people who have chosen to live in and around Cerrillos accepted that as part of their lives when they moved there. The trouble that one had to go to in order to obtain water was, in fact, a part of the attraction: It helped to discourage the sort of development that many of these people were trying to avoid. It was little enough of a price to pay for the environment they loved so much. And then, in the mid-seventies, Occidental Mining, or Oxymin, a component of Occidental Petroleum, let it be known that it was interested in obtaining copper from the ground near Cerrillos. Oxymin was not talking about mining in the traditional, deep-shaft manner, or even in stripping the earth. It wanted to get the copper by means of a brand-new process that was more chemical than it was mechanical—and that involved pouring as much as 100 tons per day of sulfuric acid, which is poisonous, into the ground. The process, said an Oxymin spokesman later, was "experimental. This was the first time it would have been done."

Not only would the acid be in close association with the water table near Cerrillos; Occidental's experiment was specifically designed to allow the acid to flow *through* the aquifer. (The company spokesman tended way from such a description, pointing out that the acid would be intercepted by drainage devices. A company-drawn schematic plan for the project, however, clearly shows the solution passing through the water table. And a company-commissioned report on the project says the main collection tunnel would be "250' or more beneath the water table.") And, to make matters worse, large quantities of water would be needed to run the process—enough, according to one estimate, to provide for the domestic water needs of 9,500 to 15,000 people. And all of this was going to happen in a place where people had trained themselves to get by on maybe 10 gallons of water per person per day.

The plan for Occidental's "Cerrillos Project," as it was known, was described in great detail in the company-commissioned study, which also included reports on its possible effects on the environment and other facets of life around Cerrillos. The report called it "an in-place (in-situ) chemical extraction of a low-grade oxide copper digest which occurs about 1.8 miles north of Cerrillos, New Mexico."

First, the porous rock which contained the copper deposits would be fractured by blasting. Then a dilute solution of sulfuric acid would be applied to the ground surface. This would percolate down through the ore, combining with the copper as it went. The solution would drip into the aquifer and then into an underground collection system which depended, in part, on the presumed flow patterns of groundwater. The resulting solution would be pumped out of the ground and further processed: Detinned scrap iron cans would be used to draw off the copper, which then would be sent to market. Oxymin estimated that its operation would last from four to ten years. In addition to the leaching process itself, roads would be built and blasting would occur. There was a report that, in order to sweeten the pot, Oxymin would reconstruct the town's water distribution system, free of charge. Contamination of the aquifer by the mining process, said Oxymin, would be prevented, but the corporation was not too clear about how this would be accomplished. The report commissioned by the company did note, however, that "Effects of the Cerrillos Project on water quality might occur if toxic leachate solutions are not properly collected and processed." And at a later point: "There is little doubt that water is the most precious of all natural resources in New Mexico, and that the proposed Oxymin project has the potential to utilize and affect the ground water resources near Cerrillos to a significant degree." But the project might also have an effect on the future of mining: "It is probable," said the report, in the stilted prose of such documents, "that resource extraction methods will increasingly turn to in-place processing of undeveloped ore bodies, provided that the Cerrillos Project and others like it prove to be economically and environmentally sound."

These finding were certainly less than reassuring to many of the residents of Cerrillos and the surrounding hills. They formed an organization named Concerned Citizens of Cerrillos and, in the manner of such single-issue, community-based groups, started producing public statements and attending hearings. In one such statement, the citizens declared that they were opposed to Oxymin's mining plans because of "the proximity to the only water supply of the . . . area and the lack of an alternative water supply; the lack of any positive assurance that this project will not permanently pollute, damage, or destroy the existing water supply; the probability of damage to historic buildings and houses (adobe and stone); the possibility of destroying existing water holes used by wild and domestic animals." Other statements expressed fears over the "untested technology" involved in the use of acid on the ground, the "unknown impact" of the blasting, the "use of prohibitive quantities of water," and, "last but not least, the failure of Oxymin to make any guarantees to the people most likely to be directly affected by their project." The Concerned Citizens organization was careful to point out that it did not oppose mining *per se* (for many of the older residents of Cerrillos had once made their livings in the mines), but rather the *sort* of mining that Occidental was proposing. Opposition came, too, from the nearby Santo Domingo Indian pueblo.

General Goodwin was not among those who opposed the project. As he explained it, he was aware that the mining might have an effect on his surroundings, but he knew Oxymin had a right to do it. "I was aware of its potential impact on me," he said, "but I also am old enough and, I think, mature enough to recognize that the world demand for copper is important and it's for the betterment of mankind. And the proposal of Occidental Mining to take copper was a logical consequence of the free-enterprise system of the United States and of the free world. Furthermore, I knew that they were legally entitled to do this." The general, who is the sort of person who is naturally inquisitive about whatever goes on around him, learned what he could about the on-site leaching process. Even though he quickly saw that the weak link was Oxymin's plan for collecting the leachate after it had gone through the aquifer, he did not oppose the project. In addition to the free-enterprise argument, he knew that Cerrillos was economically depressed and many of its jobless residents were miners. "Furthermore," he said, "I knew that Occidental Mining, if properly approached, would rebuild the water system of the village, which is antique at best and unsafe in other aspects. It's inadequate to support even the population that's there."

It was generally known that Oxymin's first step, while its applications for various permits were pending, would be to detonate an experimental blast to fracture copper-bearing rock. The blast, which had the strength of 50 tons of dynamite, was conducted just after dawn on a January, 1977, morning, and the secrecy of Oxymin's schedule did little to reassure residents about the company's good intentions. The blast, moreover, helped focus local and state attention on *all* of Occidental's plans, and a number of questions were raised by state agencies about the effects of the project on the water table. As the New Mexico Environmental Improvement Agency put it, in the unhuman style of technocracy, "the leachate collection system is central to questions of potentially adverse ground water quality impacts resulting from the project."

Opposition to what Occidental wanted to do, meantime, gathered strength. The leadership of the Santo Domingo pueblo announced that it viewed the project as a defacement of the Indians' "aboriginal land area." Others expressed fears that it would damage the state's archaeological history. Some elements of the press complained, too. The *Rio Grande Weekly* ran an article recounting the life and times of Occidental's president, Armand Hammer, and commenting that "Hammer's history of doing what he considers to be in Oxy's interest, without regard for the law or people involved, is what concerns Cerrillos and Santo Domingo Pueblo residents. Shady deals are not new to Hammer, and sometimes he's been caught."

Oxymin had little difficulty in obtaining approval from State Engineer Steve Reynolds for its plans to appropriate groundwater—about 2,350,000 gallons—for the first stages of its project. But another water matter produced a much larger obstacle. The company needed a permit from the state Environmental Improvement Agency before it could pour its acids onto the ground. The agency had to be satisfied that such discharges would not harm the aquifer. Oxymin's application for the discharge permit was the first to be reviewed publicly under the new state law that established the permit process.

In hearings at Santa Fe in July, 1977, the manager of the Cerrillos project, Robert L. Akright, testified that Oxymin's plans for the test project were "environmentally safe." Others, representing the Concerned Citizens of Cerrillos, argued that the company's processes were inadequate and could not guarantee that the groundwater would not be damaged. One of them, Marc Simmons, a historian, testified, in part: "The issue at these hearings seems to be: Are Oxymin's methods and technology, as set forth in this discharge plan, sophisticated enough to reduce the risk to acceptable levels? Presumably, when Oxymin demonstrates that its technology can control the leachate, this plan or a revised plan will be accepted. The experts will have spoken and we in the Cerrillos area will be expected to accept the fact that technology will protect us and our water supply.

". . . technology *does* have its limits. If you doubt that, then you may consult the survivors of the Teton Dam disaster, who I am certain had been assured by engineers and technocrats that that dam could not break. It did break, as you know, and many people paid with their lives. Now comes Oxymin to the village of Cerrillos, proposing to do experimental and potentially hazardous testing with acid leachate less than two miles from this small community. It offers no legally binding guarantees that it will make good on damage that present residents may suffer, and indeed, if damage did occur to the underground water table, there is no one I have found who can say with 100 per cent certainty that the damage *could* be repaired.

"If Oxymin is running any risk itself, I have not been able to determine it. On the contrary, since I am wholly dependent on the Cerrillos water system, it is I who am being asked to take the risk—I and everyone else who lives in that area. But

I do not choose to play games or gamble with my water supply when I have everything to lose and nothing to gain. Why should I and others like me be called upon to place ourselves in this unenviable position, just so Oxymin can take a few million dollars back to Denver?"

On August 26, 1977, the state environmental agency concluded that Occidental should not have the permit. In a letter to Oxymin's Robert Akright, EIA director Thomas E. Baca wrote that the firm's plans for dealing with poisonous discharges were "inadequate" and pointed out that additional information requested by the state had not been supplied by Oxymin. "Oxymin failed to demonstrate that the design of the collection system was adequate to insure the total collection of leachate," wrote Baca, "even though the Corporation relied on this assumption." He added that leachate that was not collected would have several possible avenues into the groundwater. The decision was a clear victory for the Concerned Citizens of Cerrillos, but their celebration was a guarded one. Rejection of the application for a permit did not necessarily mean Occidental would leave Cerrillos.

In the months following the denial of the permit, Occidental kept a low profile and the Concerned Citizens of Cerrillos assumed that the firm was attempting to devise ways to continue its experiment, in which it had sunk $3,000,000. Early in 1978, Concerned Citizens announced that on February 17 they would present a petition to New Mexico Governor Jerry Apodaca protesting Oxymin's continued presence. It was not to be an ordinary petition: This one would be signed by more than 200 New Mexico artists and craftspeople, including Georgia O'Keeffe, Eliot Porter, Willem de Kooning, and Fritz Scholder, and its presentation would coincide with the opening of an exhibition of Armand Hammer's art collection in the Denver Art Museum on the following day. An announcement of CCC's plans noted: "Artists, drawn by the serenity and natural beauty of this area, have traditionally made New Mexico their studio. It is the hope of the 200-plus artists represented by this petition that Dr. Hammer, noted art patron and collector, will take notice of the threat that his subsidiary company poses to the artists and residents of the Cerrillos area."

Three days later, a spokesman for Occidental Minerals announced that the firm was suspending indefinitely its project to mine copper experimentally by pouring sulfuric acid onto the ground. The low cost of copper and the high cost of meeting environmental regulations were the reasons, said the spokesman; the petition had nothing to do with the decision. A few days later, Occidental announced that it was leasing part of its Cerrillos property to an Albuquerque contractor who wanted to seek a lead-zinc vein "by conventional underground methods."

The artists of Cerrillos were relieved. They had spent much of the previous three years not painting pictures and making sculpture, or weaving or photographing nature, but fighting a huge corporation that was used to having its way. Now, it appeared that they had won; now, it appeared that they could get back to work on other things, to living their lives in a place where water was extremely scarce but where they had made their accommodations to that fact, and where they, more than most people, had taken the time to understand the precarious balance between humans and the rest of nature. It was, as everybody seemed to be saying after Occidental pulled out, a place where nature simply could not afford to let industry come in. The water was simply too precious for that.

III

Water and Pork

21

It seems incredible, considering the role that water plays in keeping humanity alive, healthy, and comfortable, but the substance has had no formal system of defenders, no great body of laws and customs that will prevent it from coming to harm. A suggestion that such a system be established was made a decade ago by a professor at the University of Southern California law school, Christopher D. Stone, in a law review article which Stone later expanded into a book, *Should Trees Have Standing? Toward Legal Rights for Natural Objects*. In the book, Stone announced that he was "quite seriously proposing that we give legal rights to forests, oceans, rivers, and other so-called 'natural objects' in the environment —indeed, to the natural environment as a whole." Stone's argument found a strong partisan in the late Supreme Court Justice William O. Douglas, a fierce environmentalist, who cited the professor's article in 1972 in a dissent in a California case known as *Mineral King*, in which conservationists tried to keep promoters of a Walt Disney amusement park from damaging part of the Sierra Nevada mountains. "The critical question of 'standing' would be simplified and also put neatly into focus," wrote Douglas, "if we fashioned a federal rule that allowed environmental issues to be litigated before federal agencies or federal courts in the name of the inanimate object about to be despoiled, defaced, or invaded by roads and bulldozers and where injury is the subject of public outrage. Contemporary public concern for protecting nature's ecological equilibrium should lead to the conferral of standing upon environmental objects to sue for their own preservation."

The logic of the professor and the Supreme Court justice is overwhelming. Just as our legal and ethical systems recognize the standing of individuals and corporations, of transit authorities and savings and loan associations, of religious institutions and accused murderers, there should be some legal assumption that applies to a pine tree, a mountaintop, a salt marsh—and, especially, to a body of water, whether it be a fast-flowing Appalachian stream, a Great Lake, a transient puddle in the West, or an underground aquifer. There should be an assumption that that substance, inarticulate and unhuman though it may be, has a right to exist, unmolested and untainted by what we might think of, correctly or not, as civilization.

Such a right does not now exist, either in law or in the minds of those who are supposed to guide society. And until very recently, there have been relatively few people who sought to intervene on behalf of water—who were sufficiently mindful of water's precarious situation that they would be willing to go into court or onto picket lines in order to protect this most precious of substances. Without the help of these people, who almost universally are known (in some cases contemptuously) as "environmentalists," water has been able to react to the assaults on it by exploiters only in very negative ways: It dries up and disappears if people use it too prodigiously, stretch it too thin. It turns, temporarily, to poison if people abuse its quality much beyond clear, easily understood limits.

Even though the simple truths of those facts have been known since the human society first roamed the world, there has been little heed paid to them. Rivers have always been treated as plunder—as convenient outlets, little more than plumbing, where water may be taken for whatever project someone thinks should be undertaken, and as convenient receptacles for the wastes of the systems that give us our all-important "lifestyles." The estuaries have been perfect for spanning with bridges and causeways, for filling in so that petroleum tank farms and gasoline refineries might be erected, for luring those with money and a yen for a second home. The lakes have served as perfect places for dumping our raw sewage, industrial poisons, and mining leftovers. Water, the universal solvent, the substance with no legal standing and very few defenders, has turned out to be the perfect fall guy, the universal victim. And it has served quite well as a convenient, low-overhead device by which fortunes might be made, by which speculators might increase their riches even further, and by which control of and title to the land, always helpful in making fortunes, might be snatched from its rightful owners. Industry and private business, as well as corporate agriculture, have done their bits to exploit water in the United States, but when it comes to wholesale destruction of the watery environment, the biggest exploiter of them all is the United States government.

The government's agencies that are dedicated to building things make Occidental Petroleum and its subsidiaries look like kindergarten competitors. The record of federal water-project construction is replete not only with accounts of flood control, hydroelectric power generation, increased opportunities for flat-water recreation and the like, but also with examples of falsification, misrepresentation, exaggeration, concealment, stupidity, greed, land grabbing, and usurpation of power without authority. There exists in our nation today no sorrier example of government's cynicism, its arrogance, its low opinion of its citizens, its willingness to improve the lot of a few at the expense of the many, and its lust for getting what it wants, even when proper analysis cannot possibly justify it, by fabricating the facts that are needed. There exists in the United States no institutionalized rip-off that has burrowed more deeply into the flesh of society than this one. In comparison to the billions that have been misspent on water projects, Watergate does, indeed, seem a "third-rate burglary attempt," and the Abscam carnival appears penny-ante. Corporate embezzlement pales by comparison. The system that is responsible for this travesty is well known, universally tolerated, frequently discussed in polite conversation, routinely assailed by politicians when they are running for office and treated with religious awe by the same politicians after they are elected. Every high school civics student knows its name: It is pork-barrel politics. It is practiced in full public view by members of the Congress and the Administration, and yet it is in the same league with industry's dumping poisons into an aquifer. The system works quite simply: The agencies that do the building dream up projects to do, usually in consultation with local movers and shakers who stand to gain financially from the projects. Members of Congress seek to get legislation passed, first authorizing, then providing funds for, the projects. Success is virtually guaranteed by the fact that members of Congress are well represented in the scheme; if a member opposes someone else's pet project, no matter how insane or destructive it may be, he or she is inviting certain retaliation. It is this aspect of the system—the fact that congressmen use their voting power over each other's pet programs to make sure that *their* favorites get money—that is the heart of pork-barrel politics. The entire process is supported financially by annual mandatory contributions from the taxpayers, and its beneficiaries are realtors, land speculators, large corporations, barge operators, construction companies, the congressmen themselves and their staffs, outboard-motor salesmen, bankers, lawyers, and those members of the justice business who specialize in serving eviction notices on farmers and other landowners. Its proponents (who could be invested with a collective title such as "the builders") never hesitate to point out also that a prime beneficiary is "the economy," inasmuch as many job slots are created by these projects, from bulldozer operator to civil engineer to motel chambermaid. And, of course (although the proponents hardly ever mention this), there is the most extensive occupational boost of them all—to the members of the eternal bureaucracies themselves.

A mid-seventies listing of those federal agencies with programs concerning water as it relates to energy alone had twenty-three names on it. The agencies and their missions ranged from the Bureau of Reclamation, which has been building and operating water projects in the Western states since 1902, to the Office of Saline Water, which was trying to figure out ways to recover energy from brines, to the Bonneville Power Administration, which, according to the listing, was involved in cloud seeding in Hungry Horse Basin, Montana, until the experiment was halted "due to heavy precipitation."

Undoubtedly, there are dozens more agencies, offices, departments, and divisions within the government that do not have direct connections with energy and that might properly be included in any list of "the builders." But the major ones—the ones that do the most building, that engage in the most exploitation and destruction, and that are most skilled at manipulating the contents of the pork barrel—are the Army Corps of Engineers, the Bureau of Reclamation (or, as it now prefers to be known, the Water and Power Resources Service), and the Tennessee Valley Authority.

The Bureau of Reclamation, or BuRec, as many know it, which is a part of the Department of the Interior, was created by the Reclamation Act of 1902, which authorized the interior secretary "to locate, construct, operate and maintain works for the storage, diversion, and development of waters for the reclamation of arid and semi-arid lands in the western United States." In testimony before Congress in 1975, a former commissioner of the Bureau, Gilbert G. Stamm, described his agency's mission as assisting "the states, local governments, and other federal agencies to stabilize and stimulate local and regional economies, enhance and protect the environment, and improve the quality of life for mankind, all through development and management of water and related land resources." BuRec's history has clearly shown that it feels the environment may be "enhanced" and the quality of life "improved" only through those other key words: "development" and "management." To wit: building dams; flooding valleys; providing irrigation water, subsidized by the taxpayers, to corporate farmers; and, in general, making sure that no drop of water west of the Mississippi runs emancipated for very long. At the end of the calendar year 1980, BuRec had 9,075 employees. Money appropriated for its Fiscal Year 1981 budget totalled $790,811,000, and BuRec was asking for a supplemental appropriation of $24,250,000. Another $74,769,000 was coming in that year from some of the users of some of the agency's projects—irrigators, electricity users, and municipalities and industries—so that the annual budget, including also carryovers from the previous year, was more than $900,000,000.

BuRec, like all of the builders, has been devoted to building for so long that it has created an astonishing definition of "the environment"—a natural world that, in its mind, is actually *enhanced* (the word that the builders use so often) by the construction of dams and irrigation canals, by the corruption of free-flowing streams into placid, warm-water reservoirs. Commissioner Stamm, in his testimony to Congress, noted during a discussion of "environmental enhancement" that "Water resource projects have many positive environmental effects. When water management practices regulate and augment low flows of rivers and streams, decrease erosion, prevent floods, eliminate waste of water, and in many instances change deserts into gardens where man can comfortably live and prosper," he said, "the result is betterment of environmental conditions."

Similar gobbledygook runs through the rhetoric of the Corps of Engineers, which, like BuRec, in recent years has had to make at least verbal concessions toward that pesky problem of "the environment." A 1977 publication by the Corps on its commitment to the environment asserts that the agency wants "to preserve the unique and important ecological, esthetic, and cultural values of our national heritage; to conserve and use wisely the natural resources of our nation for the benefit of present and future generations; to restore, maintain, and enhance the natural and manmade environment in terms of productivity, variety, spaciousness, beauty, and other measures of quality"; and "to create new opportunities for the American people to enjoy the environment and the use of our natural resources." The brochure didn't go into detail on how this last act of creation will be performed, but it almost certainly has to do with bulldozers, concrete, pork barrels, and allied tools of the enhancer's trade.

It is likely that a typical American citizen thinks of the Corps of Engineers as a regiment or so of army officers and enlisted men who build pontoon bridges in time of war and keep waterways dredged during peacetime. In actuality the agency comprises about 300 officers and 30,000 civilians, all of them terribly hard at work thinking up new excuses to stay in business. There are ample opportunities to come up with such reasons for existence, given the Corps's many-faceted official mission. According to a fact sheet on itself, the Corps maintains that its Chief of Engineers "has responsibility for investigating, developing, and maintaining the nation's water and related environmental resources; constructing and operating projects for navigation, flood control, major drainage, shore and beach restoration and protection, hurricane flood protection, related hydroelectric power development, water supply, water quality control, fish and wildlife conservation and enhancement, and outdoor recreation; responding to emergency relief activities directed by other federal agencies; administering laws for the protection and preservation of navigable waters, and emergency flood control and shore protection." Much of the decision-making power for the Corps is vested in district offices, or "field operating agencies," as headquarters calls them; they are perfectly situated to engage in congressional pork-barreling.

The Tennessee Valley Authority, too, is ever mindful of the source of the pork; in the Knoxville offices of several of its executives, maps are prominently displayed, clearly showing the congressional district lines for TVA's huge slice of the pork pie: the 40,910-square-mile watershed of the Tennessee River, which covers parts of seven Southeastern states.

TVA was created by Congress in 1933 in order to oversee the enormous task of putting the Tennessee Valley, one of the nation's more chronically-afflicted regions, on a better economic footing. The 1933 legislation sought, in its words, "To improve the navigability and to provide for the flood control of the Tennessee River; to provide for reforestation and the proper use of marginal lands in the Tennessee Valley; to provide for the agricultural and industrial development of said valley," and "to provide for the national defense" by producing munitions at Muscle Shoals, Alabama. (In fact, the law required TVA to "maintain its principal office in the immediate vicinity of Muscle Shoals," a requirement which TVA promptly ignored. It settled in Knoxville, a fact that led to a lawsuit, filed by Alabamans, that is pending in the courts.)

It is always easier and more immediately rewarding to pour cement than it is to deal with social problems, so TVA's major effort has been to turn the Tennessee River into a succession of reservoirs, with navigation locks so that commercial barges can negotiate it. In what TVA calls its "primitive state," the river curved in an arc from the western slopes of the Appalachians, in eastern Tennessee, around to the southwest, brushing against Georgia, through Alabama, then west, nicking the northeastern corner of Mississippi, and north back through west-central Tennessee and a bit of Kentucky, then joining the Ohio River for a short stretch before merging with the Mississippi. TVA threw up nine dams on the Tennessee itself, then moved in on the tributaries with nineteen more, along with another in the Cumberland Valley. Two other dams, which recently have emerged as the Authority's most disgraceful examples of pork-barrel arrogance, are being finished at the Tellico and Columbia sites. The main stated reason for all the dam construction has been to hold back water in time of flood and to provide it, from storage, when the supply is low. Another is to generate electricity—TVA's dams, along with one operated in the valley by the Corps of Engineers and Alcoa, have a total capacity of around 4,600,000 kilowatts of electricity, which the authority sells to distributors who then resell it to about 2,700,000 residential, industrial, and commercial customers in the Southeast. In all, TVA's 31 reservoirs, plus one pumped-storage plant, have a total water area of 653,400 acres, or about 1,020 square miles, which is a little less than the area of Rhode Island; they have 11,401 miles of shoreline, and when filled to the top of the dam gates they contain 7,879,996,100,000 gallons of water, or more than enough to fill 225,000,000,000 bathtubs of the thirty-five-gallon variety. They cost (not counting Tellico and Columbia) $1,465,000,000 to build. And when TVA had constructed just about every dam that could possibly be built in the Tennessee Valley, it had to satisfy the builder's most fundamental urge, that of self-perpetuation, and so it turned to fabricating electricity-generating plants fired by coal and by nuclear energy. By the late seventies, the coal-powered plants had made TVA the leading sulfur dioxide polluter in the nation. The agency put an estimated 2,083,047 tons of the harmful substance into the air each year—16 per cent of the entire national output—and when the Clean Air Act was passed, TVA argued (as it has in connection with other environmental rules) that it didn't need to obey the law.

The builders grew to their present size, scope, and strength because at one time America appeared truly to need them. The West required "opening up" to settlement and agriculture. Rivers did need "harnessing" if freighters and barges were going to get to Pittsburgh or St. Louis. Hydroelectric turbines did provide relatively simple and environmentally acceptable means of producing electricity. But many of the experts agree now that the need for continued building no longer exists. The major rivers of the nation have been dammed and re-dammed until they have become, truly, damned. Agriculture, as has been seen in the discussions of Arizona and California, no longer is apple-pie American; it is difficult to excite national passions on behalf of irrigation projects that benefit subsidiaries of oil companies. Henry P. Caulfield Jr., a political scientist at Colorado State University and the former director of the U.S. Water Resources Council, pointed out in a paper delivered in 1975 that political support for water projects has dimmed, in part, because of the new national urban majority. "Urban people, not rural people," he said, "strongly support establishment of wilderness areas, national parks, wild and scenic rivers, and fish and wildlife enhancement." (There goes that word again. Caulfield must have learned it in Washington.) The speaker recommended that Congress repeal the authorizations of the big builders and turn over much of the responsibility for future water projects to the state and local governments, with financial help from Washington in the form of grants and loans.

Such a turn of events, of course, would splinter the very staves of the pork-barrel system, and therefore it is virtually unthinkable. What *is* thinkable, however, is the idea that there are very few places left to build dams and canals. The builders know this. It presents a real problem for them. And yet the builders must build. Like sharks that must devour and rodents that must gnaw, the builders must build or they will become extinct. Every valley must be "developed," every stream "enhanced."

A few truly enormous water schemes are left, in the United States and elsewhere. Israel, the nation that perhaps is most familiar with the limits of cheap water supplies, is thinking about digging a channel from the Mediterranean to the Dead Sea. Some Japanese are considering building another Panama Canal. The Soviet Union is working on a plan to change the direction of several rivers, including two major Siberian streams, the Yenisei and the Ob, in order to provide agricultural water farther south. Reversing the rivers' flow would deprive the Arctic Sea of a considerable portion of its fresh-water intake. Some scientists have expressed concern about such a change, which would tinker with the Arctic's water salinity balance and, they say, produce drastic effects on the polar ice cap and, thus, on the world's climate.

Some of the more outlandish water projects spring from the brains of private citizens and private enterprise, but the student of the pork barrel soon learns that no project is too bizarre to attract the attention and eventual devotion of the government builders. Since the early sixties, the large California engineering and construction firm of Ralph M. Parsons Company has been promoting a scheme known as NAWAPA —for North American Water and Power Alliance, which is the entity that would be required to build and operate the most grandiose ravishment of nature in the history of the world: a series of reservoirs, dams, canals, and pumping stations that would take water from Alaska and Canada and ship it around the rest of the continent, including Mexico but mostly to the Southwestern United States, where it would be put to work, naturally, making possible more agriculture and population growth.

N. W. Snyder of the Parsons firm, in an October, 1980, speech that sought to drum up interest in the scheme again, laid down some of the basics: It would cost more than $200,000,000,000, would take thirty years to complete, could be built with conventional tools (by which Snyder meant nuclear devices wouldn't be necessary), would drain an area of about 1,300,000 square miles, would deliver 78,000,000 acre feet of water a year to the United States, would flush out the salts deposited in Western soils by the Colorado River, would produce hydroelectric power, would require the construction of 177 lakes or reservoirs, and would be profoundly influential in "the future economic well-being in North America."

Snyder is mindful that not everyone supports the scheme right off the bat. There has been some "deleterious criticism," he says, and there are those who claim that conservation should be employed before continent-wide canal building is undertaken. And, in order for the plan to become a reality, there would have to be some explaining to the politicians: "To institute and implement the NAWAPA plan," said Snyder, "may require an inordinate amount of work in the political arena as compared to the engineering work. A severe and undue conservatism prevails in the United States with regard to developments of all sorts. Required is a more progressive and liberal attitude. For NAWAPA to become a reality, three nations, 36 states, 11 provinces, and thousands of cities, counties and local agencies must cooperate. . . . Divergent views associated with the emotionally charged aspects of environmental changes need to be discussed on the basis of the major benefits to be accrued."

Robert D. Gerard, of Columbia University's Lamont Geological Observatory in Palisades, New York, had a dream almost as grandiose as Parsons'. Writing in the publication *Science* in 1966, during the height of a period of drought for the New York metropolitan region, Gerard suggested, apparently seriously, that Long Island Sound be dammed at both ends and turned into a reservoir for drinking water.

Once Gerard's dams were in place, it would take about seven and a half years for fresh water entering from Connecticut streams to decrease the ex-sound's salinity to potable levels. (Toxic wastes and the like were not discussed.) The reservoir would contain 41,800,000 acre feet of water, would have locks so shipping could go in and out, would extract $40,000,000 a year (in mid-sixties dollars) from motorists using its dams and causeways for travel between Long Island and Connecticut, would provide a great deal of drinking water, and—in a benefit that many people, including boaters, might not even know was a benefit—would delight yachtsmen with the "absence of tidal currents." Gerard's dream followed by about three decades one by John Reber, an actor and theatrical producer, for the conversion of San Francisco Bay into *two* fresh-water reservoirs by plugging it both north and south of the Golden Gate. Even the Corps of Engineers shied away from that one.

The problem with outrageous proposals such as these is

that for a lot of the builders and their confederates in Congress and the local banks and courthouses they are not outrageous at all. They fit in neatly with the beliefs and assumptions of those who build large water projects—the belief that everything should be "developed," that rivers are "primitive" or "useless" until they are "harnessed." Or, as the Corps of Engineers put it in a brochure describing its work on the Arkansas River Waterway (a channel from the Mississippi River to near Tulsa, a distance of 436 miles, with seventeen locks and dams and a continuing problem with siltation; in its time the largest civil-works project ever undertaken by the Corps), the river was a "raging torrent" with "impassable sandbars," subject to the "whims of nature," until the builders arrived and "improved" the stream for navigation, hydropower, flood control, "bank stabilization," and "channel rectification," as well as "recreation" (although pollution makes the waterway "unsafe for swimming").

Implicit in all the builders' verbiage and—particularly and most dangerously—in their actions is the assumption that water that somehow makes it to the sea is water that is *wasted*. Major John Wesley Powell, in his pioneering (at least for the white man) explorations of the Colorado River in 1869, wrote of "Mountain streams—swollen by storms in the winter, by melting snow in the spring—roaring uncontrolled into major rivers, sending floodwaters raging through entire river basins . . . wasting into the sea." Teddy Roosevelt, asking Congress to pass the Reclamation Act of 1902, said, "If we could save the waters running now to waste, the western part of the country could sustain a population greater than even the legendary Major Powell dreamed." BuRec today refers to water in California's Sacramento River that doesn't get used as "surplus flow." A New York State compendium of water resources on Long Island asserts that some 320,000,000 gallons a day is discharged from the aquifers into streams and thus into the salty waters surrounding the island, and it speaks of techniques that might be used to capture this water for "beneficial use," as if the way nature does it were not "beneficial." A scientist writing in the journal *Nature* speaks of heavy rainfalls in Poland "after which the water runs off uselessly into the Baltic." The Metropolitan Water District of Southern California, the agency which looks for, gets, and sells water all over the state's heavily populated southern portions, has this to say about the Colorado River in one of its publications: "It took billions of years to shape the Colorado, and when she was through, nature had left it unruly and rampaging, waiting for man to tame for his use . . ."

William I. Du Bois, of the California Farm Bureau Federation, was asked not long ago if he felt that river water that made it to the sea was somehow wasted. "What do you mean, 'somehow'?" he replied, with exaggerated sarcasm. "How is it used? To raise fish?" Because of the closed nature of the hydrologic cycle, he said, the same amount of water would be present in the atmosphere and on the surface of the earth "regardless of whether we put any water in the ocean or not." David F. Abelson, the director of the California Planning and Conservation League, had a different answer. "I think that viewpoint is extremely man-centered," he said, "in that it says that if it isn't being put to human uses it has no value. And I think it's not based on sound scientific evidence." Flowing rivers carry immense amounts of sediment into the ocean, he said, that nourishes beaches and estuaries; they serve as essential channels for salmon and other anadromous fishes; and "there're the aesthetic values."

For a very long time in this nation the assumption that nature exists for the benefit of humanity has prevailed. Its believers made it safely through the height of what is being called the "environmental era," and there were widespread indications, as the administration of Ronald Reagan came to power in 1981, that they would prosper more than ever before in the coming years, and that the strength of their message would be bolstered not only by the seriousness of the energy crisis but also by their ability to remind the population of some of the more stupid blunders of the technocracy as it had attempted to "save the environment." This attitude has a lot else going for it, as well: Some of its assumptions are rooted far beneath the surface of the nation's history; so far, in some cases, that they work directly on people's emotions.

John Marlin is in his early thirties, a native of Murphysboro, a town in southernmost Illinois. He has been fighting the builders, often with remarkable success, ever since he was an undergraduate at the University of Illinois and the Corps of Engineers sought to build a dam and reservoir that would threaten Allerton Park, which is used by the university as an education and research center, as well as a forest, wildlife preserve, and park. (When the Corps started planning the project, known first as Oakley Dam and Reservoir, later as Springer Dam, in honor of a politician, it was supposed to be a small storage dam that would cost less than $5,000,000. As the years passed and the pork in the barrel ripened, the project became a big, $120,000,000-plus effort. Britta B. Harris, in a detailed study of the project and the ensuing dispute published by the university's Institute for Environmental Studies, called it "a classic case of bureaucratic infighting, pork-barrel politics, and mismanagement of precious resources.")

Marlin lives now in Champaign, near the university, and he operates an organization named Central States Resources Center out of a church building. At the same time he is completing work for a Ph.D. degree in entomology. He is one of quite a few people around the country who, individually or in organizations, challenge the builders and their projects when they feel they are necessary. It would be incorrect to think of Marlin and others like him as "environmentalists" (Marlin himself sometimes refers jokingly to such activists as "the bird and bunny people"); their opposition to the unrestrained pouring of cement springs from a number of sources, some philosophical, some political, some economic, some environmental. The only name that seems to suit them all is "damfighters." Marlin seems to be one of the more articulate and good-humored damfighters; when he speaks to meetings of like-minded people he is likely to wear golden Corps insignia on his shirt collars, and he has been known to dress up in a complete, if unauthorized, Corps general's uniform, replete with mirrored sunglasses and shovel, and deliver a slide show (with the slides depicting some of the Corps's more photogenic failures) that leaves his audiences howling.

Most of Marlin's work takes place at what activists like to call the "grass roots" level, and so he is continually exposed to what he considers one of the more formidable obstacles to the reform of the builders—the unwillingness, on the part of many Americans, to believe that their own government would do this to them.

"The district colonel," said Marlin in an interview not long ago, "comes into a backwoods area of southern Illinois or North Dakota, or Kentucky, or West Virginia. He's got on the uniform of the United States Army, and he's a full colonel. He's talking to people who were in their prime, in their forties, during World War II—people with a deep amount of patriotism, who cannot conceive of the United States Army—the army that many of them helped fight Hitler with, the very army that they fought with to preserve democracy and decency —cheating them out of their land. Or taking their land for a *bureaucratic purpose*. They also don't know that the Corps of Engineers is a few hundred army officers and 30,000 civilians.

"These people also have an absolute horror of suing the government. To them, it's un-American. Can you imagine an eighty-year-old farmer in North Dakota signing a piece of paper that says, 'Joe Smith versus the United States of America'?"

Marlin flashed a look that said *he* certainly couldn't imagine such an event. "Or you take the case of somebody who built his house in 1940 for $14,000," he continued. "The Corps comes in and says, 'Well, here you are, sixty-five years old; you paid $14,000 for that house forty years ago; we'll give you $28,000.' And those people haven't been on the housing market. They don't know that a house comparable to their own today costs $50,000 or $60,000. All they think is that the government's doing them a good deed by doubling the money they paid forty years ago. And so they take the $28,000 and go looking for a house. They can't replace it.

"And there's this *progress* routine. The bulk of the voting public today grew up at a time when the Depression was more than a distant memory. A whole group of people grew up believing that dams created jobs. That irrigation canals created jobs. That we needed to make the desert bloom. That any public-works thing the government wanted to do was good for conservation. Like here in Illinois: Most of the physical work on our state parks was done by the Civilian Conservation Corps. So you have generations who grew up with the idea that moving dirt for the government was good.

"Now, since that time a lot of things have been different. For example, mechanization has turned building dams and canals and highways from labor-intensive things, which were good for employment in hard times, into capital-intensive projects where the number of jobs per dollar spent on a dam or highway is probably the lowest in the economy. Doing almost anything else is better. Building dams no longer serves a legitimate public need.

"And in terms of making the desert bloom, the last thing in the *world* we want to do right now is make the desert bloom. The country is producing more grain than it can sell or use. The capital costs of development in the West are staggering."

Marlin was warming to his subject, and it was obvious that he was not just rehashing his most recent public speech, as some frequent lecturers do, but articulating ideas that were supremely important to him. "And there's the socialistic concept," he said with a grin. "Here we have the United States of America. The Far West. Reagan Country, where everybody's a dyed-in-the-wool, pull-yourself-up-by-your-bootstraps, free-enterprise, hate-a-communist capitalist. And what do they want? In the case of a lot of these projects you have these anti-communists, these dyed-in-the-wool free-enterprise super-big corporate ranchers, and smaller ranchers who *don't* have a corporation behind them, saying, 'Well, Uncle Sam, give me an irrigation project that in effect amounts to more than a million-dollar subsidy per landowner.'

"That's the *American Way* for them! You go out to these projects and you see these same free-enterprise types saying, 'We hate communism and socialism, but oh, please, Mister Government, throw these three hundred families off their farms upriver so I can get irrigation water at a much-subsidized price.'" Marlin's eyes were blazing.

"Now, you tell me what the difference between that and outright socialism or communal communism is! It's the *government*, *allocating* the resources, *taking* from one group of people to *give* to another. You call that free enterprise? That's outright *socialism!*" By this time Marlin was thumping on the table in his crowded but neat office, and there was fire in his eyes as well as a grin of sarcasm on his face, and it was not hard to imagine the intense emotions and desires, the very fundamental human greediness, that are all excited by the prospect of dipping into the bottomless barrel of government pork.

22

The people and corporations who profit at the local level from pork-barrel politics—the contractors, bankers, and realtors—could hardly enrich themselves at all were it not for the government agencies that do the building. And the builders would have minimal power if it were not for their close relationships with the members of Congress, who, after all, are the only participants in the scheme who have access to the closest thing there is to unlimited funds: the taxpayers' pockets.

Of the three groups, the locals probably should be faulted the least. They are, after all, doing little more than taking advantage of a very tempting offer, of a game (as it is often put) that has been played for a very long time. But they *have* learned, some of them, how to bring pressures on the other two, in this system in which water has no standing, in order to get what they want. Representative Toby Moffett, writing in an environmental group's membership solicitation, has said: "Why do members of Congress go along on pork-barrel bills, or legislation posing further hazards to an environment already in jeopardy? Because so many Americans don't even bother to vote, much less complain about the way we vote. Because we are subjected to enormous pressure from politically and financially powerful interests. Because those who are battling to save our waterways, wildlife and wilderness, to protect life itself, cannot match the resources of the other side."

Representative Michael Myers of Pennsylvania shed some light on the question from another angle. Myers was one of those who were entrapped by Federal Bureau of Investigation agents and informers in the "Abscam" operation in 1979 and

1980. At one point on the videotape that the FBI made without his knowledge, one of Myers' entrappers asked him about his "connections at the State Department." Included in the representative's reply was the statement that some congressional delegations "who have key members that are involved in State are interested in something from the Appropriations Committee, where they need funding for a dam project. . . . There's a million deals; it's a trading game down in Washington, and this is the way it's done. Going on the Appropriations Committee in January, this makes me a very important guy. . . ." (Myers didn't make it to the committee; he was convicted and drummed out of Congress.)

George W. Pring was a participant in a meeting of damfighters in Washington a couple of years ago, and he explained for a questioner the nature, as he saw it, of the three-sided pork barrel. Pring at that time was a staff counsel for the Environmental Defense Fund in its Denver office; since then he moved to the faculty of the University of Colorado. As is the usual case with damfighters, Pring had a list of horror stories, of examples of the builders' art that struck him as particularly arrogant, or wasteful, or stupid, or all three. In this case the water projects were named Savery-Pot Hook and Fruitland Mesa; both are Bureau of Reclamation efforts in Colorado.

"In each case," said Pring, "you're dealing with a project that's going to cost the American taxpayers $75,000,000 to $100,000,000 to build. In each case it benefits about seventy-five to a hundred farm families. In other words, a million dollars per farm is the price you and I are paying to irrigate land that is so marginal that no *private* developer would invest good money at *any* interest rate to bring that land into production. . . . It's a ridiculous situation."

How, then, he was asked, could the perpetrators get away with it?

"Because of the Iron Triangle," Pring replied. The somewhat mysterious phrase with World War II overtones is one that is heard frequently at damfighters' meetings. Pring's questioner asked him what the triangle was all about.

"There exists in the political structure that lies behind these projects," he said, "a triangle. And at the top of the triangle is the federal agency—the Bureau of Reclamation, the Soil Conservation Service, the Corps of Engineers. Now, no agency wants to go out of business. Every agency wants to keep its bureaucrats busy, keep them from being fired or farmed out on pension. These agencies, in order to keep that way, have to keep building projects, regardless of their futility or their utility. They've got to keep building them or they will become agencies without a mission and pretty soon they'll be agencies without a budget or a staff.

"At the other two corners of the triangle are the congressional delegation that is served, and the local economic interests that benefit anytime a project is undertaken. These three parts of the triangle interact and reinforce and support each other in order to see that the projects are authorized by Congress, funds are appropriated, and they get built. Every part of that triangle benefits from building a dam, regardless of how much you or I suffer and have to pay for it. No matter how ridiculous a venture is economically, when it gets approved the agency gets another two-, three-, four,- or ten-year lease on life; the local economic interests get tremendous local quick returns. Remember, every time somebody local—businessman, banker, real estate agent, newspaper, whatever—gets something for nothing, that means *you*'ve gotten nothing for something."

Pring's enthusiasm for his subject, like John Marlin's, was clearly evident. "And *all* these local interests profit," he said. "Anytime a dam or water project is built, people have to be relocated and moved. Real estate companies make a tremendous commission; every time a person moves they make a commission on both ends, the buying and the selling. The local bank profits; all the mortgages have to be paid off. All that money gets churned back into the bank and put back out at higher interest rates; banks love these projects. Everybody figures they're going to be the ones who open up the $1,000,000-a-year bait store on the banks of the new lake that's going to be built, to rent canoes and motorboats to people. The local community thinks it's going to have a big economic and employment boom. Usually only a very few people do. But that doesn't stop that corner of the triangle from pushing as hard as possible to make the whole thing go.

"The other corner is Congress. The senators and the local congressmen derive something even more important than money, although they sure as hell line their pockets with fancy speech fees and other things from the local community for doing good by 'em. They get reelected on these things. The average congressman can rededicate the same dam for four or five consecutive elections. First, he dedicates the ground-breaking. Then he dedicates the land purchases. Then he comes back and dedicates the flood abutments. And then he finally dedicates the flagpoles. A congressman's future in many parts of the country, as the saying goes, is written in concrete."

Pring was asked if he thought the members of the Iron Triangle were really evil people. "They're not, most of them," he said. "And I've dealt with a number of different water projects in states as far-flung as Ohio and California. Ninety-nine times out of a hundred you are not dealing with truly evil, pernicious, fraudulent-type people. Mendacious, grasping—no. You're dealing with people who have two things going for them, and both of them are absolutely all-American virtues." One of those, he said, was the belief that John Marlin had discussed earlier—the feeling that it is part of *patriotism* to build dams, move water around, and make the desert bloom. "And the other thing," said Pring, "is that it's almost a virtue in this country to believe that making money off the government can't be all bad. From the person who double-dips welfare checks all the way up to the big oil company corporate official who cheats on his taxes, we've developed a nation that feels that somehow if you steal it from the taxpayer, it isn't stealing.

And you're lining your pockets with something that really isn't wrong."

The most persistent and pervasive member of the Iron Triangle, by almost everybody's estimation, is one of its federal agencies—the Corps of Engineers. This erstwhile component of the U.S. Army has a slogan, "The Corps Cares." Anyone living in the path of one of its multitudinous water projects soon discovers what it is the Corps cares about. It is certainly not the environment (despite an increasing number of pro-environmental assertions and speeches), and it is certainly not landowners and farmers. Any assessment of the Corps's recent history must conclude that the agency cares most of all about self-perpetuation and the perpetuation of the Iron Triangle.

For example, the Corps has mastered the art of the spurious cost-benefit analysis.

In order for a water project (or, for that matter, any other large public-works undertaking) to receive its authorization and funding, a case must be made for its economic feasibility. As noted before, the vehicle which is used to demonstrate this feasibility—and misused, as seems to be more frequently the case—is the cost-benefit (or benefit-cost) analysis, in which the projected costs of the planned facility are totaled up and compared with the projected benefits. If the cost-benefit ratio were 1:1, costs and benefits would be equal. As might be expected, it is in the builders' interest to come up with projects in which the benefits outweigh the costs. Inasmuch as this is impossible in some of the more grandiose and/or useless schemes, it becomes necessary to juggle the numbers. The Corps of Engineers, Bureau of Reclamation, TVA, and other members of the building fraternity have become quite adept at this.

This is accomplished in rather simple fashion by exaggerating the "benefits" and ignoring some of the costs. The cost of obtaining money for the project classically has been minimized by using an extremely low discount rate (as low as 3¼ per cent, in some cases). The project is endowed with an inordinately long economic life (as much as a hundred years, even though siltation might negate a reservoir's usefulness far sooner than that). Exaggerated claims are usually made about the number and sorts of industries that will move to the new facility and the number of jobs that will be created in order to relieve local unemployment problems. Often the economic claims are saturated in double-talk so dense as to defy translation even by a government bureaucrat. A Tennessee Valley Authority executive once explained his agency's claims of greater employment benefits in one of its projects by saying, "There are human resources that are underutilized in the four-county project area, and if the project can change the economic system for the four-county area so that these human resources can be better utilized, the difference in the productivity from subutilization or underutilization of more normalized or better utilization would be a national benefit since that would be a net increase in the total product of the national economy. . . ."

Flood control is generally counted among the benefits, as is the production of electric power. A reservoir almost always is claimed to provide water supplies for nearby municipalities, and improvement in water quality is often calculated as a benefit. The economic values accruing from navigation—the shipment of goods by freighters and barges—are counted as benefits. Recreation opportunities are almost always scheduled for "enhancement." Fish and wildlife, it is said, will prosper.

When the builders buy or condemn the land for a water project, they obtain not only the land that will be under water, but also take property for many acres around. This newly created "lakeside" land is then leased or resold, at greatly increased prices, by the builders to industry, private citizens, or speculators. Thus "redevelopment" of ordinary farmland and people's homesteads into valuable property for resale—in a way that would be "confiscation" in Russia but that here is just the great American free enterprise system, assisted by government agencies with the power of eminent domain—is figured as a project benefit.

The builders have become masters at minimizing some of the costs involved in a project, as well as at exaggerating the benefits and ignoring the possible alternatives, even though some of those alternatives might be far more environmentally sound and considerably more cost-effective than the project as originally conceived. Such manipulations are common knowledge in government. Cecil Andrus, the Carter administration's interior secretary, once commented to a *New York Times* reporter that "God knows, the cost-benefit ratios on some of these projects have been Mickey-Moused around with; the damage to the environment has been ridden over roughshod. . . ."

A coalition of environmental and conservation groups analyzed the Bureau of Reclamation's cost-benefit claims for a high dam on the Teton River in eastern Idaho and found that, using the government's own figures, the project had a ratio of at least 1 dollar spent for every 73 cents in benefits, and *that* was achieved by using the artificially low interest rate of 3½ per cent. BuRec had come up with a different cost-benefit ratio of 1:1.2. The environmentalists figured that if a somewhat more realistic (for the early seventies, when its calculations were made) interest rate of 6 per cent were used, the ratio would go to 1:0.4. These are some of the areas in which cost-benefit ratios are manipulated by the builders to their, and the rest of the Iron Triangle's, advantage:

The effects of a project on the existing land and water are ignored, if possible. The builders like to forget that private land that is inundated by a federal project is, by definition, taken off the local tax rolls. And while they are clever at inflating the alleged values of their new reservoir, little value is placed on the free-flowing stream that the reservoir replaces or on the species of fish and wildlife that will be driven away.

Although the builders are quick to come up with scientific-sounding estimates of the numbers of new industries and bait stores that will congregate on the shores of the new lake, they pay little attention at all to the thousands of acres of farmland, some of it in prime condition because it is situated in bottom-lands, that will be removed from production—and at a time when experts the world over are expressing great anxiety over the global loss of cropland. The House Committee on Government Operations, in a December, 1980, report on TVA's Columbia Dam project on Tennessee's Duck River, found that 27,500 acres of farmland would be sacrificed for the reservoir in order to provide flood control for some 9,000 acres downstream. The project's original planning documents made no "mention of the multi-million-dollar loss of farm production and farm-related business," said the committee.

Biologists R. John Taylor and Constance Taylor, writing in 1976 in the *Annals* of the Oklahoma Academy of Science, found that "Paradoxically, there are about as many acres inundated in a reservoir" in Oklahoma water projects "as are protected downstream. In most cases, the potential agribusiness yield of an entire floodplain, even receiving periodic flooding, and its adjacent upland exceeds the yield of the land protected on a floodplain below the dam. Many property owners have voiced this opinion, but land owners in a proposed impoundment area are often dismissed as uneducated individuals who do not understand the overall importance of a project."

Another cost that rarely is reflected in the official assessments of a project is the actual flood *damage* that a flood-control dam may cause. One of the things that happen to the floodplain below a dam, as the Taylors pointed out, is that the oxbows, or serpentine curves in the stream, get straightened out and lose their ability to serve as "check valves" on flooding. And when dams are built, always with the promise of flood control as one of their major benefits, people feel confident in building homes and industries downstream on the floodplain—in places where they never would have dared to build before. When the truly disastrous flood comes along (as nature has shown us it eventually will), or when impounded reservoir water upstream reaches such levels that the floodgates must be opened in order to protect the dam, the result is a man-made or man-assisted flood. As a consequence, billions are spent on building flood-control dams on major American rivers, and at the same time the cost of flood damage downstream on those same rivers is constantly rising. And, to complete this weird circle, the Corps of Engineers likes to claim that one of the "benefits" of its dam projects is the value of the structures that would not otherwise have been built in the floodplain. Brent Blackwelder, the Washington lobbyist of the Washington-based Environmental Policy Institute, has written that "many of the structures now protected by upstream dams and levees were not in place and would not have been built were it not for the dam or levee. Using the Corps's argument, almost any dam could be justified provided enough expensive developments were located in the floodplain downstream from the dam."

Recreation has found increasing favor among the builders as a means to jack up the benefit sides of their cost-benefit ratios. In addition to ignoring the recreational value of a swiftly moving stream and exaggerating the value of a warm-water reservoir, the builders have used questionable methodology in calculating the drawing power of their new projects. An estimated number of recreational visits per day, or year, is commonly used in figuring the recreational "benefit" of a reservoir. But the arithmetic generally overlooks the facts that reservoirs tend to get built in places (such as the Tennessee Valley) where there are many *other* reservoirs, that the *other* reservoirs were justified in part on the number of projected recreational visits, and that a recreational visit to New Reservoir A means one less recreational visit to Old Reservoir B or C. The major stated benefit of the Columbia Dam project in central Tennessee is recreation, although there are nine other reservoirs within fifty miles of the site. And an audit by the General Accounting Office of a Corps of Engineers plan to build a dam and reservoir in Georgia disclosed that the Corps, in an effort to inflate the recreational value of the place, was claiming that there would be as many visits to the project as there were to the most-visited Corps reservoir in the nation, a quite unlikely expectation.

When the pitch for recreation is being made, too, the builders manage to overlook the fact that other "benefits" they had to come up with in order to balance the cost-benefit ratio—hydroelectric power, flood control, and water supply—often work to the detriment of, or even cancel out, the recreation benefit. A controlled reservoir is not like a natural lake, with a fairly predictable waterline; its water level fluctuates, sometimes wildly, and when it is down, the recreation-seeking public is treated to the spectacle of boat docks and launching ramps separated from the water by a hundred yards or so of impassable red mud. The Government Operations Committee, in its report on Columbia Dam, found that in the summer the reservoir would be held at 630 feet above sea level, creating an artificial lake 12,600 acres in size. After October 15 the level would be dropped to 603 feet above sea level to leave more room in the reservoir for storage in the event of winter flooding. The winter lake would be only 4,300 acres in size. Between it and the "normal" shoreline would be more than 8,000 acres of mud flats—hardly a modern version of Walden Pond. And, said the congressional report, it was estimated that during one summer out of every four the lake wouldn't be able to make it back to its desired level because of lack of rain. At reservoirs where hydropower is a factor, summer recreation use is complicated further by the high demands for electricity to run air conditioners. When the turbines must turn, water must be drained from the recreational paradise to turn them.

Human beings are useful as variables in the cost-benefit schemes. While BuRec, the Corps, and TVA can blithely predict that industries will stream into a given project site, handing out jobs like lollipops and curing all the local chronic unemployment, they also are able somehow to minimize the costs associated with throwing people out of their homes and off their land.

The Tennessee Valley Authority's founding legislation

gives it the "power to advise and cooperate in the readjustment of the population displaced by the construction of dams" and related projects, but in actuality there is very little advice and practically no cooperation, not to mention "readjustment." Cost-benefit analyses, and the builders' working rules, fail to take into account the obvious differences between farmland and urban housing projects, between growing corn and working in a factory. Often the taking of a farm is the breaking up of a family; it can force self-reliant rural people to move to the city and to try to cope, perhaps late in their lives, with the bewildering customs and rituals of the urban life. In rural areas, land is not just a place to live on but a place to live off, and a place to be. Land is not a transient commodity, but an end in itself. Geneva Sherman, of Relief, Kentucky, testifying before a Senate subcommittee in 1979 about the Corps's techniques in running people off their land for the Paintsville Lake project, said: "To Paint Creek people, land is security. You can fall back on it whenever times are rough, not as an investment, but as a means to get by on. The land will yield a future. Its resources are money in the bank. People look to land for security in their old age, and title in land is wealth and rank passed on to their children. Many people at Paint Creek have never bought or sold land before."

Sherman referred to the Corps's methods of land acquisition as robbery. In almost every case, she said, the Corps takes its own land survey and claims that a landowner owns less acreage than his or her deed says—from 10 to 50 per cent less. In this manner, the Corps can pay less for the land it confiscates. But when the Corps is finding comparable land for those evicted, it does not do its own survey, preferring them to take the deed's word for it. A 1978 report to Congress by the General Accounting Office on the relocation practices of federal agencies found "an inconsistent, inequitable, and confusing array of differing formats, terminologies, and guidelines in 13 federal agencies' regulations, resulting in people being treated differently when displaced by these agencies."

Statistics involving people are easily manipulated in order to help out a sagging cost-benefit ratio, from the number of water-skiers and bass fishers expected at Such-and-such Lake (forget about the canoeists and trout fishers who'll never see Such-and-such *River* again) to the number of schoolchildren expected to tour a hydroelectric plant on annual field trips. These numbers are multiplied by dollar amounts that seem awfully arbitrary ($6 per schoolchild, in one project), and the result is plugged into the "benefit" side of the ratio, or perhaps refigured and replugged, until the project starts to look like an economic success. Sometimes it helps to forget. TVA, in a section of its 1972 environmental impact statement on its Columbia Dam project that was devoted to future water needs of the area, referred to a prediction that the population would hit 370,000 by the year 2075. Of course, the higher the population, the larger the amount of water that would be consumed, and the more justifiable the water-supply aspects of the dam would seem. The statement overlooked the fact that TVA itself had previously lowered the projection to 275,000. Commented the Government Operations Committee: "Had TVA revealed that . . . decline . . . it would have been compelled to re-evaluate the need for the project and its benefit/cost ratio."

23

Inflating the purported benefits of water projects is not a new technique. In 1955 the Commission on the Reorganization of the Executive Branch of the Government, known popularly as the Hoover Commission, accused the Corps of overstating the benefits of the projects it favored. The commission suggested, in vain, that the Corps's water-development powers be transferred to some other agency that would be more susceptible to Executive Department control. Nor is simple benefit juggling the only method employed by the builders in getting what they want. The Corps of Engineers and its confederates in the Iron Triangle have mastered the art and science of mounting an array of economic and political strategies to ensure that their projects, no matter how marginal, are continued and the Corps itself stays in business. Their methods include manipulation of the facts, exceeding congressionally imposed authorizations, and toadying to politicians who control the agency's appropriations.

The Corps's history is replete with examples of its own peculiar brand of responsibility, but three recent episodes demonstrate clearly the contempt in which the agency holds the American citizens and the planet's environment, particularly that portion of it that is water. In one of them, the case of the Ohio River dams, the Corps was originally authorized by Congress to exploit the river for navigation by building a series of dams and by constructing a channel 9 feet deep. Since then, and without authorization by Congress, the Corps has replaced dams with higher ones, thus changing the water level. In the process of acquiring land and easements for the dams, according to charges made by landowners along the river in a series of lawsuits still in the courts, the Corps used fraud and threats of condemnation to obtain enough land to accommodate a 12-foot channel. The deeper channel has caused severe erosion of the farmland along the river. The Corps, in reply, has said that the erosion was an "act of God," thus confirming what a lot of the agency's victims had long suspected: that the Corps of Engineers thinks it is God.

The Corps is accomplished at what is known as the "camel's nose" approach, which refers to the notion that if a camel is allowed to poke its nose into a tent, it will not be long before the entire beast is inside. In some circles this is known as the "give-them-an-inch-and-they'll-take-a-mile" routine. Or perhaps it should be the "give-them-a-gallon-and-they'll-take-the-entire-watershed" scheme. It is widely used by the builders, be they private corporations that want to strip-mine in the West or federal agencies that want to "enhance" a river out of existence. A specialty of the Corps of Engineers is getting the camel's nose into the tent by way of the unauthorized channel depth. The reasoning is simple: If Congress's wishes are ignored and a channel that was supposed to be dug at 9 feet is dug at 12, then the Corps can claim greater barge tonnage in its cost-benefit calculations. Increasing the channel will also require more work on the dams and locks on the project, which will help keep the Corps in business. Almost everyone benefits —the Corps, the barge industry (which the taxpayers subsidize at a rate that has been estimated at more than $400,000,000 a year, and which is made up of such needy corporations as Dow, Du Pont, the major oil companies, and Hooker Chemical)— everyone except the taxpayers, the railroads and other competing forms of transportation, and, of course, the water. A federal judge was unimpressed when the Corps tried the 9-versus-12-foot-channel routine on its Locks and Dam Number 26 project, which would rebuild existing structures on the Mississippi River at Alton, Illinois. Charles Richey, the district judge, said he found the Corps's statement that it didn't really plan to build the deeper channel "unworthy of belief." As for the Corps's claim that it was just doing repair work, rather than a system-wide renovation (which would require Congress's approval), the judge said, "the record is replete with contrary indications."

Perhaps the worst example yet of the Corps of Engineers' willingness to mislead the public may be found in the Tenn-Tom case. Since the forties, the Corps has been yearning to dig a ditch that would connect the much-manipulated Tennessee River, near the point where it runs briefly through the northeastern corner of Mississippi, with the Tombigbee River, which flows south in Louisiana to Mobile and the Gulf of Mexico. Ten locks and dams would be built. The Corps wants to move 250,000,000 cubic yards of dirt, more than was dug in the construction of the Panama Canal's divide cut, to provide a more direct link between the Tennessee River and the Gulf. Presently freight from the Tennessee Valley must follow the Tennessee around to the Ohio and then to the Mississippi.

When construction started in 1972 on the Tennessee-Tombigbee Waterway, or Tenn-Tom, the Corps placed its cost at $120,000,000. The present price is believed to be something like $2,000,000,000, and the ditch is only partly finished. When it is completed it will be a memorial to deceit. When environmental groups and a railroad joined forces to challenge the project in the federal courts (on the grounds that the Corps violated nine laws and was building a ditch that hadn't been authorized by Congress), they were able to obtain internal Corps documents that showed just what the engineers had been up to. Among the revelations, as gathered by *New York Times* reporter Wayne King and others, including environmental groups, were these:

· The Corps based its cost-benefit calculations for the project on a channel width that was almost twice as wide as the one Congress had authorized. Locks were included which were not on the original design. The channel depth was increased. The Corps used, again to bolster "benefits," hundreds of millions of dollars' worth of work on more than 200 miles of the Tombigbee River that was never part of the project and that had never been approved by Congress.

· The Corps misled the public about the ever-escalating costs of the project, apparently in an effort to avoid what one set of auditors called the "emotional impact" of informing the people, or Congress, that the thing was going to cost a billion dollars or more.

· When the General Accounting Office started an inquiry into the Corps's methods of dealing with financial matters, the office of Mississippi Senator John Stennis intervened and the GAO report was suppressed. Stennis is a powerful member of the Senate Appropriations Committee and of its subcommittees dealing with public works, as well as a major backer of the Tenn-Tom project. And, according to an article by *Washington Post* reporters Ward Sinclair, Bob Ratner, and Jeffrey Rothfeder, Stennis owns stock in two chemical corporations "that stand to profit from the waterway." (The *Post* also noted that the founder of one of the corporations was a "close personal friend" of Jimmy Carter.) Another audit, by the Army itself, which discovered irregularities in the Corps's stewardship of the project, was not made public.

· The Corps paraded out numerous inventions in its claims about anticipated barge traffic on the waterway. Said a report prepared by the Environmental Policy Center: "The Corps . . . calculated transportation benefits by including barge movements of goods from companies which explicitly indicated they would not use the waterway and from companies and plants no longer in existence. Were it not for the inclusion of these fabricated benefits, the benefit-cost ratio would be below unity. Thus, the Corps is justifying to Congress a multi-billion dollar investment on the basis of fictitious benefits."

· In toting up alleged benefits to the economy of the region through which the ditch would pass, the Corps engaged in more fiction writing. Ordinarily, redevelopment benefits are calculated on the basis of hiring local workers who are otherwise unemployed; the assumption is that hiring these people does not reduce productivity anywhere else in the nation, and so wages paid to such workers are not included as project costs. The Corps avoided even these questionable procedures and made three unsupportable assumptions: that a "local" worker was one who had been in the area for more than one day; that 80 per cent of the work force was "local"; and that 100 per cent of the local workers hired by the project were unemployed.

· A Corps memo written in the summer of 1975 listed the specific amounts by which each "benefit" would have to be increased in order to produce an acceptable cost-benefit ratio.

All this manipulation and deception took place in a water project whose economic foundation was a wholly unrealistic interest rate of 3¼ per cent, one which produces no hydroelectric power (and, in fact, *reduces* such power, inasmuch as it takes water away from the Tennessee River hydro dams), and one which destroys the last free-flowing river in the Mobile basin. The *Birmingham Post-Herald,* in an editorial, called Tenn-Tom "a boondoggle of epic proportions." Senator Gaylord Nelson of Wisconsin (now head of the Wilderness Society) said it was "the biggest pork barrel boondoggle of them all." An environmental group called it "a canal project for which beneficiaries cannot be found," and pointed out that the government would lose less money by stopping it in its tracks than by completing it.

The lawsuit against the Corps and Tenn-Tom was tried in federal district court in Mississippi in the late winter of 1979, and the judge ruled for the Corps. The environmentalists and the railroad pursued their suit further, and the Court of Appeals ruled in March, 1980, that, while the Corps had indeed exceeded its legal authorization, the project was too far along to stop. The camel had occupied the entire tent.

In the spring of 1981, environmental groups used the Freedom of Information Act to obtain an audit, performed by Price, Waterhouse and Company, of forty-four Corps of Engineers water projects. The environmentalists quoted the audit as showing that "Vast amounts of water sit unused and uncontracted for" in Corps reservoirs; that the Corps "has used a variety of techniques to make water artificially cheap to users, thereby insuring an enthusiastic clientele for its projects"; that power customers were given unrealistic information about the true cost of the electricity they use; and that required repayment by users of construction costs and interest is "far behind schedule," with the result that costs are shifted to the general taxpayers or to future generations.

The Corps of Engineers, while probably the federal agency that has done the most damage to the watery environment, is not the only one that uses questionable methods. An audit by the General Accounting Office, published in March, 1981, reviewed six federal irrigation projects and found that, while the water produced by them will cost the government between $54 and $130 an acre foot per year, the crops grown by the farmers on that irrigated land won't bring enough revenue to cover those costs. "The farmers will continue to buy the federal water, however, because they are charged a price below government cost," said GAO. An Interior Department study of the San Luis Unit of the California Central Valley Project, undertaken by the Bureau of Reclamation, found that the project had blossomed from a relatively simple irrigation facility to an impressive extravaganza with reservoir, canals, and pumps, all "in the absence of adequate congressional authorization," in a manner that resulted in "substantial increases in the cost." Interior's study of its own agency also found that BuRec "negotiates, reviews, and submits for approval contracts without consultation with any group other than the contracting district. All public participation takes place *after* the contract is approved by the Department of the Interior" (emphasis in original).

The Tennessee Valley Authority is notorious for its mastery of the camel-in-the-tent routine; in 1980 the House Committee on Government Operations issued a report on the scandalous lengths TVA went to in order to justify its Columbia Dam project. The committee referred to what it called the agency's "usual practice of proceeding with construction in the face of any and all regulatory constraints." The report, which provided details on cost-benefit juggling that clearly put TVA in the same all-star league with the Corps of Engineers, said that the record of TVA and of the U.S. Fish and Wildlife Service (which was supposed to consult with TVA on the project, so that endangered and other species would not be harmed) "is perhaps the best example of how difficult it is to stop, or even modify, a water project once it has started. It is a record of arrogance, bad faith and broken promises by a powerful agency and weakness and political accommodation by a less powerful one."

Columbia Dam is one of those projects that are impossible to justify by rational means, so TVA used irrational methods to make sure it would be built. In order to increase the "recreation" benefits, the agency invented a new methodology by which recreation could be quantified. Still the cost-benefit ratio remained embarrassing. TVA management, including Chairman S. David Freeman, a fairly recent appointee who came into office making good-guy noises about how the era of dam building was over, was requested by the Office of Management and Budget to ask the TVA staff to investigate alternatives to the dam. The staff *did* identify some alternatives that were cost-effective, even considering what the Government Operations Committee called the "juggling of numbers that worked to the economic benefit of the project as planned." But then management—identified by the House committee as Chairman Freeman and Richard Freeman, a TVA board member—rewrote the staff report "behind closed door." Said the Committee on Government Operations in its 1980 report:

"In the course of being reviewed by the two Freemans, the report emerged as a totally different document. The changes rendered at the 'unofficial' board level prompted the TVA staff to reject the suggestion that the final report be released as a TVA 'staff study.' Consequently, the final report was issued as a study 'Prepared by the Tennessee Valley Authority.'" Management's changes, said the committee, included using some non-staff estimates when they suited the purpose of furthering the project and deleting some of the expected benefits that might accrue from an alternative project. The reasons advanced by the ultimate authors of the report for promoting the dam, said the committee, were "at best specious and in some instances demonstrably false." (S. David Freeman has since been succeeded as chairman by Charles W. Dean, Jr., a Reagan appointee. The two Freemans remain as board members.)

A favorite ploy of all the builders, whenever they are confronted with overwhelming evidence of the worthlessness of the projects they are promoting, is to fall back on what might be called "the Devil-made-me-do-it" arguments. We're just doing what Congress tells us to do, says the Corps, ignoring its own role of considerable leadership in thinking up the projects, promoting them in Congress, and then monkeying with the statistics to make them appear worthwhile. S. David Freeman of TVA, testifying before a subcommittee of the Government Operations Committee, spoke of the Columbia River and Tellico dams as "projects on which the Congress has directed us to proceed," and the casual inference might be that TVA is, indeed just a handmaiden of those people in Washington, forced to perform acts which it knows to be indecent, forced to build projects which its chairman refers to, as he did once in the case of a nuclear breeder reactor, as a "turkey." Such a notion ignores the fact, said the committee report, "that Congress supported the [Columbia Dam] project over the years at the specific recommendation of TVA" and also that "TVA has the unilateral right to drop projects," a right that it had exercised before.

Similarly, TVA is one of the more professional practitioners of what might be called the "mea culpa-let's-let-bygones-be-bygones" routine, which is a cousin of "the Devil-made-me-do-it" and a subcategory of the "camel-in-the-tent" tactic. As practiced with near-perfect skill by David Freeman, it consists of equal portions of admitting that your agency has been doing wrong for years, carefully absolving yourself of any blame for this, and urging everyone to forget about the past and get on to the serious business of the future (for TVA, this has consisted in recent years of talking about solar energy, of "harnessing" the power of the sun as well as the Tennessee River). The argument is remarkably similar to that advanced by the leaders of the chemical industry in discussing the toxic waste issue. (Irving S. Shapiro, the chairman of Du Pont, it may be recalled, had suggested, "Let's start with today, not worry about who did what in the past.") Freeman, explaining to Congress why he hadn't reconsidered the clearly wasteful Columbia Dam project after he came into office in August of 1977, replied: "The Congress continued to direct us to build it, and we have 50,000 employees and a power program with $3,500,000,000 cash flow, more paper, and more live issues. I have chosen to spend my time putting together the nation's strongest energy conservation program, getting the solar program off the ground, and numerous other things."

Freeman *has* been able, in speeches he's made in the valley and around the nation, to pause from time to time to acknowledge TVA's faults *before* he took over the helm. The agency bears much of the blame for industrial water pollution, he has said, and the problem of lowered oxygen levels at TVA reservoirs is a serious one. On the subject of strip mining, Freeman has said, "We burn an awful lot of Appalachian coal in our power plants, and that has left an awful lot of ugly land as a result over the years. TVA got religion a little late on strip mining and I think we're at the stage of the game now where we're finally trying to work with the Department of Interior and others. But there is a legacy, a horrible legacy, of strip-mined land that is an embarrassment to me." On the destruction of farmland, Freeman has asserted: "Each year more and more of our prime farmland is being gobbled up by the developers and the fast-buck artists and no one—at least no one here in the Tennessee Valley—is doing anything about it." He did not dwell on the fact that TVA itself was one of the hungriest developers and fast-buck artists.

An essential component of the "mea-culpa-bygones" routine is the Look to the Future. Hardly an announcement comes out of TVA these days, or hardly had Freeman made a speech, without the point being made that the agency now views its mission as leading the nation out of the quagmire of the energy crisis. Having dammed practically every river, stream, and brook in the Tennessee Valley, having courted the extinction of species and fouled the water and poisoned the air, TVA would now have us forget about the past and concentrate on a future in which it shows us how to develop synfuels, how to insulate our homes, and how to capture the energy of the sun. The most overwhelming of the builders' characteristics— and just about all of their characteristics are quite overwhelming, by design—is their instinct for their own survival, even at the expense of everything else.

It was not at all difficult for them to survive a frontal attack by a president of the United States. For the builders, Jimmy Carter's effort to impose a new water policy on the nation, and to eliminate or tone down a few of the more wasteful water projects, was just another routine obstacle, easily overcome; no more of a challenge than an environmental impact statement or a GAO audit, a mountain range or a pleasant bend in a meandering river that needed to be straightened out, "enhanced."

Carter left office in January, 1981, of course, with not only his water program but also a number of his other initiatives unimplemented. But it may be instructive to recall, in outline, what happened to the Carter water policy. For at least the issue was raised. For the first time, the nation was asked to seriously consider what it was doing to its water, in terms of quality, quantity, and environmental and aesthetic implications. It quickly became clear that the issue was too traumatic for the nation (and especially for the corner of the Iron Triangle represented by Congress) to handle. But when it is raised again, perhaps the nation will find itself closer to being ready for it. It *will* be raised again, because America is running out of clean, cheap water.

Soon after taking office in January, 1977, Carter announced that nineteen water projects overseen by the Corps, BuRec, and TVA were not necessary, were too expensive, or were too harmful to the environment, and that he was opposing their further funding in the federal budget for Fiscal Year 1978. And the new President delivered a message on the environment in which he declared that one of the nation's pressing domestic issues was the "establishment of a national water resources management policy." The United States, he said, needed a "comprehensive reform of water resources policy, with water conservation as its cornerstone."

The catalogue of nineteen projects, which was immediately dubbed Carter's "hit list," later was expanded to thirty-two projects, then shrunk considerably as Congress reacted in horror and outrage. The legislators restored most of the President's cuts and Carter signed the legislation, although his supporters probably could have sustained a veto. Brock Evans, the director of the Sierra Club's Washington office, called Carter's actions "a betrayal," and said "the President caved in." It was not an auspicious beginning for a President who wanted to reform the nation's water policy.

Carter went to work on the other aspects of his new water policy, and on June 6, 1978, he sent the reform to Congress. The program he envisioned was remarkably far-reaching and thorough (although it appeared to shy away from anything that might upset agribusiness, and it refused to deal with the issue of the ridiculously low interest rates that are factored into cost-benefit calculations). It contained four major elements:

The first sought to make federal water projects more economically and environmentally sound through such devices as requiring that conservation be figured into the planning, requiring that non-structural alternatives be considered in the planning process, and revising the existing means of figuring (or fabricating) costs and benefits. A professionally staffed review board, presumably insulated from the Iron Triangle, would pass judgment on proposed projects. Carter also wanted state-federal cost sharing for water projects; this, the President reasoned, would make non-structural alternatives more attractive to states once they were paying part of the bill.

The second major element was conservation of water. Here, Carter didn't go into much detail, but he at least raised the question that so badly needed raising. The third element was getting the states more involved in water not only through cost sharing but also through federal grants that would promote the planning of water projects at the state level. Carter's fourth point involved avoiding damages to the environment. "Sensitivity to environmental protection," he told Congress, "must be an important aspect of all water-related planning and management decisions. I am particularly concerned about the need to improve the protection of in-stream flows and to evolve careful management of our nation's precious groundwater supplies, which are threatened by depletion and contamination."

As Congress was considering the President's proposals, it also was dealing with a new public-works budget. In the spring and summer of 1978, Congress managed to increase the number of water projects, including eight that Carter had managed to kill the previous year. This time Carter vetoed the bill; Congress sustained the veto; and the House and Senate quickly passed a substitute appropriations bill that excluded funding for most of the disputed projects.

In the following year, 1979, Carter sought to implement portions of his water policy. When he tried to remove from the Corps of Engineers the power to plan projects and calculate their cost-benefit ratios, and to place it in the hands of a new Department of Natural Resources, the reaction from the Iron Triangle was so severe that the plan was dropped almost immediately. Carter, the White House told the press, "believes it is too controversial for Congress to handle this year." (Another report was that the President was dropping the plan in exchange for votes on the Strategic Arms Limitation Treaty.)

In February of 1980, a $4,200,000,000 water projects bill, redolent of juicy pork from the eternal barrel, was pending in the Senate, and Carter was talking about vetoing it. He called it "a travesty—wasteful, destructive, and expensive," and declared that "I do not intend to allow this proposed legislation to become law." By the following fall, Carter apparently had changed his mind; he signed an appropriations act that provided funds for three dams that had been on his original hit list (the Yatesville Dam in Kentucky, Columbia Dam in Tennessee, and Orme Dam in the Central Arizona Project), along with a number of other of the builders' more infamous undertakings: the Tennessee-Tombigbee Waterway, Locks and Dam Number 26, Dickey-Lincoln in Maine, and new construction on the Central Arizona Project. In return, Congress gave Carter very little of what he wanted. It refused to go along with the very important review-board idea and it declined to make changes in the way costs and benefits are figured. Carter, upon signing the appropriations act on October 1, 1980, referred to the legislation as "a constructive compromise among contending interests," even though it was difficult to see who, other than he himself, had compromised. There was, said the President, much in the bill that departed "significantly from my water resource development policy." An example, said Carter, was the need for an independent review agency "to insure that projects are planned and designed as both economically feasible and environmentally acceptable." He would work with Congress on furthering that goal, said Carter, "next year." But a little more than one month later the electorate turned

Carter out of office, and by the beginning of the next year Carter was home in Georgia, replaced by a President who had once blamed trees for air pollution and who chose as his Secretary of the Interior a man who clearly saw the environment as another set of "resources" for the builders, miners, and irrigators to exploit.

The builders, meantime, continued their assaults on the environment, but occasionally they got caught. In March, 1982, a federal district judge in New York City rendered a stern decision in a suit brought by environmentalists and community groups against the promoters of a supremely wasteful project called Westway. It would spread 4.2 miles of the most expensive highway on earth along Manhattan's Lower West Side, filling in a portion of the Hudson River in the process. Whatever the project's purported transportation uses, it clearly was also a convenient means by which private developers could create new, expensive real estate at public expense.

The judge, a Nixon appointee named Thomas P. Griesa, found that the Corps of Engineers had violated several laws in issuing a permit allowing the filling of a section of the river that it called a "biological wasteland." The judge said the Corps had overlooked the objections of three other federal agencies, had ignored its own data showing the landfill area to be an important wintering place for juvenile striped bass, had withheld information, and had acted in "total noncompliance" with the law. "The total failure of the Corps to comply with [its] obligations," said Judge Griesa, "has been demonstrated beyond any question." A spokesperson for the Corps said he was "embarrassed" by the findings.

24

And there is Tellico, the saddest example of the builders' art.

The Tellico project represents practically everything that's wrong with the federal water agencies and their attitudes toward, as well as their treatment of, Earth and the water that flows on it. Despite the fact that the project could not be justified even by its promoters' most strenuous manipulations, it was built. The Tennessee Valley Authority, acting on behalf of Congress and the local delegates to the Iron Triangle, clearly disregarded regulations, common sense, and simple decency in order to complete a project that had no advantages for anyone other than the builders and the speculators. In the process TVA destroyed one of the last free-flowing streams in the region, obliterated the remains of an ancient culture, threw people off their ancestral homelands, ruined great tracts of prime farmland, and deliberately destroyed what was believed to be the only habitat of a unique species of fish. And, in the end, a President of the United States who wanted to be remembered as an environmentalist, who wanted to reform the process by which the builders were ruining the land, who once said the three or four best days of his political life were the ones he spent going down a wild river on a raft—this President of the United States not only surrendered himself to the powers of pork-barrel politics, but also gave up for destruction yet another piece of the tattered planet.

Tellico happened in easternmost Tennessee, in a valley roughly equidistant from Knoxville and Chattanooga but tucked away from the corridor of traffic, industry, and pollution that connects the two cities. It is an area of low ridges and rolling pasture, at the place where the Little Tennessee River, only half tamed as it tumbles down from the North Carolina mountains, joins the series of reservoirs that TVA has manufactured from remnants of the once mighty Tennessee River. The junction is in the lowlands, about 800 feet above sea level. Just a few miles to the east, past the achingly long Chilhowee Mountain, and Happy Valley Gap, and Polecat Ridge, among a hundred other places high and low, rise the Great Smoky Mountains, thrusting as much as a mile more toward the heavens. As TVA had thrown dam after dam across everything in its region that moved and was wet, the last dozen or so miles of the Little T, as it is known, had taken on a virtual uniqueness. Its water was swift and cold and relatively pure, an increasingly rare combination that encourages trout and other species that can survive only in a clean environment. Almost every other body of water within TVA's purview had been imprisoned behind dams; had grown fat and sluggish and warm, its floor covered with silt and its oxygen depleted; and the trout and other aquatic life that serve so well as ecological sentinels died out.

TVA's own staff reported that the Little Tennessee area was "one of considerable archaeological and historical value." More than 250 archaeological sites have been identified there, providing evidence of human habitation dating back over a period of 10,000 years. The valley was also one of the homes of the Cherokee Indians, who had several villages there. One, a capital, was named Chota; another, Tanasi, is believed to have been the place that provided Tennessee with its name. There is, said the TVA staff, "evidence of the occurrence of some of the earliest traits of cultural development in eastern North America."

But TVA management suffered from a terrible compulsion to build dams. Since 1936 the agency had been drawing up plans for the Little Tennessee. At first they included throwing a dam across the Little T where it joined the Tennessee River, then sending the Little T's waters off by way of a canal to

another TVA reservoir, Fort Loudon, just a few hundred yards
to the east. The alleged benefits included flood control, improved navigation, and the pushing of more water through the
electrical generators at Fort Loudon Dam. The "Fort Loudon
Extension," as the project was then known, was estimated to
cost $10,700,000. When World War II began, it was put on the
shelf. Later, when it was brought down and dusted off, TVA
added some features to build up the cost-benefit ratio—mostly
industrial, commercial, and residential development around the
lake that would be created—and to raise the estimated cost to
$41,000,000. A centerpiece of the project would be the con-
struction of a planned community, Timberlake, which would
serve as sort of a TVA-built, taxpayer-financed company town
for the Boeing Aerospace Company, which TVA hoped to lure
to the site. By 1963, when TVA officially proposed the construction of the Tellico Project, as it now was known, its benefits
were said to break down this way: 38 per cent for recreation,
19 per cent for shoreline development, 6 per cent for "enhancement of fish and wildlife," 11 per cent for hydroelectric power,
11 per cent for navigation, 13 per cent for flood control, and 2
per cent for water supply. TVA claimed the project would
create 6,600 jobs, 4,000 of them in industry and the rest in
trades and services.

TVA's promotion of Tellico coincided with the swelling
of great national interest in environmental matters, and so an
unprecedented degree of controversy followed the project
through the sixties. Critics of Tellico placed great emphasis on
the loss of the river, of the Indian homesteads, and of the
agricultural land. Such arguments hardly bring tears to the eyes
of the keepers of the pork barrel, however, and in 1966
Congress appropriated funds for the project, whose cost was
now estimated at $45,000,000. Construction began the following
year, as did acquisition of the land, or the "grabbing" of it, as
it is known to many in Tennessee. TVA appraisers, threatening
condemnation and expensive legal battles and often so good at
their work that they could judge the value of a 100-acre farm

without leaving their automobiles (it is called a "windshield appraisal" in the business), assembled about 38,000 acres of land, along with existing buildings, for which they paid out some $22,000,000. Of that total only 1,841 acres represented the area of the actual river. Much of the remainder had been officially categorized as "prime farmland" or "land of statewide importance for agriculture."

TVA, true to arrogant form, did its best to ignore the National Environmental Policy Act of 1969 and, in particular, that portion of the law that required the filing of environmental impact statements. The act was as important, in its way, to the nation's new appreciation and understanding of and commitment to the environment as the various civil rights acts of earlier years had been to race relations. It required that there be included in every proposal for federal action that significantly affected the quality of the human environment a "detailed statement" of the anticipated "environmental impact of the proposed action." The statement would include, among other things, an examination of possible adverse consequences, a list of irretrievable commitments of resources that would result, and a discussion of possible alternatives to the proposed action. The environmental impact statement, or EIS, for short, has developed as a prime tool for environmentalists in challenging, and at the least slowing down and forcing a public examination of, public works and other projects that they deem to be harmful. Demands for environmental impact statements have been made, as well, by those normally considered to be on the other side of the fence, including irrigators in California. The act's creation of a Council on Environmental Quality was another step in the right direction. Under the Jimmy Carter administration, the Council was one of the few government agencies that seemed to be genuinely concerned about enlightening the public and the government on environmental matters, and its annual reports on the state of the environment and on the nation's dealings with it became valuable reference works.

When environmentalists brought a federal suit in 1971, charging that TVA had not filed a proper EIS, the agency responded that it was not subject to the National Environmental Policy Act. The courts disagreed and construction at Tellico was halted for twenty-one months while TVA produced the statement. In it, TVA found it necessary to demonstrate that there were, in fact, a couple of viable alternatives to the project as originally conceived. What TVA wanted, the agency had calculated (with the help of some very fancy methodology), would cost $1,507,000 a year to operate and would return $5,903,000 a year in benefits. One of the alternatives, which consisted of restoring the Little T to the status of "scenic stream," would cost $82,000 a year and return $129,000. Abandoning the project altogether would cost nothing, according to TVA, and return $101,000 a year in benefits. (Later, a report by the General Accounting Office pointed out several flaws in TVA's methods of calculating costs and benefits. "Our analysis," said GAO, ". . . showed the assumptions and logic used by TVA to estimate some benefits are not valid predictors of Tellico benefits. In some cases the methodology did not conform to federal guidelines for estimating the benefits of water projects and, in other instances, statistical projections were not valid." For example, in figuring the benefits of "scenic stream" status, which TVA did not want, the agency managed not to add in benefits from continued use of the land for agriculture, or from the historical and cultural worth of the land, or from fish and wildlife. GAO concluded that TVA's numbers were so old and its methodology so shaky that "we do not believe the benefit projections are representative of the actual benefits that would be derived if the project is completed." TVA's response to the embarrassing document from GAO was the predictable camel's-nose act: The project was so close to being finished, said the agency, that it should be finished.)

In August of 1973, there was a discovery that was to profoundly affect the Tellico project and the attitudes of the builders and their fellow members of the Iron Triangle. David

A. Etnier, a professor of zoology at the University of Tennessee, was snorkeling in the Little Tennessee River about seven miles upstream from the point at its mouth where the Tellico Dam would soon be in place. Etnier was one of several scientists whose interest in the river and its environs had taken on a new and considerably more urgent quality: The river soon would be impounded, and if those who chronicle and catalogue life on this planet wanted to learn the secrets of the long, meandering valley, they would have to do their work quickly. Before it was all over, archaeologists would be using the crudest of instruments—backhoes and bulldozers, instead of trowels and camel's-hair brushes—to unearth signs of earlier civilizations; and piles of bones from the Cherokees, the earlier residents who had treated the environment (and their dead) with considerably more respect, would be hastily dumped in basements at the university.

Etnier's work was cleaner. While suspended in the water over a gravel shoal, he saw a small fish he had never seen before. He captured it in his hands, collected some more, and soon concluded that it was a fish called a darter, of the subgenus *Imostoma*, genus *Percina*—a relative of the perch. (Eventually the fish would be classified as *Percina (Imostoma) tanasi*, after the Indian village that had been situated on a bend of the Little Tennessee.) The nation was soon to know the fish as the "snail darter"—or, through the courtesy of media that seem compelled to reduce everything to a cliché, the "tiny snail darter." The fish rarely grew longer than three and a half inches, and its adult weight was about 5 grams, or .176 of an avoirdupois ounce. The darter was brown, with faint green tracings and four distinct brown markings, called "saddles," and a white belly. It was soon determined that the snail darter spawned in Coytee Shoals, several miles upstream from the Tellico Dam site. The current carried their larvae downstream to slower-running water, where they hatched and grew into tiny fish. As the darters matured, they fought the current back toward their spawning beds and the cycle was renewed. The darter's life span was about three years. As scientists probed more and more deeply into the life of the small fish, it seemed that *Percina (Imostoma) tanasi* lived only in the Little Tennessee River and that its population could be numbered in the several thousands.

Only a few months after Etnier's discovery on the Little Tennessee, Congress enacted the Endangered Species Act of 1973, which requires, in the words of a government agency, the "identification and protection of habitat that is critical to continued existence of endangered species." The snail darter was an immediate candidate for inclusion on what has become known as the Endangered Species List, a compilation of creatures and plants whose existences are threatened by humans' relentless exploitation of Earth. TVA fought such a designation, utilizing its usual argument that it was above the law. Aubrey J. Wagner, who preceded David Freeman as head of TVA, said at one point that "In our rush to correct decades of environmental neglect, we have tended to place man's needs in a changing, complex world somewhere well down our list of environmental priorities." At about the time the endangered species argument was developing, the Tellico Project slipped a notch in priorities, too; Boeing Aerospace decided to back out of the company-town scheme, and the mythical town of Timberlake was never heard of again. By then, the Tellico project was said to be 75 per cent completed, and its estimated cost had risen from $41,000,000 to $100,000,000.

The discovery of the snail darter, and the nation's discovery that species were worth preserving, led to the fish's inclusion on the list in November of 1975. They also led opponents of the Tellico project into a course of action that has become quite celebrated, as well as misunderstood, by fellow environmentalists, builders, and the general public alike. It started one day in 1974, when a young member of the University of Tennessee law school faculty, Zygmunt Plater, was talking with a student. Plater was teaching a course in environmental law, and the student wanted to discuss a possible subject for a term paper. "The student said he had taken a fish biology class," recalled Plater a few years later, "and he said that his professor had discovered a three-inch fish that was an endangered species, right in the middle of the Tellico project. Did I think that would be a decent subject for an environmental law term paper? I told him that I thought it was going to be a good deal *more* than that. And of course it was." What Plater, a soft-spoken former Peace Corps member, got started was the celebrated Snail Darter Case. In February, 1976, a lawsuit was filed on behalf of environmentalists and the fish to enjoin the Tennessee Valley Authority from completing the impoundment of the Little Tennessee River, on the grounds that it would destroy the "critical habitat" of the fish, in violation of the Endangered Species Act. Zyg Plater, who argued the environmentalists' case all the way to the Supreme Court, said later that "from the very beginning I knew that, in the law, we had them absolutely dead to rights. Section Seven of the act says you cannot destroy a species, and you have to consult on alternatives to avoid destroying a species. TVA was going to destroy this species, and they refused to consult. So I knew we had them on the law, and I knew we had them on the biological facts. It was absolutely clear. But there was much more, and that's the problem. The only story that the media ever covered was fish-versus-dam. Every story was about the little David and the big Goliath, Little Fish versus Big Dam. The way it was covered, they never looked at the *battlefield* of David and Goliath."

Plater was quite correct about this. As key assertions and decisions were made in the case, television news shows invariably flashed on their screens graphic creations depicting a tiny, chubby, and somewhat stupid-looking fish, superimposed on a representation of a huge dam (actually, the Tellico was a minnow as dams go). *The New York Times* declared in a headline: "Controversy Over 3-Inch Fish Stalls the Mighty T.V.A." The *battlefield* that Plater mentioned was hardly ever mentioned, and that, he said, was the absolutely clear lack of need for a Tellico project at all.

"The reservoir is not hydroelectric," said Plater. "There are no generators. They only have a little canal that leads water to another lake and produces 23 megawatts, which is peanuts. It wasn't flood control, and it wasn't irrigation. It was to create a hypothetical industrial city that would be built along the lake. They talked about barge traffic, but the economists told me that barges would not be attracted. And recreation. This is the sixty-ninth dam in the area. There are twenty-four existing reservoirs within sixty miles. But they talk about this as recreation—eliminating the last clean-flowing big trout river, a fantastic river. This is the last such river that's left. You can drink the water from it."

These issues were not the ones that were argued in the courts, however. By the time the matter got before the Supreme Court, in the spring of 1978 (with the project 90 per cent complete and its cost now estimated at $116,000,000), the question was strictly one of endangered species.

The Carter administration demonstrated its interest in the case (and its disdain for the environmentalists) by sending Attorney General Griffin Bell in to argue for TVA, even though TVA's large battery of lawyers was perfectly capable of providing self-defense. Bell offered a pair of strange arguments, ones with no known foundation in U.S. law: that the Endangered Species Act should not be applied to projects that were close to completion when the existence of the species was discovered, and that Congress had demonstrated its intent that the dam should be finished, no matter what the Endangered Species Act said, by its continuing appropriations of money for the project. Zyg Plater argued that there was no legal precedent for this sort of "amendment by authorization." An unusual aspect of the trial was that Interior Secretary Andrus was allowed by the administration to disagree with the Bell-Carter position, in writing.

Griffin Bell's appearance before the highest court was widely interpreted (undoubtedly correctly) as a not so subtle hint from President Carter that, despite the joys he got from rafting down wild rivers, he intended to cast his lot with the builders. Conservative newspaper columnist Patrick J. Buchanan, writing during the trial, said that Bell's appearance was "Mr. Carter's coded signal that the White House has added up the respective numbers and is putting distance between itself and the environmental movement." The environmentalists, continued Buchanan, were "Dominantly young, well-educated children of the upper middle class and the rich" who had "tasted affluence since they were 10, have tired of Chablis and Brie, and are casting about for heroic weekend causes into which to cast themselves. Instead of signing up for the Abraham Lincoln Brigade and going off to fight Franco as the old leftists did, the new leftists take the weekend off to fly to Canada to save the seal pups."

The Supreme Court delivered its ruling on June 15, 1978: The Tellico project must be stopped because of the Endangered Species Act. David beats Goliath, echoed the media immediately. The ruling came on a 6–3 vote, with Associate Justice Lewis F. Powell, Jr., in the principal dissent, demonstrating his ignorance of the Tellico battlefield by writing about "the adverse effect on the people of this economically-depressed area." (About the only people who would be hurt would be TVA's bureaucrats, land speculators, and motorboat salesmen.) Powell demonstrated further ignorance by expressing the fear that conservationists might be able to block federal projects elsewhere because of "a water spider or a cockroach." Both majority and minority opinions noted that Congress might want to pass legislation exempting the Tellico project from the Endangered Species Act; and, in fact, such legislation was even then in the works.

One such attempt at a legislative remedy, which soon became law, created a review group, called the Endangered

Species Inter-Agency Committee, to deal with matters of "irresolvable conflict" between the Endangered Species Act and federal projects and programs. Zyg Plater referred to it as "a bureaucratic extinction committee which plays God." The God Committee met in January, 1979, to consider the Tellico case. When one of its members, Charles Schultze, the chairman of the President's Council of Economic Advisors, began to make a comment on the matter, environmentalists feared the worst. Schultze, a tough-looking, almost gruff man, was not likely to be the sort of person who'd fly off to save seal pups, much less spiders and cockroaches. But he shocked the environmentalists by declaring (in words that went largely unreported by the press, but that Plater and others recorded) that "The interesting phenomenon is that here is a project that is 95 per cent complete, and if one takes just the cost of finishing it against the [total] benefits . . . it doesn't pay, which says something about the original design." The God Committee then voted unanimously to stop the Tellico project on economic grounds, rather than out of compassion for the snail darter. Zyg Plater was quoted as saying that the decision "proves that government, when enlightened, can work."

Government, when unenlightened, works with equal efficiency. Legislation made its way through Congress to exempt the Tellico project from the Endangered Species Act. Representative John J. Duncan, a Republican whose district encompasses Tellico and TVA's headquarters, delivered a speech to his fellow legislators that contained several arguable assertions (such as one that a "successful transplant" of the snail darter was being carried out on another river; the success or failure of a transplant takes several years to assess) and that demonstrated what seemed to be an utter contempt for nature: "I hope we will not overlook the human considerations of this controversy," he said. "Should a worthless, unsightly, minute, unedible minnow outweigh a possible injustice to human beings?" (Duncan was not the only one to malign the small fish and, furthermore, to malign it incorrectly. An editorial writer at *The New York Times* referred to the snail darter as "that tiny minnow.")

The Iron Triangle, under attack now, moved swiftly. TVA produced a report on the possible alternatives to the original project that had the additional effect of demonstrating how worthless Tellico had been. The report said, among other things: "At the heart of the dilemma here is a conflict between creating a reservoir to generate electricity or preserving the rich bottomland to grow food. Both resources are essential and becoming increasingly scarce. Who is to say which is the most important? (*sic*)" (Although TVA was now claiming big electrical benefits, the measly output of the water Tellico would add to another dam's turbines remained measly. TVA claimed Tellico would add 200,000,000 kilowatt-hours per year to its capacity. To use one kilowatt, someone would need to burn ten 100-watt light bulbs for only one hour each. In 1981, Consolidated Edison, which furnishes electrical power to 2,700,000 residential customers in the New York City area, sold 7,723,440,000 kilowatt-hours.)

The Cherokees were dealt with in traditional, straightforward white-man fashion. Their lawsuit challenging the project on the grounds that it deprived them of their religious rights was turned down. (TVA's argument against them was that they didn't own the land!) And on June 18, 1979, Congressman Duncan quietly slipped in a rider to the appropriations bill that specifically exempted the Tellico project from the provisions of the Endangered Species Act or any other law. There were few members of Congress present, and the measure passed on a voice vote. On the following September 10, the Senate reversed positions it had taken twice before and voted, 48–44, to authorize completion.

Interior Secretary Andrus warned that if the Tellico exemption stayed in, he would urge President Carter to veto the appropriations bill. But the exemption stuck, and Carter did not veto it. On September 25, 1979, the President signed the act closing the dam at Tellico and seriously jeopardizing the life of the snail darter. Zyg Plater was to say, later, that it was the first time in the history of the world that mankind had *deliberately* taken steps to exterminate a species.

The President signed the act in a somewhat sneaky fashion. He was conducting a "town meeting" in the Queens borough of New York City, and thus was about as far removed as he could be from reporters who had a clear understanding of what was happening. (The *Times*, in its story the next day, referred to Tellico as a "hydroelectric project," which it clearly was not.) There was immediate speculation on why he had done it. An official White House line was that Carter didn't veto the measure because he didn't want to goad Congress into weakening or abolishing the Endangered Species Act. Carter spoke of his "clear belief in the principles" of the act, as well as his promise to "enforce it vigorously," even as he signed the act that facilitated the extinction of a species. There were reports, somewhat more believable, from other quarters that Carter had made a deal with Tennesseans that involved his swapping the only known remaining habitat of the snail darter for their support of the Panama Canal treaty.

TVA moved quickly after the President signed the legislation. The agency evicted people from their land, bulldozed their homes, and, on November 29, 1979, under cover of darkness, closed the gates in Tellico Dam and the water level started rising. Not long afterward the well-stocked TVA Map Sales Office on the ground floor of TVA's headquarters in Knoxville began selling a chart named "Tellico Lake Recreation-Fish Attractor Map." It depicted, in a scale of one inch to half a mile, the *new* Tellico Lake, with places where fish —the more sluggish fish of warm waters, not the trout that once lived there—could be found. There was no mention on the map of the place, a little upstream from Bacon Bend, where the adjacent Cherokee villages of Chota and Tanasi could be found. They were under water. And there was no indication, of course, that *Percina (Imostoma) tanasi* had ever existed.

(The snail darter may yet endure. Late in 1980, David Etnier reported that he had found some of the fish in another body of water—South Chickamauga Creek, many miles to the south, near Chattanooga, and a year later he reported finding three more groups of the fish, in Alabama and Georgia.)

In February, 1980, the Tennessee Valley Authority asked the State of Tenneessee to lower its water-quality standards for the newly born Tellico Lake. Since the Little Tennessee had been a free-flowing, cold-water trout stream, with no industries and therefore very clean water, such a change in the standards would have to be made before industries that TVA said would be built on the side of the new lake could legally discharge their effluent into it. A TVA publicist was quoted as explaining that "It's basically a case where the classification has to catch up to the facts of the matter."

And two years after that, David Freeman had fully incorporated Tellico into the "mea culpa" routine. TVA, he told a meeting of conservationists in March, 1982, had "refused even to evaluate any alternatives to Tellico. It simply refused to consider the archaeological significance at Tellico, or the fish and wildlife that would be disrupted, or even the food-producing value of the 16,000 acres that were to be submerged under Tellico reservoir."

25

TVA would prefer that everyone now forget the Tellico fiasco and concentrate instead on the future. The era of big dam building is over, TVA officials have said, knowing that every conceivable big dam has been built. We are "getting back to our roots," says Mohammed El-Ashry: TVA is "trying to be a conservation and a development agency, providing the development while at the same time protecting the environment."

Mohammed El-Ashry used to run the Denver office of the Environmental Defense Fund. Born in Egypt, he has spent most of his life in the United States and most of his professional life working for the environment. He is tall and handsome, with neat gray hair and intense, intelligent eyes. In September of 1979 he left EDF and joined the TVA staff as Director of Environmental Quality, where part of his job is to advise the general manager and TVA's board on environmental matters.

He could not have come to Knoxville, said El-Ashry, if it had not been for the fundamental change that occurred in TVA at about the time Jimmy Carter made S. David Freeman its chairman. Before, he had never dreamed of working for the government, much less TVA (which his environmental organization had sued, in the Columbia Dam case), said El-Ashry in the summer of 1980. "But over the last two years, things have changed dramatically at TVA." When he visited the agency for an interview, he said, "I realized that the commitment for environmental quality is here, and it has been very exciting to become part of the change that is taking place and that will be taking place in the environmental area." It was, he said, a "natural progression" from working for a private environmental group. "There were these things that we had been advocating that government ought to do. Now we are going to be part of it."

El-Ashry's enthusiasm for TVA and its potential does not diminish when he is confronted with questions about Tellico. He had the stock "the-Devil-made-us-do-it" TVA answer for Tellico, the answer that ignores TVA's own record in promoting the worthless project: "Tellico was a decision that was made by Congress. TVA was only fulfilling the mandate of Congress to close the gates. Congress passed it, the president signed it, and it became law. So if we're going to go on the past—the past is very grim. I was not in favor of Tellico. But Tellico is a reality now, because of the law. Congress passed it and the President signed it." There is more in TVA's history with which El-Ashry felt uncomfortable: "It was TVA's idea not to put any [sulfur dioxide] scrubbers on the power plants," he said. "And it was TVA's idea to build fourteen nuclear power plants, and it was TVA's idea to build the hundred and some dams that are there. That is true. That's the past of the agency. And I did not join the past of the agency. I'm joining the future of the agency. *That's* what I'm here for."

And the future, he said, is using the "tremendous expertise" that TVA has developed over the years to assist the residents of the Tennessee Valley in demonstrating that development and the environment can exist, side by side, in balance.

There are some, however, who are more skeptical about TVA's future. Tom Johnson, the executive director of Tennessee Citizens for Wilderness Planning, which opposed Tellico and other such water projects, said not long ago that the only improvement in TVA, in his view, was in the top management. "There is not a basic change in attitude," he said. As for TVA's frequent claim that it's out of the dam-building business, he says, "I think they probably are, at least on the big projects, because there really aren't any sites left. There's not much left they can do to us."

Alfred L. Davis would like to see something done to TVA.

He would like to see the agency go out of business. Davis, a tall, athletic-looking man, runs Davis Tractor and Equipment Company in Philadelphia, Tennessee, not far from the flooded bottomland. His family farm, one that his great-grandfather built in 1864, was taken by TVA for Tellico, although only a portion of it was actually needed for the lake. TVA will sell the rest, at a considerable profit, to an industry or, perhaps, to a well-to-do Knoxvillian or Nashvillian who wants a summer home or a condominium.

"TVA's got the power next to God around here," said Davis one day in the summer of 1980, as Tellico Lake was filling. "They can do whatever they want to, according to the courts. A court case with TVA is a real joke, because when you go to court with them, they'll do anything: lie, steal, whatever." Davis was one of those who fought TVA's land-grabbing methods in court, and lost. There are many reasons he opposes Tellico, some personal and some philosophical and some based on the easily-arrived-at conviction that the project was a supreme waste of the taxpayers' money, but the thing that bothered Alfred Davis the most is what TVA has done to the land.

"We love the land," he said, in a soft, almost delicate-sounding voice (it seemed all the softer for the huge tractors and combines and harvesting machinery that surrounded him). "There's something about ownership of the land that's undescribable. I think that people who never own any land miss something. . . . I don't know if it's more powerful than the love of a woman, but there's something about the ownership of the land—a farmer has a responsibility to take care of the land. You have *ownership* for your lifetime, but you have an *obligation* to leave the land in better shape than you found it. Your real good farmers do that. The people that's out for the dollar don't.

"The land is the backbone of the country. I think the real bad thing with Tellico is that we lost 16,000 acres of the best farmland in the world."

Davis talked on a while about what TVA had done—the

agency's techniques for appraising and obtaining the land would make even a non-landowner angry—and he displayed an intimate knowledge of the speciousness of TVA's claimed benefits for the project—and then his visitor asked him if he had gone back to his family farm since the lake started rising.

"I've been back two or three times," he said. "I almost want to cry. You drive down there, and what used to be a big river bottom, it's now water, twenty feet deep. That's the part that's hard to take. And the old barn that Granddaddy built, water's standing where it was. There are a lot of people who just don't go back." Then Alfred Davis looked out the window of his office, in the direction of what used to be the Little Tennessee River.

"I'd like to see the lake drained," he said quietly, and then he paused a moment to let the thought sink in. "We may never see it in our lifetime, but it *will* be drained. By the year 2000, everybody predicts, we will consume every bit of food that we can produce. Some people don't believe that. But we're directly involved with agriculture. People who aren't involved think that we have just an endless supply of food. We don't. It's not that way. By the year 2000, we'll be hard-put for land. Someday they're going to have to drain that lake so we can grow food again."

Zyg Plater lost his job. After he argued the snail darter case before the Supreme Court, he was denied tenure at the University of Tennessee law school. "My contract wasn't renewed," he explained later. "And the reason that I was given by one of the people who voted against me was that I did not 'adequately understand the moderation expected of a Tennessee law professor.' I was an activist. But I was also, I think, an intellectual, a scholar, and I did more work in the research of the theories, in my work, than most people. It was quite clearly a political feeling that I just wasn't fitting in. That's okay." He moved to Michigan shortly thereafter and continued teaching.

More recently, in the spring of 1980, Plater was one of the

speakers at a conference at Ramapo College, in Mahwah, New Jersey. The subject of the meeting was "Water and the Public Interest," and it attracted a small but concerned group of women and men who were interested in a spectrum of water issues, from fighting dams to catching midnight polluters. Plater wore a light tan, utilitarian suit and a checkered shirt. He was obviously a practiced speaker, with the ability to modulate the volume of his voice in a way that makes his listeners feel, during the moments when he is almost whispering, that they're being let in on important, almost secret, thoughts. The young professor's subject was "The Water Crisis," and he chose to approach it with the question, "What have we learned?" during the last years of lawsuits, of environmental awareness, of controversies such as Tellico.

"Well," he said, "it seems to me—and this sounds simplistic —we've learned that water reflects." There was laughter from the audience. "Water reflects," Plater repeated. "But what does it reflect? It reflects the heart of our government. It reflects politics. It reflects economics, it reflects ethics. It seems to me that if you look at water, you will find that it indeed incorporates everything that we are about as a society. Looking into water is not just an intellectual inquiry. It is an inquiry that goes to the heart of this particular society. . . .

"Abandon hope if you do not want to think politically. If you care about flowing water, if you care about drinkable water, you will become a political analyst perforce. The pork barrel, it seems to me, is, day in and day out, just short of patriotism as *the* single most forceful power within government to make Presidents, congressmen, and governmental agencies respond." The nation was full of projects, he said, that never should have been built but that are built, "because they're tied into the system of agency, congressional, and financial subsidies. Marginal projects get built because they are not marginal politically.

"Let me say something, though, about the marginal economics. You will become economists, as well. Most of you perhaps already have. In fact, environmentalists, it seems to me, are the *real* economists today. You cannot understand the economics of Hooker's dumping chemicals into a stream or into a land area that leaches into a stream just by looking at the corporate economics. Economics, properly viewed by environmentalists, has to look at the economics of water *downstream*—the cost of water which is lost but which is very hard to measure. . . ." Plater talked for a while about Tellico—about how the environmentalists who had brought the case had tried from the beginning to explain to the public the economics of the project, but how the media always seemed to end up with a picture of the tiny snail darter superimposed on the giant dam and the David-and-Goliath cliché. Then Plater's voice became almost a whisper again:

"Never before in human history have we *consciously* chosen to exterminate a species from the face of the earth. God help us, we have *done* it a thousand times. But this was the first time we did it consciously. I don't think that point was ever raised in the public media in this country."

A little later, Plater returned to his original question: "What have we learned?" It was necessary during the New Deal, he reminded his listeners (most of whom had not been born until long after Franklin Delano Roosevelt's policies had become firmly institutionalized), that the government assume the role of "chief protector of the public interest." That meant agencies to oversee and supervise and regulate. But the agencies, the regulators, gradually became part of a system that involved just them and the regulated. The Iron Triangle was born, the pork barrel perfected. But more recently, the public has entered the equation. "Twenty years ago," Plater told his audience, "it would have been astounding to think that a citizen had standing to sue the Corps of Engineers on an entire wasteful project. But now there are all kinds of opportunities to sue against official action on many different levels, in the courts but also within the agencies. I see many people like us walking into state agencies and testifying—

raising not only emotional pleas but also having done their homework. Raising the embarrassing questions that neither the agency nor the regulated industry wants raised. I've seen a high school class change the nature of a political decision. In the old days it was 'The business of government is business. The market rules.' Then it became 'The government will protect us *against* the market when the market is excessive.' And now it's 'People are learning to protect themselves in legal ways against the market's excesses and the excesses of the agencies that were put there to do the job.'"

Someone once traced the politics and development of a large number of nations, Plater told the audience, and concluded that the one constant was water. "If you follow the development, the dispersion, the politics, the law of water," he said, "you will understand a society in a way that you could by following no other variables. It seems to me that that makes it pretty clear that what we're involved with, ultimately, is government. And when we, as citizens, try to apply our intellects and our activities to the kinds of things I've been talking about—political analysis, economic analysis, legal analysis and involvement, and informational analysis—then we *are* government. And it seems to me that if democracy has meaning and prospect, then the politics, the economics, the law, and the involvement of people in *water* is ultimately a bellwether for democracy, for the way our congress will work and the sort of quality of life all of us will have, forever.

"It's a lot of work, and, I'll tell you, it's depressing."

At about the time Zyg Plater was saying that, S. David Freeman, TVA's chairman, the man who had said the era of big dam projects in the Tennessee Valley was over, was visiting China. He was the United States' signatory in an agreement in which the U.S. will help China design four large hydroelectric projects. News stories about the signing said an outgrowth would be the eventual prospect of big financial deals with American firms.

IV

The Future

26

And so what will be the future of our most precious and abused resource?

It is clear that if we continue to treat water as we have treated it in the past, that future will be dismal indeed, both for water and for us who depend on it for survival. Even a general notion of the sheer magnitude of the crisis is ample cause for worry. But our self-imposed ignorance of the situation makes it even more frightening. It is an ignorance compounded by our reluctance to probe very deeply, to learn for ourselves the dimensions of the problem, to pay attention to the lessons of the past. It is an understandable reluctance, for there is always the chance that what we discover will confirm fears far too horrible to acknowledge—will confirm that we have gone too far; that we have drunk already an irreparable dose of the toxins; that we have, worst of all, poisoned generations that have not even been born. But it is a reluctance that must be overcome, in the name of the planet's distant future, if not for our own.

The horror stories continue to be told. The nation was almost convulsed by tales of toxic dumping and drinking-water contamination in the summer and fall of 1980, but then other crises, other events claimed the headlines. The chemicals were still there, though, leaching through the soil toward the aquifers and traveling through the aquifers toward the wells and streams. In July, 1980, the town of West Milford, New Jersey, accepted a free offer of "oil" from a tank-cleaning firm. The thick, oily substance was sprayed, several inches deep, on unpaved roads, some of them bordering water supplies.

The substance kept the dust down, but residents complained of headaches and nausea. Newspapers reported that state investigators knew, as early as the end of August, that the "oil" contained toxic chemicals, but the residents were not informed until the end of October, when state cleanup crews came to scrape the substance away. No one has explained what caused the delay, but officials did learn that the "oil" contained high concentrations of PCBs, lead, arsenic, chromium, nickel, mercury, cadmium, and selenium.

The General Accounting Office released a report in March, 1982, that said the nation's drinking water supplies are getting more dangerous. Some 28,000 community water systems, or 43 per cent of the total, had violations in 1980 of federal health standards, said the GAO. The auditing agency also noticed another trend that has become increasingly alarming in the water crisis: the operators of the systems were not telling the public about the problems they were discovering in their water. Of 146,000 violations of standards reported in 1980, said the GAO, the public had been informed in only 16,000 of the cases.

As 1982 began, two electronics firms in the region south of San Francisco known as Silicon Valley, for its concentration of high-technology industries, revealed that toxic chemicals had leaked from their factories and contaminated water supplies. In one of the cases, four months elapsed between the time the leak was discovered and the time the public was told.

In Greenville, Mississippi, in the fall of 1981, some 354,000 gallons of what was described as a "potentially toxic chemical" were reported missing from a storage terminal. The chemical turned up under 40 feet of water in a local lake.

Vandals attacked an oil company's electric pump north of New York City in late 1981, and as a result several thousand gallons of fuel oil flowed into a stream that feeds one of the city's drinking-water reservoirs. Some got into the reservoir itself.

The New York Public Interest Research Group reported

in October of that year, after a three-year investigation, that more than 500,000,000 gallons of water contaminated with various chemicals were flowing into the Niagara River each day. An estimated 380,000 people drink water from that river, which serves as part of the border between the United States and Canada, not far from Love Canal.

Also in the fall of 1981 the Justice Department charged more than three dozen individuals, waste haulers, and chemical companies with disposing of toxic wastes at Price's Landfill, a 22-acre pit a few miles from Atlantic City, New Jersey, and near the well field the city uses for its drinking water. Private wells in the area were contaminated, said the government, and the chemicals were said to be heading toward the dozen wells that supply the city.

Price's Landfill, said the Environmental Protection Agency, was "the most severe environmental problem in the country." Among the defendants named in the civil action were the landfill operators (one of whom was quoted in the press as saying the state of New Jersey knew and approved of what had gone on), firms that hauled the wastes to the site, and firms that had contributed their wastes to it. These included such well-known names as Chemical Control Corporation (of Elizabeth, New Jersey, fame), Union Carbide, Honeywell, Hoffmann-La Roche, Krylon, and Procter and Gamble.

The Justice Department's complaint summarized the situation at the landfill this way:

"Hazardous wastes sent to the site during its active operation [which started in 1968] were accepted for disposal in an unlined pit which is surrounded and underlain by highly permeable sand deposits. Hazardous wastes are leaching through the sand deposits into the groundwater beneath the landfill and are contaminating nearby residential drinking water wells. These contaminants are migrating in the direction of and are likely to enter the water supply wells of Atlantic City's public water system which are located down-gradient from the landfill.

"This action arises from the imminent and substantial endangerment to public health and the environment which the defendants' conduct in creating, handling, storing, treating, transporting, and disposing of solid or hazardous waste has caused, contributed to, or permitted to exist."

According to the government's complaint, solid and liquid hazardous wastes, including "industrial chemicals, septic tank and sewer wastes, sludge, grease and oil," were "transported to, discharged, deposited, dumped, and placed in the landfill. Some liquid chemical wastes were poured directly into the landfill and allowed to soak into the sand underlying the site. Other chemical wastes were buried in 55-gallon drums."

Since the landfill was not lined, and since the wastes were poured onto highly permeable sand, the chemicals reached the groundwater, which is 10 to 20 feet below the surface, said the Justice Department. Private wells that serve families nearby were already contaminated, said the complaint, and the Atlantic City wells, the closest of which was 3,400 feet away, were threatened.

The chemicals involved are practically a roll call of the substances that are attacking America's water. The Justice Department complaint said the following had been discovered in monitoring wells and private wells near the landfill:

· Benzene: Scientists have established a "risk level" of .66 part per billion of this solvent. If that calculation is accurate, it would mean that benzene in that concentration could be expected to cause one additional case of cancer in each population of one million people who had been exposed to it. Water sampled from a well near Price's Landfill had benzene in concentrations almost 12,000 times the "risk level," according to the government's complaint.

· 1,2-dichloroethane: It has been found in concentrations of more than 140,000 times the risk level.

· 1,2-trans-dichloroethylene: In a monitoring well it was found at almost 97,000 times the risk level.

· Vinyl chloride: 38 times the established level.

· Trichloroethylene: More than 44 times the risk level in one well.

· Chloroform: Almost 358 times the risk level.

· Arsenic, cadmium, lead, nickel, mercury: These heavy metals, all of them highly toxic, have been found in the wells, according to the complaint.

The government's suit asks the federal courts to require the defendants to provide funds for studying the extent of the damage done at and around Price's Landfill; to provide potable drinking water for those denied it; to prevent further migration of the chemicals through the aquifer; to clean up the wastes that have migrated already; and to reimburse the government for its expenses. News articles on the matter referred almost offhandedly to what it would cost to "clean up the aquifer," and yet the fact remains that neither government, nor the system of jurisprudence, nor science knows how to do that. As Thomas H. Maugh II pointed out in a 1982 survey of the hazardous-dump calamity in *Science*, there is little in the way of scientific knowledge, law, or technology that prepares us for dealing with contaminated aquifers. The only solution may be to abandon them.

And with each aquifer that is abandoned, our supply of cheap, clean water declines a little more.

As insoluble as the situation at Prices' Landfill seemed— and, for that matter, as insoluble as it seemed in New Jersey in general—it was rich, lush Florida, by one way of reckoning, that was even worse off. When EPA in the fall of 1981 released its compilation of what it called the nation's 115 worst hazardous waste sites, industrialized New Jersey was second in number of sites, with 12. Florida led the entire list with 16 sites. EPA said it figured Florida was in the most danger because its aquifers were so close to the surface and its population so concentrated. Florida had the added burden in 1981 of coping with another below-average amount of rainfall.

The infrastructures of the nation's older cities continue in their slow, certain collapse. Once victory was declared in

New York City's "drought"—the one that was caused less by lack of precipitation than by a delivery system that leaks like a colander—interest in preparing for the next shortage evaporated. New York and a dozen other cities could desperately use a set of new pipes, but the builders prefer to construct their billion-dollar projects in places where they aren't needed at all, and at the expense of nature, agriculture, property rights, relations with Canada and Mexico, and, most especially, water.

The pork barrel continues as the all-time favorite gathering place of politicians, and water continues as the barrel's chief ingredient. Some members of Congress mounted an effort in 1981 to slow or halt the Tennessee-Tombigbee Waterway project, but numerous deals were cut in the Capitol and Congress voted to continue pouring money into the ditch.

Ronald Reagan was elected to office on promises to cut government spending to the bone, and he kept his promises—at least when the spending concerned welfare, nutrition, environmental protection, and a large collection of other programs that are referred to as "social" but that actually are far more intimately involved in the nation's character and well-being than spending for military defense, which Reagan wanted to increase. In his February, 1982, budget message to Congress, Reagan recalled that when he had taken office a year before, the economy "was in the 'worst mess' in half a century."

But now, he said, Congress and the administration had met the challenge: "Fundamental and long-overdue remedies were proposed and put in place. Together, we enacted the biggest spending and tax reductions in history."

The remedies did not, however, include any significant changes in the public water business. Reagan asked for a decrease of 6 per cent in the Fiscal Year 1983 budget of the Corps of Engineers, to $2.7 billion, but most of the reduction came from the normal "winding down" of several big projects, according to an administration official. The Corps was managing to keep busy, meantime, with 284 water projects that will cost (at least, if experience is any guide) an officially estimated $26 billion.

Reagan asked for $950 million for the Bureau of Reclamation. This represents an increase of 23 per cent over BuRec's previous budget and, as Margot Hornblower pointed out in *The Washington Post*, the rise would be even greater than the one requested for the Defense Department. In all, Reagan asked for $3.82 billion for water projects and promised Western states that a request would come along later for $43 million more. Interior's James Watt helped out by affirming that "We are committed to new projects."

Development and growth, too, proceed in ways that add mightily to the water crisis, causing the loss of cropland at the rate of more than four square miles a day. And the forests fall, and the new homes and Burger Kings and hospitals and schools get built in the floodplain, in the foolish belief that we have tamed the rivers.

We continue to mine for minerals that we call "precious," or "semiprecious," or in some cases not "precious" at all but merely useful, and in the mining process we manage to poison and waste the substance that is most precious of all. When we are not mining minerals, we are mining water itself at rates that cause the land to collapse. A state-written document in California estimates that by the year 2000 that state will pump from almost 1,000,000,000,000 to almost 2,000,000,000,000 more gallons of water out of the ground than the amount that is naturally recharged. The lower figure, points out the state, "is equivalent to the annual demand by the combined population of Los Angeles, Ventura, Orange, and San Diego Counties." The overdrafting, in California as in every other place where it occurs, requires greater expenditures for energy to pump it out of the ground, and it contributes to intrusion of the freshwater aquifers by salty seawater.

One of our earliest concerns, when the environmental movement was born such a relatively short time ago, was the deplorable condition of our rivers. Thanks largely to such legislation as the Water Pollution Control Act of 1972, much has been done to limit the discharge of pollutants into the streams. Almost annually there are news stories about how a species that once departed a certain river for a cleaner habitat or spawning grounds—the shad, or the salmon—was "coming back." That has been an occasion for great joy, both for the people who fish for those species for pleasure or for profit and for those who welcome the return as a sign that the rivers are running cleaner. But there is a darker side to the home-coming. As a United Nations document pointed out recently, "the fish now returning to rivers in the northeast United States after avoiding those waters for years because of pollution are not fit to eat, in many cases: They contain high levels of toxic chemicals."

Water seems to be making a comeback as an efficient carrier of disease—or it may be that modern detection methods are simply finding waterborne disease where before it could not be discovered. An article in *The New England Journal of Medicine* reported the finding of several cases of cholera, a diarrheal disease that causes rapid dehydration and sometimes death in humans, in southwestern Louisiana, and suggested a connection with the eating of crabs from the waters of the coastal marsh. Popular thought in America had long classified cholera as one of those diseases, like smallpox and polio, that belonged to the unenlightened past.

The federal government's Centers for Disease Control, which maintain what they call a "largely passive surveillance system" to keep track of water-related outbreaks of disease, reported in January, 1982, that during the year 1980 they had received notices of sixty-six "outbreaks of acute water-related disease associated with drinking water, non-potable surface water, and recreational water." Fifty of the outbreaks concerned water intended for human consumption, and they were said to have affected 20,008 people. Said the centers: "This is the highest number of outbreaks and cases related to potable water reported in any year since the current surveillance system began in 1971." Half of the states in the nation reported at least one outbreak each. The agency said its surveillance system provided information on "but a fraction of the number of outbreaks that actually occurred."

Despite our widespread newfound appreciation of the coastal environment, the destruction of estuaries continues. It is as unthinkable to destroy a tidal marsh as it is to destroy the habitat of an endangered species, and yet we do it all the time, hiring lawyers to find the loopholes for us and, if that fails, simply amending the laws.

Just a few years ago, when our young were celebrating their alienation from the world of unjust war, as well as such notions as peace and love, and were often using hallucinatory drugs in the process, one of American society's fears was that some crazed hippie might dump some LSD into a municipal reservoir, just for the fun of watching an entire city "get high." Now the fear has been realized—exotic substances *have* been introduced into our water supplies—but the perpetrators are industry, along with inept government officials, and nobody wants to talk about it. Again, the reason may be that we simply do not want to know the extent of the damage.

America's horror stories are the world's, and the world's are America's, for with water, more than any other issue, the fortunes of the nation and the planet are aligned. Worldwide, the most pressing water problems are disease (the UN has estimated that domestic water supplies are hazardous to the health of at least a quarter of the globe's population) and hunger (460,000,000 people are considered "permanently hungry"). But the rest of the world's methods for dealing with those problems too often resemble those which haven't worked in the United States, the most developed nation: Dams are being built that will do more harm than good; unwise development and badly planned agriculture result in a decline in the available cropland and an increase in waterlogging, salinization, and alkalinization. Groundwater depletion is a world problem as well as a California, Long Island, and Arizona problem.

Taken together, the world's water dilemmas, when added to a growth in population that is more pronounced in the less developed countries, all add up to a crisis of considerable proportions. Even though there will still be 369,820,250,000,-000,000,000 gallons of water on Earth, it will still be unevenly distributed, and some of it will arrive too quickly and some will arrive too slowly. This has always been the case, but never before has Earth functioned so close to its carrying capacity. *The Global 2000 Report* of 1980, the one requested by Jimmy Carter to assess the world's environment through the end of the century, found that "There will apparently be adequate water available on the earth to satisfy aggregate projected water withdrawals in the year 2000; the same finding holds for each of the continents. Nevertheless, because of the regional and temporal nature of the water resource, water shortages even before 2000 will probably be more frequent and more severe than those experienced today." Further, said the report:

"Fresh water, once an abundant resource in most parts of the world, will become increasingly scarce in coming decades, for two reasons. First, there will be greater net consumption . . . so that the total supply will decline. Second, pollution and the impacts of hydraulic works will effectively limit the uses of fresh water—and therefore, in effect, the supply. The deterioration of river basin catchments, especially as a result of deforestation, will increase the variability of supply, accelerate erosion, damage water development projects, and degrade water quality. It seems inevitable that the function of streams and rivers as habitat for aquatic life will steadily be sacrificed to the diversion of water for irrigation, for human consumption, and for power production, particularly in the less developed countries. . . . scarcities and conflicts are becoming more acute, and by the year 2000 economic, if not human, survival in many industrial regions may hinge upon water quality, or water supply, or both."

One possible advantage shared by some nations is their joint dependence upon important bodies of water. This may encourage them to recognize their problems, if not to do something about them. In 1980, seventeen nations signed an agreement to start cleaning up the Mediterranean Sea, a body of water with a very sluggish self-flushing action. During the same year, marine scientists from states bordering the Persian Gulf met to discuss research on the Gulf's shallow waters and little-explored ecology. But relatively little is being done on a global basis to deal with the environmental problems of the oceans. It has taken delegates from around the world more than six years of attendance at the United Nations Law of the Sea Conference to reach a tentative agreement on a treaty regulating the exploitation of ocean-floor minerals; a treaty dealing with pollution might take forever. And yet, as the American Chemical Society has pointed out, "The sheer size of the marine environment makes it potentially the biggest water pollution problem of all."

So we are left, then, with a future that is not very promising. And if anything, the situation is likely to be worse than recent predictions would have it. Problems with the quality of water quite likely will be greater than anything we know today, simply because of the slow-moving nature of groundwater. Hooker Chemical started dumping its wastes into Love Canal in the fifties, but they did not come to the surface, literally or figuratively, until the seventies. And Love Canal was a relatively shallow trench. The toxic substances that have been discarded more recently may not reach our water supplies for dozens of years. Even then the full impact may not be known; cancer is a relatively slow-acting disease, and so the true price of our poisonous profligacy may not be paid by our bodies, and our children's bodies, until decades after that. A study of Long Island notes that water taken now from the wells extending into a certain aquifer reflects "the quality of water that entered the groundwater system since the late 1940s," and that a century may pass before water from the surface of the land leaches down to the lower portion of the island's major aquifer in the center of the island. From there, it may take 800 years to travel laterally to the wells along the barrier beaches on Long Island's southeastern coast. Given only the degree of poisoning that is *known* to have gone on on Long Island in recent years, then, the prospects for the next *century* are indeed frightening. As Occidental Chemicals' environmental official at the Lathrop, California, plant put it in one of his internal memos on what the plant was doing to its neighbors' wells: "Fortunately heavy organic pesticides are often tied up by absorption on soil. . . . However, given enough time and enough flushing of water through the soil the materials will transfer deeper and deeper into the ground until eventually they come out on the other end. Granted this takes years and might never come out in a concentrated enough form to hurt anyone but if it ever does, the responsibility for any damage to human or animal life is with the person who authorize [sic] the leaching of materials in the first place."

A further complication is radioactivity. As conventional energy production becomes more and more expensive, the temptations undoubtedly will grow to rely more heavily on nuclear energy. But no one has the slightest idea of how to properly dispose of radioactive waste, and when there is a problem with nuclear power it almost always is also a problem of water. Three Mile Island is in the middle of the Susquehanna River; one of the engineers' first proposals, when the nuclear accident occurred there in March, 1979, was to vent contaminated water into the river. That idea was scotched, fortunately. Two years after the accident happened, all the highly radioactive water still had not been drained from the reactor. There is the problem in radioactive materials, as in toxic wastes, of the extreme longevity of the poisons that are created. It has been pointed out that some of the by-products of nuclear reaction have half-lives that are about five times as long as Earth's recorded history. Almost all of the chilling proposals for "disposing" of these materials involve storing them in the skin of the earth, and therefore in close proximity to the groundwater. Salt mines have been suggested, as have holes in rocks in the Antarctic and encapsulation in sheets of polar ice. They are all excellent devices for putting the future out of sight, and thus out of mind, for a little while, at least.

Again, it is a disquieting, almost terrifying prospect— the promise of a United States of the not so distant future in which present-day Long Island and California have become the models: a nation that uses groundwater supplies that serve also as the final resting places for toxic chemicals, hazardous wastes, and all the other effluent of an enterprise system that is without conscience or much morality, plus the overdoses of pesticides and herbicides that are the legacy of an agribusiness that has forgotten its classical obligation to the land; and a nation that ships its surface waters around like parcel post, taking it from the fertile valleys and pouring it onto the deserts, ever eager to subsidize the user, the potential user, the builder, the congressman who's running for reelection, the oil company, the miner, the speculator. It is almost enough to make one give up.

But, as Gardner Hunt said at that hazardous waste site in Gray, Maine, with the topo map spread out on the hood of his car, the map that looked so green and full of wilderness, but that concealed groundwaters full of chemicals we only lately have heard of—as Gardner Hunt said, it does no good to stick our heads in the sand. We must do something, for the sake of our children if for no one else.

There is, as there almost always is, an *if*. There is an *unless*. It is not too late to salvage our water and our future, *if* we start right now to do the right things and to undo the wrong things of the past. The premier conclusion of *The Global 2000 Report* was that, "Barring revolutionary advances in technology, life for most people on earth will be more precarious in 2000 than it is now, unless the nations of the world act decisively to alter current trends."

A good start would be to assemble what little we know about water, inasmuch as one of our fundamental problems with the substance is our ignorance about it—our tendency to take water so much for granted that we do not even notice the damage we inflict on it. It is painfully easy to total up what we know that *doesn't* work.

We know that, where the quality of water is involved, we cannot trust industry to regulate itself. It is too much to expect that industry and business, trained to respect the "bottom line" and nothing else, will behave any differently when the purity of water is involved. There are cases on record in which a particular company has even poisoned *itself* in its pursuit of the bottom line. Surely we cannot expect corporations to refrain, voluntarily, from poisoning the rest of us.

We also know that we cannot rely on government to protect us from the bad things that can happen, and that are happening, with water. Government's response to problems of water quality has been frightening in its inadequacy, and its dealings with quantity issues have been a symphony of bad judgment. Proper *planning* for water matters in even the near future has been minimal, partly because water so rarely stays within any specific political jurisdiction. How may the future of human dealings with the Mississippi River be properly planned, when a thousand communities think they own a piece of it? In this case, as in many others, the federal government is the logical planning agency, but shockingly little is being done at that level. A few of the states have devoted far more energy and brainpower than Washington to assessing their present water status and future water needs. In New Mexico, much progress is being made in plotting permissible development and growth on the basis of existing water basins. If the water isn't there in a certain section of Santa Fe County, for example, the county's General Plan seeks to impose a lid on more development. The Texas State Water Plan, a thick compendium of what is known and projected about water in that geographically diverse state, is a model of planning. "To fail to plan well," states the Texas document, "and to fail to develop water resources according to the schedule required by population, technological, and environmental change, has social and economic costs of practically inestimable magnitudes. The failure to plan and implement timely water-resources programs, with today's large population and elevated economic level, is to invite economic and social crises that have a high probability of resulting in disaster for Texas."

The Texas plan is cited by United Nations officials as an excellent example of water planning. But there is no true, comparable United States Water Plan. It seems incredible, but virtually all of our decisions about growth, production, development, industry, agriculture, and *life* are made without any formal examination of the essential ingredient, water. According to some experts, the global Green Revolution, in which fertilizers and new, highly productive varieties of grain were supposed to change the shape of agriculture and bring an end to starvation, became a failure because nobody happened to figure water into the equations.

The evidence of government's failure is miserably apparent. But we also know that there can be no solution for our problems of water without the energetic entry of government into the crisis—without a quality and intensity of leadership that is far greater than what we have had so far.

We know that we cannot trust most politicians within a country mile of a pork barrel, and we know that we cannot trust the builders—the Corps of Engineers, Tennessee Valley Authority, Bureau of Reclamation, or any of the others. We particularly cannot trust them to be the agencies who build the projects *and* provide the economic justification for them. To do so is to assign the fox the task of guarding the hen house, multiplied by 10^9.

We know that waiting around for the problem to go away will not work, and neither will feigning ignorance about it.

The problems of toxic substances in our drinking water, and reduced quantities of available water due to waste and lowered quality, will not go away unless we take deliberate steps to make them go away. Anything else is kin to returning to the riverside after the flood has wiped out our homes, trying to fool ourselves into thinking that it won't happen again; or like immediately forgetting, on the day the hard rains break the drought, everything we lately had learned about saving water. And the longer we wait to begin solving the problems of water, the greater will be the costs.

We know, or should have learned by now, that we are wasting our precious time if we sit around waiting for some dramatic breakthrough, some technological discovery that will solve our problems of water quality and quantity. This may be the most difficult acknowledgment for Americans to make, for we are a very spoiled people, not much used to facing hard and undramatic facts, particularly those that affect our comfort. As a nation, America *has* produced a lot of breakthroughs, from the invention of the automobile and the airplane to the creation of the transistor, integrated circuit, and fast-food emporia. But the hard and undramatic facts as they stand now, and as they are likely to remain, are that the breeding of an acid rain-resistant trout is not the proper solution to the problem of acid rain, any more than gasohol made from corn is going to bring back 32-cents-a-gallon automobile fuel and solve the energy crisis. We will have to learn to work with what we have; and, while we have a great deal, it is not as much as we have always fooled ourselves into believing it was.

A case in point is our ongoing romance with desaliniza-tion. It is technically feasible, and has been for some time, to convert salty seawater into water that is sufficiently "fresh" for humans to drink. One of the processes by which this is accomplished is called reverse osmosis, in which the saline water is made to lose most of its salts when it is forced under pressure through a fine-pored membrane. Another process, the one that most people probably imagine when they think of "desalinization," is basically one of distilling seawater—boiling the salt water, capturing the vapor that rises from it, and condensing it into droplets of water that is, for all intents and purposes and as far as humans are concerned, "pure." The process is straightforward and relatively simple (enough so that sailors cast into the sea in lifeboats can rig solar-powered stills that produce enough drinking water to keep them alive), and it is in regular use in many parts of the world where a natural supply of potable water is unreliable. Israel is particularly adept at producing useful water in this fashion, and has helped to make desalinization a relatively well-known process. When the issue of water quantity comes up elsewhere in the world, including the drier portions of the United States, one of the questions almost always raised is: What about desalinization?

One answer is that desal (as the water people refer to it) works, but it works only at a price, and that price is often much higher than most users are willing to pay. The process, like many others that promise to solve civilization's current problems, requires large quantities of energy, and that means large quantities of money, as an employee of the desal plant serving the Florida Keys explained to a visitor not long ago. Mrs. Judith Weigell, who worked for what then was named the Florida Aqueduct Authority, explained the technique at the agency's desal plant on Stock Island, in Key West, a facility which produces 2,300,000 gallons of potable water every twenty-four hours "with everything working right." The plant is 105 feet long and is made up largely of some 400 miles of ⅝ inch-diameter titanium tubing, which is used to condense the vapor. Three wells near the ocean draw saline water into the plant, where it runs, at the rate of six feet per second, through fifty separate stages. There it is injected with various chemicals that remove gases, foam, acids, and brine and adjust the water's pH; then the water is sent into a two-story-tall evaporator that heats, then condenses, the substance. Finally the water goes into large storage tanks and then into the homes and businesses of the Keys' citizens. Weigell, in walking her visitor through the process, referred to its result as "the product." "When the product is a distillate," she said, "it's *too* pure, and people don't like it. So we put it in post-product treatment tanks, which are filled with marl—coral—and it picks up minerals from it." The one component of the Key West operation that makes desalinization seem less like a wave of the future and more like a relic of the past is the fact that all that water has to be heated to above the boiling point. The plant's boiler produces 135,000 BTUs of heat energy, and it runs on copious quantities of Number 6 bunker oil, a substance which, like water itself, was hardly a matter of conscious thought just a few years ago but which now is recognized as the very heart of many of the problems of the Western world.

27

We know, too, not only that we must be very leery about placing our blind trust in the big breakthroughs that may never come, or in some sketchily defined future, but that we must end our blind faith in the ways of the past. In many of the components of modern life, but particularly in environmental issues and *quite* particularly in water matters, the old ways of doing things, or perhaps of *not* doing them, have become highly suspect. A lot of the clichés by which the nation grew, and which were used to excuse some really relentless and destructive exploitation, must now be abandoned: the idea of TVA as the savior of a region; of the Corps of Engineers as the objective instrument of progress; of the inherent *goodness* involved in making the desert bloom; of the essential *rightness* in the damming up of a river; of the unquestionable *purity* of water that falls from the sky or that comes out of a well.

An interesting and pertinent example of this sort of questioning of the old rules may be found in the current dispute over organic chemicals in drinking-water supplies, sometimes referred to as the chlorine–trihalomethanes–granulated activated carbon controversy.

There has been concern for some time about the chemicals that might be found in drinking-water supplies, of course, but inquiry into the matter took on a new importance with the release in 1974 of a study by Robert H. Harris titled "The Implications of Cancer-Causing Substances in Mississippi River Water." The study was published by the Environmental Defense Fund, which refers to itself as a non-profit "national coalition of scientists, lawyers, and economists working to protect environmental quality and, consequently, human health." Harris, who has a Ph.D. degree in environmental science, was a scientist on EDF's staff; more recently, during the Carter administration, he served as one of the three members of the Council on Environmental Quality. His paper reported finding, in the words of an EDF summary, "significantly higher rates of bladder and gastrointestinal cancer in communities drinking contaminated water from the Mississippi River." The communities in question were in and around New Orleans. At about the same time Harris's report came out, the Environmental Protection Agency released results of tests it had performed on New Orleans drinking water, in which it found sixty-six chemical compounds. The compound found in the highest concentration was chloroform. Chloroform, once used in anesthesia, has been listed by the National Cancer Institute as one of twenty-three "carcinogens and suspect carcinogens in drinking water" in the United States.

The reports produced considerable consternation, both in New Orleans and at the national level, and they have been credited with leading to the passage in Congress of the 1974 Safe Drinking Water Act, as well as the issuance by EPA of a set of national drinking-water standards. The standards did not deal with the question of organic chemicals in water, however, and the Environmental Defense Fund brought suit against EPA to force action. EPA responded, in January, 1978, with a series of proposed regulations to control suspected carcinogens in drinking water. Administrator Douglas Costle declared: "This marks the start of the first large-scale effort in history to deal with organic chemical contaminants in drinking water. It will initiate changes in our approach to protecting and assuring the quality of the water we drink, and will give the American public an 'insurance policy' against the dangers associated with chemicals in our water." Costle specifically praised those whose job it had been to keep the water clean all along—the professional waterworks engineers. "The outstanding record of the American waterworks industry in virtually eliminating infectious water borne disease in this country is a matter of history," he said. "We are confident in their ability to meet this new and emerging challenge."

The new challenge had to do, in part, with chlorination, the traditional method chosen by the waterworks people to disinfect community water supplies. For years, they had used chlorine to counter bacterial and viral contamination, and in the process had practically removed the names of a lot of deadly diseases from Americans' vocabularies. But what was newly discovered was that chlorine reacts with naturally occurring materials in the water—materials such as humus—to form synthetic organic substances called trihalomethanes. Several THMs, as they are called, are suspected of producing cancer in test animals. Among them are chloroform, dichlorobromomethane, and bromoform. (More recently, according to a 1981 article in *Science*, a "new class of potentially hazardous chemicals," previously not included on the researchers' lists of things to worry about, "appears to be present in drinking water throughout the United States." The chemicals, known as dihalocetonitriles, or Dhans, had been missed in earlier analyses because they were destroyed by the usual testing methods. New techniques, including one called two-dimensional gas chromatography, revealed the presence of Dhans in water supplies in various parts of the nation. Some of the compounds in the class, said *Science*, were believed to be dangerous; one was believed to be a mutagen and others were said to be capable of breaking down into carcinogens.)

EPA's regulations proposed to do two things: set safe limits for concentrations of THMs in water supplies (along with monitoring for them in the supplies) and require some communities to filter their water through granular activated carbon (or GAC) to remove synthetic organics that might come from upstream. Some of those organics might include THMs as well, since industry has used them as solvents and in the production of dyes, pesticides, drug, cough medicines, and toothpaste, and has discarded them, like most everything else, into the nearest river.

The Environmental Protection Agency's announcement was like a bomb dropping on the professional waterworks establishment, which responded with strong attacks on EPA, on Robert Harris, and on the entire GAC process. The professionals clearly did not want anyone else telling them how to protect the nation's drinking water. Almost two dozen private and public water utilities that were members of the American Water Works Association formed a group, which they called the Coalition for Safe Drinking Water, and hired a law firm to argue against EPA's proposals. Members of the law firm of Baker and Daniels, of Indianapolis and Washington, published a three-part assessment of the situation in the *Journal* of the American Water Works Association in which they assailed the high cost of the GAC program; expressed doubts that the amounts of chemicals found in water supplies really posed health risks; pointed out that the program as EPA wanted it had not been tested and could not be compared with activated carbon processes presently in use in Europe and in the U.S. food and beverage industries; said that the process might actually put deadly heavy metals *into* the water supply and that there might be other unwanted side effects; noted that the process would burn lots of energy; and repeatedly made the point that chloroform had not been found to produce cancer in *humans*. (That last argument is one that is encountered frequently when researchers announce that such-and-such substance has been found to cause cancer in laboratory animals. Human volunteers for cancer experiments are relatively hard to come by, of course. In its *First Annual Report on Carcinogens*, published in July, 1980, the Department of Health and Human Services' National Toxicology Program commented on this dilemma: "Science and society have not arrived at a final consensus on the definition of a carcinogen, either in human population or in experimental animals." The judgment involved in seeking such a definition, it said, "rests on a knowledge base that is fluid and evolving. However, prudent public health policy dictates that regulation of possibly hazardous substances should not have to wait until there is human evidence of cancer. It is important that evidence from experimental animals be used because society cannot wait until cancer occurs in a population to learn that there is a serious health problem.")

The waterworks people's attack was aimed, naturally, at what its authors saw as EPA's unscientific rush to embrace a new, untested, and potentially expensive technology. But it was also an attack on the new environmental-minded people, such as those at the Environmental Defense Fund, whose arguments strongly suggested that the traditional guardians of our drinking water weren't doing their jobs well enough.

A New Orleans physician, Edward S. Hyman, wrote an article in the *Journal* of the Louisiana State Medical Society attacking Harris's methodology and what Hyman apparently felt was all this unjust criticism of the professionals by those he termed "newcomers to the discussion." These he termed "itinerant advocates," "activists," "cultists," and "sensationalists who achieve stardom by being the darlings of certain elements of the press." "There is no way to control these dramatists after they have achieved a doctorate," wrote the doctor, who then returned to what appeared to be his basic theme: that the water professionals are the only ones fit to deal with water problems. "Instead of launching a nationwide experiment involving untested technology with potential hazards of epidemic proportions, and without the dire urgency to justify it," he wrote, "the EPA should turn over the task of improving the technology to serious, qualified scientists who would deliberate in serious scientific meetings and literature and would give us better technology."

Jacqueline M. Warren saw it from a different perspective. She was an attorney at the Environmental Defense Fund and worked with Robert Harris on the original challenges to EPA. (More recently she has been at the Natural Resources

Defense Council, which, like EDF, combines the talents of scientists and lawyers.) "Part of it has to do with a certain professional pride in the water supply industry," she said in an interview not long ago. "These are the people who oppose the regulations, the changes. They're the ones who've been providing 'the safest water in the world for the last fifty years,' and all that—the water authorities and water commissioners and water boards. They strongly resent any suggestion that they haven't done the best possible job. And rather than say, 'Okay, in general we solved the cholera and typhoid problems, now we need to get onto this other problem'—rather than say that, they say, 'It's not a problem.' You have to consider that it's a real insult to them, really, for people to come out and say, 'You haven't done a good job.' "

The mayor of New Orleans, meantime, was attempting to understand both sides of the issue. In an August, 1978, letter to an EPA official, Mayor Ernest N. Morial noted that "New Orleans is the city where organic contamination of drinking water first became a visible national issue and where it remains a matter of serious concern for us. The New Orleans area has *one of the highest cancer rates* in the country, and we are anxious to do what we can to reduce this rate as soon as possible" (emphasis in original).

But, added Morial, there are some questions about the seriousness of the organic chemical problem and about the efficacy of the granular activated carbon process which EPA wanted to impose. The mayor, like many of those at the local level, raised also the question of cost. There have been enormous variations in the estimates of what the GAC process would cost. Some of them are quite astronomical. Wrote Morial:

"The major implementation question to be resolved is who should pay for the required new treatment facilities. The proposed regulations presume that the required capital and operating costs will be financed at the local level through higher water rates. However, since the installation and use of

. . . GAC filters is apparently designed primarily to remove synthetic organic chemicals present in the water as a result of up-river industrial discharges, agricultural runoff, and other sources of water pollution, it seems only fair that the burden of removing these chemicals should be borne by those who put them there, not by the people of the City of New Orleans.

"The costs of controlling pollution are legitimate costs of production, since waste disposal consumes a valuable resource —clean water. Therefore, these production costs should be borne ultimately by the users of products which cause such pollution. It would be grossly unfair to require the citizens of New Orleans to subsidize the production costs of items consumed by a regional, national, or international market. . . . The cost of removing pollutants from drinking water should be borne by the industrial and agricultural concerns whose operations make this removal necessary. . . . Until such a reimbursement system is established, however, it will be necessary for the federal government to provide financial assistance to cities impacted by these new regulations."

New Orleans has not, to date, had to come up with the cash to install a new granular activated carbon filtration system. EPA's proposed regulations on THMs—setting standards for them and requiring communities to monitor them— have been promulgated, but the suggested rules for GAC have gone nowhere, no doubt because of the concentrated reaction from the water-supply industry. Nothing has happened with them, said an EPA official not long ago, "and there's nothing in the wind on them either."

New Orleanians continue, however, to drink water (unless they buy it from a store) that comes from the Mississippi River, at the end of a long, long body of water that is used as a sewer by communities and industries from Minnesota to Louisiana. The last few miles, the line of petrochemical plants below Baton Rouge, are particularly frightening. Some of this stream, an average of 135,000,000 gallons a day of it, is captured by the Sewerage and Water Board of New Orleans, an independent city agency, in four-foot pipes that thrust out into the river. The water is given an initial shock dose of chlorine at the river, then piped back to a treatment plant where potassium permanganate is added to combat offensive tastes and odors; ferrous sulfate is added to precipitate the chemicals together so they can settle out; lime is added to soften the water; another shot of chlorine is added to disinfect the substance; and then the water is distributed to the city's residents. When they are through with it, their sewage is treated and put back into the river.

Stuart H. Brehm, Jr., says there's no problem with the city's water quality. "I drink it all the time," said Brehm, who is the director of the Sewerage and Water Board. "Right now, the Mississippi River's passing somewhere in the neighborhood of between 500,000 and 740,000 cubic feet of water per second past Canal Street." He motioned toward the window of his office, on an upper floor of New Orleans' City Hall. "That's one lot of water. Multiply it out: A cubic foot is seven and a half gallons of water, and that's not per hour or per day; that's per *second*. That's one hell of a lot of water. You could put a gallon of arsenic in the thing upstream and it would be diluted. Which leads us to the point that the quality of the raw water is really only the problem of taste and odor control. It's no big sweat. It really isn't." Brehm's visitor sipped, as did Brehm, a cup of coffee that an assistant had brought in. The coffee tasted strongly of the chicory that New Orleanians favor, but the taste of the water, particularly the chlorine in it, was strong as well.

The visitor asked about the chlorination-THM controversy, and Brehm responded immediately with an attack on Robert Harris. He was a "character from the Environmental Defense Fund," said Brehm, who "came out with spectacular, ludicrous statements regarding cancer. . . . Let me explain something to you. See, the water industry as a whole is a very passive group. They go about their business of giving people good water, and they make damn sure among themselves that it's good water. And there are some cases where there've been slips, naturally. But it really wasn't until the Harris–Environmental Defense Fund attack on drinking water—and it was a pure *attack*—that the water industry really got together. Before, it had been a loosely connected group of people who went about their business doing what they knew was best—not *thought* was best, but what they *knew* was best—because they'd been doing it for quite a length of time and had seen the results." Brehm took another sip of his coffee, and it seemed almost as if he did it to demonstrate how good and reliable New Orleans' drinking water was.

A few floors below Stuart Brehm's office in City Hall is the office of Gino Carlucci, who was Mayor Morial's director of the office of environmental affairs, Carlucci is a young man, with a neat beard, who is trained in urban and regional planning. In addition to water matters. Carlucci keeps up with, and advises the mayor on, issues of air quality, noise, the recovery of resources, and disasters. Carlucci is a strong supporter of the proposition that the industries and municipalities upstream that contribute to the pollution of New Orleans' drinking water should also contribute to cleaning it up. "It's like you lived next door to me," he said, "and I cut my grass and raked it all up and then said, 'This is going to cost me too much money to take to the dump; I'll just throw it over the fence into your yard.'" He added that, while plenty of other places in the nation had water problems, too, "We probably are a little bit worse off than other places. We're at the end of the river, and 40 per cent of the country drains into that river."

And, he said, that fact did bother him a bit—obviously more than it concerned Stuart Brehm upstairs. It bothered him so much, in fact, said Carlucci, "that I don't drink the water. I buy bottled water. I have it delivered to my house, which is what a lot of people in New Orleans do." He was concerned about the poisons that might be in it, he said, but even if New Orleans' water were proved to be pure, he'd buy his water in bottles because of the odor and the taste of the mixture that comes out of the end of the Mississippi's long, troubled pipe.

28

There are other things we have learned.

We have learned that there is no place to hide. There is no corner of the nation (or of the world, for that matter) that can claim immunity from water contamination. The places that once were considered pristine, the few remnants of America's frontier—Maine, Alaska, parts of the Southwest—have, in fact, become particularly susceptible to exploitation and contamination for the same reasons that they have been considered "untouched"—lack of population and abundance of space have made the frontiers very attractive to those who would strip-mine, build outlandish projects, and dump their toxic wastes. Pennsylvania's lovely Allegheny Mountains, the clear lakes of the Adirondacks, the windblown New Mexico high desert, and any meandering stream or river on the continent—they all have become as liable to poisoning as the filthiest urban gutter.

It may be that some of the places that have had the worst records will turn out to be the leaders in according water the attention it deserves. California, for all its compulsion to ship water around to places and people who really don't deserve it, nevertheless is facing the problems of water and is engaged in ongoing debates on it. Florida, another symbol of developmental excess, is seriously trying to avoid becoming "another Florida." Even New Jersey, which is quite likely the toxic waste capital of the nation, is at least working harder than most states to identify and control those poisons. Michael Greenberg, a professor in community development and urban planning at Rutgers in New Jersey, noted not long ago in an interview that "One of the reasons why there's a lot of negative publicity about New Jersey's water supply is that New Jersey happens to be one of the few states that actually makes an effort to determine the quality, with respect to toxic substances, of its water supply. There are many other states in which the people may be drinking water that's contaminated, but in fact if their state governments don't go out and spend the money to explore, to check to see if the water *is* contaminated, the people don't find out. New Jersey, because it's trying harder than the other states, is getting a bad rap for it. We find more problems simply because we look for them."

We have learned that in the case of water, to a degree matched by practically nothing else on the planet, everything we do is a trade-off. Just as the 1.4×10^9 cubic kilometers of water that we have moves perpetually through the perfectly balanced hydrologic cycle, anything we do to the water, or to the environment that affects our water, will have repercussions somewhere and sometime else. If we want our highways to be free of ice in the winter, we put salt on them, and we get chloride contamination of our groundwater. We want poisons that will kill grasshoppers so that they will not interfere with our food supplies, but we also dump those poisons on the ground and, in essence, run the risk of poisoning ourselves as well. Some of us propose that problems of water shortage be solved by technology such as reverse osmosis and desalinization; but such processes use enormous amounts of energy. A terrifying prospect is that those who trade heavily in the promotion of technology as a magical solution for all our problems will be successful in convincing the policy makers that *every* facet of human life and the environment may conveniently be figured into a cost-benefit ratio. If and when that happens, the results will be just as unfair and preposterous as the ones the Corps of Engineers produces when it wants to build a dam or a waterway: Clean water for poor and black people will somehow be not as important as clean water for well-to-do and white people; agribusiness's need for water will somehow outweigh the right of a stream to run free; scientists and bureaucrats will discover that a certain predictable amount of cancer from the water supply is cost-efficient and tolerable in our growing, vibrant society.

We know, or should know, that the era of cheap water, like the era of cheap energy, is over; and that with it have gone our innocence and naïveté about water. It was nice while it lasted, this assumption that a turn of the faucet handle will produce pure water in boundless quantity, but now that time is gone. Economics will control the future of water, whether we like it or not. A Geological Survey document puts it this way: "As increases in water use deplete the easily developable supplies, more costly additional supplies are being sought. As the costs of water go up, water resources become more and more like other economic commodities for which there are supplies, demands, and a pricing and marketing structure to balance the supplies and demands."

It is not an idea that is easy for humanistic-minded people to like, for it conjures up highly likely images of the wrong people's being in control of the economics of a substance that is absolutely essential to human life—the wrong people being, in all likelihood, the members of the petroleum cartel, the leaders of the chemical industry, and the other stalwarts of the great American free enterprise system that has shown such contempt for water up until now. The opportunities for corruption, abuse, and political and economic capital are unlimited. They are even more alluring than those in the public-works water business run by the Iron Triangle, and *that* is probably the biggest fleecing of the general public in the history of the world.

But the fact remains: Decent water will never again be a free good. That question is now beyond argument. The best we can do, now that we know that economics will be the controlling factor in the future, is to try to keep that control out of the hands of the wrong people.

The economics argument also appears to overlook the aesthetic side of water, and that too may bother the humanist.

It is basically, inherently *wrong* to poison water, to ruin fine streams, to waste water that is clean enough to drink, to build dams and canals that exploit water needlessly. But that argument and a quarter will get you only a one-way trip on the Staten Island Ferry. The future of water will be decided, not by aesthetics, but by economics. Fortunately, there are some who believe that the most economical uses of water are also those that preserve best the aesthetic values of water. David Abelson, of the California Planning and Conservation League, said not long ago: "I think if you go to the Stanislaus River, or the Pitt River, or the north fork of the Feather River— places where dams and major power plants are proposed—and take a look at the rich, integrated, ancient systems that are thriving up there, you may find that there's a real question about man's sensitivity when, for such marginal uses as watering his sidewalks, he would wipe out a million-year-old system without regard to the collateral impacts that would result." Some people, he said, will be swayed to respect water when the environmentalists and others explain to them what it is they stand to lose if water doesn't receive respect. "But I think, being a realist in the world that we're living in," he added, "that the more meaningful indicator will be economics. The beauty of the position we're taking on the issues of water in California is that the path that we are advocating is actually economically advantageous."

The path that is being promoted by Abelson and many others who are concerned about the future of water is conservation. It is an obvious key component in solving the water crisis and in avoiding future problems. It is the obvious way to provide the equivalent of a vast, previously untapped reservoir of clean, potable water. It is as obvious as elementary school mathematics: halving the demand for water (or anything else) is equal to doubling the supply. Every serious examination of what is happening to water today, and of what threatens to happen to it tomorrow, comes to the conclusion that conservation is of extreme, possibly of premier, importance. And yet the subject is studiously ignored by politicians, leaders, builders, planners, agriculture, and industry, and their unwillingness to seriously pursue it is a leading contributor to the crisis.

Of course, they pay lip service to conservation. For Jimmy Carter, what the country needed was "comprehensive reform of water resources policy, with water conservation as its cornerstone." Edmund G. Brown, Jr., the governor of California, held a news conference in January, 1979, to accept a report from his commission reviewing water rights law, and he commented: "I believe water is more important than energy. . . . The only question is whether we have the wisdom and the foresight to act as stewards for the future or are we just going to consume away the present like the other masters in civilizations bygone . . . that have collapsed into the dustbin of history. . . . If we build new projects, and if we haven't learned how to use our water, we will continue . . . the overdraft, and bring more land into production and continue stealing from the future. . . . There is this gigantic conspiracy of the present to steal from the future, and since the future hasn't any news reporters or legislators or lobbyists, nobody knows about it."

The State of Arizona published a handsome document, part of its State Water Plan, that was devoted exclusively to conservation. The quantity of water available in Arizona, it declared, "is finite and current use rates cannot continue forever. Water conservation will help bring the state's water supplies and uses into balance." Conservation, said the document, "can be practiced in Arizona without creating financial hardships or major changes in life style."

In New York City, as the shortage of water got increasingly serious in the first months of 1981, Mayor Koch and other city officials urged conservation on the citizens. Koch threatened to humiliate water-wasters by announcing their names publicly (a technique he earlier had applied to men who patronize prostitutes) and led schoolchildren in recitations about how they were going to force their parents to use less water while brushing their teeth.

It all sounded good (if, in the case of New York, a bit heavy on the humiliation, but that has become a Koch trademark), but it was mostly hot air. Jimmy Carter did little to promote conservation beyond talking about it, and he signed legislation that actively *ordered* the waste of millions of acre feet of water. Jerry Brown, the nation's leading guru of the "era of limits" philosophy, went on to support the construction of California's foremost water-transportation boondoggle, the Peripheral Canal project, which will rob the state's north of additional water and ship it south to make the desert bloom even more.

Arizona's commitment to conservation turned out to be more paper than real. C. Laurence Linser, the planning chief of the Arizona Water Commission, explained in an interview that the state's water conservation document was "developed in a hurry when the hit list came out." (He referred to President Carter's original list of water projects that should not receive funding. Some components of the Central Arizona Project were on the list.) "The governor wanted us to come up with a plan to demonstrate that we were conscientious," said Linser with a smile. And in New York City, while Mayor Koch was teaching conservation slogans to schoolchildren, his parks commissioner (generally thought of as one of the brighter members of the city administration) was using millions of gallons of potable water to make artificial snow in Central Park to promote a "winter festival" that was sponsored by a sporting-goods store. Fire hydrants were running open around the city, as they do all the time, and the Koch administration was making minimal effort to locate and shut off underground leaks that have run for years. Uncounted millions of gallons poured out of abandoned, city-owned buildings whose plumbing hardware had been taken by thieves, cut off at the pipes.

Conservation is, in short, a nice topic for politicians to be in favor of, but a difficult one for them to grasp and embrace. A 1974 federal report of a meeting of state representatives to discuss water conservation noted that "Everyone agreed efficiency was a good idea, but acceptance of specific methods produced something less than consensus." Other surveys have shown that those in industry and agriculture pay little attention to saving water until its cost becomes an issue with them. As the Arizona conservation document says: "Water conservation is rarely practiced solely for the purpose of saving water."

But conservation of water is *easy*. It can be practiced without pain or suffering or deprivation, even without sacrificing one's precious "life style." While this is a fact that is not widely appreciated by agriculture, industry, or politicians, millions of individuals who have felt a need to save water understand it quite well. Their motives have ranged from a desire to cut the water bill (as in southern Florida), to the knowledge that they were in the midst of a real drought, one in which the water really could run out (as in northern California in the late seventies), to an understanding and acceptance of the fact that there isn't any water to waste (as in Cerrillos, New Mexico, and many other communities), to the feeling that wasting clean water is simply immoral (as in countless homes around the country). Enormous savings in water can be accomplished by simple, almost unnoticeable changes in, or additions to, the daily routine. A dime-sized metal disc with a hole in it, placed in a bathroom shower head, reduces the volume of water passing through a shower without affecting the experience of getting clean. Devices, some of them homemade, for reducing the amount of water stored in a toilet tank may be installed and easily forgotten (although one of the techniques that is frequently mentioned, a brick in the tank, is a bad idea, since the brick can crumble and jam up the plumbing. Water-filled plastic milk jugs are much better). Not flushing a toilet that has been used for urination is not as disgusting as it first sounds, and taking a plastic bucket into the shower with you to catch the runoff, for use in flushing toilets, feeding houseplants, filling humidifiers, and the like, can quickly become part of one's routine.

Conservation could produce immense savings, in terms of

water and of dollars, if it were practiced on a national level. Water that is conserved is water that does not need to be impounded behind Corps of Engineers dams or shipped around in Bureau of Reclamation canals or stored in deep, expensive tunnels beneath Chicago. Conserving water also means spending less money on the energy that is needed to pump it out of the ground and over mountains (and in the home and industry, saving water means using less *heated* water, which further reduces expense on energy). David Abelson cites a California Department of Water Resources estimate that "through a *modest* program of conservation—substantially less than what we're recommending—you could save California on the order of 10,000,000 barrels of oil a year. And using 1976 dollars, both in terms of their value and in terms of what the price of oil was at that time, there would be $100,000,000 a year in consumer savings."

One way to conserve water is to reuse it—or, strictly speaking, to reuse it a little sooner than we normally do, inasmuch as all the water on Earth is constantly being reused, and the water Mayor Koch uses to brush his teeth was used by billions of other people, animals, fish, birds, and plants before him. There already are some programs in operation which involve spreading treated waste water on the ground in order to allow it to recharge the aquifers below. Some other efforts aim at using waste water—often called "gray" water, or water that has been used but which doesn't contain fecal matter—for irrigation and in industry. These processes are still in the early stages of development, and there is a lot to be learned—in particular, about what happens to water as it drifts down through the ground to the aquifers. If artificial recycling of water in this manner results in damage to the aquifers, lasting harm will be done. Scientists are particularly concerned about the presence of viruses in such water. The *British Medical Journal* commented in 1978 that "The demands on water are increasing so rapidly because of population expansion and industrial needs that recycling of domestic waste and sewage is practically inevitable in the future. The presence of viruses in sewage effluent, streams and rivers, lakes, and other waters is an important health hazard with the increasing contamination of surface water." Such recycling, however, is inevitable if we are to avoid serious water shortages brought on by a combination of increased user demand and decreased supply because of pollution.

One area in which conservation will *not* be appreciated is the Iron Triangle, and particularly that part of it that resides in the District of Columbia. It will not be easy to explain to the bureaucrats that their destructive, wasteful services are no longer needed (President after President has promised to do that; the bureaucrat-builders have always won). Perhaps another approach would be better: putting the builders to work building the *right* things for a change; letting them train their expertise and naked power on the problems of toxic waste sites and trihalomethanes and New York City's need for a third water tunnel. Zyg Plater has referred to this notion as "building a better pork barrel." Whether one is built or not, the agencies that feast on the pork will find *something* to do, for they must build in order to stay alive. The Central Arizona Project is far from complete, but the Bureau of Reclamation is already talking about enlarging it. A Bureau publication states: "Although Central Arizona Project water will lessen the impact of continued ground water overdraft to maintain the existing economy, by the end of this century, or before, additional water will be needed to stave off water bankruptcy." The Tennessee Valley Authority is lusting after various energy projects, including solar power. And the Corps of Engineers speaks of its "new environmental consciousness" but also has its hungry eye on what it estimates to be 12,000 possible hydroelectric sites in the Northeastern part of the nation.

The marvelous thing about water conservation is that, even though the idea induces paralysis and chronic backbone failure in politicians, the people seem to accept it without many qualms at all. There are parallels in the public's response to two recent events—an apparent shortage of gasoline and other petroleum products and rises in the cost of credit that were so great the usury laws had to be amended. With scarcely more than vague hints at leadership from their elected officials, the people reacted by driving less and ending their dependence on gas-guzzling Detroit automobiles and by charging less on their credit cards. In both cases they cut back so much that the political leadership got seriously concerned about effects on the economy, by which it meant the oil companies and the banks. (Alfred E. Kahn, who was billed as the Carter administration's "inflation fighter," was quoted during the credit crisis as saying, "All of us were taken by surprise and to some extent disconcerted by the extent of the reaction.") Once again, the people were well ahead of their "leaders."

It is equally clear that the people are perfectly willing to save water. It helps if they have the proper leadership and if they receive sufficient information on *how* to save it, but those are not essential. One of the essential lessons that was learned during the California drought of 1976–77 was that individuals and families could cut their consumption of water greatly without destroying or even seriously rearranging the rest of their lives. "It is clear," said a state report on the drought, "that Californians can carry on nearly all domestic activities with little more than a minor crimp in lifestyles, [and] with a rather substantial reduction in water consumption."

Conservation of water, whether it be done by a retired couple in a Miami suburb or a conglomerate that wants to remove copper from the ground, amounts to little more than learning to *care* about water. A learning process is required because water has been such a free good for so long, a substance so easily taken for granted, used, and then splashed unceremoniously onto the ground or into the nearest stream— such an unseen, unnoticed, and unloved component of our lives that we have hardly known it was there. If there is one thing we should know about water now, it is that it is important. It is not free. We cannot continue to exploit it. Water will have to have standing.

The political leaders of the United States, their senses dulled by too frequent attendance at the orgies around the pork barrel, have not yet caught on to this. But many others have— ordinary people, most of them; some young and some old, some "hippies" and some legionnaires, some radicals and some Birchers—and they are the ones who provide the hope for water. Some of them call themselves "damfighters," and some are "conservationists," and others are "conservatives," and a surprisingly large number of them are "housewives." The one thing they all have in common is a respect for water.

They hate to see it wasted. They hate to see it misused, particularly by those who misuse it for their personal gain. They know that water has a marvelous ability to absorb the effluent of humankind and then, given enough time, to cleanse itself for use again and again—but they also know that if that marvelous ability is abused, is strained too far and taken too much for granted, water will become a poison. And they fear what that water, if it becomes poison, may be like for future generations, and sometimes for their own children.

These people may not normally subscribe to anthropomorphism, but in the case of water they know the substance has so many human characteristics, and is so much a part of us all, that it might as well be human. Water is infinitely wise and all-knowing; it has been here since soon after Earth began, and it has seen everything there is to see, has been part of everything that ever was. But at the same time water is innocent. When it falls from the sky in fat April drops or thin feathers of snow, or when it foams its way down a stream, or pushes mightily along a broad river, or dwells silently beneath the ground, water is almost naïve; gullible; passive. Each time nature cleanses it and returns it to us, it comes to us like a week-old kitten, trusting us as fellow constituents of life, of the cycle of nature on the planet. And yet we foul it and waste it and cast it aside, and we ignore the clear fact that even water's forgiving nature has limits and that the time may come, and *will* come if we are not more respectful, when the water will not be drinkable. It will still be there. It will even be called water. But we will not be able to drink it and continue living.

Together, the people who feel this way about water have given it a standing that it has never enjoyed before. They have spurred governments into action when the governments clearly would have preferred to remain lethargic. They have taken on the most formidable opponents in the nation—the bureaucracies, the enormous corporations, and the builders—and they have gone into their battles after having done their homework and, to the amazement of practically everyone, including themselves, they sometimes have won. In the vacuum left by poor national, state, and local leadership, these people have taken over the battle to rescue water. They know that the battle cannot be won without the wholehearted involvement of government, but until that comes, they are the leaders.

They have a sneaking fear, some of them, that their leaders may very well do nothing at all about water until catastrophe—an epic man-made drought, a crushing man-made plague, or a combination of the two—forces them to act. This fear, as pessimistic as it sounds, may be the most logical one at the moment, and it certainly has a solid historical basis. But these people keep trying anyway.

By and large these people are doing what they are doing reluctantly, for they were not brought up to be public nuisances or to challenge roomfuls of army colonels. But, like others before them in conflicts over civil rights, the unjust war in Vietnam, and the human rights of a dozen different minorities, they have overcome their shyness. They have told themselves that they were doing it temporarily, for they also had jobs to go to, classes to attend, mouths to feed. But they have done it energetically and enthusiastically and tirelessly, because they had no alternative. It is their *drinking water* they are fighting for; the stuff of their very lives.

29

For the housewives in Gray, Maine, it was an unexpected entry into a new world—one populated by state officials, local politicians, a lot of very skeptical people, camera crews, reporters who phoned at all hours—a world that they had glimpsed only on the television set.

Cheryl Washburn was the daughter of an army family that settled in Maine in 1964. Her husband, George, is a salesman for a company that makes biscuits. They have two young children. She was in her early twenties when a neighbor first noticed that the laundry, which was done in the well water that all the houses in East Gray used, was discolored and smelled funny. Cathy Hinds, another neighbor, was from Portland. The house in Gray was the first for her and her husband, Greg, a sign maker for the Maine Turnpike, and their two children. Both women referred to themselves, in an interview in 1979, as "domestic engineers."

When tests showed what was in the water that the Gray families were drinking—trichloroethylene, trichloroethane, methylene chloride, dimethyl sulfide, acetone, and alcohol—Washburn and Hinds were shocked. But there was more that bothered them: In March, 1977, Cathy Hinds had a miscarriage. In December, 1978, she delivered a baby boy. He died two days later, on Christmas Day. "And the rest of us," she said later, "have had kidney problems, infections where we don't know where they're coming from; respiratory problems, where you have difficulty breathing; nervous disorders. Some people were treated with tranquilizers. Some had visual problems, a loss of feeling in extremities, skin problems like rashes, dizziness, loss of balance." The obvious source of these problems, the women thought, was the chemical waste site a few hundred yards away from their homes and water wells.

At first, Washburn and Hinds felt isolated, felt that they were impotent to deal with the problem beyond recording everything that happened in a spiral notebook that had a color photograph of a flower on its cover. The local health officer, they said, did an excellent job of trying to arouse interest in the water situation, but there was little other official action. One day they saw a television documentary on toxic wastes, called "The Killing Ground," by the American Broadcasting Company, and they realized that they were not alone. They formed an organization, EPIC, for Environmental Public Interest Coalition, in June of 1979. Soon they started getting telephone calls from people in other communities who had discovered that they, too, were drinking strange chemicals and who wanted to know what they could do about it. Neither of the Gray women had experience in organizing. They were not the sort of people who had tired of Chablis and Brie and who were rushing around saving seal pups. But they found that they didn't need very much experience. "People who have a problem," said Cathy Hinds, "like to talk to other people who have the same problem." The women built up a correspondence with their counterparts at Love Canal, with officials of the National Wildlife Federation, with Congressman Albert Gore, Jr.

At first, they said, the State of Maine was reluctant to agree that Gray had a problem. "Like us," said Hinds, "the Department of Environmental Protection was ignorant. But we're no longer ignorant and they shouldn't still be the same way." After the state had gotten officially involved in closing the waste site—Gardner Hunt, the director of the state's water lab, was the official who was most concerned with the Gray situation—the women discovered that children were using the chemical dump as a playground. "Hunt said there were some things still there but that they were buried," recalled Cathy

Hinds, "but it sure didn't look like that to us. We called the press and held a press conference at the site and demanded that it be made safe. We put a lot of pressure on Mr. Hunt, and he said he'd put up a fence, but he wasn't sure about when. *Eventually* was what it sounded like. We made more noise and they did it according to our deadline, which was within two weeks. On the very last day of the two weeks they did it. Mr. Hunt probably thinks we're a couple of bitches. We think a lot of what he does is a bunch of p.r. crap."

(Actually, Gardner Hunt refers to the two women as "the ladies." When he was asked about the state's role in detecting and sealing off the hazardous waste site in Gray, he pointed out that traditionally his department, and corresponding agencies all over the nation, had concerned themselves not with groundwater supplies but rather with surface waters. "These are the waters that show," said Hunt, "because that's where the public attention has been directed. I think the ladies are partially correct," he added. "Prior to this problem, we didn't pay the attention to groundwater that we do now." One big difficulty, he said, was that "The public essentially wants a zero risk" in its dealings with water and other elements of the environment. "But on the other hand, we're not in a position as a society yet to be able to assure a zero risk. The ladies are demanding all the answers, the zero risks, and they come to us for the answers, and we just don't *have* the answers now. Society doesn't have the answers."

(Would the state have acted as quickly and as thoroughly, the state official was asked, if Cathy Hinds and Cheryl Washburn had not been so persistent? "I've said this many times before," replied Gardner Hunt, "in public and in private: The squeaking wheel gets the grease. It is axiomatic." Eventually the state brought its own suit in the McKin site case.)

The two women sat at the dinner table in Cathy Hinds's house, the spiral notebook with the history of Gray's water problems open before them. Their children played nearby and goldfish scooted back and forth in a bowl. Cheryl Washburn noticed that the visitor was staring at the fish. "We watch them to see what happens to them," she said. "It's local water."

One of the bad things about the experience with the water in Gray, she said, was having to seal her backyard well—the one that tapped into the groundwater—and tie onto the town's water lines when they were extended to East Gray. "Losing the well," said Washburn, "was like losing some of your independence. It's like the well represented some kind of *freedom* for us. It meant we didn't have to depend on other people as much. . . . Whenever anybody takes a little bit away, it's like you're not free anymore. We've been through a bad time with water, but now we know how to survive. If it happened again —if something like a pipe broke, or something else that cut off the water—we'd know how to handle it. We'd know how to cope."

Will their experience happen to others? the women were asked.

"It's inevitable," said Cathy Hinds. "And it's going to have to happen to people before they learn about it."

It *has* happened to many people, all across the nation, in the short time since Cathy Hinds said that, and virtually everywhere that the water has been threatened, people have banded together and formed organizations to fight back. As often as not, they have been rebuffed and mistreated, and very often misled, by the governmental agencies—particularly at the state level—that are supposed to protect them. In northeastern New Jersey, streamwalkers patrol the fetid, but once clear, brooks and rivers that industry has turned into sewers. A Ralph Nader offshoot called the New York Public Interest Research Group has provided the leadership (where state and counties have clearly failed) in doing research on toxic waste problems in the Hudson River and on Long Island. The latter place may turn out to be the nation's most serious environmental disaster.

The State of New York and the government of the United States were engaging in a childish and scurrilous game of blame-pinning on the question of relocating families made victims by the Love Canal tragedy, and each side was demonstrating its ability to treat the tormented families—tormented not only by poisonous chemicals but by a heartless series of "reports" and "studies" as well—as political pawns, when some of the families rebelled against their oppressors and took federal hostages. They locked up two EPA officials, a press officer and a physician, until agents of the Federal Bureau of Investigation arrived. A few hours later, President Carter declared the families' situation a federal emergency, and the victims started getting some relief.

Across the nation, Americans who were outraged at the Reagan administration's attacks on virtually everything that hinted at environmental protection turned to the established organizations, such as the Sierra Club, the Wilderness Society, and the National Audubon Society, in unprecedented numbers. The religious zeal with which Reagan's Secretary of the Interior, James Watt, pursued the handing over of the environment to business interests served particularly well as an organizing tool for those interested in saving Earth. The National Audubon Society became unusually vocal in its attacks on what it called "hydropork" schemes that pour billions into projects such as the Tennessee-Tombigbee Waterway and the Columbia Dam project.

Landowners opposing the Corps of Engineers' plans to run 1,800 people off 21,000 acres of land to build a pork-barrel project, Stonewall Jackson Dam in West Virginia, started selling their land off in three-square-foot sections (for $10 a lot) to frustrate and complicate the Corps's paperwork when it started condemning the land. When women in Cape May County, New Jersey, realized that a lot of miscarriages were occurring, they formed an organization called the Concerned Parents Association to disseminate information. They gathered statistics on birth defects and put pressure on state health officials to test their water supplies. In Woburn, Massachusetts, the scene of some of the nation's worst toxic chemical contamination, citizens got the runaround from officials before they made enough noise to attract attention. An EPA lawyer told *Washington Post* reporter Martha M. Hamilton that he had discerned a trend in which people who feel they've been hurt by environmental pollution from industry or other sources have been getting together and suing. "It's a very interesting trend," said the lawyer, "different people looking to enforce environmental law for different reasons. It's not because they're do-gooders, but people who have been harmed."

Another trend involves those different people's not only getting together but also getting together and doing their *homework* before taking on a polluting industry or a government agency that wants to destroy a valley or ruin a river. As never before in American history, citizens have learned how to use the tools provided by government itself—the Environmental Impact Statement, the agency regulations, the laws of the land, the public hearing process—to challenge, delay, and in many cases defeat public-works projects and private industry efforts that are dangerous to the environment. In the "old days" of just a few years ago, these projects never would have been challenged. The change has been phenomenal, and it has been widespread, covering every area of the nation, and it has occurred with practically no comparable widespread public notice. Almost overnight people who respect the environment, who feel that water should have standing, have learned how to deal with government and the exploiters on their own terms and on their own levels.

There are few of these people who know how to do their homework as well as the aforementioned John Marlin, director of the Central States Resources Center in Champaign, Illinois. Marlin is the young man who sometimes wears Corps of Engineers insignia and who so obviously enjoys taking on the Corps in a battle; by one count, his organization has stopped twenty-five Corps projects in one year. Marlin explains his attitude, which borders on what used to be called the "military

manner," by declaring that in his line of work, which is dam-
fighting, and in which the people Marlin considers the good
guys are greatly outnumbered by Corps colonels, bureaucrats,
barge owners, and land speculators, all of whom he frequently
encounters at public meetings, "the psychology of a situation
like that militates against anyone who comes in with a humble
attitude. I like to walk in there with a look on my face, even
though I'm outnumbered four hundred to one, that says, 'All
right, you turkeys, one at a time or all at once?' "

Marlin was at a damfighters' meeting in Washington in
1979, a featured speaker in a session on organizing techniques,
and he went into considerable detail on the subject. The first
thing you do when setting out to stop an unwise project, he told
his audience, is to learn as much as possible about it. Then it is
essential to identify your potential allies and enemies. Often
the allies turn out to be landowners, including farmers, as well
as the "bird-and-bunny people." Sometimes the two groups
have conflicting philosophies and may never have worked
together before, or even met each other. Once, when Marlin
needed to organize a meeting of the two groups in a dam fight
(for tactical reasons the meeting could not be publicly
announced), he had to ask all the participants to stand next to
the left taillights of their automobiles at 8 p.m. in the parking
lot of a certain restaurant. "There was a conglomeration of
farmers and hippies and environmental types and housewives
and professors," he recalled, "all standing in the parking lot of
Sandy's restaurant by their left taillights, and that's how we
knew who we were. That's how we started."

"The next thing you've got to do," continued Marlin, "is
find who your *enemies* are. Now, you know that the agency is
your enemy. And I mean that in a military sense. ENEMY.
They're trying to run you off your land. They're trying to
destroy your heritage. Whatever it is that you've got, when
they're done with you you won't have it. There is no difference
at all between the Corps of Engineers, or the Bureau of
Reclamation, coming in and flooding the land and running

people off and bulldozing the houses, and Attila and his Huns coming through an area. The people are just as gone. They may not be dead. But much of their spirit, their cohesiveness, and their tradition die in the process of the government's taking over an area which for generations supported those people. So think of them as the enemy."

Next, said Marlin, "figure out what your objectives are, and keep that as general as possible to minimize the amount of conflict you're going to have within your own organization." And a group fighting a water project should come up with a number of alternatives to it, rather than one specific alternative, which would invite a specific attack. "One of your biggest advantages when you fight a project," he said, "is that you have a specific target. You know exactly what to fight. You don't want to give the other side the same advantage." Marlin was sounding very much like an experienced military officer about to lead his troops into battle.

And cultivate spies, he added. "We have a lot of spies within various agencies who send us things in plain brown wrappers. On almost any project you will find somebody in any agency who really finds it a bad project. . . .

"You've got to understand that your project comes to you because of and through *political* processes. You fight a dam project on *political* grounds. Engineering, technical terms, legal things, those sorts of things are useful and they're very important, and they have their place. But your number one project is usually political." He explained the nature of the Iron Triangle, and reminded his audience that no politician is too small, no elected office too insignificant, for damfighters to approach and lobby. "In most cases," he said, speaking of the politicians, "they are not sinister people. They're trying to do things that help their constituents. You cannot expect a politician who's supported a project since he was on the city council somewhere to suddenly change his position just because a bunch of farmers and bird-and-bunny people say it's a bad project. You've got to *educate* them and give them a politically viable way to change their minds. New evidence. New studies. Changed economic situations. You've got to approach them with the attitude that you can convert them and if, after several years of not converting them, it looks hopeless, then you try to remove them."

Marlin advised his listeners to form organizations that are democratic but that leave room for quick maneuvering and response by executive committees at the top—a distinct advantage in dealing with bureaucracy, which is set up in precisely the opposite fashion. Only one person should be deputized to deal with the press. "It keeps your story straight," he said. "It keeps the information flowing through one area and prevents unauthorized enthusiasts and crackpots who join your group from using your group's name."

When dealing with the Corps of Engineers, he advised, aim at the senior civilians and forget about the colonels, since "The Corps changes colonels more often than most people change underwear." And (here Marlin seemed even *more* like a commander lecturing his troops) keep the hair short and the beards trimmed.

"Your image is the most important thing you have in a public fight," said Marlin, whose own blond hair was just a bit shorter than most everyone else's in the room, even those who were obviously not bird-and-bunny people. "One of my cardinal rules is: Keep your hippies off TV. Now, that's not a very nice thing to do to well-meaning people who look like leftover Berkeley radicals, but it is the only way to deal effectively with a state and a populace who no longer identify with leftover Berkeley radicals. We use people who have a free lifestyle for research, transportation, writing, press releases— anything but being in front of a camera. Why do we do that? It's very simple. If you take a cross section of the population, especially where I operate in the Midwest, they do not like beards if they're frizzy. They do not like granny gowns, and they do not like the braless look. Keep those people off television and out of the newspapers and you'll be miles ahead."

Marlin was nearing the end of his talk, and although it had run for quite some time, no one in his audience seemed the least bit restless or bored. Many of his listeners, both bird-and-bunny folk and those who were damfighters because of conservative political convictions, had been taking detailed notes on what Marlin was saying.

"Work together," said the speaker. "You've got a dam in your county, and somebody's got a dam project in the other county. Talk to each other; compare notes and tactics. The Corps can't hold a hearing in Illinois or Indiana anymore without people from six or seven different projects showing up and warning each other about how awful it was here, and about what they tried to do there, and saying, 'Yeah, Colonel, we heard *that* before.'

"And always remember that the game is *political.* Don't sue anybody until you have to. When you sue somebody, you spend money on lawyers. And worst of all, after they have that big headline, SUIT FILED, very often the media don't want to hear about the other aspects of the project because 'It's in the courts.' They lose interest.

"Research is great. But when you get into it, there'll be the one hydrologist on your side and the government will have eight or nine on its side, at the taxpayers' expense, and they'll overwhelm you by out-experting you. So organize. I don't mean to belittle the research aspects or the legal aspects. They're very important. But realize the limitations. *This is a political game. These other things are just on the side.*"

Marlin's commitment to his work is beyond question (he has often said that he views the controversies and challenges in which he engages as the equivalent of war), but there are others whose lives are wrapped up in the water crisis in almost spiritual ways. Frank Welsh, the director of the citizens' group opposing the Central Arizona Project, once had the ultimate in job security—a civilian position in the Corps of Engineers—and gave it all up. Until then, he said, he had been "the eight-to-five, you-are-how-much-you-make-type person." One reason for the change was Arizona: "I just love it here," he said. "I'm part lizard. I love the warmth." Another was the knowledge that he was doing the right thing in opposing a project that will damage nature and that is economically unsound. But working for a citizens' group that opposes a public-works project is not the most financially rewarding job in the world. In order to survive, said Welsh, "I have accepted being what I call 'independently poor' as a way of living."

Mark Dubois was willing to give his life for water.

In 1979, Dubois was thirty years old, a Californian of striking appearance—he stands six feet eight inches tall—with piercing brown eyes and a neat beard and a body so spare and adorned with such simple clothes that a visitor might assume he had sworn some religious oath of poverty. The river Mark Dubois was willing to give his life for is the Stanislaus, one of the last remaining wild rivers in California—or, for that matter, in the nation. The Stanislaus tumbles down out of the Sierra Nevada southeast of Sacramento; it is dammed as it enters the foothills, but before it turns into a reservoir it provides an immense environment (called, by those who study such things, a riparian habitat) for a great variety of creatures and vegetation, as well as for humans who like to tear down through whitewater in rafts. It was the aim of the Bureau of Reclamation, which planned to operate the dam project, and the Corps of Engineers, which was to oversee the construction, to enlarge the reservoir by creating a New Melones Dam. The builders promised more water for irrigation in California's rich Central Valley, along with increased hydropower. The opponents of New Melones, among them a Sacramento-based group to which Mark Dubois belongs, Friends of the River, argued that the project was not economically sound, that the amount of electricity generated would be negligible, and that "the most precious stretch of the river," a wild nine miles running east from a point known as Parrott's Ferry, would be destroyed.

One day in the spring of 1979, as the Corps was raising the level of the reservoir, Mark Dubois slipped into the canyons above Parrott's Ferry and chained himself to a rock. His friends informed the Corps, the state government, and the press that Dubois was there and that if the water continued to rise he would be drowned. They would not reveal where Dubois was. The Corps stopped filling the reservoir, and after a week in the wilderness Dubois came out—but only after an assistant to Governor Brown produced a document saying the state would monitor the water level at a point, agreed to by state and Corps, that would not flood the canyon.

Not long after he released himself from the chain, Dubois spoke in Sacramento about his feelings for the Stanislaus and about why he had done what he did.

"I'd been spending the last fifteen years of my life up in that canyon," he said. "It was my first place where I had the freedom of growing up—of being in my own space and in getting to know a place. It became more of a home to me than I could ever imagine. To me, it's been a *person*." He first went to the Stanislaus to explore its limestone caves. Later he returned to run commercial rafting trips down the river, including some in which city kids "who didn't have a chance to go many places" spent summers on the river.

Before long, Dubois realized that he owed something to the canyon, which was coming under attack by the builders. So he joined with Friends of the River, and they tried to save the river by "going through channels. Going to hearings; things like that—letter-writing campaigns, working on an initiative to save it." There were setbacks. Once, said Dubois, he was convinced that all the reasons that cynics give for *not* taking on public issues were valid. "We had always been taught not to get involved in the system; that it doesn't work; that big money buys the answer. Well, all of a sudden we had been shown

that all that old garbage was true." Then there were some suc-
cesses, and most of them were achieved through administrative
channels, in state and federal government. But slowly, deliberately, certainly, the other side was winning. The water was
rising. Dubois visited the Stanislaus again.

"I just felt all the energy of that canyon, and that canyon
had given *me* so much energy, and I knew that I would have to
make a statement to help people realize how much life is being
destroyed." And so Mark Dubois went to a hardware store and
bought what he needed, and then he went to the canyon and
found a big chunk of bedrock. "I took a star drill," he said, "the
kind the old miners used to use, and a sledgehammer and I
made a little hole in the rock. I hated drilling a hole in the rock.
But I didn't want to chain myself to a tree because I knew
they'd cut it down. I wanted to stay there. When the chain was
wrapped around my leg and attached to the rock, I had just
four inches of movement. I knew that if they found me and I
had a long chain, they'd just move me over and cut the chain.
I used the most expensive lock I'd ever seen."

The water continued rising, and by the time the Corps
reacted to Dubois's demonstration, realized that it couldn't find
him in all those woods, and stopped filling the reservoir, it was
about a foot and a half from his feet. Dubois said later that he
was very confident that he would not drown.

He was asked, after it was all over, what he thought had
been accomplished. He replied: "Each time before, I said, 'I'll
try the administrative channels,' and I did, and I lost. Friends
of the River tried, and we lost every time. So this was the last
chance. I was hoping that maybe a few bureaucrats would get
their butts in gear and do the right thing. I was basically hoping
that responsible people would do what they were supposed to
do.

"I'm talking about the bureaucrats, the administrators. And
Colonel [Donald] O'Shei, who ran the project for the Corps.
I knew he had a choice about whether the water would rise,
and I knew that he would do whatever he thought was right.

I thought that maybe some other people might put pressure on him to flood it. But I also knew that I had a lot of respect for him, and I knew that he values life. He doesn't value the life of the *canyon*; he can't relate to that. He has his construction schedules, which he implements fully."

In a sense, Mark Dubois failed in his effort to rescue the river. The builders eventually got their way. But in another sense, he won a great victory. His obviously sincere action in chaining himself to that rock touched and moved an uncounted but important number of other young people—people of the late seventies, of an era characterized more by cynicism and selfishness than anything else—by their encounter with his idealism, and the idealism has spread. Particularly in California, now, one encounters groups of younger people gathered in the same makeshift offices as those that once served the movements to end racial discrimination and the Vietnam war. Like their predecessors, they research the issues and plan the strategies and lobby the policy-makers. Partly because of people like Dubois, and partly because of Dubois himself, saving rivers has become a legitimate cause.

Joanne Foster found out about the water in her town from the same television show that the women in Gray had seen— ABC's "The Killing Ground." At the end of the program, when it ran in March, 1979, there was a list of communities with problems of toxic wastes. Southington, Connecticut, was one of them.

Joanne Foster, who is a wife, mother, and substitute schoolteacher, is not the sort of person who sits back and lets events overtake her. Once she got tired of all the breakdowns her automobile was suffering, so she bought a motorcycle. The day after she learned from a network television program that Southington had a problem with toxic wastes, she read *The Hartford Courant*, which covers Southington, very closely for more information. There was none. After three days, Foster called a reporter on the paper and asked what was happening.

The response was the reporter's interviewing Joanne Foster and writing a story about "one resident's concern."

"I'm normally concerned about things like this," she explained later. "Just in general. But I wasn't a member of any environmental groups or anything like that. Not *then*. I was just a concerned and informed television viewer. I was interested in what the public issues were. This was my first exposure to the fact that something like this was so real and evident. That was the beginning of my public consciousness."

What caused that beginning was the discovery that hazardous chemicals had contaminated part of Southington's drinking-water supply, which is obtained from wells. The apparent source of the chemical, said Foster, was local industry —specifically, a firm named Solvents Recovery Service of New England.

Other citizens of Southington read the newspaper story about "one resident's concern," and they called Foster and asked what they should do. It was obvious that a meeting had to be held. Like John Marlin's dam opponents, the residents hadn't met before; they agreed to wear something purple on their shoulders, said Foster, "so we could identify each other." Out of the meeting and subsequent gatherings came a formal organization, the Southington Citizens Action Group. And there came the discovery, which was surprising to some, that many people in positions of leadership, elected and appointed, wanted to downplay the problem. "You call your town council members," she said, "and a few of them say, 'Yeah, I heard about that; let me know what you find out.' Call the water department, and you can't get through—the lines were really busy." She also called the state Department of Environmental Protection and learned that Solvents Recovery's disposal methods had been the subject of investigation. Slowly, but with some certainty, the local officials responded to the citizens' pressure. Public meetings were held. Facts came out. Joanne Foster, and the others with new public consciousness, learned how water in Southington was obtained and distributed. At one point they discovered that one of the public wells had been quietly shut down a year previously after it had been found to be contaminated.

Help, in the form of warm bodies from Yale University to conduct legal research, came from an organization named the Connecticut Fund for the Environment. In the summer of 1979 the fund filled a thick petition with the federal Environmental Protection Agency, demanding action. Later that year the government brought lawsuits against Solvents Recovery and another firm, charging them with contaminating the underground water supply of the town of Southington by improper storage and dumping of chlorinated hydrocarbon wastes. The suit asked for an injunction against further dumping, remedial action on what had been done already, and prevention of future damage.

Joanne Foster felt good, in a way. "We were disappointed that the officials didn't take the initiative," she said. "We had to provide the pressure." But it was good to know that the people in Southington had discovered the problem and had taken steps to deal with it. Many other communities have not progressed that far along the road to awareness. "And we *know* that it's going on all around us," said Foster. "We absolutely *know*. We are lucky that we found out about it."

Had she ever felt, though, that it would be somehow nicer, that it would make life less complicated, *not* to find out what was down there in the aquifer?

"No," she replied instantly. "I will never *not* fight for something. I think of people like that as fatalists; people who think they have no control over things. I'm not a fatalist. I will do what I can and fight for what I can. But I won't ever sit back and say, 'Accept it; there's nothing you can do about it.' I'll *always* find something to do about it, I think."

In fact, Joanne Foster found something else to do about water in Southington. There was a vacancy on the town's water board, which has six members. Foster applied for the job and was appointed to it. She then became Water Commissioner Foster of Southington, Connecticut, as well as a concerned resident.

Later she expanded her horizons further. Foster left the water board to become a lobbyist at the state level for the Connecticut Fund for the Environment, and she found that she liked lobbying very much. She also became involved in environmental issues for the Connecticut League of Women Voters.

The town of Southington dug new wells, and the government's suit against Solvents Recovery dragged on. Charges against the other original defendant were dismissed. Joanne Foster said in early 1982 that she was "very worried" about the Reagan administration's attitude toward the problems of toxic contamination. "I'm worried that they might want to pull out," she said. In the case of the Southington suit, it appeared that she had ample cause for concern. An EPA lawyer, a member of the new Reagan team, explained in February, 1982, that the government was still trying, after more than two years, to negotiate a settlement in the suit. "At the moment we're in an elongated negotiation posture," he said, in the language government agencies use to explain why they have accomplished nothing.

Ellen Stern Harris has challenged the agency that has been called California's second most powerful decision-making body, surpassed only by the state legislature. It should not be a surprise that this agency is involved with water. It is the organization that has made the southern California desert bloom with fruit trees, office buildings, corporate agriculture, freeways, and Mercedes-Benzes.

The Metropolitan Water District of Southern California was created by legislative act in 1928 as a quasi-public body to find water to supplement the existing sources for the state's south coastal plain, which included wells, runoff from the

mountains, and an aqueduct completed earlier this century by
the City of Los Angeles that brings water from the Owens
Valley on the eastern slope of the High Sierra. If left to its
own devices, the area would receive an average of 14 inches of
rainfall a year. But southern California has not been left to its
own devices. Promoters and speculators and politicians learned
early on in California that bringing water artificially into the
semi-arid environment was as close to *creating* expensive real
estate as human beings were likely to ever come.

The District arranges for and purchases water in mind-
boggling quantities and then sells it, at wholesale, to the cities
and communities which it comprises. Each of those jurisdictions sends at least one representative to the board of directors
of the MWD, as it is commonly called.

The MWD is immensely powerful, simply because water
is so valuable in southern California and because the agency
controls so much of that water. Nearly 11,000,000 people, or
about half of the state's population, live within the MWD
service area, a countryside that is laced with aqueducts, reservoirs, distribution lines, tunnels, and canals. Like the roots of a
willow tree, the Los Angeles area searches restlessly for water
to feed its growing habit of people, agriculture, and industry,
and the roots stretch northward to well beyond San Francisco
Bay and as far to the east as the sadly emasculated Colorado.
Fortunes are spent pumping the water down the aqueducts
and over the mountains into the Los Angels area.

Like all builders, the Metropolitan Water District is constantly searching for rivers to dam, sources to tap, and new
ways to spend money. And, although it functions in a place
where water's preciousness is especially obvious to most people,
the MWD seems to be less than preoccupied with the notion
of conservation. Its headquarters building on Sunset Boulevard
in Los Angeles, which is a far more opulent-looking structure
than the typical repository of public workers, has well-watered
lawns outside, a lush atrium, and absolutely no sign inside
that its owners are interested in conserving water. The rest-

room facilities, for example, are of the water-wasting variety rarely seen in modern public buildings. The District's own cafeteria is better appointed than most non-subsidized restaurants, and the District has caused its own official seal to be richly inscribed on the plastic food trays. The feeling a visitor might get is one of power, mixed with more than a little arrogance.

At the same time that it seems to be celebrating all the good things that happen when copious amounts of water are poured onto the desert, MWD also is constantly reminding its citizens that they cannot take water for granted. Such a reminder, one might logically think, would form the basis for a comprehensive program of conservation, but in southern California it serves rather as a foundation for arguments that more and bigger projects need to be built. A favorite effort is the Peripheral Canal, which, MWD keeps reminding people, is essential because anticipated cuts in the amount of water California will get from the Colorado (because of the court decision restoring to Arizona some of its historical entitlement to the river flow) will mean that southern California must come up with more water from somewhere, and so why not from northern California, where there are still some rivers that are running "needlessly" (i.e., free) to the sea? A few years ago the MWD published a pamphlet titled *Is Southern California Running Out of Water?* in which Earle C. Blais, its chairman, informed the citizenry that "The answer, unfortunately, is a very real 'Yes.'" Blais based his conclusion on the proposed cutback in Colorado River water and on increasing population in southern California, and he raised the spectre of another drought for the region. Conservation was useful, he said, but it "can amount to only a small fraction of all that Colorado River water we'll be losing."

A system such as the one operated by MWD is destined to have critics, but few of them have been as articulate as Ellen Stern Harris. For one thing, most critics are outsiders of one form or another, but Harris has conducted her critiquing from inside the district's board of directors, where, until March, 1980, she served as a representative from Beverly Hills. Harris sat not long ago in a restaurant just off the currently fashionable Rodeo Drive in Beverly Hills (an eating place where status-y bottled water costs more than beer) and traced her recent, tempestuous, and mostly satisfying history.

"I started out as a wife and the mother of two young children," she said in her ebullient style, "and became divorced, went to work for the Center for the Study of Democratic Institutions, listened to all those people sit around and pontificate. And I said to myself, 'Oh, you are such a lucky person, Ellen, sitting at the feet of the great minds of our time,' and the more I listened to them, the more I realized bullshit was being espoused." The center was situated in Santa Barbara, where the blowout of a coastal oil rig on January 28, 1969, made environmentalism a very pertinent, and permanent, issue for many Americans. But the center, said Harris, "wasn't paying any attention to any real-life problems" such as that. So she moved on and held a number of jobs in the environmental field, and in the process she learned a lot about the workings of government. She became a member, and the vice chairman, of the state's Coastal Zone Commission, which is the planning agency for coastal development and preservation. She put together a coalition of citizen organizations, the Council for Planning and Conservation, and she published a periodical account of what was happening in the field.

Her newsletter caught the eye of editors at the *Los Angeles Times*, and they asked her to write a column, which was titled "Consumer Advocate" and which ran once a week for seven years. Harris is proud of the fact that she "heavily researched" her topics. "It wasn't just about how I felt when I got out of bed," she said. It seemed quite fitting that, with her knowledge of consumer matters, her community, Beverly Hills, appointed her in January, 1978, as its representative on the Metropolitan Water District's board of directors.

Harris was appalled at the workings of the MWD, especially at its tendency to lavish money on self-promotion and executive travel, and before long she was letting her *L.A. Times* readers know what was happening. In one column published in the summer of 1978, she laid out a temperate but detailed report of some of the issues raised by MWD critics other than herself. These included questions about the district's public relations department, which cost more than a million dollars a year; about first-class travel and luxury accommodations for MWD directors attending conferences; about the fact that, while citizens conserved during the drought of the late seventies, the district raised the rates they had to pay; and about the differential rate structure that favors agriculture at the expense of domestic, municipal, and industrial water users. After the column ran, Ellen Stern Harris was fired by the *Los Angeles Times.*

Harris believes she knows the reason: "The Times-Mirror Corporation owns one of the largest single contiguous pieces of agricultural land in California. Their support for the Metropolitan Water District's policy is very much intertwined with their own corporate goals, and that is the importation of water for which they pay very cheap prices and for which the rest of us pay very high prices."

(The newspaper's view of what happened was that Harris seemed unable to separate her two roles—those of a personal advocate and those of a journalist—when writing her column. "We wanted a question-and-answer-type column," said Shirley Taylor, an associate editor, one "in which the writer is not personally involved," and Harris did not supply that need. The editor said the decision to terminate Harris's column was made "without any consideration of the *Times*'s agricultural land" holdings. Of course, Harris was hired to do the column in the first place on the basis of her personal advocacy for consumer causes.)

Harris has managed to stay busy. She has complained to

a grand jury about the MWD's behavior, and she conducted a consumer affairs program on radio, and she continued serving out her term as Beverly Hills's somewhat out-of-the-ordinary representative on the Metropolitan Water District board. "I'm a minority of one on a fifty-two-member board," she said in the spring of 1980. "Every vote would be unanimous, practically, if it wasn't for me." She disagreed with the majority on matters of nuclear power, on blind devotion to the Peripheral Canal project, and, most of all, on MWD's own internal behavior. She continued to make noise about conservation. ("Let me tell you the difference between *talking* conservation and truly enacting it," she said. "At the MWD, the officials go around depressed every time it rains. It means the water sales go down.") After she left the MWD, Harris did consumer affairs broadcasting for cable television, and she has taught courses at the University of California at Los Angeles on the concentration of power in the hands of the media.

And she has continued to talk about the future of southern California, and to consider a future that is *not* built on endlessly increasing supplies of water taken from some other part of the planet. She was asked if she believed there were something environmentally immoral about making the desert bloom, and she replied:

"Do I consider it immoral? I don't think the morality of it is any longer something that I can address myself to, because it is a *fact*. There's already an enormous civilization in southern California. Everybody agrees it can't revert to the desert. But you are going to see it do just that. When 1983 comes, the energy portion of the state water project [the legal instrument by which water is bought, sold, and shipped around California] will expire, and new contracts will be negotiated. At the current energy price levels, we are anticipating a tenfold increase in the price of water. Let me tell you what is going to happen to all the lush gardens around here. It's going to be incredible. You're suddenly going to see a new appreciation for California native brush and plants. Where there are lawns you're going to see gravel. Where there are trees you will see cacti. And it will change the face of this civilization. It's really going to be interesting."

And if all of this comes to pass in the way Ellen Stern Harris thinks it will, perhaps the California desert will, for once, bloom naturally.

Rae Ely is deceptively soft in voice and manner, a southern woman who is at home among the sophisticates of Charlottesville, Virginia, and the surrounding green, rolling hills where people still, on occasion, use horses to chase foxes. But she is pure hell in a fight, as several giants of industry can testify.

Ely has done a great deal to protect Green Springs, Virginia, an unincorporated community not far from Charlottesville, from those who would strip-mine it. Green Springs rests gently on some 14,000 acres in the flattened cone of an ancient volcano. The cone now is hardly visible even to those who know what to look for; it has been filled and replaced by a lush environment of rolling hills and green pastures that looks more like a painting than reality. The greenness is there because there is a great deal of water just beneath the cone's surface. And the water is there because of the existence, in Green Springs, of a huge deposit of vermiculite. Vermiculite is a very absorbant mineral used in agriculture and in construction and in the home, where it may be employed to catch the droppings of house cats: cat litter.

There are mansions and farms and fine-looking homes in Green Springs today; the place is so close to unique that the Interior Department has designated it as a National Historic District, calling it "a textbook of Virginia's architecture up to the period following the Civil War." Green Springs also offers a potential textbook example of a terrific place to strip-mine for vermiculite. For this reason several mining outfits, including the multinational chemical firm W. R. Grace & Company, have become attracted to Green Springs. Another, smaller company, Virginia Vermiculite, entered the picture later. It was headed by a man named Robert Sansom, who worked at EPA during the Nixon administration.

Rae Ely and others in Green Springs—most of them were women, as are very many of the participants in the battle for water—did their homework and they fought the invaders. They lobbied for Historic Site designation, which would help protect the area from disfiguring exploitation. Ely hired an airplane and flew over Grace's South Carolina plant and brought back color slides that showed what a vermiculite strip mine looked like—a moonscape. The women held bake sales, house tours, and barbecues to raise money to pay their lawyers. They bought stock in Grace and went to stockholders' meetings and asked embarrassing questions. They maintained close relations with the press. And in the end, they apparently brought W. R. Grace & Company to its knees. The firm has not lately expressed a desire to do any strip mining in Green Springs.

But the fight was not over. Virginia Vermiculite went to court to challenge the Historic Site designation, and, in the summer of 1980, a federal district judge in Richmond ruled in the firm's favor. (He was Robert R. Merhige, Jr., the man who officiated at the Kepone settlement.) The judge found that the Interior Department lacked detailed standards for designating the place as a historic landmark.

Rae Ely and her confederates swung back into action. They announced their plans to appeal the decision, as might be expected, but they did something else that was more effective: They got friends in Congress to draft legislation that had the effect of revalidating all previous Historic Site designations. Ely, who called it a "technical amendment," said it went through Congress without many representatives actually knowing what they were voting for. Jimmy Carter, with about a month left to serve in office, signed the legislation, and Green Springs was once again saved. (Later Judge Merhige ruled that the new legislation was adequate to enforce the designation.)

Sansom, of Virginia Vermiculite (who by then had become Ronald Reagan's chief advisor on the future of the Tennessee Valley Authority), cried foul. He told Ben Franklin of *The New York Times* that neither he nor others who had been fighting the Historic Site designation had been made aware that Congress was considering such legislation.

When it became known that the strip miners had been zapped once again, Rae Ely was asked about her techniques. She was in Charlottesville now, a mother and wife who had decided to go to law school in her late thirties (and the first law student at the University of Virginia to be admitted without an undergraduate degree). Wasn't what the protectors of Green Springs had done—in effect, sneaking through legislation while nobody was looking—a lot like what the *other side* did? Wasn't it, in fact, a great deal like what the promoters of Tellico Dam had done?

She replied sweetly. "We learned early on," she said "that the way to win was to look at our enemy and figure out his game rules, and then use his game rules against him. And it's worked like a charm. My, aren't they clever to have figured this technique out, and to have shared it with us!"

There is one lesson that is quickly learned by anyone who signs on to protect the watery environment, and that is that the other side never quits. A victory for water is never a complete one, because those whose livelihoods depend on exploiting it never give up. The government builders never give up, not only because it costs them nothing to keep plugging away at their projects, but because even the act of plugging away keeps them alive and on the payroll. The miners, dumpers, irrigators, and speculators never give up because the financial return from winning is so enormous. As this is written, the level of the Stanislaus River is rising again because the Corps of Engineers never gave up (and because the leaders of state and federal government lacked the conviction and the courage to stop it).

The miners came back to Cerrillos, New Mexico.

Oxymin left, but a sixfold increase in the price of uranium brought prospectors to the vicinity, and the coalition that had gathered itself to fight the copper mine grew uneasy again. The people who had come to Cerrillos because they felt the rest of the world lacking what Cerrillos had—the people who were not only willing, but actually *wanted*, to live in Cerrillos on its own terms, hand-fetched water and all—they started doing their homework on uranium. As is always the case, the government officials who should have been keeping their eyes on the situation (federal, this time) did nothing until the community started making noises.

And then came Gold Fields. It is a mining corporation, a multinational operation based in England, and in the fall of 1978 it started stripping the top off a mountain near Cerrillos for a gold-mining project. Like Oxymin, it wanted to collect its mineral by "modern" methods—by scooping up ore, placing 3,000 tons of it per day on a flat space called a "leaching pad," pouring a leaching solution on it, collecting the gold, and dumping the remains into a canyon. The leaching solution would be a mixture of cyanide and lime. At least 26,000,000 gallons of precious water would be required per year for the process. (Later, the figure was raised to about 106,000,000 gallons.) Gold Fields did all the usual things: It promised that its operation would create jobs. It assured the residents that it would not harm the environment. An aerial photograph of the operation which appeared in a newspaper was a study in desolation. Gold Fields started demolishing the mountain without obtaining a blasting permit. By the time it was caught, of course, the damage had been done. Gold Fields was fined $300 for the violation. The procedure, said Dierdre Hazelrigg, one of those who had come to live with Cerrillos on its own terms, was a familiar one: "They go ahead and tear things up and ask questions later, whether they get their permit or not."

This time, General Goodwin was not on the side of the industry, and neither was his wife, Kiki. "They've developed a process that works better than anything else here," she said, referring to Gold Fields. "And that's the process of *fait accompli*."

She and the general were sitting in their handsome ranch house with the big picture windows. Inside there were dozens of mementos of their career before they retired to Cerrillos—photographs of old army friends; a collection of the general's swagger sticks; many, many books. Outside, a sudden, violent downpour started. Before, the land had been dry as a bone, but now the Rio Galisteo, which runs by the ranch, had become torrential. As is common in this water-conscious part of the world, the Goodwins thanked their visitor for "bringing us the rain."

"I'm not fighting against the fact that Gold Fields, the world's largest gold-mining conglomerate, wants to take gold out of the Ortiz Mountains," said General Goodwin, "where they have leased land and have the right to take it. But I do object to what they are going to do to the water." He explained that, under the laws of New Mexico, both his ranch and Gold Fields existed in a "closed basin"—a geological setting in which it was assumed that all the water was spoken for. The Goodwins had spoken for, and paid for, theirs. Now Gold Fields wanted to take more than 100,000,000 gallons out of it each year. "There is no available water here," said the general.

His visitor kiddingly accused the general of going over to the side of the "young people" (or, as a very few still put it, "the hippies"). He replied, in his slightly formal, but always responsive, way: "I enjoy very much including among Mrs. Goodwin's and my coterie of friends around here those whose whole life style, whose whole upbringing, whose whole outlook and ambition are completely different from ours. It's refreshing. I enjoy it very much. Deirdre Hazelrigg is a fascinating young woman. Young Ross Lockridge is rising rapidly in my evaluation because I realize that his way of doing things, which is quite antithetical in most cases to mine, is equally successful and perhaps even more so. And I'm beginning to wonder whether my education, my experience, wasn't considerably more limited than I know it was."

A mile or so away and an hour or so later, Deirdre Hazelrigg, Ross Lockridge, Annie Murray, and several other Cerrillos residents—the "young people"—sat in a sun-washed house that looked out on the Ortiz Mountains. The sudden rain had long gone, and the ground was dry again. But some of the water, precious little of it, had soaked into the earth. There would be just enough to support the life that was there—animal, vegetable, and human.

To the south, there was a huge puff of smoke and then, a few seconds later, the sound of an explosion. "Gold Fields," said Ross.

"We're not trying to react in a panicky way to hold up the quote-unquote 'progress' that's already in the works," said Deirdre Hazelrigg. "But rather we're trying to influence the perspective of the state about what's valuable for it in the long run. This state's really a baby. It's really naïve when it comes to a sense of its development. It's getting its idea of how to develop from *other* states in the Union, when actually that might be totally outmoded. We may be the only ones left with the resources and the scenic beauty to stay alive in the slightly different culture that's on its way."

How, she was asked, would she describe that "slightly different culture"?

"Slightly more respectful," she replied. "With an awareness that our resources are finite. That to be energy-conscious isn't just some elitist thing for environmentalists to push and practice. That the planet's small and that a lot of people are going to have to begin recognizing that fact. That a certain quality of industrial progress is now old-fashioned, is outmoded by the conditions."

And is New Mexico a good place for that sort of different culture to be born—in a place where there is a constant reminder of the preciousness of water?

"Anywhere is," she said. "But, sure, New Mexico is a good

place. Because it's relatively unspoiled. It also has powerful money interests, so there are pressures both for and against its being born—against that state of mind. But it seems worth working for."

Index